MAKING SENSE OF

AUTISTIC
SPECTRUM
DISORDERS

MAKING SENSE OF

AUTISTIC
SPECTRUM
DISORDERS

Create the Brightest Future
for Your Child with the
Best Treatment Options

JAMES COPLAN, M.D.

BANTAM BOOKS
NEW YORK

Copyright © 2010 by James Coplan, M.D.

Published in the United States by Bantam Books, an imprint of The Random House Publishing Group, a division of Random House, Inc., New York.

BANTAM BOOKS and the rooster colophon are registered trademarks of Random House, Inc.

Library of Congress Cataloging-in-Publication Data
Coplan, James.
   Making sense of autistic spectrum disorders : create the brightest future for your child with the best treatment options / James Coplan.
       p.   cm.
   Includes bibliographical references and index.
   ISBN 978-0-553-80681-6   ebook ISBN 978-0-553-90717-9
   1. Autism in children.   2. Autism—treatment.   I. Title.
   RJ506.A9C672 2010
   618.92'85882—dc22   2009047842

Printed in the United States of America

www.bantamdell.com

9 8 7 6 5 4 3 2 1

First Edition

This book was designed by Diane Hobbing

Dedicated to tomorrow's children

Acknowledgments

> If I have seen a little further it is by standing on the shoulders of Giants.
>
> —*Isaac Newton, 1676*

As a fellow at the Johns Hopkins Medical School from 1977 to 1979, I had the privilege of meeting Leo Kanner and hearing him speak. He was as insightful then as he had been in 1938, when he met the first of eleven children whom he described as representing "pure-culture examples of *inborn autistic disturbances of affective contact.*" In the seventy years since that first patient encounter, Kanner's observations birthed the entire field of autism care and innumerable advances in autism research. Over the thirty years of my own career to date (1979–2009), I have witnessed the discovery of fragile X, the invention of noninvasive brain imaging techniques such as the CAT scan and MRI, the mapping of the human genome, and the slowly expanding clinical panorama of the autistic spectrum as we know it today. Without these clinical insights and tools of basic science, I would be groping in the dark, perhaps even blaming autism on "refrigerator mothers." Thus, my first debt is to those who came before me. If my work proves to be of value, that value will have been achieved mainly by juxtaposing and linking the insights of my predecessors in a new way.

I thank my dad, a polymer chemist, who was instrumental in developing products ranging from nylon to the membranes used in artificial kidney machines. My dad's legacy goes beyond his passion for science, however, and extends to his passion for justice and his ability to see the world not just as it is but as it *should* be.

I thank my teachers, some of whom must have known, even before I did, that here was a physician-scientist in the making. I include in this list not only my science teachers but also those who taught me to appreciate the works of Sinclair Lewis (creator of Martin Arrowsmith, the conflicted idealist), William Carlos Williams (a pediatrician who wrote of medicine as well as affairs of the heart), and J. D. Salinger (Holden Caulfield's imagined "catcher"—rescuing babies before they tumble over the brink—is a role model for many a pediatrician).

I thank my former collaborators, Cate Church and Abbas Jawad, who provided assistance at critical points in the development of the 3-D model of ASD that forms the heart of this book.

This book could not have been written without the invaluable support of Janet Deatrick, PhD, FAAN, associate program director of the Center for Health Disparities Research of the University of Pennsylvania School of Nursing. My appointment as a scholar in residence at the School of Nursing has enabled me to roam the world's libraries—surely a trip Aladdin would have envied.

Special thanks to Julie Silver, MD, director of the course on writing for medical authors at Harvard Medical School. It was Julie who demystified the process of transforming my wish to become an author into a series of concrete steps that have culminated in this book. I highly recommend her course to any budding medical authors.

I thank my editors: Toni Burbank, Philip Rappaport, and Angela Polidoro at Random House, and David Sobel. Their patience with a novice and their ability to see the book hiding inside my verbiage have been most welcome. I also thank the staff at Random House and Bantam Dell who shepherded this book through the process from manuscript to finished product with unstinting enthusiasm. I thank my colleagues and the parents of my patients who offered constructive criticism of the manuscript or assisted me in other ways, including Jon Farber, Paul Rogers, Steve Glazier, Mary Barbera (author of *The Verbal Behavior Approach*), Lisa Rudy (editor of About.com), Stacey Groder (moderator of ASA Philly), John and Sandy S., Piper J., Heidi F., Leslie and Jeremy A., and many others whose names must remain unmentioned due to confidentiality issues.

A big thank-you goes out to the service providers in the Philadelphia region who gladly gave of their time and permitted me (with parents' permission) to observe many of the therapies described herein, including Kristine Quinby, MEd, BCBA, and the staff of Potential, Inc.; Judith Horrocks, PhD, and the staff of the Timothy School; Wilma Dorman, OTR, and the staff of OTR, Inc.; Maureen Hugel and the staff of Theraplay; Jennifer Paget, MS, RDI-program-certified consultant; Nancy Allard and the staff of Fitz-All; Eric and Dana Pollack of Little Wonders; and many others.

I thank my friends, especially the Friends of the French Press Guy. Bill Wilkinsky enabled me to envision myself as a published author and then challenged me to turn that vision into reality. And for several years, all of you listened to my ups and downs, always asking "How's the book coming?" as if you were inquiring about a developing child.

I thank my staff at Neurodevelopmental Pediatrics of the Main Line. My friend and colleague, Judith Watman, LCSW, wears several hats around the office, including chief of moral support. She and my receptionist, Maureen Isakov, have at various times either waited patiently or gently hounded me to finish my dictations and go through my mail, knowing that writing a book can be both addictive and time-consuming.

I thank my agent, Jeremy Katz. Jeremy has been my biggest booster as well as guide and frequent hand-holder. No pilot ever had a better wingman than Jeremy. I wouldn't be here if it weren't for you. (Special thanks to Juniper P.'s mom, who put the two of us in touch.)

There is no way I can adequately express my tremendous gratitude to the families who have entrusted the welfare of their children to me. For reasons of confidentiality, I cannot mention you by name—but you know who you are. I have learned something from each and every one of you. I thank your children also. They did not volunteer to come to see me; that was your decision. But they are no less deserving of my thanks because of that.

I thank my own children. You have been my admirers, my pupils, my critics, but most of all my teachers. From you I have learned that life is an open-book exam and that the only place to look up the answers is within my own heart.

Finally, and most importantly, I thank my wife. Someone once said, "Old friends are the best friends, because they know where you've been." We've been through a lot these past thirty-eight years, and I cannot imagine having taken this journey with anyone but you. To be blessed with your companionship all these years is more than I might have dared to hope for . . . and all I had to do was ask.

Ardmore, Pennsylvania
2009

Contents

PART II: THE WORLD OF INTERVENTION SERVICES   143

Introduction

Who Am I, and How Can I Help You?

Learn from the mistakes of others. You don't have time to
make them all yourself!

—Anonymous

"Oh, Tommy, look at the trains!"

I watch from my office door as a preschool child, accompanied by
his parents and grandmother, enter my waiting room. Tommy does not
reply or even look at his dad. Instead he darts over to the trains, picks
up one, and lies down on the floor with it. He presses his face against
the rug so that he's eye level with the train, and studies the wheels as he
rolls the train car back and forth. He takes no notice the next time his
dad calls out to him, but instead rolls onto his back, twirling the little
train wheels in front of his face.

I usher the parents into my office, leaving Tommy in the waiting
room with his grandmother. (I require both parents, plus an extra
adult, to attend initial evaluation sessions. This gives the parents some
quiet time with me at the beginning and end of the evaluation. It also
gives me a chance to see how the child and his or her parents handle the
challenge of being separated from one another.) I direct the parents to

the sofa; my social worker and I sit down across from them in a couple of chairs, and I get things started.

"Thank you for coming. What are your concerns?" I ask. "What are your goals for coming to see us?"

"He has delayed speech," Tommy's mother begins, and immediately I see her eyes redden and a flush appear on her face. "I'm so worried because he doesn't look at us or even notice us. He seems to be in his own little world. I've been reading on the Web, and I think he has autism." At this point she cannot hold back her tears.

"Sometimes I think my wife reads too much," Tommy's father says as he puts a consoling arm around his wife. "I think Tommy will speak when he gets around to it. My mother says that I didn't speak until I was three. And as for his behavior, well, he's just a boy."

I've been at this a long time, and in these first brief moments with this family I have already begun to think that the mother's fears may be justified. Three hours later, after careful observation and examination, I am convinced that Tommy does indeed have autism. My social worker and I have been through this painful process many times and are prepared for the flood of questions that come pouring out: *Why did this happen to our child? How bad is it? Can anything be done? Will he ever be normal? If not, how can we at least maximize his potential? Does he also have special medical risks? Could this happen again if we have other children? What do we do now?*

Autism—a condition commonly grouped under the heading *autistic spectrum disorder (ASD)* along with *pervasive developmental disorder, not otherwise specified* and *Asperger syndrome*—is a devastating diagnosis. There is really no way you can prepare yourself for the shock of learning that your child has ASD. You must suddenly revise your expectations for your child's future and your own. At the very least, things that you once took for granted as part of your child's future— independence, a career, marriage and raising a family—are now called into question. And as if the emotional impact of receiving a diagnosis of ASD isn't enough, you suddenly find yourself faced with a bewildering maze of complex treatments and unproven therapies, with seemingly no consensus among the experts as to what course is best.

There are many people offering you advice, so why should you listen to me? Let me answer that question in two ways, professionally and personally. At a professional level, I am a developmental pediatrician, meaning that I specialize in helping children with developmental disabilities. I have specialty certification in general pediatrics, plus subspecialty certification in neurodevelopmental disabilities and developmental-behavioral pediatrics. (These are two pathways leading to professional expertise in child development for pediatricians and—in the case of neurodevelopmental disabilities—for child neurologists as well.) I have spent the last thirty years working almost exclusively with children with developmental disorders, including mental retardation, learning disabilities, cerebral palsy, hearing loss, and ASD. For eighteen years I was the only university-based neurodevelopmental pediatrician for the two and a half million people in central upstate New York. After that, I spent seven years as director of a federally funded training program in developmental disabilities at The Children's Hospital of Philadelphia. I have published numerous professional articles in medical and pediatric journals, mainly on the subject of early language development and the causes of language delay. Throughout that time, I have maintained an active clinical practice for children with developmental disabilities. I have also remained committed to teaching medical students, residents, and fellows.

At a personal level, I am the sibling of an individual with special needs. I remember my great-grandpa Joe holding my infant sister on his knee (I was in elementary school at the time), asking my father and stepmother, "Why doesn't she talk?" Later, I remember how every year my sister's playmates would surpass her, and a new crop of younger children would become her playmates for a year or so, until they too outgrew her. When I was in high school, I bought my sister a book of poetry—*Now We Are Six* by A. A. Milne (author of *Winnie-the-Pooh*)—as a birthday present. I felt uncomfortable with the title, but somehow I knew that the book was written at her level, even though it was her twelfth birthday. I also watched my parents struggle with the implications of my sister's mental retardation. In those days, there was no such thing as Early Intervention (created in 1986) or free and appropriate public education (created in 1975). Instead, my parents—and other parents in the same circumstance—were left to find, or create, resources for themselves. My dad, for example, became the second president of the local chapter of the Association for Retarded Children, what we know today as the ARC.

My parents also pursued many blind alleys—promised cures that turned out to be bogus. So, at a personal level, I have been motivated to write this book in part by a desire to provide you with the kind of guidance that my parents never had.

You need straight talk about the present (*What do we do now?*) and the future (*What kind of life will our child lead?*). There are more services available today than my parents could have dreamed of fifty years ago, yet there are also more blind alleys. Especially in the field of ASD, there are scores of self-appointed "experts," promising things they can't deliver, sowing seeds of guilt or false hope, and sapping your resources at a time when you need to remain focused on getting the most out of every moment and every dollar. This is where my technical expertise can help you. And, having personally witnessed and experienced some of the pain that goes along with having a child with disabilities, I want to help other families come through the experience a little better off than ours did. Looking back on my life as the sibling of an individual with a disability and my career of working with families of children with special needs, it's clear to me that some families adapt to the birth of a child with disabilities in a healthy manner, while others do not. This brings me to the final reason for writing this book: my desire to make some sense out of my own life. In sorting through my own personal and professional experiences, I hope to pass on some wisdom that will help you in the course of your journey.

I approach each new patient with three areas of inquiry: the child, the "system," and the family. First I want to figure out what's going on with the child. Of course I want to arrive at the correct developmental diagnosis. (I've encountered children with deafness or physical disability who were misdiagnosed by others as having mental retardation. I've also seen children with autism labeled deaf, and vice versa.) As a physician, also I want to identify—if possible—the underlying medical factors that have led to the child's developmental disorder. Second, I want to help families to select the appropriate therapies, and to navigate the maze of special education and health care that we call the "system"—even though it's more of a patchwork quilt than an organized system. Third, I want to see how the family is doing. In order for any child to achieve his or her full potential, the family as a whole needs to be on an even keel. This is particularly true for a child with special needs, who is less able than a normally developing child to compensate for family factors that may be out of balance. I'm also interested in averting collateral damage—to the parents, their marriage, or the mental health of the siblings—as the impact of the child's disability ripples through the family.

This book roughly parallels the way I work with families. Part I focuses on the child and deals with questions such as *What is ASD? Why did this happen? Can it happen to us again? What about my child's future prospects?* Part II focuses on the many different forms of intervention for children with ASD. My goal here is to enable you to become a smart shopper. You only have so much time, money, and energy. You need to allocate your resources in a way that will benefit your child the most. I will give you a set of criteria that you can apply to all therapies to see if they measure up to certain basic standards of credibility, safety, and therapeutic benefit, before you spend money on them, or subject your child to them. In Part II we also cover behavior management and medication. While medication should never be used in isolation from behavioral measures, it can be a godsend for alleviating behaviors that are beyond your child's control. Part III focuses on the family. In a very real sense, the family is my patient. This is one reason why I insist that both parents be present at the initial evaluation. This is also why I ask parents, "What will you tell your other children?" Children with ASD do not remain children forever either: *Where will my child live as an adult?* is a question that's on every parent's mind. One of my roles is to help families plan ahead, for the time when neither they nor I will be on the scene. The book closes with a glossary (in addition to learning about autism, and the ins and outs of the service delivery system, you will need to learn a whole new vocabulary), a list of resources, and several appendices. Look for the (i) symbol throughout the body of the book, which indicates that additional information on that topic is available in the Resource List. For those of you who are academically inclined, I have also included citations to some of the scientific articles mentioned in the text. These citations are also in the Resource List.

The field of ASD is changing so rapidly that I can do no more than help you to jump on board. This is a wonderful thing, since it reflects the pace of progress—even though it means that parts of this book will become dated all too quickly. What will not change, however, is parents' love for their children, and the commitment on the part of parents and pediatricians to help each child achieve his or her full potential. Since embarking upon my career as a developmental pediatrician, I have helped thousands of families travel the path of having a child with special needs. As many times as I've taken this journey, the road is never quite the same twice, and I know that for you, this is probably the first time. So let us begin together.

PART I

THE WORLD
OF THE CHILD

Chapter 1
Patterns of Development

Our child is off the beaten path.
—Parents of a child with autistic spectrum disorder

Three Young Friends

I'd like you to meet three youngsters who can help illustrate the many facets of autistic spectrum disorder (ASD). I've referred to these children as friends, not because they know one another (they are all fictionalized, composite versions of patients of mine, as are all the patients mentioned in this book), but because the children whom I evaluate eventually come to regard me as their friend. The best way to get a child to reveal himself or herself to me, and to work with me, is to befriend the child. Sometimes this means getting down on the floor and playing with the child (I'm always wearing out the knees of my slacks). Sometimes it means letting the child explore the train memorabilia in my office, or letting him or her play with various sensory toys I keep stashed away (a battery-operated spinner, blinking rubber balls, etc.). And at all times it means respecting children and accepting them for who they are, even as I may try to reshape their behavior into more adaptive patterns.

You'll meet these three children as I did, when their parents brought them to me, and perhaps you'll get a sense of how a developmental pediatrician approaches the process of assessing a child, getting to know the family, and determining the next steps. In later chapters we'll come back to these three children, to see how their stories have progressed. As you will see, all three of these children are boys. Males outnumber females with ASD about three to one. There are plenty of girls in this book, but for these three examples I've kept the gender the same, in order to avoid confusing severity with gender-related issues.

Kevin, Age Thirty-Three Months

This visit starts like so many others. "Kevin has delayed speech" is the first thing Kevin's parents tell me. "He jabbers like he's speaking a foreign language. We think he understands us when we say no, but he usually doesn't listen to us when we speak to him or ask him to do things. He tunes us out. For a while we thought he might be deaf, but the audiologist said his hearing is fine. He manages to get his point across by pulling us where he wants us to go, and then putting our hand on what he wants."

"Is there anything else that worries you?" I ask.

"He has this weird fascination with people's earlobes. Whenever we hold him, all he wants to do is stroke our earlobes. And he is the master of routines. At bedtime, we have to do things exactly the same way each night, or he flips out."

"What does he do for play?"

"He loves his beads-on-a-wire toy. That can keep him busy for hours. Or flipping through the pages of a book—not really looking at the story, just flipping the pages. Or rolling one of his toy cars back and forth and watching the wheels go around. When he gets really excited, he spins himself around, or walks on his toes. He does like to be tickled or be chased by his dad around the room as a game. But otherwise he'd rather sit by himself and play with the beads."

Just these first few snippets of conversation with his parents have me concerned. They've already mentioned several warning signs of ASD: rigid, repetitive behavior; fascination with spinning objects; limited play skills; odd physical mannerisms; and across-the-board language delay.

As for his other skills, Kevin's parents report that he is finger-feeding (a seven-month skill) but still not using a spoon, a critical milestone that he should have reached eighteen months ago. When I ask what Kevin does with crayons, they immediately reply, "Oh, we can't give him crayons! He would just eat them." Toddlers normally transition from using a crayon as a teething object to using it as a writing implement around twelve to fourteen months of age, the same age at which they learn to use a spoon. Kevin's delayed use of the spoon and crayon as tools worries me. ASD alone would not account for this deficit, raising the possibility of global cognitive delay, and an eventual diagnosis of mental retardation.

On examination, Kevin makes virtually no eye contact, and his vocalization is limited to crying. He follows no verbal commands with or without gestural cues from me (such as putting out my hand while saying "Give me . . ."), and he doesn't copy me when I build with blocks or draw with a crayon. He is not being uncooperative. Rather, he is unaware of me or my intentions. He's cut off from others, incapable of being either cooperative or uncooperative.

On the other hand, Kevin interacts directly with the test materials as long as he isn't required to observe or copy another person. We call this *stimulus-driven behavior*. In other words, the physical aspects of the item itself "drive" the child's behavior; it's almost as if the shapes "want" to go into the holes, or the bell "wants" to be rung. The child responds directly to the object without any need to relate to the adult. This is normal in a seven-month-old shaking a rattle or a sixteen-month-old fitting shapes into a shape sorter. By Kevin's age, however, a child's behavior and use of objects should be much more attuned to social cues, and the functional use of an object—driving a train, feeding a doll, looking at a book, or imitating a grown-up—rather than merely interacting with an object at the level of its physical properties. Preschool children with ASD generally do well on stimulus-driven tasks but stumble when they have to take cues from another person. I've seen many children with ASD complete complex shape-matching tasks such as puzzles, yet fail on the simplest imitative task, such as stacking two blocks. It's not that the child doesn't know how to stack; the missing link is the child's inability to appreciate that he or she is expected to imitate an action modeled by the adult. Kevin successfully completes the pegboard task (designed for children of fourteen to sixteen months), but it's strictly between him and the pegboard. Rather than looking up for approval after completing the task, he twirls one of the pegs in front of his eyes. Based on Kevin's developmental history, my observations, and the results of standardized tests, I diagnose Kevin with autism. Based on the history of delayed adaptive skills (not using a spoon as a tool, for example), I also diagnose developmental delay.

Darryl, Age Twenty Months

"We're worried because he doesn't speak," Darryl's mother begins, "He babbles and says 'mama,' but sometimes he says 'mama' because he's distressed or uncomfortable, not just to mean me." Delayed speech in early childhood is the concern or symptom I hear about most often from parents. However, I'm interested in comprehension as well as speech. I want to know if Darryl recognizes his own name. (Typically, infants respond selectively to their own name at around nine months.) "I think so," Darryl's mother says, "although sometimes he acts as if he doesn't hear us."

I ask more questions. Does he follow simple commands, like "Come here" or "Give me..."? Children typically start following commands at about twelve months, but Darryl's mom tells me he started doing so only a month before the visit. I make a mental note that his receptive language may be delayed, along with his speech. Does he play gesture games, like patty-cake or peek-a-boo? I ask. "He occasionally copies us, but he never starts it himself," his mother replies. (A normally developing child will start enjoying such games at seven to nine months, just copying the parents at first, and will generally start initiating these activities by ten to twelve months.)

Next I ask if he points and then looks at his parents. Pointing is a critical communication activity, parallel to speech, and typically emerges at about the same age, that is, around twelve months. "No," his parents tell me, "and he doesn't look where we're pointing either." At this point, I'm becoming concerned that Darryl not only has delayed *speech* but delayed *language,* a more global problem encompassing speech, listening comprehension, and understanding of visual or non-verbal communication.

I turn to fine motor and adaptive (self-care) skills, which are important clues to a child's overall mental development. For example, the ability to use a spoon is more than just a fine motor skill; it also reveals cognitive development, because the child understands the function of the spoon as a tool. Darryl's parents tell me that he learned to use a spoon at around fourteen months, which is right on schedule, and is now cooperating with dressing and undressing by inserting his arms in the sleeves of his clothes. This is good; Darryl's non-language-related adaptive skills and fine motor skills are emerging on schedule, which gives me some assurance that his level of general intelligence may be normal. As for gross motor skills, Darryl walked at fifteen months and began running at eighteen months—the upper limit of the normal range.

Next, I ask about play, an important developmental activity that reflects a child's motor, cognitive, and language abilities simultaneously. Darryl's parents are able to engage him, and he loves to listen to stories. Less promisingly, they describe him as "fascinated" by lights and fans, as well as stop and exit signs. He studies objects out of the corners of his eyes, "obsesses" over opening and closing closet doors, and memorizes videotapes. When he is excited, he flaps his hands or clenches his fists.

When I examine Darryl, I find him alert but difficult to engage. He makes only brief, inconsistent eye contact, and his vocalization is limited to occasional babbling. I ask him, "Where's the ball?" and in response, he smiles at me, turns, and retrieves a tennis ball, demonstrating an ability to follow one-step commands with no gestural cue. At other times, however, I find it almost impossible to engage him. He gravitates to the illuminated exit sign in my waiting room, flapping his hands in excitement. I test Darryl's problem-solving abilities—putting shapes into holes, retrieving hidden objects, and so on—and these cluster around the sixteen- to eighteen-month level. He is generally calm, with occasional bursts of agitation.

Based on the developmental history, my observations during testing, and the results of various standardized tests, I diagnose Darryl with pervasive developmental disorder, not otherwise specified (PDD-NOS).

Teddy, Age Seven Years

Teddy was referred by the guidance counselor at his elementary school for behavior problems in class and at recess. Teddy's parents seem perplexed, explaining that their son is bright and highly verbal, but there is something "off" about his social interactions, and the other kids act wary of him.

"Teddy doesn't understand the unwritten rules of the playground," they lament. "He doesn't know how to go up to another child and start a conversation or join in with other kids' play. Sometimes he thinks he is another kid's best friend when he hardly knows the child. At other times he thinks other children are being mean to him when no insult was intended. We've always felt that Teddy was a bit different from other children, but it was never a problem until he started school."

When I probe further into his history, things become a little clearer. "He was a high-needs baby, always fussy," his parents tell me. "Later, when he was able to get around, he was very curious about how things worked. One thing would take over for a while, then he would move on to the next thing. At first he was fascinated by ceiling fans. When he was three years old, he used to nag us to take him to Home Depot and Sears so he could study the fans. Then he was into trains, then airplanes. For the past year or so, he's been fascinated by the *Titanic*, reading books about it and making models of it with the cushions and bar stools in our den.

"He's always been a talker. By his first birthday, he was making two-word phrases, and he was speaking in sentences by a year and a half. But sometimes he asks the same question over and over, or dwells on the same topic forever, like the *Titanic*. By his third birthday, he started teaching himself to read. But all he wants to read about is the *Titanic*."

As I do in every interview, I ask about Teddy's fine motor and adaptive skills, and learn that Teddy has struggled with coordination. "He couldn't get the hang of using a spoon until eighteen months, and even now he's messy. He couldn't do buttons until his fourth birthday, and he still can't tie his shoes or cut food with a knife and fork. Handwriting is a huge challenge for him." As for his gross motor skills, I learn that he walked at fourteen months and could run at two years, but he couldn't pedal a tricycle until age five, when all of his cousins were riding theirs at three (the usual age). "And he's still afraid to ride a bicycle," his father adds, "even with training wheels."

When I examine Teddy, I can see what his parents mean by his interactions being "off." He tends to look over my shoulder as he answers my questions. He crowds into my personal space, coming almost nose to nose with me. One time he even blows a raspberry in my face.

I sense his behavior not as testing limits, as might be the case in a child with normal development, but as reflecting a lack of awareness of social boundaries. His activity level is increased and his attention span is decreased for a child his age. He does indeed have fine motor clumsiness. He can answer simple factual questions, such as "How many legs does a dog have?" He also has some remarkable talents: not only does he know his birthday, he also can tell me which day of the week it fell on last year. (This is called a *calendar savant skill,* from the French word *savoir,* meaning "to know." Some children with ASD have remarkable savant skills in isolated areas, such as calendar facts, schedules, and similar list-based information.)

Teddy is verbal and uses grammatically appropriate sentences, but his tone of voice is another clue that he has a problem. His speech is stilted, mechanical, and formal—he sounds like a little professor. The only time he becomes animated is when I steer the discussion to ocean liners, at which point he launches into a lengthy lecture on the sinking of the *Titanic.* I diagnose Asperger syndrome (AS) on the basis of Teddy's developmental history, his behavior during the examination, and the results of standardized testing.

WHAT'S IN A NAME?

Most physicians speak of *Asperger syndrome* (without the apostrophe) rather than *Asperger's syndrome.* The condition is named for the pediatrician Hans Asperger, who in 1944 described children with a specific group of behavioral patterns, but he doesn't own it! Psychiatrists and the nonmedical community still embrace the apostrophe.

On the Spectrum

You don't need a laboratory test to spot your mother in a crowd. You recognize her by a pattern of features—what her face looks like, how she walks, how she sounds, what she wears, and so on. Some medical conditions are recognized in the same way; without a specific laboratory test, doctors need to rely on a pattern of symptoms to arrive at the correct diagnosis. *Syndrome* is the term doctors use for a pattern of clinical features (physical characteristics, unique behaviors, or particular complaints) that occur together. Some syndromes have a confirmatory laboratory test, while others do not. For example, Down syndrome (DS) is diagnosed on the basis of several distinctive physical features (slanted eyes, flat nasal bridge, short fingers, and so on) as well as a specific lab test (which detects an extra copy of chromosome 21). Tourette syndrome, on the other hand, is diagnosed purely on the basis of history and observation: multiple tics, including vocal tics, for at least twelve months. Like Tourette syndrome, autistic spectrum disorder is diagnosed solely through the developmental history plus observation of the child's behavior—there is no lab test. We have lab tests for some of the underlying medical disorders that can *cause* ASD, but there's no laboratory test for ASD itself.

ASD is not only a syndrome; it's also a *spectrum disorder*. That is, the symptoms of ASD vary in intensity, from severe to very mild. Kevin, Darryl, and Teddy all have problems in similar areas—language, repetitive behavior, and social interaction—but the severity of their difficulty and the presence or absence of other features (fine motor clumsiness, normal intelligence, increased or decreased verbal output) varies. Physicians and psychologists rely on these differences in order to distinguish between autism, PDD-NOS, and Asperger syndrome. Children with any of these three diagnoses are said to be "on the spectrum." In this book, I will use the term *autistic spectrum disorder* to refer to these three conditions.

(i)   See the Resource List for additional information on the different forms of ASD.

Off the Track

If a train arrives thirty minutes late, we'd say it was delayed. The word *delayed* means the same thing in railroading and child development terms: behind schedule. A train that's delayed is traveling its normal route and will pass through all the expected stations, just later than expected. Likewise, a child with delayed development hits all the expected milestones, just later than usual. Now let's suppose that instead of the train being late, one of its wheels has gone off the tracks. Even if the train arrives at the station right on time, there's still a problem. And even if it's running on time, a train that's derailed train may wind up in the ditch: something that should never happen. Child development too can go off the track. Like our derailed train, a child whose development has gone off the track demonstrates behaviors that would never occur in the course of normal development. We refer to development that's gone off the track as *atypical*. A couple of examples should make the difference between delayed and atypical development clear. A two-year-old child whose vocalizations consist of repeated syllables such as "la-la-la-la," who recognizes his or her name, and who has just begun to play simple gesture games such as patty-cake and peek-a-boo is manifesting *delayed* language; his or her language behavior is similar to what we would see in a normally developing nine-month-old. There's still a problem, because the child's language is quite delayed, but the behaviors themselves are normal (that is, they would be perfectly typical in a nine-month-old). In contrast, a two-year-old child who is nonverbal except for continuous recitation of TV commercials has *atypical* language development; there is no age for which this pattern of language development would be considered normal. This child's language does not resemble that of a normal but younger child. Instead, it has gone off the tracks.

Atypical development in ASD may be glaringly off the track, as we saw with Kevin, who was totally in his own world, or it may reveal itself in more subtle ways, as with Teddy, who was interested in other people but did not know how to go about interacting with them. Some children with ASD demonstrate normal or even advanced skills, but these skills emerge in the wrong sequence—for example, identifying alphabet letters before saying "mommy" or "daddy." This is the developmental equivalent of putting on one's shoes before put on one's socks. The child's development is literally out of order. This form of atypical development may be especially difficult to recognize, because skills that emerge prematurely may seem like signs that a child is gifted, rather than clues that the child has a developmental problem. We saw this with Teddy, whose phenomenal memory, calendar skills, and early reading ability gave the impression of superior intelligence. (Some children with AS *do* have superior IQs, but in many cases, their savant skills are isolated "splinter skills" rather than indications of across-the-board brilliance.)

Autism; pervasive developmental disorder, not otherwise specified; and Asperger syndrome are diagnosed on the basis of behavioral symptoms. Over the years, numerous scales and checklists have been created in an attempt to provide a standardized way of making these diagnoses. However, since there is no biological "anchor" for these conditions, there is no way to prove which scale is best. This is very different from, say, marketing a new pregnancy test: It's easy to judge the accuracy of a pregnancy test, since the condition itself—pregnancy—can be verified by a means other than the test. Not so for ASD, where experts argue about the proper criteria for making the diagnosis. This will change as brain imaging and genetic testing enable us to look beyond the symptoms of ASD to the underlying biology, but for now, symptom checklists and behavioral measures are the best we have. The checklists most often used by physicians are published by the American Psychiatric Association in its *Diagnostic and Statistical Manual, 4th Edition,* commonly referred to as the *DSM-IV.* The *DSM-IV* contains checklists for autism, Asperger's Disorder (what we refer to as Asperger syndrome), and pervasive developmental disorder, not otherwise specified. The *DSM* checklists code each symptom as "present" or "absent," making no provision for symptom severity (see Appendix I for the specific items on the *DSM* checklists). In addition to applying *DSM* criteria, I use the Childhood Autism Rating Scale, or CARS. The CARS covers many of the same behaviors as the *DSM.* The difference is that CARS permits me to rate each behavior on a point scale, from 1 (normal) to 4 (severely atypical). The CARS looks at fifteen developmental areas, so the best possible score is 15 and the worst possible score is 60. The cutoff for autism is 30. Children with atypicality that stops short of fully expressed autism usually have CARS scores in the mid- to high 20s. In the clinical vignettes above, Kevin's initial score on CARS was 45; Darryl's was 28. With Teddy, I used a different measure, the Asperger Syndrome Diagnostic Scale (ASDS), to quantify his atypical features, such as his pedantic, adultlike speech. In addition to the *DSM,* CARS, and ASDS, there are many other diagnostic instruments in use. See Appendix III for more information on test instruments.

Symptom Areas

The symptoms of ASD fall into four areas:

- Difficulty relating to others
- Atypical language
- Repetitious behavior
- Abnormal sensory and motor processing

Nobody knows why these very different kinds of symptoms occur together; there is no "autism center" in the brain that controls these four areas, as far as we know. However, the clustering of symptoms is so striking that in most cases the overall pattern is diagnostic—even though the child's symptoms in any one area might be mild enough to escape detection if considered separately. First we'll take a close look at these four symptom areas. Then I'll introduce you to a couple of underlying cognitive deficits—"theory of mind" and "central coherence"— that will help you tie many of these symptoms together.

Relating to Others

All through my pregnancy, I was looking forward to meeting him. Now he's four years old, and I still don't feel that I've met him.
—Mother of a preschool child with autism

A child's *failure to connect* troubles parents more than any of the other symptoms of ASD. Commonly, parents describe their child as being in his or her own little world. "Our child is *among* us but not *with* us," one mother said. A child who doesn't participate in the regular give-and-take of social and emotional relationships is essentially closed off from others. This lack of reciprocity may be evident from birth, progressing from poor eye contact as an infant or toddler to difficulty in mastering interactive play as a preschooler and then to an inability to see things from another person's point of view as a school-age child (or, for that matter, as an adult). Impaired social reciprocity is not a black-and-white problem. Like trying to pull in the signal from a distant radio station—sometimes it's crystal clear, at other times it's full of static—the ability to engage a child with ASD may fade in and out: perfect eye contact one minute, "in his own world" the next.

Eye Contact

Normal infants would rather look at faces than nearly anything else. Children with ASD tend to lack this preference. Some actively avoid eye contact, turning away when parents move into their field of vision and try to engage them. Others make brief eye contact but only on their own terms, meaning they may initiate eye contact but don't respond when someone else attempts to initiate it with them—something I call "one-way eye contact." Children with ASD also fail to engage in joint attention, meaning they cannot be prompted to look at something together with an adult, nor do they point at a desired object and then look back at the adult to seek recognition.

ENGAGEMENT IN NORMAL AND ATYPICAL INFANTS

Thirty years ago, during my training, I watched a video that left a lasting impression on me. In the video, a three-month-old baby sits in an infant seat, facing his mother. Mom and baby are smiling back and forth at each other; the baby is making happy gurgling sounds, and Mom is talking to the baby in a soft voice. Suddenly, on instruction from the experimenter, the mother's face goes blank and motionless. The baby leans forward, still smiling, trying to reengage his mother, but to no avail—her face remains a frozen mask. Over the next minute or so, the baby's efforts become more frantic. Eventually the baby curls up into a little ball, cries, turns away, and spits up. Suddenly Mom becomes interactive again, smiles, and reassuringly reaches out to soothe the baby; he gradually regains his composure. The entire episode lasts only moments, but it seems like an eternity. This is the famous "still-face experiment," which psychologists have used for decades to study infant development (for example, the ability of a premature infant to engage with its caregiver) and to look at mother-child interaction (for example, the effect of maternal depression on the quality of infant development). Watching this tape, it's clear that babies are eagerly seeking adult engagement and become greatly distressed when a response is not forthcoming.

Fast-forward to 2007. Rebecca Landa, director of the Center for Autism and Related Disorders at the Kennedy Krieger Institute in Baltimore and an associate professor at the Johns Hopkins University School of Medicine, is making videotapes of babies born to parents who already have had one child with ASD. Each of these babies has about a one-in-ten chance of being on the spectrum too. (We'll have more to say about recurrence risk in a later chapter.) By taping these high-risk babies from birth, Dr. Landa has collected a library of videotapes of children who ultimately get a spectrum diagnosis. These tapes are the exact opposite of the still-face experiment. Now it is the mother who is doing everything possible to engage the baby, while the baby stares off into space. Unfortunately, unlike the mothers in the original still-face setup, these babies do not suddenly snap out of it.

Personal Space

Children with ASD often give mixed signals when it comes to respecting or even understanding personal space—the unwritten rules of social interaction that relate to appropriate physical boundaries between people. Often children with ASD don't like to be held or to receive physical affection, yet at the same time they may invade the personal space of others, adults and peers alike. Occasionally children with ASD can be extremely clingy, typically with one person. The analogy of a thermostat may be useful here. A thermostat has to sense the temperature in a room correctly in order to regulate it. If the thermostat is broken, the room may become either too hot or cold. In the same way, a child with ASD may seem to run hot and cold, squirming out of his parents' arms one moment, only to run up and hug a stranger the next. Children who give me no eye contact may happily climb into my lap and fiddle with the contents of my shirt pocket, but I might as well be a statue to them. A child with ASD might hug too hard or push his or her way through a group of peers as if the other children weren't even there. It's easy to mistake this kind of behavior for aggression, but it isn't, just as climbing into a stranger's lap isn't necessarily a show of affection. All of these behaviors stem from the child's lack of awareness of personal space.

Social Reciprocity

At each level of development, a person with ASD struggles with interpersonal skills—the ordinary back-and-forth interactions of daily life. The toddler with ASD may ignore other children in the Mommy and Me gym class. As a preschooler, the child may not know how to engage in interactive play, preferring to run around the perimeter of the playground by himself. If the child does engage with other children, turn taking and sharing are difficult. Doing what the other child wants to do, instead of continuing one's own play, is a challenge. At birthday parties, the child with ASD is likely to go off in a separate room rather than remain with the rest of the group. When the child with ASD gets to school, following the teacher's requests—"Everybody come sit down, it's circle time!" for example—is a problem. It's not that the child with ASD is disobedient (although it's often misperceived as that). Rather, the child just doesn't understand the importance of joining the group, or may be totally fixated on some activity that's of interest only to him- or herself. Negotiating unstructured social settings (playground, cafeteria, school bus) can be challenging. Making and keeping friends is also a problem. Adults with high-functioning autism or Asperger syndrome have difficulty with the nuances of social interaction, making it challenging for them to sustain intimate personal relationships. Career advancement can also be a problem. The father of one of my patients with ASD, with subtle atypicality himself, told me that he had lost several jobs because of his inability to sustain eye contact with his boss.

Language Development

Language is a symbol system for the storage of information and communication with others. Communication takes place by various means:

1. Auditory expressive (making ourselves understood through speech)
2. Auditory receptive (understanding the speech of others)
3. Visual (expressing and receiving nonverbal signals)

This is an oversimplification, but it gives us a place to start when comparing normal language development with language development in children on the autistic spectrum.

Auditory Expressive Language Milestones

Auditory expressive milestones emerge in a predictable pattern. At about one or two months, infants with normal development begin to coo, making open vowel sounds for vocal pleasure. (The "melody" of vocalizations—the way their inflection rises and falls—is known as *prosody*. More on prosody later in this chapter.) By three months, infants will listen quietly as the parent speaks, then coo in response. At four or five months, they start making raspberries, blowing bubbles, laughing, and uttering single syllables such as "ba" or "goo." Strings of repeated syllables, such as "da-da-da," "la-la-la-la," and "ma-ma-ma" appear at seven to nine months.

One day the child accidentally shortens these utterances and produces "dada" or "mama." Instantly the parents respond with massive positive reinforcement, even though the child has no idea what those sounds mean, or even that they have meaning. Gradually the infant comes to associate these sounds with the appearance of a friendly giant. The most significant breakthrough occurs around ten months of age, when the child realizes not only that different sounds—"dada" or "mama"—produce different people but also that these sounds *stand for* these people. That is, the child discovers that arbitrary sounds have meaning. (The ability to attach meaning to, or extract meaning from, words is known technically as *semantics*. We'll come back to this term in later chapters.)

By twelve months of age, most infants can produce at least one word in addition to "mama" or "dada." By eighteen to twenty months, the typical infant can correctly and consistently use at least fifty words without parental prompting. By twenty-four months the child begins combining words into novel two-word phrases, such as "Want bottle." (Phrases such as "I love you" or "All gone" are learned as a single unit and do not count.) Toddlers are usually forming three-to-five-word phrases by age two and a half, and by this time their vocabulary is so big that parents can no longer count the words. At three, children can

produce grammatically appropriate sentences and carry on brief conversations. Normally developing three-year-olds can also fib, engage in
verbal make-believe, and understand verbal humor—skills that are remarkably difficult for children with ASD to master.

Auditory Receptive Language Milestones
Infants go through an equally predictable sequence of auditory receptive
milestones in the first year of life, beginning with alerting to a voice as
newborns, turning to a voice at three to four months, and turning to
nonverbal stimuli such as the sound of a bell by five months. Between
five and nine months of age, infants become better at localizing sounds
in their environment, turning directly to the source of the sound. They
begin responding selectively to their own names by nine months (right
around the same age at which infants begin to produce "mama" and
"dada"). Around this time, they begin to recognize "no," and they start
responding to simple verbal commands that are accompanied by visual
cues, such as a parent saying "Give it to me" while holding out a hand.
By twelve to fourteen months, normally developing infants are responding to one-step verbal commands without an accompanying gesture. By
sixteen to eighteen months, infants can point to several body parts on
command. By two years of age, a normally developing toddler can perform two different, unrelated, and unrehearsed commands in a row (for
example: "Put away your shoes, then go sit down at the table"), and by
three years of age they can follow three-step commands.

Parents sometimes come to me claiming that their child "understands everything," but on close questioning it turns out that this is true
only because the parents have broken everything down into a series of
one-step commands. Following a single one-step command is a twelve-
month receptive language milestone. Following an infinite number of
one-step commands, although very functional in terms of day-to-day
living, is no better than an eighteen-month receptive language level.

Visual Language Milestones
Brief eye contact should be present within the first few days of life. By
two months of age, most parents report that their infants recognize
their faces. Normally developing infants engage in games such as patty-
cake or peek-a-boo by nine months. These games reinforce social reci-

procity and encourage the infant's use of gesture as a means of interacting with his or her caregivers. At this age, infants also begin to wave bye-bye in imitation of others or in response to a verbal prompt. By ten months, infants begin to wave on their own, and they use simple, informal gestures such as raising their arms to indicate a desire to be picked up.

By their first birthday, infants initiate, rather than just imitate, gesture games, and begin pointing to desired objects. They also develop what's known as *joint attention:* The infant points to a desired object, then looks up at his or her parents, to make sure they are looking at the object too. Likewise, the infant will follow the direction of an adult's eye gaze or point, to discover what the adult is trying to show them.

Put all these skills together—gesture games, single words, following commands, pointing, joint attention—and you see the early stages of interactive two-way communication. The child not only recognizes and interprets signals from others but also can make him- or herself understood by generating sounds and gestures with communicative intent. (The technical name for this ability to use language socially, as a means of communicating with others, is *pragmatics.*) Consider the huge difference between the nine-month-old who may cry, slap the table, or reach for an object and the twelve-month-old who calmly points at the object while engaging a parent's gaze, perhaps while uttering "bottle." That's significant progress.

Language development in ASD is not just delayed; it's gone off the track. The atypical quality of language development in ASD can be traced to deficits in pragmatics and prosody.

Pragmatics
As we have pointed out, pragmatics and prosody are identifiable from earliest infancy. Most adults, without even realizing it, speak to babies in a high-pitched, lilting tone of voice. When a three-month-old listens to the singsong voice of an adult and then coos or babbles back, a form of "conversation" is taking place. There is an interaction, an exchange. The gesture games that a nine-month-old plays with an adult—patty-cake, peek-a-boo, so-big—involve the same kind of social reciprocity. The first words an infant uses, such as "mama," "bottle," or "up," have pragmatic value, connecting the child to important people, objects, or

Table 1.1 Normal Language Milestones

Age	Auditory Expressive	Auditory Receptive	Visual
1 month	Coos	Alerts to voice	Recognizes parents
2 months			
3 months	Vocalizes back to parents	Turns to voice	Recognizes common objects (e.g., spoon)
4 months	Babbles—single syllables ("ba," "da," "goo," etc.)	Turns to the side to locate sounds	Improved visual tracking
5 months			
6 months	Laughs Blows bubbles	Turns over and down to sounds below eye level	Horizontal tracking Vertical tracking
7 months	Babbles—strings of syllables ("la-la-la," etc.) Uses "mama" and "dada" but not always specifically		
8 months		Turns directly down	
9 months		Understands "no" Recognizes own name Follows one-step command with parental gesture	Imitates gesture games
10 months	Uses "mama" / "dada" as label for the correct parent		Upraised arms to signify desire to be picked up
11 months			
12 months	First word to refer to other than mother, father, family, pets	Follows a single one-step command without gesture	Initiates gesture games Points to desired objects
14–18 months	Single-word vocabulary increases	Points to body parts on command; follows several one-step commands	
24 months	50+ single words, two-word phrases	Follows two-step commands	
30 months	3–5 word phrases		
36 months	Sentences; fibs, verbal make-believe, verbal humor		Finger counting

actions in his or her environment. The child realizes that using the right word or pointing to a desired object produces a specific result. In the same way that children learn to use a spoon to feed themselves, they discover that words too are tools that they can use to manipulate the behavior of others, and that that language has a payoff. Unfortunately, these pragmatic skills are impaired or absent in a child with ASD.

Problems with pragmatics take a number of different forms. Some infants and toddlers with ASD do not acquire speech at all. Others begin producing single words but fail to grasp the pragmatic *value* of language as a means of getting their needs met, so their early words dwindle and disappear. Some children remain verbal, but their speech consists of recitation of memorized material—a feat parents sometimes mistake for superior intellect. If your child memorizes the alphabet or recites lists of names or numbers or other random facts, it may seem impressive, but language like this lacks the pragmatic value of a simple "mama" or "ball." The parent of one such child summed it up perfectly, declaring, "Our child talks, but he doesn't communicate."

Some children with ASD repeat words or phrases (the technical term for this is *echolalia*). This can include *immediate echolalia,* repeating the other person right on the spot (the adult says, "Do you want a cookie?" and the child immediately echoes, "Want a cookie?"); *delayed echolalia* (the child says "Are you okay?" after falling down, repeating what others have said to him or her in the past); and *scripting* (the child goes around the house reciting chunks of a favorite DVD or TV program).

As children with ASD approach school age, they usually begin to develop some spontaneous speech, although it is usually connected to their immediate needs, rather than conversational. The child may begin to use common phrases in a socially appropriate context. For example, the child might say "Let's go" when he or she wants to terminate an activity. We also see verbal *perseveration*—the incessant repetition of the same statement or question. In time, spontaneous utterances usually increase in length and complexity, and the child will engage in simple verbal exchanges.

Many children with ASD become fluent but continue to struggle with the more subtle, abstract dimensions of language, such as fibbing, jokes, and verbal make-believe. Their use of, and response to, speech remain literal. One of my patients, a seven-year-old girl with PDD-

NOS—we'll call her Sally (not her real name)—accuses her four-year-old brother of "lying" whenever he engages in verbal make-believe (pretending to be a fireman, for instance). For Sally, something is either true or false, and that's it. The idea of deliberately tinkering with the truth, for fun, is inconceivable to her. Additional pragmatic skills include turn taking and checking in with the other person to see if he or she understands and is still interested in what we have to say. Children with ASD typically lack these skills. The child with ASD often talks *at* rather than *with* another person, jumping right into a topic with no introduction and going on at length without noticing whether the listener is following along.

Prosody

Infants coo and babble, with variations in pitch, volume, and rate. In effect, they are warming up for spoken language by practicing the melodies and cadences that they hear around them. By twelve to eighteen months of age, babies produce *jargon:* long strings of different syllables, with rising and falling inflection, that sound like a foreign language. Sometimes you can pick out real words embedded in the jargon: "Jalamabadaga*mommy,* dabakalapata*daddy.*" As toddlers begin to produce actual words and phrases, they learn how to inflect these as well, to convey meaning that goes beyond the literal translation of the words themselves ("Want it *now,*" for example, to show emphasis). Children with ASD display various distortions in prosody. The speech of a child with ASD may go from too soft to too loud, the rhythm may be stilted or mechanical, or the child's speech may have a singsong or robotic quality. Ironically, the only time the child's prosody may sound normal is during an episode of echolalia or delayed echolalia, when the child is imitating someone else. In the case of Asperger syndrome, the child's speech is pedantic (the so-called little professor), with a condescending tone, as if the child is talking down to the other person. In my experience, well-preserved prosody is a good prognostic sign. Just as my stepmother used to take my temperature by kissing me on the forehead to determine if I felt warm, I take a child's "ASD temperature" by listening to the melody of his or her speech. The more natural the prosody, the better the prognosis.

Receptive language development in children with ASD is equally impaired. They may act deaf, even though their hearing tests fine. They may fail to respond to their own names, even though they may be keenly aware of the faintest nonhuman sound, such as the droning of an airplane. Children with ASD are usually delayed in being able to follow verbal commands, although as they get older they usually begin to follow highly practiced commands given in a familiar context. Sometimes during an office visit parents will say, "He does it for us at home, Doctor; we don't know why he won't do it for you in the office." What happens is that the child learns to respond to a command given in a consistent way, in a particular setting, and cannot generalize the skill to another setting or another speaker. (One reason why children with ASD are drawn to videos and DVDs is that the speech and gestures are always exactly the same each time.)

Just as children with ASD can't bring appropriate inflection to their own speech, they can't read cues in the prosody of other people's speech either. This leads to obvious difficulty with receptive language. You know how many meanings you can convey with the simple phrase "Come here," depending on your tone of voice—anger, affection, impatience—but to the child with ASD, these different tones may all sound the same. Your child will have difficulty reading your underlying meaning (or sense your emotional state) because he or she can't read prosody.

Finally, visual language skills are also off the track, starting with eye contact, which may be absent or odd in some way: "My child seems to be searching for me rather than looking at me" and "My child is looking *through* me rather than *at* me" are frequent comments from parents. The nine-month-old baby with ASD does not engage in age-appropriate gesture games. Children with ASD are not able to use visual language to offset verbal language delays. The twelve-month-old may point to items of interest but does not use pointing as a way of communicating with his or her parents. Toddlers with ASD don't employ joint attention by pointing to what they want while making eye contact with Mommy or Daddy. Instead, the child may physically lead his or her parents to the object, or may take the parent's hand and place it on a desired object. "My child uses my hands like surgical instruments," one mom told me. Another told me she kept her own hands clasped behind her head to encourage her child to speak instead of directing her by taking her hand.

Body language is another form of visual communication. Your child with ASD may have as much difficulty reading your body language as he or she has in reading your verbal prosody, making it that much more difficult for your child to gauge your mood or intentions, compounding his or her difficulty with social interactions.

Interestingly, while children with ASD usually struggle to read body language or vocal tone, they have more success with the printed word. Many children with ASD teach themselves to read, although the process is sometimes completely mechanical: Like a reading machine, the child can convert the printed page into spoken words, but with limited understanding of what it means (this is termed *hyperlexia*). The child is unable to paraphrase the text in his or her own words and may be unable to answer questions about the material unless he or she exactly duplicates the phrasing in the text itself. Later, as the child begins to attach meaning to the printed word, the child will continue to have difficulty extracting information that is only implied by the text. The child with ASD may excel at reading tasks in elementary school but suddenly run into trouble in middle school, where reading for inference becomes required: As the saying goes, in elementary school we learn to read; after that, we read to learn.

Repetitious Behaviors

There is nothing inherently wrong with repetition. "Practice makes perfect," my stepmother used to say, and what is practice but repetition? Repetition of a task or a song or a game also makes it familiar and comfortable, creating a sense of security. But repetitious behavior in children with ASD is excessive, sometimes extreme, and indicates cognitive rigidity.

Children with ASD engage in repetitive behavior for various reasons. Sometimes repeating behavior over and over, like a phonograph needle stuck in a groove in the record—what we call *perseveration*—is a symptom of neurologic impairment, the same way that seizures or paralysis of a limb after a stroke represent symptoms of neurologic impairment. In children with ASD, perseveration is often coupled with its opposite, *impulsivity*. Like alternating between fever and chills when you have the flu, the child with ASD may go back and forth, showing perseveration one minute and impulsivity the next. This can be a real challenge!

Sometimes what looks like perseveration is actually a coping strategy. Imagine you are blind. You'd probably be pretty upset if somebody rearranged your furniture. In this case, your desire to keep the furniture arrangement in your house unchanged wouldn't represent neurologic impairment. Rather, it would be a *compensatory strategy* on which you rely because you cannot see objects in the physical world. Similarly, children with ASD rely on routines as a way to compensate for their inability to see the meaning of day-to-day events.

Finally, some children engage in repetitious behavior for comfort. Most of us do this from time to time—we rock babies to sleep, or we soothe our own jangled nerves in a rocking chair or gently swaying hammock. In the same way, the repetitive behaviors of a child with ASD help the child calm himself, though the behaviors are more extreme. It's good to keep this in mind when we lose our patience with these behaviors, which can be annoying, and which clearly mark the child with ASD as being "different."

Types of Repetitious Behaviors

Repetitious behaviors in ASD fall into two broad categories, mental and physical. Mentally repetitious behaviors appear to be driven by an underlying thought or idea, while physically repetitious behaviors (also called *stereotypical behaviors* or *stereotypies*) do not seem to be rooted in a particular thought but are strictly physical mannerisms.

Mentally Repetitious Behaviors

• *Insistence on sameness.* If you've seen the film *Rain Man,* you may remember Dustin Hoffman's character, Raymond, insisting that he's "got to see Judge Wapner," or that Tom Cruise's character purchased the wrong brand of underwear. Such behavior may be apparent at a very early age. You may not be aware of a particular routine that your child has set up until you inadvertently interrupt it, seriously upsetting him or her. Perhaps you drove home by a different route and your child had a meltdown in the backseat. Or perhaps you tried to brush your child's teeth before, rather than after, washing his or her face. Only after blundering do you realize that this is something your child has memorized and needs to perform exactly the same way every time.

- *Difficulty with transitions.* Your child may get stuck on the activity of the moment, becoming agitated if you try to move him or her on to something new. This is not ordinary childhood stubbornness; lack of adequate preparation for the transition may throw your child into a panic.
- *Stereotyped play.* Children gain mastery of the world through play. Play skills emerge in a predictable pattern, along with other cognitive, social, linguistic, and physical milestones. Children with normal development learn about the world through play, exercising their imagination and cognitive abilities as well as honing their social skills through role playing. In contrast, the play of a child with ASD has a repetitious, rote quality. The child with ASD is more likely to spend hours carefully arranging his or her toys than to use them as they were intended. He or she may become fascinated with mechanical objects or odd items such as rubber bands or bits of string, manipulating them for their sensory qualities, rather than using them as part of make-believe play. For instance, a preschooler with ASD might dangle a toy telephone from its cord and watch it spin, rather than pretend to talk on it. As one dad astutely observed, "Our child wants to play with the wrapping paper, not with the toy inside."

Children with ASD gravitate to activities that are highly predictable, and information that can be cataloged—particularly visual information: a fascination with geometric shapes, numbers, or letters of the alphabet; an aptitude for puzzles, electronic games, and computers. They may respond to videos, but want to watch the same one over and over, anticipating what's about to happen on-screen, or repeating dialogue from the video ("scripting") at other times. As they get older, many children with ASD develop a large body of knowledge on a particular topic, like a mental database—a long list of facts and figures like state capitals, animal species, or bus routes. This affinity for catalog-type information may create the appearance of precocious development when in fact it is a symptom of atypicality.

Physically Repetitive Behaviors
- Hand flapping
- Finger twiddling

Figure 1.1 Repetitious Behavior in Children with ASD *The toddler on the left can barely walk but already is demonstrating the tendency to line up objects. The eight-year-old who produced the page on the right was fascinated with math facts and produced page after page of similar material.*

- Toe walking
- Spinning
- Running laps—around the perimeter of the room, back and forth across the room, around the house in a circuit, and so on.

Physically repetitive behaviors vary in intensity from child to child. Often these behaviors seem to serve a role as stress reducers or as a form of self-stimulation, giving rise to their common name: "self-stim" or "stimming." These behaviors are most evident during the preschool years and usually become less prominent as the child gets older, although they may reemerge from time to time when the child becomes very excited or upset.

Sensorimotor Processing

Up to this point, we have covered three of the four core symptom domains in ASD: social skills, language, and repetitive behavior. The fourth area, *sensorimotor processing,* was treated for a long time as a diagnostic stepchild, largely ignored by the medical community. There are probably several reasons why this has been the case. Although abnormal sensory processing and fine motor clumsiness are common in ASD, they are not unique to ASD. That is, they may be seen in other conditions, such as learning disabilities and attention deficit disorder (unlike, say, impaired eye contact, which is seen almost exclusively in ASD). Partly for this reason, sensorimotor impairment was set aside as a diagnostic feature of ASD. Furthermore, psychiatrists and psychologists have traditionally focused on "things of the mind," leaving "things of the body" for others to deal with. How could something as "low level" as sensorimotor function be related to ASD, a disorder of mental function? As it turns out, however, things of the body are interwoven with things of the mind in ASD.

Children with ASD process sensory input differently than everyone else. Like personal space or attention span, your child's ability to perceive sensory input is under the regulation of a kind of thermostat. If this thermostat malfunctions, your child may over- or underreact to such input. As a result, a stimulus that another child would regard as innocuous may register with your child as exaggerated and unpleasant. Conversely, some stimuli that other children would regard as offensive or painful may not register with your child at all.

Every time you or I experience a physical stimulus, our brains link that stimulus to past events and associations: *Is this sensory experience pleasant or unpleasant? Familiar or unfamiliar? Intense or faint? Originating within my body or coming from outside?* This is how we "know" that something feels good or bad, for example. Children with ASD have difficulty forming these links, or building up a library of past events to draw upon. Think about how surprised you felt the last time you picked up a glass of water you expected to be full but it turned out to be nearly empty: Since you expected it to be heavier than it really was, your arm probably jerked the glass up into the air, perhaps splashing water around. This is an example of a mismatch between your mental expectation of a stimulus and the physical reality of the stimulus itself. Now imagine going through life experiencing such mismatches at random moments throughout the day: Something you expect to be hot turns out to be cold, something you expect to be mild turns out to be intense, and so forth. This may be what it's like for your child. In fact, adults with ASD have written about the painfully exaggerated nature of sensations they experienced as children. No wonder children with ASD often have very regimented ideas about which stimuli to let in and which ones to fend off.

Hearing

Children with ASD often have extremely variable responses to sound. For example, they may appear to be deaf to their parents' voices but acutely aware of the distant drone of an airplane. Frequently, they find sharp or high-pitched sounds very unpleasant. Applause, crowd noise in a gymnasium, guests singing "Happy Birthday" at a party, or the sound of a vacuum cleaner or kitchen blender might make your child very agitated. Children with ASD often cover their ears in anticipation of an unpleasant sound, or when they are excited or upset.

Vision

Children with ASD are frequently drawn to repetitive visual patterns. For example, they are often attracted to spinning objects or those with complex geometric patterns such as chain-link fences. Children with ASD may also engage in visual self-stimulatory behavior such as looking at a light while waving their fingers in between the light source and their eyes, looking at objects from odd angles, or studying their own shadows or reflections for prolonged periods of time. Conversely, some children with ASD manipulate objects without looking at them, acting almost as if they were blind.

Touch

Children with ASD often crave deep pressure, but at the same time may be highly averse to light touch (clothing tags, for example) or gooey things on their hands. They may engage in tactile sensory-seeking behaviors such as rubbing or licking objects or people. Even when most other forms of social interaction may be absent, children with ASD usually enjoy roughhousing and being tickled.

Smell

Some children with ASD sniff objects, including inedible ones, as a way of exploring them. They may be acutely sensitive to certain smells.

Figure 1.2 Visual Self-Stimulation *This child was content to stare at the blinking blades of a battery-operated spinner indefinitely.*

Pain

The pain threshold may be dramatically increased or decreased in children with ASD. Reaction to bumps and bruises may be delayed, absent, or exaggerated.

In addition to experiencing distortions of the traditional senses (hearing, vision, touch/pain, and smell), children with ASD often have problems with food selectivity and regulation of fear—complex behaviors that are closely intertwined with sensory processing.

Food Selectivity

Food selectivity in ASD goes far beyond ordinary "picky" eating behavior and can be viewed as a combination of two atypical traits: *insistence on sameness* and *abnormal sensory processing*. Sometimes there is a discernible pattern, based on the sensory quality of the food: One child may reject anything that is cold or crunchy, while a second may reject anything that is sticky and gooey and yet another may only eat foods of a certain color. Sometimes the distinctions can be quite fine, based on differences that are imperceptible to most people: Fries from Burger King may be acceptable, while fries from McDonald's may not. (The parents of one of my patients tried to wrap food from McDonald's in Burger King paper, but the child was not fooled.) Sometimes the child will eat only in a certain location in the home or from a certain dish, or foods cannot touch one another on the plate. Individual items, such as animal crackers, must be whole, with no broken-off limbs. All of these distortions of eating behavior can turn mealtime—normally a pleasant event in the daily life of the family— into a nightmare.

Fear

Some children with ASD are totally fearless, running into the street or climbing onto high structures with no hesitation whatever. Conversely, some children with ASD display intense and unusual fears (for example, one of my patients has a terrible fear of video screens; another is afraid of falling leaves), and once a child has become afraid of something, it may be nearly impossible for him or her to unlearn the fear of that stimulus in the future.

Motor Clumsiness

Many children with ASD are clumsy. Children with Asperger syndrome, in particular, are commonly awkward, and test poorly on IQ measures that tap processing speed (the ability to execute fine motor tasks quickly and accurately). The reasons for this are not clear.

Underlying Cognitive Deficits

Until now, I've been talking about problems in four discrete areas—social skills, language, repetitious behavior, and sensorimotor processing. Now let's consider two mental abilities that cut across these four areas. The names for these mental abilities—*theory of mind* and *central coherence*—may sound mysterious, but they're actually very simple ideas, and they tie together a lot of the problems we've been describing up to now. And—as you will see in Part II—these underlying abilities point the way to intervention strategies.

What Others Are Thinking: Theory of Mind

We know without being told that other people have thoughts and feelings that are different from ours. Most of us are also reasonably good at figuring out what someone else is thinking and feeling as we are interacting with them. Is the other person smiling or frowning? Nodding in agreement or folding his or her arms across their chest and tapping their foot? Leaning forward or turning away? We take in all of these signals as the interaction unfolds. The realization that other people have thoughts and feelings of their own, combined with our ability to make a good guess as to what someone else is thinking and feeling as we interact with them, constitutes *theory of mind*. It's easy to see how many of the social problems experienced by children and adults with ASD can be traced to their difficulty with theory of mind. Starting in infancy, the child with ASD experiences an inability to read social and emotional cues, such as facial expression, body language, and tone of voice. During early childhood, a child with ASD might laugh inappropriately when someone falls, or may not realize when he or she is provoking another person, not sensing the rising tension until it is too late. For the school-age child with ASD, this misinterpretation of social clues often leads him or her to believe that another child is their best friend or that the other child "hates" them, when in fact the two children have little or no relationship of any kind. Most painful of all, the child with ASD may not learn from experience, since he or she doesn't get the impact of his or her behavior on others. Developing friendships, attracting a mate, and holding a job all depend upon theory of mind skills.

Theory of mind deficits also affect the language abilities of a child with ASD. When we speak to another person, we consciously or unconsciously monitor how the other person is receiving our words, constantly updating our impressions over the course of an interaction, based on signals of understanding and engagement, or boredom and distraction, or whatever, from our conversational partner. Conversely, with limited sensitivity as to how their speech is being received, children and adults with ASD often seem to be speaking *at*, rather than *with*, other people. They have difficulty connecting with another speaker in a real give-and-take dialogue, instead launching into monologues on topics of interest only to themselves.

Not only do children with ASD have a hard time with turn taking, but their language is also literal and concrete. Normally, verbal make-believe, verbal humor, and fibbing all emerge around three years of age. All three depend upon the child's theory of mind skills. Verbal make-believe reflects the child's ability to engage in role playing ("I'll be the good guy and you be the bad guy") or to attribute personality traits to inanimate objects (causing Thomas trains or stuffed animals to "speak" to one another, for example). Children with ASD, who have a hard time understanding that real people have inner thoughts and feelings, find this type of play to be exceptionally difficult. We saw this earlier in the chapter in the example of Sally, who accused her younger brother of "lying" whenever he engaged in verbal make-believe. Verbal humor and fibbing both depend upon the speaker's ability to misdirect the listener; in a joke, we surprise the listener with the punch line, while in a fib, we try to leave the misdirection standing. Not surprisingly, children with ASD don't make good liars. Not only are they not good at lying, many of them don't understand why anyone would engage in such an activity.

In addition to enabling us to sense how someone else is feeling, theory of mind enables us to consider other people's intentions—why they do the things they do, and the ability to anticipate their next move. Without theory of mind, the behavior of others can appear random or arbitrary. Imagine how anxious you would be if you were thrust into a social situation where you were suddenly unable to predict what anyone was about to do next. The ability to read the intentions of others is also a safety measure: Without this ability, we cannot sense when someone is trying to take advantage of us. As the child with ASD enters

One Big Happy

Figure 1.3 Theory of Mind *This cartoon evokes a smile because the little girl, Ruthie, does not quite grasp theory of mind. Grandma has told Ruthie to bluff, but Ruthie is not very good at it. She understands the notion of bluffing at a superficial level, but she gives herself away because she cannot anticipate the effect of her declaration ("Okay, I'll bluff") on her listeners. This is normal for a preschool child, and Ruthie appears to be about four or five—the age when children begin to master the fine art of fibbing. But even very bright teenagers (or adults, for that matter) with ASD have difficulty anticipating the effect of their declarations on others. The individual with ASD may engage in simple denial ("No, I didn't do that"), but fabricating complex lies is difficult or impossible.* (By permission of Rick Detorie and Creators Syndicate, Inc.)

adolescence and early adulthood, he or she becomes rather easy prey, as other people recognize and exploit this lack of awareness.

Seeing the Big Picture: Central Coherence

Central coherence is just a fancy way of referring to our ability to see the big picture. When you look out at a scenic vista, your brain doesn't say, *Look: A tree, and another tree, and a third tree....* Rather, your brain says: *Look: a forest.* This ability to pull together all of the thousands of little details into a larger whole is known by psychologists as central coherence. Our brains are driven to achieve central coherence, and most of the time we do so effortlessly, never giving it a conscious thought. Persons with ASD, however, have difficulty achieving central coherence, leaving them with a piecemeal view of the world. They notice countless tiny details but miss the big picture—especially the larger social meaning of events.

Remember our discussion of insistence on sameness as a coping strategy? Without theory of mind and central coherence, the entire world becomes chaotic. For the child with ASD, all the little pieces fail to come together into a coherent, meaningful whole, and the motiva-

Figure 1.4 Absence of Central Coherence *In addition to standardized testing, I assess a child by a variety of informal measures. One of the most revealing is to go through a storybook from which I've previously removed all of the printed text, and ask, page by page, "What's going on in this picture?" For a school-age child, a typical answer on this page would be "The boy is writing a letter." After studying this picture for several minutes, one of my patients with ASD (a six-year-old with normal nonverbal IQ) declared solemnly, "The kitten is on the boy's back and is about to eat him." He could not grasp the context and misinterpreted the one element in the picture to which he had been attracted—the kitten staring over the boy's shoulder. Without central coherence, he saw the picture as a collection of individual elements, not an organic whole.* (From SEVEN LIT-TLE POSTMEN by Margaret Wise Brown and Edith Thatcher Hurd, copyright 1952, renewed 1980 by Random House, Inc. Used by permission of Golden Books, an imprint of Random House Children's Books, a division of Random House, Inc.)

tions for other people's behavior are a total mystery. Almost in desperation, the child imposes whatever order he or she can, usually on the basis of what you or I would consider irrelevant details—sorting objects by color or size, or always taking the same route to a particular destination. The child gravitates to these details because they provide some kind of reliable landmarks. They don't have "meaning" as you and I would define the word, but at least they offer something the child with ASD can rely upon.

TEMPLE GRANDIN ON THEORY OF MIND

Temple Grandin, author of *Thinking in Pictures,* a memoir of her life with autism, once likened herself to "an anthropologist on Mars": a scientist studying the behavior of an alien species, trying to understand how the members of that species communicate with one another—passing invisible messages back and forth, whose meaning she can only guess at. The neurologist Oliver Sacks' collection of essays *An Anthropologist on Mars* takes its title from his interview with Grandin. Grandin's book and Sacks' interview offer insight into the mental and emotional function of adolescents and adults with limited theory of mind skills.

Table 1.2 Symptoms of ASD

Developmental Domain ↓	Decreasing Atypicality or Increasing Age →		
	Severe / Youngest	Moderate / Older	Mild / Oldest
Relating to others	• No eye contact • No physical affection • Cannot be engaged in imitative tasks	• Intermittent or "one-way" eye contact • Seeks affection on own terms • May invade personal space of others (not true affection) • Intermittently engageable in imitative tasks	• Good eye contact • Shows interest in others but does not know how to join in • Rigid: has difficulty if he or she perceives that rules have been broken • Easily engaged in imitative tasks

Table 1.2 Symptoms of ASD (*cont'd.*)

Developmental Domain ↓	Decreasing Atypicality or Increasing Age →		
	Severe / Youngest	Moderate / Older	Mild / Oldest
Language • Pragmatics • Prosody	• Nonverbal • No response to voice • May act deaf • No use of gestures • May use hand-over-hand to guide caregiver to desired objects	• Echolalia • Delayed echolalia • Stock phrases • Verbal perseveration • Odd inflection • Some use of visual modalities (symbol cards, sign language)	• Speaks fluently but lacks understanding of verbal nuance • Difficulty with theory of mind tasks: fibbing, humor, framing conversations, conversational repair
Repetitious behaviors • Mental • Physical	*Mental* • Extreme distress if routines are changed or when required to transition from one activity to another • Fascination with odd objects *Physical* • Frequent stereotypies and self-stimulatory behavior (flapping, spinning, twiddling objects, etc.)	*Mental* • Diminishing level of distress; may accept verbal preparation for changes in routine • Repetitious play (lining up objects; letters or numbers; etc.) *Physical* • Stereotypies and self-stimulatory behaviors are infrequent but emerge when excited	*Mental* • May demonstrate conscious awareness of preference for repetitious behaviors; easier to self-modulate • Play remains repetitious but repetitive quality is more subtle; reoccupation with odd topics *Physical* • Stereotypies and self-stimulatory behavior are rare or absent
Sensorimotor processing • Intense aversion or attraction to all types of sensory input • Fine motor clumsiness	• Auditory: hypersensitivity to noise, or may act deaf • Visual: fascination with visual patterns, looks at objects from odd angles, or may not look at objects at all • Tactile: rubs, licks, mouths objects; craves deep pressure, averse to light touch • Olfactory: sniffs nonfood items • Food selectivity • Increased/decreased pain threshold • Unusual fears or fearlessness • Difficulty with fine motor tasks	Same, but with diminishing intensity	Same, but with diminishing intensity

Summing Up

Autistic spectrum disorder is the shorthand term for a collection of symptoms in four areas: social skills, language, repetitious behavior, and sensorimotor processing. Table 1.2 summarizes the atypical features seen in children with ASD. The degree of a child's atypicality in one area does not necessarily correspond to the degree of his or her atypicality in other areas. A child might have mildly impaired social skills, for example, but severely impaired sensory processing skills, or vice versa. Symptoms in some areas may be detected only as part of a broader pattern of atypicality; viewed by themselves, they might not attract any attention at all. Remember Teddy and his fixation on the *Titanic*? Many of us are fascinated by the *Titanic*, but that doesn't mean we have ASD. Teddy's behavior changes from a quirk to a symptom when placed within the context of his other atypical features.

Finally, don't panic if some of your child's behaviors presently lie all the way over to the left-hand edge of the table. The column headings correspond to decreasing atypicality *or* increasing age. Your child may have symptoms in the leftmost column at this time because of young age rather than because of the intrinsic severity of his or her ASD. Over time, virtually all children move *to the right. No one moves to the left.* (The only exceptions to this rule are children with seizure disorders or progressive neurologic or metabolic disorders.) For the overwhelming majority of children with ASD, therefore, this table can be used two ways: as a snapshot of where the child is today, and as a road map of where the child may be tomorrow.

Chapter 2

Getting a Diagnosis

First Steps

Up until now, your uncertainty, along with your hope that everything would turn out all right, may have stopped you from investigating the possibility that your child may have ASD. It's less upsetting to attribute your child's speech delay to recurrent ear infections, to believe that your child is just ignoring you, or to think that he or she is revealing a naturally independent nature than to consider a diagnosis of ASD. Your child's behavior may be inconsistent, "off" one moment and normal the next. You and your partner may be of different minds about your child, with differing levels of concern. Well-intentioned grandparents or other relatives may fail to see the problems that you see, or say that you or your partner were "just like that" at the same age. If you are a first-time parent, you may not have considered the possibility of ASD until now, because you have no basis for comparison with normal development. (Many parents have told me that it was only after their second child was born that they realized how odd their first child's development had been, and that they would have been in to see me much earlier if their child with ASD had been born second.) At some point, though, your worries will win out over all of these defenses, and you will suddenly feel an urgent need to act. Then what?

If you suspect ASD, make an appointment with your child's primary care physician. When making the appointment, tell the receptionist or nurse what you are worried about, so that the doctor can allot sufficient time for the visit. Try to have your partner accompany you to the visit. Before the visit, go to the First Signs website (www.firstsigns.org) and fill out the M-CHAT, a popular screening test for ASD. Share the results with your child's doctor at the time of the visit. Bear in mind, however, that *screening test results only indicate if your child is at increased risk for ASD. Screening tests cannot be used to establish or rule out a diagnosis.* That requires a formal evaluation. This is where you need experts to help you—even if you are a physician or psychologist yourself. There's a saying I learned in medical school: The doctor who treats himself has a fool for a patient. Don't try to be your own child's diagnostician!

(i) See the Resource List for additional information about obtaining a diagnosis.

Assuming that your child's primary care physician shares your concerns, you will probably leave his or her office with two tasks: getting an official diagnosis, and getting services. Ideally, you would be able to achieve both of these goals quickly and efficiently. Sadly, this is often a challenge, due to lack of resources and fragmentation of services within the medical and educational systems. There are often long waits at university-based diagnostic clinics. Getting services started is a bit easier, but without an ASD diagnosis you may not be able to get everything your child needs. I wish I knew how to remedy this state of affairs, but it's a societal problem, having to do with our priorities, and allocation of resources.

Your child's evaluation consists of two parts, a developmental evaluation and a medical evaluation. These cover separate but related issues. The developmental evaluation takes a descriptive approach, focusing on your child's skills and delays: *Does my child have ASD? What is my child's level of intelligence? Does my child have sensory issues, fine motor problems, or other areas of concern?* The medical evaluation, on the other hand, searches for the underlying cause: *Why does my child have a developmental problem? Are there associated medical issues that could affect my child's general health or life span? Is this a genetic problem, and if so, what is the chance that my partner and I could have another child with similar issues?* (Or: *I'm through having kids, but what about my children's children?*) The combined information from both types of evaluations will enable you to develop a comprehensive plan for your child and family's future.

Developmental Diagnosis

Professionals best qualified to make a diagnosis of ASD include:

- Physicians (MDs)
  - Child neurologists
  - Child psychiatrists
  - Developmental-behavioral pediatricians
  - General pediatricians
  - Neurodevelopmental pediatricians
- Child psychologists

Physicians typically arrive at a diagnosis of ASD by combining clinical observation with parental history and application of *DSM* criteria (Appendix I). Psychologists are more likely to base a diagnosis of ASD on the results of standardized tests (Appendix III), placing somewhat less emphasis on the parental history than physicians do. The two approaches complement each other and usually lead to similar conclusions, although in borderline cases professionals may disagree, not because they see different things in your child, but because the scales or tests they use don't place equal emphasis on the same developmental signs. (As we shall see, quibbling over minor differences in a child's diagnosis—such as whether it is autism or PDD-NOS, for example—are less important than addressing the big picture: the need for remediation in the areas of social reciprocity, language pragmatics, cognitive flexibility, and sensorimotor processing.)

Other developmental specialists can evaluate specific skills. They may have more experience in their areas of specialization than either the physician or psychologist, but they are not qualified to make a diagnosis of ASD. These include:

- Occupational therapists (OTs): assess fine motor and sensory processing ability
- Physical therapists (PTs): assess gross motor skills
- Speech/language pathologists (S/LPs): assess language
- Early childhood education or special education teachers: assess a child's language, self-care, social, and academic abilities

The assessment process results in a detailed profile of your child's strengths and weaknesses across a range of domains, as well as his or her degree of atypicality. Observations from a variety of professionals with a range of special skills ensure a more detailed and accurate picture of your child than a snapshot by just one person at one point in time.

Recommendations for your child's developmental intervention will be based on your child's developmental diagnosis. Your understanding of your child's developmental status will help you answer key questions: *What is the best way to teach my child? How do I optimize his or her long-term potential? Which therapies, and for how many hours a week, will best serve my child? Are there coexisting behavioral issues that we need to address as part of the intervention program?* Since so little controlled research exists that can help answer these questions, you and your doctors and therapists will often have to rely on your combined judgment. The clearer your understanding of your child's needs and the better your understanding of the various therapies, the wiser the choices you'll be able to make.

LOCATING RESOURCES

1. Contact your nearest hospital-based department of pediatrics.
2. Search the Association of University Centers on Disabilities website (www.aucd.org) for the nearest Leadership Education in Neurodevelopmental Disabilities (LEND) or University Center of Excellence (UCE) program.
3. Contact your local county health department (typically, the early-intervention provider for children from birth to age three) or your local public school (for children over three).
4. Contact your local chapter of the Autism Society of America.

5. Do a Web search on the following terms (include your area code, zip code, or state to limit the results to providers near you):
   a. Developmental pediatrics*
   b. Neurodevelopmental disabilities*
   c. Developmental-behavioral pediatrics*
   d. Child psychiatry
   e. Child neurology
   f. Child psychology
6. Check out Wrightslaw: www.wrightslaw.com. Their Yellow Pages for Kids (www.yellowpagesforkids.com) lists many providers of evaluation and therapy services.

* There are two medical subspecialties devoted to children with special needs: neurodevelopmental disabilities (NDD; for pediatricians and child neurologists), and developmental-behavioral pediatrics (D-BP; for pediatricians only). Pediatricians with certification in D-BP or NDD are commonly referred to as "developmental pediatricians," although there is no actual board certification in developmental pediatrics. I am certified in both NDD and D-BP.

Medical Diagnosis

Why Get a Medical Diagnosis?

A medical diagnosis will not change the fact that your child has ASD. And—despite what you may read on the Internet—there are no proven medical cures for ASD. Nonetheless, there are good reasons to get a medical evaluation.

A physician can help you connect the dots between everything you'll hear from all the different therapists who will be seeing your child, as well as the reports from other physicians (genetics, for example). Only a physician with broad training can speak about your child as a whole person, rather than a collection of symptoms—delayed speech, delayed play skills, sensory integration disorder, and so on—identified by different professionals.

The physician's ability to synthesize medical and developmental information, combined with his or her long-term involvement with your child's care, puts him or her in the best position to address the question of prognosis: *What can we expect in the future?* (More on this in later chapters.)

A physician can provide continuity of care. Your child will "age out" of the zero-to-three service system on his or her third birthday and move on to preschool (typically, covering the window from three to five years of age). At five, your child will transition yet again, this time into elementary school, leaving the preschool special education system behind. Someday your child will transition from elementary school to middle school, and from there to high school. All the while, your child's developmental features will be slowly evolving, and—in most cases—improving. At some point, your child will have changed so much that it may be impossible for a new teacher to imagine what your child looked like as a preschooler, or to understand the connection between your child's early developmental picture and his or her current needs. Sometimes the older child with mild residual atypicality is misperceived as willfully disobedient or inattentive. The teacher doesn't perceive the child's ASD because it is no longer severe, and the relationship between the bad old days and your child's present level of function is not immediately obvious. This creates the risk that your child will be dealt with inappropriately (for example, as a "discipline problem" rather than a child with mild residual atypicality). As good as your child's teachers and therapists may be, years from now, only you and your child's physicians will be able to look back and comprehend the complete picture of your child's growth and development.

Often you will need a physician's diagnosis of ASD in order to obtain services such as medical assistance (which is provided on the basis of the developmental disability, regardless of family income, to defray medical costs such as laboratory testing).

ASD is just a shorthand label for a collection of symptoms; *there's always an underlying biological cause.* If the physician identifies a specific cause, you can link up with other families of children with the same medical condition for support and information and to learn from their experiences. Awareness of a specific medical diagnosis enables you to stay current with ongoing research that may be relevant to your child.

A specific medical diagnosis may occasionally play a role in the choice of developmental therapy. This is the case if your child has a condition that is associated with a particular cognitive or behavioral profile, such as 22q11.2 deletion syndrome, Smith-Magenis syndrome, fragile X syndrome, or Angelman syndrome. Each of these medical disorders is associated with specific behaviors (self-hugging, hand wringing, inappropriate laughter, etc.), for which there are specific behavioral interventions.

Although there are no medical treatments for ASD itself, there are medications that help with selected symptoms, such as impulsivity, compulsive/repetitive behavior, agitation, anxiety, and so forth. Careful use of medication may assist your child in achieving his or her full potential. (See Chapter 12.)

A medical diagnosis can alert you to the presence of associated medical problems that may accompany your child's ASD. Knowing the medical diagnosis will enable you to anticipate, rather than react to, the emergence of these problems.

Finally, having a medical diagnosis is intimately tied up with the question of recurrence risk: *If this happened to us once, how likely is it to happen to us again? What about our children's children?*

Look for a doctor who will work with you as a partner in your child's care. I have seen thousands of children in my years of practice, but each one for only a few hours at a time. Through clinical experience, I've learned a great deal about the range of normal and abnormal variation in child development. Parents, however, know their own child better than I ever can. I need them as much as they need me. Each of us has a unique piece of the puzzle, and together we can assemble these pieces to the benefit of the child.

What to Expect in a Medical Evaluation

The evaluation should be calm and unhurried. You should feel that the physician has listened patiently and carefully to your story. If both parents are involved in the child's care, both should be present for the evaluation.

Look for the doctor to cover these elements during the evaluation:

1. *Medical history.* Difficulty getting pregnant, fertility therapy, drug or alcohol exposure during pregnancy; prematurity; complications at delivery (there is almost no such thing as "silent" brain damage—if your baby went home from the hospital with you at two or three days of age, then the chances of him or her having sustained a birth injury that gave rise to ASD are nearly zero); your child's medical history after birth (illness, surgery, trauma).

2. *Family history.* The health, developmental, and mental health history of the extended family (subtle issues with language, learning, or social skills are common in the extended families of children with ASD, as are mental health conditions such as anxiety disorder or depression; see Chapter 3).

3. *Social history.* Parents' level of education and occupation; family support systems.

4. *Physical exam.* Growth parameters (height, weight, and head circumference); identification of congenital malformations (one major malformation that affects health, such as heart defect, or three minor malformations that are purely cosmetic, such as shape of eyes or fingers, suggest a problem with fetal development during the first three months of pregnancy, when the organs of the body are being formed); a complete neurologic exam (tone, strength, reflexes, coordination, etc.).

5. *Neurodevelopmental testing.* An assessment of mental status, including attention span, cooperation, activity level, emotional state, and engageability; cognitive abilities (language, problem-solving, and academic skills if the child is over five); atypicality (using the *DSM* criteria and various rating scales). Often, a young child with ASD will be neither cooperative nor uncooperative, but simply does not understand that he or she is being tested; an experienced examiner will be aware of that possibility and refrain from concluding that your child cannot perform the task at hand.

6. *Review of outside records.* School progress reports, Individualized Education Programs (IEPs), formal IQ, language or occupational therapy assessments, and so on.

7. *Laboratory testing.* Basic genetic and metabolic studies (see the box "Fact and Fiction in Lab Testing").

Once this comprehensive picture is complete, the doctor should be able to provide, either directly through or other team members, information about therapy services, behavior management, emotional support services for you and other family members, assistance with long-term planning, and any relevant medical advice. The doctor should provide you with a full report in a timely manner. Likewise, the

FACT AND FICTION IN LAB TESTING

There are a small number of lab tests that are generally considered to be appropriate elements of the diagnostic evaluation of a child with ASD. These tests point to known medical disorders, most of which have been proven to cause ASD. Some practitioners urge parents to perform a large battery of nonstandard tests that seem scientific but are generally a waste of money (and an unwarranted intrusion on the child). These tests often do not point to disorders proven to cause ASD, or even to recognized medical disorders of any kind. Since most tests are designed to flag the highest and lowest 2.5 percent of all results, if you do enough tests you're bound to find some that come back high or low. Therefore, even interpreting the significance of a generally accepted test that comes back out of range can be a challenge. The results of nonstandard tests are usually of little value insofar as the diagnosis or treatment of ASD is concerned, whether they come back normal or abnormal.

Generally Accepted as Part of a Diagnostic Evaluation for ASD (Additional Tests May Be Indicated if Particular Symptoms Are Present)

- **Genetic testing:** chromosomes (karyotype), fragile X, single nucleotide polymorphism (SNP), tests for specific genes (PTEN, MECP2, etc.)
- **Biochemical testing:** sodium, potassium, chloride, CO_2, glucose, pyruvate, lactate, NH_3 (ammonia), plasma amino acids, acyl carnitine profile, urine organic acids
- **Audiology:** behavioral audiometry, brain stem evoked potentials, otoacoustic emissions (*not* tests for "auditory sensitivities")
- **Ophthalmology:** eye exam by a pediatric ophthalmologist (not an optometrist)—the interior of the eye is actually brain tissue,

so a good look at the eyes often provides clues as to brain development

- **Imaging studies:** magnetic resonance imaging (MRI), and in selected instances magnetic resonance spectroscopy (MRS—a newly emerging tool to identify certain inborn metabolic errors by identifying abnormal accumulation of lipids or lactate in the brain)
- **EEG:** generally not indicated, unless the child is in the midst of a regressive episode or if seizures or Landau-Kleffner syndrome (see Chapter 3) is suspected

Not Generally Accepted as Part of a Diagnostic Evaluation, but May Be Appropriate Within Specific Research Protocols

- **Allergy and immunology:** immunoglobulins (IgG, IgA, IgM, and specific subclasses), anti-gliadin antibodies, fibrillarin, myelin basic protein, measles/mumps/rubella antibody titers
- **Chemistry:** urine peptide levels (casomorphin, gliadorphin), purine and pyrimidine metabolites, copper, ceruloplasmin, zinc, mercury, other metals (in blood, urine, or deciduous teeth), metallothioneins (metal-binding proteins), folate (folinic acid) levels
- **Functional MRI (fMRI):** a way of measuring which parts of the brain "light up" during different mental tasks; holds great promise but at present is in its infancy and should be used only in research settings

No Generally Accepted Clinical or Research Indication in an Evaluation for ASD

- Stool culture for yeast, parasites, or other organisms
- Stool or hair studies for metals
- Urine culture
- Red blood cell elements

doctor should feel comfortable communicating with your child's school or therapy program, if you wish.

The doctor should ask to see your child periodically, to monitor his or her progress against the original findings. *Has your child made the expected amount of progress since the last evaluation? How good is the "fit" between your child's developmental abilities and the developmental services your child is receiving? Have any behavior problems arisen? How are you and your partner coping? What about the other children in the family?* These are the kinds of big-picture questions a developmental pediatrician will typically explore with you.

Occasionally, parents come to me hoping to obtain an evaluation without informing their child's primary care physician. As a matter of policy, I will not undertake an evaluation unless the parents give me permission to communicate with their child's regular doctor. Any medical consultant should *always* keep the primary care physician in the loop. What if the consultant discovers something that is medically crucial, or a significant piece of family history that has a bearing on other children in the family? Your child's primary care physician is ultimately responsible for all aspects of your child's care—not just the narrow piece addressed by one consultant or another. If you don't trust your child's primary care physician with my report, then why are you going to him or her in the first place?

(i) See the Resource List for additional information on medical testing for causes of ASD.

An Office Visit

Let me take you through the specifics of how I conduct an evaluation. As I mentioned earlier, parents are my first critical source of information; nobody has observed the child more closely or over a longer period of time. Prior to the day of the appointment, parents are asked to complete a questionnaire detailing the facts of their child's situation, as well as their concerns. My second critical source of information, if the child is attending school or receiving services, is the child's educational staff. Teachers and therapists are trained observers and have had the chance to work with the child day after day, month after month. No matter how good an examiner I may be, I am limited to seeing a child for a relatively brief glimpse (even though a three-hour appointment is long by medical standards). So, in addition to the parent questionnaire, I ask the child's teachers and therapists to give me a brief report of their observations of the child. I also get copies of any prior medical or developmental testing.

My assessment begins as soon as the family enters the office. (In addition to both parents, I request a third adult, to watch the child when I need to speak with the parents.) How does the child react to his or her new surroundings? Does the child become agitated or fearful? If so, does he or she make any direct appeal to the parents such as looking them in the eye and pleading to leave? How easy is it for the parents to soothe the child? My waiting room is filled with toys: alphabet blocks, a dollhouse, books, puzzles, hand puppets, a train set, and more. Generally, the child settles down after a couple of minutes, at which point my social worker and I invite the parents into my office, leaving the child in the waiting room with the third adult (typically a grandparent). After my social worker and I have reviewed the developmental history with the parents, I leave my social worker to complete the psychosocial portion of the family history and I spend about thirty minutes with the child in the waiting room, observing the child at play, and attempting to get myself invited to participate in whatever he or she is doing. Does the child play with the toys, and if so, is the play developmentally appropriate (engaging in imaginative play with the dolls or hand puppets, for example)? Or does the child's interaction with the materials have a mechanical quality (lining up the alphabet blocks, or rolling a train car back and forth while studying the wheels)? Does the child take note of me? Am I able to insert myself into the child's play activities? I also watch how the child approaches (or fails to approach) other adults during play. Does the child bring toys to me or to the third adult, or ask for help?

When my social worker has completed the psychosocial interview, she and the parents emerge from my office. This gives me another opportunity to observe the child's social behavior. Does the child acknowledge the return of his or her parents, or does the child remain engrossed in whatever he or she is doing, seemingly oblivious to his or her parents? At this point, I bring the child and parents from the play

Figure 2.1 Diagnosis by Trains *My social worker and I have often remarked, only half jokingly, that we can make a diagnosis of ASD by observing what a child does with the trains in the waiting room.*

The engineer. *Andrew is fascinated by geometric designs, such as the checkerboard pattern on a tablecloth or the herringbone pattern in the brick walk leading up to his preschool. Here's Andrew, lying on his side in the waiting room, clutching several crayons. Rather than using them to draw, he is comparing them to the geometric design of the toy bridge from the train set.*

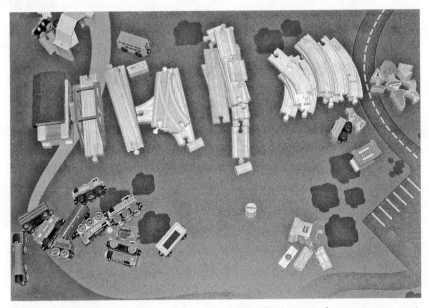

The arranger. *Ralph arranges things. At home, he lines up his toys in a specified order. If one toy is missing, he becomes frantic. His parents no longer give him multicolored breakfast cereal, because he sorts the individual pieces by color and has a meltdown if they try to interrupt him before he has sorted everything in his bowl. Ralph's way of "playing" with the trains is to neatly sort the pieces by category (bridge sections, switches, straight track, curved track, livestock, locomotives, etc., each in their own pile).*

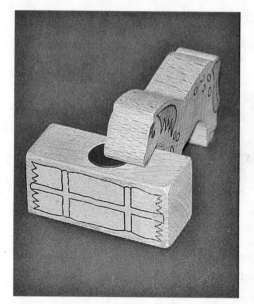 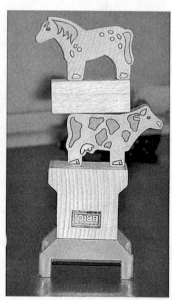

Normal play. *Meanwhile, Ralph's sister, who has typical development, busied herself in imaginative play, depicting (left) a horse "drinking" from a pretend water trough and (right) a statue in the park.*

Of course, we cannot really make a diagnosis of ASD just on the basis of a child's play, but children reveal themselves through play in a way that standardized testing cannot begin to capture.

area into the exam room. How does the child handle this transition? Some children become very upset if I interrupt whatever they're doing with the toys. This is useful diagnostic information. As I tell parents, my job is not to see a child's best; rather, my job is to see a child's *typical* behavior. Is the child behaving in the way the parents would have predicted, given the situation in which we have placed the child?

In the play area, my job is to tag along after the child. In the exam room, the roles are reversed, and the child's job is to imitate actions modeled by me. Often, getting the child to pay attention to me can be a challenge. I use tangible reinforcers such as crackers, visually arresting stimuli including toys that blink or spin, or tactile input such as tickling and hand-over-hand guidance. If the child is lying on the floor, I get down on the floor next to him or her. Many children with ASD are attracted to singing—even mine—so sometimes I give that a try. "The Itsy-Bitsy Spider" is always good, since it combines song with hand gestures.

Often, none of these efforts works. Even if I can't get the child to focus on me, the test materials themselves may grab the child's attention. Many children gravitate to the materials, such as a board for placing shapes into holes, because the items themselves "speak" directly to the child (*stimulus-driven* is the technical term). In contrast, I may fail utterly in my attempt to get the child to copy a circle with a crayon. To copy, the child must first understand that his or her expected role at that moment is to observe and copy the grown-up. Understanding what the adult wants is a theory of mind task. A child can't fulfill expectations that he or she doesn't understand. It's not a matter of refusal or inability. Rather, the child may not realize that he or she is being expected to perform. Items such as the shape sorter, however, are self-explanatory; the child is drawn to them because of their intrinsic properties as physical objects. Anything that requires the child to attend to and then copy me, however, can prove nearly impossible.

I go through a series of verbal and nonverbal tasks. I generally start with a nonverbal task, since children with ASD generally do better with these, then I alternate between nonverbal and verbal items. Nonverbal tasks include copying designs with blocks or crayons or fitting shapes into the right holes in a board. For older children, or children with a higher level of development, I might give a more complex figure-drawing task, or a test involving matching geometric patterns of steadily increasing complexity.

For verbal tasks, I use a variety of formal and informal measures of vocabulary, language use, and other expressive and receptive language skills. If the child is able, I look through a picture book with him or her and ask simple questions such as "What's happening in this picture?" to see if a child can understand the relationships between the characters, rather than just focusing on the details (see the example in Chapter 1). I do not give formal IQ tests; most physicians, myself included, are not trained to give them.

Throughout all of this, I'm observing every detail of the child's behavior: eye contact, attention span, anxiety, agitation, stereotypical movements, and so on. I watch to see if the child can handle frustration by shifting gears or if he or she gets "stuck" on an incorrect response.

At the end of my assessment, I compare my observations with the descriptions given by the child's parents and teachers. If all three sets of data line up, I am usually in a position to make a diagnosis and lay out a plan of action. Where the data are in conflict or unclear, I may have to refrain from making a diagnosis, even while laying out a therapy plan. This is also the type of situation in which I will send a child to a psychologist for additional testing. There is no way to rush the process, and sometimes we have no choice but to conduct serial observations over a period of several months before matters clarify themselves. Under- and overdiagnosis are the twin evils in my profession. The key is to have a set of action items that the parents can get working on, without either rushing to judgment or adopting a head-in-the-sand attitude. Parents want the truth, but they also respect the diagnostician who can say "I'm not sure yet"—as long as the family can get going in the meanwhile. "Wait and see" *without* an action plan is never an acceptable answer.

Summing Up

Your child's future well-being depends upon implementing the right therapies. This, in turn, requires the right developmental diagnosis, profiling your child's strengths as well as his or her areas of greatest need. It's also essential to determine whether there are any underlying medical issues that have the potential to impact negatively on your child's development. Comprehensive evaluation, therefore, should include both medical and developmental components. Having a medical diagnosis may enable you to link up with other parents of children whose ASD arises from the same biological cause, enabling you to tap into the collective wisdom and experience of all the families in the group. Having a medical diagnosis is also essential to providing you with information about recurrence risk. Finally, only you and your child's physicians will have a long-term perspective on your child's development. This becomes more important as time passes and your child's symptoms fade. Only someone who has a long-term relationship with your child will be able to view current problems within the context of your child's long-term development. Look for a knowledgeable physician who is both compassionate and technically skilled. He or she will be a member of your child's team for the long haul.

Chapter 3
Why My Child? A Medical Primer

Parents of a child with ASD usually want to know why this calamity has befallen their child. *Is it my fault? Could it have been prevented? If this happened to us once, can it happen to us again?* All of these questions and more may be weighing on you. In this chapter we will review what is presently known about the causes of ASD, and the recurrence risk faced by parents who have already had one child on the spectrum. In Chapter 4 we will review the facts behind the "explosion" in ASD, as well as various unproven but widely alleged causes for ASD. My hope is that these two chapters, along with Chapter 14 ("Sense and Nonsense in the Treatment of ASD") will enable you to critically examine claims that you will run into in the media, as well as claims made by purveyors of various therapies for ASD.

What Causes ASD?

Asking "What causes ASD?" is a bit like asking "What causes fever?" The answer, in both cases, is "lots of things." The single biggest factor is family genetics, which accounts for about 80 percent of all individuals with ASD (Figure 3.1). The remaining 10 to 20 percent of individuals with ASD have an underlying medical disorder that has caused their ASD as part of their medical condition. Some children

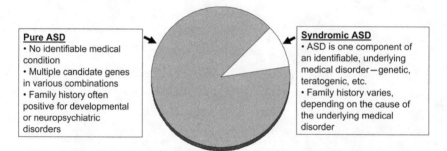

Pure ASD
• No identifiable medical condition
• Multiple candidate genes in various combinations
• Family history often positive for developmental or neuropsychiatric disorders

Syndromic ASD
• ASD is one component of an identifiable, underlying medical disorder—genetic, teratogenic, etc.
• Family history varies, depending on the cause of the underlying medical disorder

Figure 3.1 Proportion of Children with Pure ASD or Syndromic ASD *Some children have ASD alone, and in others ASD is one element of an underlying medical disorder. In the former instance, there are no other apparent problems, hence the term* pure ASD. *In the latter instance, ASD—itself a behavioral syndrome—is one facet of a larger medical syndrome. Therefore, we call it* syndromic ASD.

with ASD are clearly atypical from birth, and some appear to stagnate or regress. Rarely the cause of the regression can be identified; usually it cannot. In this chapter I will give you an overview of the science as it stands today. Keep in mind, though, that the science is constantly evolving.

Proof of Causation

How do we know that something is true? Or, in the case of ASD, what shall we accept as evidence, to establish proof—or at least a reasonable likelihood—of causation?

Establishing causation is typically a three-step process. The first step often is an isolated case report or chance observation: "I saw someone carrying a folded umbrella, and ten minutes later it started raining. I wonder if umbrellas cause rain." The second step involves determining whether the suspected causative factor really precedes the bad outcome more often than would be expected by chance alone, or the original observation was just a fluke. To answer this question, we need to move from isolated case reports to screening entire populations—for example, observing one thousand consecutive pedestrians on Main Street, noting how many of them are carrying umbrellas, then documenting the frequency of rainfall within the next thirty minutes. If the relationship that was observed in the first isolated case reports holds up, then we have established an *association:* The proportion of people carrying folded umbrellas really *does* go up just before it rains. But associations by themselves are not proof of cause and effect. After proving the existence of an association (the more people we see carrying folded umbrellas, the greater the likelihood of rain within the next thirty minutes), the final step is to manipulate the risk factor to see if we can reproduce the problem—handing out umbrellas to try to make it rain, for example, or, in the case of a medical condition manipulating some biological variable, to see if we can affect the frequency of occurrence of the disorder. If we can alter the rate of occurrence of the disorder by manipulating the suspected risk factor, then—but only then—the risk factor becomes a known or probable cause. Of course, it would be unethical to manipulate a risk factor to see if it causes ASD in children. Instead, researchers compare large groups of children—some with ASD and some without, some who were exposed to the risk factor and some who were not—to see if the proportion of children with ASD among those exposed to the risk factor differs from the proportion of children with ASD among those who were not exposed to the risk factor.

There are different ways to go about such comparisons. The key is to have comparison groups that are comparable in all ways *except for the presence of ASD or exposure to the risk factor.* If we observe a difference in the proportion of children with ASD between the two groups (those exposed to the risk factor and those who were not exposed), we can use statistics to tell us how often that difference might have occurred just by chance (without going into the math, the larger the difference, the less often a difference of that size would occur just by chance). If there's less than a 5 percent likelihood of the observed difference occurring purely by chance, then we say that the difference is "statistically significant." *This still does not prove causation,* but the less likely the difference is to have occurred by chance alone, the stronger our suspicion becomes that something *other than chance* is behind the difference. (In fact, science rarely proves anything to be absolutely true. What science does is demonstrate that alternative explanations for observed events, such as the workings of chance, are highly improbable.)

As strange as it may seem, in some cases we also have animal models for ASD. Animals engage in well-defined forms of social behavior: sniffing or grooming one another, responding in characteristic ways to one another's vocalizations, congregating in groups (think of how cute the gerbils at the pet shop look, huddled together in their glass enclosure), and so forth. By modifying certain genes, or by exposing animals to certain chemicals in the womb, scientists can disrupt these normal social behaviors in highly predictable ways, or induce unusual behaviors such as repetitious, nonfunctional activity. No one would say that these animals have ASD, but the parallels to human behavior are striking, and researchers have discovered that children with the same genetic defects or prenatal chemical exposures develop full-blown ASD. Thus, along with statistical modeling based on large samples of children, animal modeling is a powerful tool to help determine probable causation of ASD.

Known or Probable Causes of ASD

Family Genetics: Pure ASD

As mentioned earlier in this chapter, most people with ASD have pure ASD, that is, ASD without an identified coexisting medical disorder. The first clue to a genetic cause for this most common form of ASD came forty years ago, from the study of twins. Researchers noted that if one member of a pair of identical twins has autism, the other twin has roughly a 60 percent chance of having autism, and more than a 90 percent chance of having some degree of atypicality, such as impaired eye contact, difficulty in social situations, or an intense interest in some repetitive behavior. If one member of a pair of fraternal twins has autism, the other twin has about a 10 percent chance of having autism. This is much less than the risk for identical twins, but still greatly increased compared to the background risk of about 1 in 150. (Ordinary siblings of a child with ASD also have about a 10 percent likelihood of being on the autistic spectrum.) The fact that identical twins are so much more likely than fraternal twins to share a diagnosis of ASD strongly suggests a genetic factor, over and above the fact that twins share the same environment in the womb. Likewise, the fact that fraternal twins and ordinary siblings of a child with ASD face about a 10 percent risk of having ASD also suggests a genetic factor, since this is a fifteen-fold increase over the background risk for ASD of 1 in 150. A rule of thumb seems to be that the more closely a child is related to a person with identified ASD, the greater the risk the child will also have ASD.

Our genetic code is made up of about thirty thousand genes, 50 percent of which are expressed in the brain. So far, of those fifteen thousand genes, scientists have identified a few dozen that are known or suspected of causing ASD, as well as milder forms of atypicality (nonverbal learning disability, semantic-pragmatic language disorder, broad autism phenotype) and non-ASD neuropsychiatric disorders (anxiety disorder, depression, obsessive-compulsive disorder, bipolar disorder, alcoholism). We will have more to say about nonverbal learning disability (LD), semantic-pragmatic language disorder, and broad autism phenotype in Chapter 5. For now, note that *phenotype* means the way someone looks on the outside, as opposed to *genotype,* which refers to that person's genetic makeup. The term *broad autism phenotype* therefore implies that there can be many different underlying combinations of genes (genotypes), each of which leads to the same outwardly visible behavioral traits (phenotype). In fact, there are probably hundreds of different genes or combinations of genes capable of giving rise to each of these conditions. This continuous reshuffling of the cards is what accounts for the fact that all of these conditions occur with increased frequency in the extended families of children with ASD (Figure 3.2).

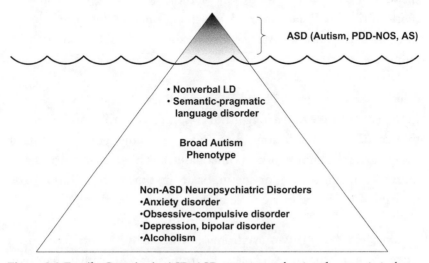

Figure 3.2 Family Genetics in ASD *ASD represents the tip of a genetic iceberg. All of the other disorders shown here occur with increased frequency among the siblings, parents, and extended family members of the child with ASD.*

In addition to illustrating the strongly genetic basis for ASD, another implication of family studies is that there is no bright line between "normal" and "abnormal." Atypical traits appear to be widely distributed in the population as a whole; it's only when we get to people with a high dose of genes for atypicality that we start talking about "disorders" rather than "traits." We'll come back to this point in Chapter 4, where we discuss the so-called explosion of cases of ASD, and Chapter 5, where we discuss the long-term prognosis for children with ASD.

One final note: The term *pure ASD* is slightly misleading. Their ASD is "pure" to the extent that it is not accompanied by major structural malformations (heart disease, for example), mental retardation, or other readily identifiable physical, developmental, or medical signs. However, many of these children probably have underlying abnormalities of brain development or subtle biochemical markers, although thus far such markers have eluded detection by current methods of investigation.

Syndromic ASD

About 10 to 20 percent of the time, ASD—itself a syndrome—occurs as part of a broader medical condition. Many of these medical disorders or syndromes are so rare that even most physicians have never heard of them, and a complete discussion of these conditions is beyond the scope of this book. However, it's worth considering the various broad *categories* of syndromic ASD, as well as some of the more common examples.

Genetic Syndromes with Physical Abnormalities

In this category we find a long list of conditions due to abnormalities in the genetic blueprint. In some cases, one or the other parent is a carrier for the genetic abnormality. In other cases, the abnormality arises as a mutation within the egg or sperm, or at the time of fertilization. You probably have heard of a couple of these conditions already:

Down syndrome. Down syndrome is caused by the presence of an extra chromosome (three copies of chromosome 21, rather than two, hence its technical name: trisomy 21). Children with Down syndrome have a characteristic facial appearance, with almond-shaped eyes, a flat nasal bridge, and a prominent tongue, as well as short fingers, low muscle tone, mental retardation, and (in many cases) heart disease. Most children with Down syndrome are cheerful and extremely social. A significant minority, however, have ASD. Why this is so—since they seem to have the same genetic error as other children with Down syndrome—remains a mystery. For additional help, turn to the National Down Syndrome Society at www.ndss.org, and enter *autism* as your search term.

Fragile X syndrome. Fragile X syndrome is due to a *mutation*—a spelling error that changes the meaning of the genetic code—on one of the X chromosomes. (Remember from high school biology: Females have two X chromosomes, and males have one X and one Y.) This condition gets its name from the fact that the abnormal X chromosome has a little section that looked as if it might break off, when researchers first spotted it under the microscope thirty years ago. It doesn't break, but the name has stuck. Fragile X affects both males and females, but males are usually more severely affected, since they have only one X chromosome, while females have a second, normal X chromosome that partially offsets the problems stemming from the defective X. Older boys and adult males with fragile X characteristically have a broad forehead, large ears, large testicles, loose joints, and mental retardation, often accompanied by developmental features of ASD. Girls and adult females with fragile X may not show any physical abnormalities, and their developmental issues are usually milder, ranging from no symptoms at all to mild mental retardation. There is also something called the fragile X pre-mutation, which can cause anxiety and obsessive behavior in males and females, as well as premature ovarian failure and infertility in women. For reasons too complicated to explain here, the maternal grandfathers of children with fragile X are at risk for Parkinson-like symptoms (difficulty with gait and balance). For additional information, go to the National Fragile X Foundation: www.fragilex.org.

Rett syndrome (RS). RS is a degenerative disorder that primarily affects girls. Affected girls appear normal at first, but by six to eighteen months they begin losing language and social skills. Repeated hand-washing or hand-wringing movements are common. At this point, many of these girls meet behavioral criteria for ASD. Unlike children with garden-variety ASD, however, these children continue to lose abilities, with slowing of motor development, unsteady gait, unusual breathing patterns during sleep, and slowing of brain growth. This phase can last for several months, followed by a leveling off of abilities in later childhood. As adulthood approaches, slow deterioration of physical abilities sets in, and the affected individual is left wheelchair-bound and severely incapacitated. It was originally believed that whatever caused RS must be lethal in males, since RS was observed almost exclusively in females. All that changed in 1999, when the specific cause of RS—a mutation on the X chromosome (MECP2, at a different site than the fragile X mutation)—was discovered. With the genetic cause at hand, it became possible to test for the mutation directly, rather than relying on physical and developmental symptoms alone to make the diagnosis. About 85 percent of girls with a *clinical diagnosis* of RS (that is, a diagnosis based on the developmental history and physical examination) test positive for the MECP2 mutation. It's not clear whether the remaining 15 percent of girls with a clinical diagnosis of RS have a mutation that's below the level of detectability or whether they have some other mutation producing a *phenocopy* of RS (that is, having the same phenotype as RS but different genotypes). The RS mutation is usually sporadic, meaning that the recurrence risk is very, very low. This is good news for parents of a daughter with RS, since it means that their ability to have more children is usually unclouded by worries of having another daughter with RS. One surprising discovery has been the range of expression of MECP2 mutations in males, including long-term survival with only mild disability. Even though the mutation in males appears to be the same gene as in females, the clinical picture in males is not that of RS (same genotype, different phenotype). Why this is the case is unknown. For additional information, go to www.ninds.nih.gov/disorders/rett/detail_rett.htm or www.rettsyndrome.org.

Genetic Syndromes with Metabolic Abnormalities (Inborn Errors of Metabolism)

The cells in your body are equipped with an elaborate set of metabolic machinery. The actual "workers" in the machinery are called "enzymes." There are thousands of enzymes, all under genetic control. Defects in the formation of these enzymes can lead to disordered metabolism. Some inborn errors of metabolism have been proven to cause ASD, and others are suspected of doing so.

Phenylketonuria. Phenylketonuria (PKU) was discovered in 1934. Newborn screening for PKU (a blood test) was introduced in 1962. The underlying problem is a deficiency in a specific enzyme within the body, leading to the buildup of phenylpyruvate—a potent neurotoxin. Left untreated, PKU can cause autism and mental retardation. Fortunately, PKU is treatable by putting the infant on a lifelong diet severely restricted in its phenylalanine content. (The artificial sweetener aspartame breaks down into phenylalanine in the body. That's why diet drinks sweetened with aspartame bear a warning label for persons with PKU.) PKU is a recessive disorder, meaning that the child needs to inherit two copies of the gene—one from each parent—in order to be affected. This also means that parents with one child with PKU have a 25 percent risk of having another, since they are both carriers for the genetic defect. Untreated PKU is extremely rare in the United States because of the high acceptance of newborn screening.

Mitochondrial Disorders

Mitochondria are tiny energy-producing structures found inside almost all cells in the body; think of them as tiny little blast furnaces. Within mitochondria, glucose is combined with oxygen (oxidized), releasing carbon dioxide, energy, and a toxic by-product known as reactive oxygen species (ROS). Fire is another example of oxidation. In a fire, oxidation takes place very quickly, and the energy is released directly into the environment as light, heat, and ROS; the flame from a fire is essentially a cloud of ROS. Within mitochondria, oxidation takes place more slowly, and though some of the energy is released as heat, most of it is recaptured and stored, to be used elsewhere within the body. Mitochondria go to great lengths to prevent ROS from escaping, because—like an open flame—ROS generated by mitochondrial oxidation attack tissues, causing cell damage and death. The principal means of detoxifying ROS is via specialized enzymes and antioxidants. Despite the body's best efforts, however, some ROS leak out of the mitochondria and attack other parts of the cell. Damage to cell walls impairs cell function and leads to cell death; damage to DNA in the nucleus of the cell can cause cancer or genetic mutations. Leakage of ROS out of the mitochondria goes by the term *oxidative stress*. A certain amount of oxidative stress happens in all of us, all the time; chronic oxidative stress is believed to be one of the key factors driving the normal aging process. This explains why antioxidant supplements are so popular!

In mitochondrial disorders, energy generation is deficient, due to the malfunction of one or more mitochondrial enzymes. Instead of oxidizing glucose to carbon dioxide, the end product of oxidation is frequently *lactate* (also called lactic acid). The amount of energy generated by oxidizing glucose to lactate is only about 10 percent of what would be obtained by oxidizing glucose to carbon dioxide. Therefore, people with mitochondrial disorders are chronically energy deficient. The organs of the body with the highest energy demand (brain, muscle, heart, eye) are always teetering on the edge of failure. This is why muscle weakness and neurologic degeneration are common symptoms in mitochondrial disorders. Elevated blood lactate is the classical "calling card" of mitochondrial disorders, but it may not always be present. Often, people with mitochondrial disorders squeak by, with marginal but tolerable blood chemistries, as long as they are in good general health. But a sudden metabolic stress—surgery, injury, or a simple viral infection with fever—can tip them over into a metabolic crisis.

Medical evaluation for mitochondrial disorders includes measuring lactate and amino acid levels in the blood. MRI (magnetic resonance imaging), sometimes including a special form of MRI called MRS (magnetic resonance spectroscopy), may show accumulation of lactate within the brain. Eye exams and EKGs sometimes reveal findings suggestive of a mitochondrial disorder. Sometimes a skin or muscle biopsy is necessary in order to measure mitochondrial enzyme activity directly.

Known mitochondrial disorders occur in about one in four thousand children in the general population. When groups of children with ASD have been screened, elevated lactate has been reported up to one in fifteen, suggesting an increased frequency of mitochondrial disorders in children with ASD—although the precise metabolic diagnoses have not been established. Looking in the other direction, ASD has been identified in children with confirmed mitochondrial disorders. These data strongly suggest a role for mitochondrial disorders as the cause of ASD in some children. For more information on mitochondrial disorders, go to the website of the United Mitochondrial Disease Foundation, www.umdf .org, or the Cleveland Clinic website, http://my.clevelandclinic.org/ disorders/Mitochondrial_Disease/hic_Mitochondrial_Disease.aspx.

Teratogens

Any chemical or physical agent that can cause damage to the unborn baby is known as a *teratogen*. German measles (rubella), now rarely seen because we immunize children against it, can cause malformations, including brain damage, deafness, mental retardation, and autism, if a pregnant woman catches the virus and it passes through her system to the unborn child. The antiseizure drug valproate (valproic acid), if taken by the mother during pregnancy, can cause autism in her unborn child. Thalidomide, a drug once sold in Europe as an over-the-counter sleeping pill, causes limb deformities, brain malformations, and autism. (Thalidomide is available today by prescription for treatment of certain rare medical conditions.) Babies born to mothers who are alcoholic have an increased risk of ASD, but this may be because of shared genetic risk factors: The same genes that predispose an adult to develop alcoholism predispose the child to have ASD, rather than a toxic effect of alcohol exposure in the womb (see Figure 3.2).

Malformation Syndromes of Unknown Cause

The causes for many syndromes have not been worked out, even though the syndromes themselves are well known. Some of these syndromes give rise to ASD in addition to medical complications. Most are rare and beyond the scope of this book. For resource information, you can go to the National Organization of Rare Diseases (www.rare diseases.org), or the websites for specific disorders.

(i) See the Resource List for additional information on causes of ASD.

Risk Factors and Associated Conditions

In the preceding section, we discussed known or probable causes of ASD. In this section I will be speaking about conditions that have been associated with ASD, although no cause-and-effect linkage has been established. As the science unfolds, some of these factors will move up the list as causal mechanisms are worked out, while others may be scratched from the list as we discover deeper, underlying problems that account for both the association and the ASD.

Male Gender

Newborn mortality is higher and life span is shorter in males compared to females. Many genetic disorders are seen more commonly or expressed more severely in males—hemophilia, muscular dystrophy, and color blindness, to name a few. Mental retardation and learning disabilities are more common in males than females. Finally, ASD is more common in males. The ratio usually cited is four boys with ASD to every girl, but it's not that simple. Look back at Figure 3.1. If we were to examine the sex ratio of each portion of the chart separately, we would find that boys with pure ASD outnumber girls four to one. But in the smaller group of children with syndromic ASD, the ratio of boys to girls is far lower—about two to one. Stated another way, *the more severe the autism, and the more severe the associated medical problems, the closer the sex ratio comes to being equal.* Among children with ASD plus seizures or mental retardation, for example, the sex ratio is about two to one, and the National Autism Society (England) reports a ratio of *adult* male to adult female clients with autism of two to one. The presumption is that persons with severe atypicality will be more likely to remain on the radar screen as adults, compared to persons with mild atypicality. The two-to-one male-to-female ratio among adults with ASD receiving services is thus a clue about the relative severity of ASD between the sexes. Therefore, we have not one mystery on our hands but two: Why is there a male predominance for ASD overall, and why, at the more severe end of the spectrum, does the male predominance all but disappear?

At the more severe end, Rett syndrome occurs almost exclusively in females, but RS is a rare disorder—there aren't enough girls with RS to account for the shift in sex ratio. Down syndrome occurs equally in males and females—another factor that may work to equalize the sex ratio at the syndromic end of the spectrum. Are there other, as yet unidentified, medical disorders that occur more frequently or create more severe problems among females? Or perhaps there is some unrecognized disorder that is lethal in male fetuses, so only the females survive to develop with ASD? We just don't know. We have the opposite riddle to explain at the other end of the spectrum: Why are there so many more males than females with pure ASD? Perhaps there are just as many females as males with the same underlying biological disorders, but their symptoms are different (same genotype, different phenotype). Fragile X acts this way: Boys with fragile X tend to have ASD, while girls may have an anxiety disorder or no symptoms at all. And finally, is there something about being male that is inherently a risk factor? In fact, the answer to that question is yes. There is a growing body of evidence that prenatal exposure to male hormones—regardless of gender—is a risk factor for ASD. In laboratory animals, exposing male or female fetuses to testosterone (a male hormone) affects their later social behavior. Certain endocrine disorders result in the production of excess male hormone, by female as well as male fetuses. Girls with these disorders show an increase in atypical behavior. Likewise, the offspring of women with polycystic ovary syndrome (PCOS)—a disorder associated with increased production of male hormone—may to be at increased risk for ASD, presumably because the fetus was exposed to the mother's male hormones during pregnancy. There are some interesting physical clues to support this theory as well: The ring finger is longer than the index finger in most people, but this disparity is greater in males than females due to fetal exposure to testosterone (why testosterone causes the ring finger to grow longer than the index finger is a total mystery). Males with ASD have the highest ring-to-index-finger ratio of all, suggesting that they had superelevated testosterone levels during fetal life. At present, however, we don't have a fully satisfactory explanation for the striking imbalance of males to females with pure ASD.

Parental Age

Father's age and mother's age are each risk factors for having a child with ASD. With every successive decade, the risk of having a child with ASD goes up by a factor of about 1.3. Parents in their thirties are 1.3 times as likely as parents in their twenties to have a child with ASD;

parents in their forties are about 1.7 times (1.3 × 1.3) as likely as parents in their twenties; and so on. The reason is unknown; one theory is that it may be due to the steadily accumulating number of mutations in the parents' eggs and sperm due to chronic oxidative stress.

Infertility and Artificial Reproductive Technology

Infertility itself is often a marker for underlying genetic or medical disorders that can cause ASD. For example, premature ovarian failure and infertility are seen in women with the fragile X pre-mutation. If they succeed in conceiving, they have an increased risk of bearing children with ASD. Likewise, as we've noted, the offspring of women with polycystic ovary syndrome (PCOS)—a condition frequently associated with infertility—seem to be at increased risk for having ASD. Another speculation is that autoimmune or inflammatory causes of infertility might also be at work in some instances, giving rise to ASD in the offspring.

What about artificial reproductive technology (ART)? Many couples with infertility turn to ART in order to have children. Does ART pose any additional risks? Manipulating the sperm and egg by the technique of intracytoplasmic sperm injection (ICSI) in order to achieve fertilization can sometimes disrupt methylation, the process that turns individual genes in the fetus on and off. Disrupted methylation can produce fetal overgrowth (abnormally large offspring) and specific malformation syndromes. One uncontrolled case series reported an increased risk of ASD among babies conceived following ICSI. Whether ICSI truly increased the incidence of ASD, however, is unknown at this time. This is an area of research interest, with more data sure to be forthcoming in the near future.

Perinatal Events

Prematurity and certain medical complications at birth are associated with an increased risk of ASD. For example, in one recent study, bleeding into the cerebellum (the region of the brain at the back of the skull) stood out as a risk for ASD. This is interesting, since we know from children with other disorders that abnormalities of the cerebellum are associated with an increased risk of ASD. However, some of these data are based on the Modified Checklist for Autism in Toddlers (M-CHAT)—

a screening tool, not a diagnostic test. Abnormalities on the M-CHAT may indicate overall delay or neurologic impairment rather than ASD.

Any claim that a child's ASD is due to perinatal events needs to be viewed with caution. First, there is almost no such thing as silent brain damage. Just being slow to pink up in the delivery room is not an indication of brain damage. Complications sufficient to cause brain damage almost always produce multiple organ failure (kidney shutdown, for example) and land the infant in intensive care. Furthermore, complications in the delivery room often represent the playing out of cards dealt months earlier, in the form of genetic risk factors or fetal exposure to viral infection, drugs, or alcohol. Abnormal fetuses come to delivery with reduced physiologic reserves and may require resuscitation at birth, but resuscitation at birth does not prove birth injury. Therefore, even when perinatal complications occur, such events should never be uncritically accepted as the cause (or at least as the *sole* cause) of a child's developmental problem. Simply blaming birth events without looking for other factors during early pregnancy or in the family history runs the risk of missing a disorder with a known recurrence risk.

Macrocephaly

Large head size (macrocephaly) is the physical trait most commonly found among individuals with ASD. Interestingly, the head circumferences of infants destined to have ASD are not unusually large at birth. Over the course of the first year of life, their head circumferences migrate to the upper percentiles on the chart. The emergence of macrocephaly thus immediately precedes or coincides with the appearance of atypical features. Cause and effect? No one knows for sure, but we have some tantalizing clues. In a few cases, a specific genetic mutation on the PTEN gene has been identified as the cause of macrocephaly; mice with the same mutation demonstrate abnormal social behavior, suggesting a cause-and-effect relationship between genetically triggered neuronal overgrowth and abnormal development. Macrocephaly of unknown cause also seems to run in the family members of some children with ASD. Macrocephaly is thus a physical sign that is trying to tell us something about the underlying biology of ASD, but for now, that message remains hard to decipher.

Regression

I knew there was something different about him from the moment they handed him to me in the delivery room. I nursed him for the first nine months, and in that entire time he never looked up at me once.
            —*Mother of a child with nonregressive autism*

He seemed fine up until his first birthday: smiling, laughing, babbling, and doing all the other things his sister did at those ages. Then, around his first birthday, he changed: He just went into himself.
            —*Mother of a child with regressive autism*

Autistic regression was first described in 1887, yet to this day remains a murky topic, with more questions than answers. What is it? Even getting a clear definition is harder than you think. What causes it? Does the outcome differ for children with regressive versus nonregressive ASD? As with so many other questions pertaining to ASD, the answers are not all in. Here's what we know so far.

About one-quarter to one-third of parents of a child with ASD report regression, with loss of previously acquired speech and social skills, typically between fifteen and twenty-four months. Parents are often adamant that everything was perfectly fine up until the regressive episode. However, a closely taken history often reveals otherwise. Take, for example, a recent patient of mine. Jeremy is a handsome, husky thirty-two-month-old who was referred to me by his primary care pediatrician for evaluation of atypical development. When I saw Jeremy, he was using around two dozen words, primarily to label objects of interest to himself (bus, truck, etc.) rather than to initiate social interaction. He was also echolalic. Receptively, he inconsistently followed a few familiar one-step commands. Visually, he did not make use of index finger pointing. Instead, he would guide his parents hand-over-hand, or go and get a preferred object himself. He also displayed a host of other atypical features such as insistence on routines, stereotypical movements, and sensory aversions—all clearly symptoms of ASD. The parents stated that Jeremy's development had been normal as an infant; they first became concerned when he was about eighteen months of age because of developmental regression, with loss of language and social skills. However, on closer questioning, they indicated that Jeremy had not called his father "Dada" until eighteen months of age, and he had never responded appropriately to his own name when called. Normally, both of these skills are well developed by age nine to ten months. Thus, although Jeremy's parents dated the onset of his "regression" to eighteen months of age, he had clearly been delayed for at least nine months prior to that.

Whether we are talking about regressive or nonregressive ASD, research studies have repeatedly shown that the child's symptoms often precede the parents' concerns by many months—sometimes years. This is especially true if the child with ASD is the parents' firstborn, giving the parents no basis for comparison. (As I mentioned earlier, many parents say to me, "We would have been here sooner if he were our second child. We didn't pick up on things until later. But now that we have another child who is developing normally, we can see how different he was even during the first year of life.") One way this has been studied is to look at home movies of children with confirmed ASD that were shot months or years before the parents were concerned about the child's development. Expert reviewers are easily able to pick out the autistic-to-be children from control movies of normally developing children.

This doesn't mean that some children don't deteriorate in the second year of life. There do seem to be two groups of children with ASD: Some are dramatically abnormal from earliest infancy, and others slow down, stagnate, or lose skills—but whether these children were ever perfectly normal remains unclear. In many cases, as we saw with Jeremy, subtle abnormalities in language and social interaction precede the period of obvious regression by months to years. Following the regressive interval, children with regressive ASD as a group appear to be somewhat more impaired than children with nonregressive ASD, but the long-term prognosis does not appear to differ from that of children with nonregressive ASD who have the same level of impairment. In other words, for most children, regression appears to be a one-time event, rather than the opening salvo in a steadily downward course.

In most cases, the cause for the regression is unknown. As discussed, regression and the emergence of macrocephaly frequently coincide. Occasionally Rett syndrome or an inborn error of metabolism can be identified. Seizures are frequently associated with regression, although it often remains unclear as to whether the seizures are actually the cause of the regression or whether the seizures and regression are both due to some deeper problem. Immunizations are often blamed for regression, although, as we will discuss in Chapter 4, there are no reliable data to back up this claim.

Seizures

Seizures (or convulsions) consist of a sudden change in level of consciousness or other bodily functions (movement, sensation, behavior) due to uncontrolled electrical activity in the brain. At one extreme, a seizure may consist of generalized stiffening, jerking movements of any part of the body, interruption of breathing, and color change, followed by limpness. At the other extreme, a seizure can be quite subtle: nothing more than a few seconds of staring off into space, with a temporary arrest of body movements. Although seizures are often terrifying for a parent to watch, they usually do not cause brain damage, and they are almost never fatal.

The most commonly quoted estimate is that about 25 percent of children with ASD also have seizures. However, with the broadening of the definition of ASD and the inclusion of many children with milder forms of the disorder, the prevalence of seizures among children with ASD has probably declined. (We will have more to say about the epidemiology of ASD in Chapter 4.)

The best way to diagnose a seizure disorder is to observe the child having one (live or on videotape). An EEG is not as helpful as you might think. Many children with bona fide seizure disorders have normal EEGs. Likewise, some children with abnormal EEGs have never had a seizure. The key question is whether the abnormal blips on the EEG correspond to a simultaneous change in the child's level of function. Staring spells are a tough problem, since children with ASD are prone to stare off into space just because of their ASD. Sometimes a child may undergo simultaneous EEG and video monitoring. If an episode of blank staring captured on camera coincides with a burst of squiggles on the EEG, it's probably a seizure.

Can seizures cause ASD? That's a straightforward question with a complicated answer. Often symptoms of ASD precede the onset of seizures by months or years, suggesting that both the ASD and the seizure disorder are symptoms of some shared, underlying abnormality of brain development. Occasionally the onset of seizures and symptoms of ASD coincide (technically, this is called *autistic epileptiform regression*). The location of the seizures within the brain may disrupt certain functions, or circuits, as a result of which the child begins to show autistic symptoms. The best known example of this is Landau-Kleffner syndrome (LKS), an uncommon but fearsome condition in young children (typically, ages three to seven), who suddenly act deaf, lose speech, and may develop autistic-like behavior. About 75 percent have outwardly visible seizures, and on EEG all have severe abnormalities in the temporal lobes—the part of the brain that controls auditory awareness and language comprehension. The theory is that the electrical "storm" in the temporal lobes disrupts the child's ability to perceive sound or language normally; that's why the child loses speech and acts deaf. As with regression of unknown cause, however, a certain proportion of children with autistic epileptiform regression were developmentally abnormal before the onset of seizures. Even in Landau-Kleffner syndrome, it's not exactly clear whether the seizures have caused the autistic-like behavior, or whether the seizure disorder and the autistic behavior are both symptoms of some underlying malfunction of the brain. Saying that LKS causes autism just moves the question back a step: What is it about this child's brain that is causing his or her temporal lobes to fire off in the first place? In some cases a specific cause for the seizures can be identified. In many cases, however, the cause for the seizures remains unknown (idiopathic). The presence of epilepsy (recurrent seizures) is a wild card that makes it difficult to give a clear prognosis developmentally. Most children with ASD make steady progress, but the child with epilepsy is subject to setbacks when his or her seizures flare up.

If a child is having visible seizures, these need to be controlled with medicine. There is no consensus on whether to treat a child with anticonvulsant drugs just because of spikes on the EEG, in an effort to "normalize" the tracing. Likewise, there is no clear consensus as to whether anticonvulsant drugs improve developmental outcome, aside from the indirect benefit of bringing the seizure disorder under control. Anticonvulsant drugs carry risks of their own (liver toxicity, and—in intellectually normal subjects with an isolated seizure disorder—

cognitive impairment). So it's no light matter to simply put a child with ASD on anticonvulsants just because the EEG is abnormal or in the hopes of improving the ASD (rather than for seizure control).

A full discussion of the causes and treatment of seizures is beyond the scope of this book. Visit the following websites for additional information: www.epilepsyfoundation.org and www.nlm.nih.gov/med lineplus/seizures.html.

Where Is Autism?

With all this talk about what ASD looks like, and what can cause it, you'd think we would know where, exactly, ASD is hiding in the brain. But the embarrassing fact is, we don't—although we have lots of suspects.

- *The cerebral cortex.* We commonly think of the uppermost layer of the brain—the cerebral cortex or "gray matter"—as the center of reasoning. The frontal lobes are associated with complex abilities such as future planning, insight, and judgment, and the temporal lobes are associated with language. Since ASD impairs insight and

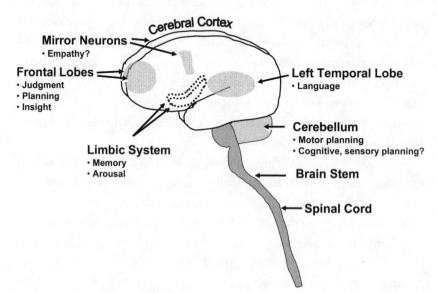

Figure 3.3 The Brain, Viewed from the Left Side

language, the logical assumption would be that ASD arises because of a problem with the frontal or temporal lobes, and indeed there is exciting new evidence of cortical impairment in ASD, but not in the expected place.

• *Mirror neurons.* If you watch a spider crawling up someone else's arm, your own skin will begin to prickle. In fact, the same neurons will fire in your brain as in the victim's brain. Likewise, if you watch someone else try to thread a needle, the neurons in your own hands and fingers will fire as if you were performing this task yourself. The nerve cells responsible for this are called *mirror neurons* and are located a bit farther back from the frontal lobes, along the surface of the cerebral cortex. As our mirror neurons fire, in a sense we literally go through the same motions or feel the pain of the other person. One theory proposes that our ability to feel empathy—to sense the emotions of others—is due to this mirror neuron system. It's only a short leap from there to the idea that defective mirror neurons can impair theory of mind and lead to ASD, and in fact people with ASD do appear to have defective mirror neurons. (See the fascinating book *Mirroring People* by Marco Iacoboni for a detailed discussion of the possible relationship between ASD and mirror neurons.)

• *Limbic system.* The limbic system is made up of several structures deep within the brain that regulate emotions (specifically, arousal and rage) and memory. The limbic system is part of our "old brain," dating back tens of millions of years, as opposed to the cortex, which is a relatively recent development from an evolutionary standpoint. The limbic system is responsible for assigning meaning to different scents—animals can literally smell danger, and for humans scents can evoke powerful emotional responses. A distinct group of children with ASD are "sniffers," smelling all sorts of objects in the environment—each crayon before putting it to paper, their mother's hair, the seat cushion after someone stands up, or anything else with which they come into contact—with an intensity usually seen only in bloodhounds. My hunch is that these children have limbic system dysfunction. Limbic abnormality also probably contributes to the heightened (or blunted) level of fear manifested by many children with ASD.

• *Cerebellum.* The cerebellum is tucked below the cerebral cortex, at the back of the skull. When I was in medical school, we only thought about the cerebellum when it was malfunctioning, which we'd know because the patient had jiggling eye movements (nystagmus), tremor, or an unsteady gait (ataxia). Otherwise, the function of the cerebellum was a big mystery. Now we know that the cerebellum is involved in mental activity, although we're still not sure exactly how. There are as many connections between the cerebellum and the cortex as there are between the brain itself and the rest of the body. What information passes back and forth between the cerebellum and the cortex, and how the disruption of these pathways might figure into ASD, is still unclear. It's intriguing to note, however, that the most commonly observed brain abnormalities in persons with ASD are in the cerebellum.

• *Brain stem.* The brain stem is the "stalk" that attaches the brain to the spinal cord. Like a complex series of toll gates, the brain stem regulates the flow of traffic between the brain and the body. Earlier in this chapter we mentioned that animals engage in highly predictable social behaviors, and that these behaviors can be disrupted by genetic alteration or by exposing the animals to selected chemicals during pregnancy. Anatomic defects in the brain stem have been identified in children with ASD following exposure to specific drugs (thalidomide and valproic acid). In animal models and in human children, these anatomic abnormalities are strongly associated with autistic or autistic-like behavioral changes—a clear example of a teratogen producing both anatomic and behavioral changes.

There are many competing theories as to the nature of the brain malfunction in ASD, each supported by a reasonable body of evidence. Probably each theory is true for some children. Someday we'll be able to divide ASD into brain-specific disorders: Johnny might have "cerebellar-cortical ASD" while Billy has "limbic-temporal ASD," and so on. And we'll be able to trace the cause of the brain malfunction to specific biological factors. One hundred years ago, all fevers were looked upon as pretty much the same, and even if we knew the cause, we didn't have any antibiotics to treat the problem. Today we look back on those times with smug satisfaction: "How little they knew back then about infectious disease!" Someday people will look back on current neuroscience with similar wonder at how little was known about ASD "way back then" in the early twenty-first century.

Could This Happen to Us Again? Recurrence Risk

One of the questions parents often ask is "If this happened to us once, what are the chances it could happen to us again?" (Or "What about our children's children?") Genetic evaluation seeks to determine the precise cause for a child's ASD and provide parents with information about their child's specific medical condition as well as recurrence risk figures. Unfortunately, at present we can do this only for the 10 to 20 percent of children with syndromic ASD—and then only if the cause of the syndrome can be identified. For these families, the recurrence risk of ASD is tied to the recurrence risk of the underlying medical disorder. If the child has Rett syndrome, for example, the recurrence risk is very small, since most cases of RS are due to a new mutation arising at the time of conception, rather than a mutation that's been inherited from one or the other parent. In contrast, if the child has fragile X syndrome, then the risk of having another child with developmental problems is somewhere between 25 and 50 percent. For the children with pure ASD, we can only go by the average recurrence risk, which is around 10 percent. This figure may be an underestimate, however, for two reasons: First, many parents of a child with ASD stop having children, thus cutting down the apparent recurrence rate in the published literature. Second, some of the recurrence data are old and based on a narrow definition of autism. If we could rescore the old data using present diagnostic criteria, the recurrence rate would probably be higher, since many children with mild atypicality who were passed over in the original analysis would get scored today as recurrences.

REASONS FOR GENETIC TESTING

You may say, "I'm not having any more children" or "I don't believe in abortion, so genetic testing is not for me." Even if you do not plan to have more children, or you would never consider termination of a pregnancy, there are still many good reasons to take your child for genetic testing:

1. *Medical care of your child with ASD.* Some conditions that give rise to ASD carry medical risks. Knowing your child's genetic diagnosis will enable you to provide your child with optimal medical care.

2. *Parent support.* With the advent of the Internet, there is a parent support group for virtually every medical diagnosis, no matter how rare. Knowing your child's specific medical (as opposed to developmental) diagnosis will enable you to connect with other parents of similarly affected children. Such parents will be a source of strength and information for you.

3. *Developmental intervention.* Certain medical conditions are associated with specific developmental or behavioral profiles. Knowing your child's underlying medical condition may lead to the implementation of developmental or behavioral strategies tailor-made for children with that condition.

4. *Peace of mind.* Sometimes just knowing why your child has ASD can provide peace of mind.

5. *Unplanned pregnancy.* You may not be planning on having more children, but accidents happen. There are few things more stressful than going through a genetic evaluation of your child with ASD when you find yourself unexpectedly pregnant. Get the testing done when you are not under time or emotional pressure.

6. *The next generation.* Your other children (assuming you have any) will someday want to know whether they are carriers for a genetic disorder with a recurrence risk to them and their own offspring-to-be. Even if you do not contemplate having more children, someday they may.

Summing Up

In this chapter we have taken a brief look at the current state of the science in terms of our understanding of the causes of ASD, the locations within the brain that give rise to the functional behavioral disturbances of ASD, and the recurrence risk faced by families who already have one child with ASD. Along the way we have briefly considered what constitutes a reasonable standard of proof of causation. In some ways, those few paragraphs are really the most important part of the entire chapter—the frontiers of what we know will advance, but the underlying principles that enable us to go from chance observation to likely cause will remain unchanged. Keep those principles in mind as we shift our attention in the next chapter to the realm of speculation.

Chapter 4

Speculative Causes of ASD, and the Autism "Explosion"

In this chapter we will review various speculative causes of ASD. These are theories that have not passed the basic tests for likely causality that we outlined in Chapter 3. Before getting into these speculative causes, however, we will review two assumptions—both false, as it turns out—that underlie most of these unproven theories: first, that ASD is a new disorder, and second, that we are in the midst of an autism epidemic. Once we deflate these assumptions, the energy goes out of the claims for most of the speculative causes of ASD. There are a few caveats, however, that need to be addressed before some of these claims can be laid to rest.

Is ASD a New Disorder?

These children are self-contained and self-absorbed. They speak in the third person, with frequent echolalia. [They are] bright in their expression, often active in their movements, agile to a degree, fearless as to danger, persevering in mischief, petulant to have their own way. Living in a world of their own, they are regardless of the ordinary circumstance around them. [Many of them have] a fascination with music or an extraordinary memory.

—*J. Langdon Down, 1887*

These words perfectly describe the children in my clinic today, but in fact they were written more than 120 years ago by the British physician J. Langdon Down. Down was referring to a group of patients with an extraordinary range of abilities and disabilities—children who could memorize numbers, musical compositions, or vast sections of *The Rise and Fall of the Roman Empire,* yet were unable to interact with their caregivers. Some of the children Down described were affected from birth: "I know nothing more painful than the long motherly expectancy of speech; how month after month the hopes are kept at high tension, waiting for the prattle that never comes. How the self-contained and self-absorbed little one cares not to be entertained other than in his own dream-land, and by automatic movements of his fingers or the rhythmical movements of his body." Others were normal at birth, but their condition worsened over time (what today we call autistic regression): "Intelligence dawned in the accustomed way... [but then] a change took place.... [They] lost their... brightness [and] took less notice of those around them."

In Down's time, *moron, imbecile,* and *idiot* were the accepted medical terms for what today we call mild, moderate, and severe to profound mental retardation. Down coined the term *idiot savant* (*savant* from the French verb *savoir,* meaning "to know") to describe children who displayed amazing memorization skills on one hand and profoundly impaired daily life skills on the other. Looking back now, it seems clear Down was describing children with autism plus splinter skills—isolated feats that depend upon powers of memorization rather than reasoning ability.

Long before Down's patients lived Victor the "wild boy," who was discovered in 1800 wandering in the woods outside the town of Aveyron, France. Victor was nonverbal. He showed people what he needed by leading them by the hand, and he showed a strong preference for meticulous order—all classic signs of autism. The belief in Victor's day was that he had been raised by wolves (like Romulus and Remus, the mythical twins who founded Rome). More likely Victor was a boy with autism who had been abandoned by his parents. Or perhaps he had run off and become lost in the woods—"elopement" remains a common problem in children with autism to this day.

THE BIRTH OF DEVELOPMENTAL PEDIATRICS AND SPECIAL EDUCATION

J. Langdon Down (1828–1896) served for many years as the physician in residence at the Earlswood Asylum, a residential center for persons with developmental disabilities, and he presented his observations in a series of papers given before the Medical Society of London in 1887. In addition to providing the first detailed description of autism, Down was the first to describe a group of children with mental retardation and unique facial features, which he called "Mongolism." Today we call this condition Down syndrome in his honor.

Across the English Channel, Victor's care was entrusted to Jean-Marc Itard, another physician with an interest in bettering the lives of those with developmental disabilities. Itard, in turn, enlisted the aid of his medical colleague Édouard Séguin. Séguin founded the world's first school for people with disabilities, and in 1846 he published *Traitement moral, hygiène et éducation des idiots* (Mental treatment, hygiene, and education of idiots). In 1850 Séguin immigrated to the United States, where he continued his work.

Down, Séguin, and Itard created the fields of developmental pediatrics and special education, raising the care and education of people with disabilities to the level of a respected profession—a tradition that I am privileged to carry on today.

Around the time French physicians were puzzling over Victor, we find records from the American physician Benjamin Rush (one of the signers of the Declaration of Independence and founder of American psychiatry) of a calculator savant named Thomas Fuller, who could figure out a person's age to the *second*, including adjustments for leap years. (We don't know if Fuller had other autistic features as well.)

Reaching back further still, we find the curious case of the Scottish nobleman Hugh Blair of Borgue (1708?–1765), whose eccentric behaviors (limited social skills, insistence on having the same seat in church, ability to recite lengthy sections of the Presbyterian catechism from memory despite having poor overall language) have been attributed to Asperger syndrome. Indeed, so many prominent figures throughout history have displayed odd behavior that it has become almost a parlor game to try to "diagnose" famous cases (http://en.wikipedia.org/wiki/People_speculated_to_have_been_autistic). A nice book has even been written on the subject, which you might want to use to help introduce your child with ASD to his or her diagnosis: *My Book of Autism Heroes* by Jennifer Elder.

ASD has almost certainly been with us for a very long time, but only recently has it been specifically identified and differentiated from mental illness (schizophrenia, manic-depression, etc.), or other forms of cognitive impairment such as mental retardation. As we shall see, it is the very process of identification and differentiation from other disorders that has contributed to the "explosion" of ASD.

Epidemic or "Explosion": What's the Difference?

Incidence and Prevalence

When people talk about an "explosion" of cases of ASD, they frequently gloss over the difference between incidence and prevalence. The *incidence* of a disorder refers to the rate at which new cases are occurring. *Prevalence,* on the other hand, is a proportion, measured as the percent of the population at one instant in time who have the condition in question. An *epidemic* is defined as an *increase in incidence* (for example, the number of new cases of influenza per week). There is no one-word synonym for an increase in prevalence. Incidence and prevalence can be influenced by many things other than changes in the disease itself, including methods of case-finding, and the exact boundaries of case definition (that is, what counts as a "case").

It would be nice if I could quote you some solid figures for the incidence and prevalence of ASD, but those figures are not available, because we do not perform *active surveillance* for ASD: With a few notable exceptions, no one is going door-to-door, canvassing entire geographic regions, to directly measure prevalence. Instead, we are forced to rely on secondhand data, primarily from schools (we'll discuss the inaccuracies of such data in a moment). According to these data, the prevalence of ASD among schoolchildren today stands somewhere between 1 in 150 and 1 in 100. We have no idea of the prevalence of ASD among adults in the United States, because no one has looked. We have no way of knowing incidence, since we cannot measure the rate at which children with ASD are being born (there is no newborn screening test), and we have no way of determining the exact time of onset of ASD in older children (so we cannot calculate how many children "came down with ASD" during any given time frame).

"Autism 100 times more common than 20 years ago," shouts a newspaper headline. What the paper should say is "The prevalence of ASD, using the current definition and case-finding methods, is 100 times higher than it was using the old definition and case-finding methods," but of course, that's not going to sell as many newspapers. Let me take you through some of the misconceptions that go into the misleading headlines. We'll talk about various factors that have led to an increase in the *prevalence* of ASD, including:

- Broadening definitions of ASD
- Broadening federal service and reporting requirements for children with ASD
- Improved case-finding

These are factors that have resulted in an increase prevalence but they tell us nothing about *the rate at which babies with ASD are being born,* or *the rate at which children are regressing in the first three years of life;* the sum of these two values would tell us the *incidence* of ASD. We'll also talk about the "missing" adults with ASD, another argument commonly raised to prove that we're in an epidemic.

Broadening Definitions of ASD

Changes in case definition can have a profound effect on prevalence. Let's say we want to determine the prevalence of tall stature (that is, the proportion of tall people) in a given population. The first thing we need to do is define what we mean by *tall*. If we define *tall* as anything over seven feet, the prevalence of tall people will be around 1 in 1,000. Then let's say we change the definition; under our new rules, anyone over six feet ten inches qualifies as "tall." Suddenly the prevalence of tall stature jumps, perhaps to 1 in 250. If we revise the definition again, this time to six feet six inches, the prevalence jumps again, maybe to 1 in 100. Simply by broadening the definition, we've created a tenfold jump in prevalence, but *no one is one inch taller than before.* This is exactly what has happened with ASD.

Infantile autism did not appear in the *Diagnostic and Statistical Manual of the American Psychiatric Association*—the standard for making a diagnosis—until 1980, even though Leo Kanner published his landmark paper on autism all the way back in 1943. Prior to 1980, physicians used the term *childhood schizophrenia* to cover a vast range of disorders, from delusions and hallucinations to what we now call ASD. When the diagnosis *infantile autism* was finally introduced in the third edition of the *DSM,* or *DSM-III,* in 1980, it was limited to children with severe impairment: pervasive lack of responsiveness to other people, gross deficits in language development, and bizarre responses to various aspects of the environment (see Appendix I). The *DSM-III* also included the category "Autism, residual state," to include children who once met criteria for fully expressed autism but who no longer expressed all of the symptoms. PDD-NOS first appeared in the *DSM* in 1987, replacing "Autism, residual state," which was then removed. PDD-NOS included not only children who had once met criteria for full expression of infantile autism but had outgrown their initial symptoms but also children with milder forms of atypicality who had never met full criteria for infantile autism in the first place—a significant broadening of the scope of the disorder. Asperger syndrome made it into the *DSM* for the first time in 1994, encompassing children with even milder atypicality. (The term *ASD,* emphasizing the spectrum aspect of the condition, is still not a formal *DSM* diagnosis.)

The earliest surveys included only children with severe "Kanner-type infantile autism" and yielded prevalence estimates of about 2 to 4 children per 10,000. Now, however, the prevalence data encompass the complete range of ASD, including many children who never would have qualified for an autism diagnosis in the past. It's no wonder that the prevalence has jumped radically. In 2007, the Centers for Disease

Control reported that 1 child in 150 met the criteria for autistic spectrum disorder. That's a hundred-fold jump in prevalence, compared to the rates I was taught in medical school. But that doesn't mean that there's been an increase in the incidence of ASD, that is, the rate at which infants with ASD are being born or the rate at which older children are undergoing autistic regression. There are no studies that show a change in the incidence of ASD. In fact, there are very few studies of incidence at all. Why not? Because we can't go to the delivery room and count how many children with ASD are being born per year. And (with a few exceptions, discussed below) we generally don't know the rate at which children in the first three years of life are slipping into autistic regression. The sum of these two rates would give us the incidence—the overall rate of occurrence of new cases of ASD. But we don't have these numbers. All we have are the data showing how many children in school carry a diagnosis of ASD. *For all we know, the incidence of ASD could actually be going down, even as prevalence is going up due to broader case definition and improved case-finding.* I am not suggesting this is so, but it is perfectly possible.

Federal Service Requirements for Children with Disabilities

We take Early Intervention (EI) and universal public education for granted today, but it wasn't so long ago that these didn't exist. In the 1950s and 1960s, when my parents sought help for my sister with mental retardation, they were told by their local public school system, "We have nothing for her." The first federal law mandating free and appropriate public education for all children over the age of five, regardless of the presence of disabilities, went into effect in 1975. Special education for infants, toddlers, and preschoolers was mandated only in 1986. Prior to that time, infants and children with special needs were off the radar of the public school system. It stands to reason that once public schools faced the requirement to educate all children, the number of children in the school system with disabilities would rise.

U.S. Department of Education Definitions, Reporting Requirements, and Funding

The Education for All Handicapped Children Act, passed by the U.S. Congress in 1975, marks the beginning of public education for children with disabilities in this country; since 1975, the number of children with disabilities of all kinds in the public schools has shot up. However, in the past twenty years, not only has the "pie" of children with special needs gotten larger, but the "slice" comprising children with ASD has gotten bigger relative to the rest of the pie. Why?

The first part of the answer may surprise you. In 1975, when Congress enacted the Education for All Handicapped Children legislation, autism did not make the list of disabling conditions. Schools were only required to serve—and report back to the government—children with the following diagnoses: mental retardation, hard of hearing, deaf, speech impaired, visually handicapped, seriously emotionally disturbed, orthopedically impaired, other health impaired, deaf-blind, multiply handicapped, or learning disabled. In the eyes of the federal government, autism did not exist. It was not until 1990 that the federal government added autism to the list—almost half a century after Kanner's landmark 1943 paper, and ten years after the appearance of *infantile autism* in the *DSM-III*. (Incidentally, the law was also renamed at that time, from the Education for All Handicapped Children Act to the Individuals with Disabilities Education Act—IDEA). Just as physicians had mislabeled autism as "childhood schizophrenia" until the *DSM-III* came along, prior to 1990 ASD had to be labeled by educators as something else: typically "emotionally disturbed" or "other health impaired." I remember those days. I hated seeing schools mislabel children, but the diagnosis of autism was simply not on their checklists. Once the autism label became available under federal education law, the number of children identified with autism in the school system had nowhere to go but up. In addition to classifying newly diagnosed young children correctly, there was a one-time backlog of older children already in the system, from kindergarten through age twenty-one, who could now finally be reclassified as having autism. As part of the change in federal definitions of disability, and subsequent regulatory changes by the Office of Special Education Programs (OSEP) of the U.S. Department of Education, beginning in 1992 schools were required to report the number of children with autism served. These changes in the federal definition of disability and in reporting requirements led to a huge jump in the number of children identified with autism in the schools, beginning from a pre-1990 baseline of zero. This is a huge increase in *prevalence,* but it had nothing whatever to do with *incidence.*

The second major change in federal law was the creation of Early Intervention. It's hard to imagine a world without EI, isn't it? But Early Intervention has only been around since 1991 (the law was passed in 1986 but came into effect in 1991). Beginning in 1991, EI (for children from birth to age three) and preschool special education (ages three to five) suddenly began identifying even more children with autism, producing another big jump in the number of children served under this label. Children who previously would not have come to the attention of the school system until kindergarten entry—by which point their atypical features might have faded to the point where they would not have been considered for a spectrum diagnosis—suddenly began receiving services, and diagnoses on the autism spectrum, as toddlers and preschoolers.

The third change in the educational system was driven not by changes in federal law but by changes in the medical definition of autism. Remember that the *DSM-III* (1980) described autism as a severe disorder with continuous, bizarre features. The two subsequent editions of the *DSM* (*DSM-III-R* and *DSM-IV*) broadened the diagnostic criteria for autism and introduced PDD-NOS (1987) and Asperger syndrome (1994). Like their medical counterparts, school psychologists began applying these newly available diagnoses to children with milder and milder forms of impairment, leading to yet another surge in the number of identified children (prevalence). Today, the majority of children with ASD have IQs in the normal range—a reversal of what used to be the case in the 1980s and 1990s. My hunch is that the broader criteria for an ASD diagnosis are now pulling in children with normal IQ who never would have received an ASD label in the past.

The most recent change in the educational system has been the trend to allocate funding and resources for children with ASD—smaller class size, provision of an instructional "shadow" in the classroom, and so on—that are not provided to children with other disabilities. This creates a powerful incentive to seek an ASD diagnosis regardless of the child's actual disability. I sometimes find myself wrestling with this issue. If I diagnose a child with PDD-NOS, he or she will be eligible for more services than if I diagnose the child with a nonqualifying condition such as a nonverbal learning disability. The incentive to assign an ASD diagnosis as a means to gain access to educational services may be driving another jump in the prevalence of children with an ASD diagnosis, without having anything to do with the incidence of the disorder.

In summary, therefore, over the past thirty years several factors have kicked in, each of which has led to an increase in the prevalence of ASD (see Table 4.1 and Figure 4.1). The most dramatic rise in prevalence followed the recognition of ASD by the federal government in 1990. So, has there been an "explosion" of cases—that is, increased prevalence? Definitely. Is there an epidemic (increased incidence)? No—or at least we have no evidence to support the claim.

Where Have All the Adults Gone?

If we're not in an epidemic of autism, why don't 1 in 150 adults have ASD—the same prevalence as we see in children? Don't all these "missing" adults prove that we're in an epidemic? This argument is flawed for several reasons. First, it ignores the natural history of ASD. No one

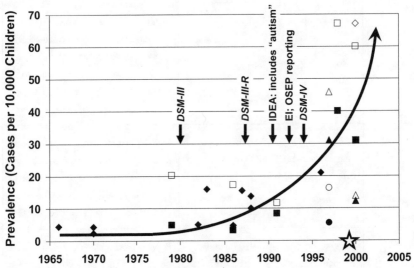

Figure 4.1 Factors in Prevalence of ASD *Changes in diagnostic criteria and federal law, and removal of most mercury from vaccines (☆) versus prevalence of ASD. Notice the huge jump in prevalence immediately following the inclusion of "autism" as an eligible diagnosis for federal funding under IDEA (1990) and the changes in OSEP reporting requirements (1992). We will have more to say about mercury later in the chapter.*

Table 4.1 Factors Affecting Prevalence of ASD

Year	Event	Comments
1975	Congress enacts Public Law 94-142, the Education for All Handicapped Children Act.	First federal law requiring the states to provide free and appropriate public education to all children older than 5 years, regardless of disability.
1980	*DSM-III:* First appearance of *infantile autism* and *Autism, residual state* for children who once met criteria for infantile autism but no longer do.	*Autism* is defined by six mandatory, severe criteria, including pervasive lack of responsiveness to other people, gross deficits in language development, and bizarre responses to various aspects of the environment. Diagnosis limited to severely impaired children. *Autism, residual state* is limited to children who once met full criteria for autism but now have milder symptoms.
1986	Congress enacts PL 99-457, commonly referred to as the Early Intervention Amendments to PL 94-142.	Extends free and appropriate public education to children ages 3–5, mandated to take effect by 1991 (Section 619, Part B), and creates Early Intervention for children from birth to age 3 (Section 619, Part H). Leads to greatly increased level of service to children from birth to 5 years of age.
1987	*DSM-III-R: Infantile autism* is replaced by *autistic disorder*; PDD-NOS replaces *autism, residual state.*	PDD-NOS is more inclusive than *autism, residual state,* since it encompasses children who never met the full criteria for autism as well as children who once met such criteria but improved over time.
1990	Congress enacts PL 101-476 (another amendment to PL 94-142). Education for All Handicapped Children Act is renamed Individuals with Disabilities Education Act (IDEA). For the first time, autism is included as an "eligible disability."	Prior to 1990, children with autism were typically served under a variety of other labels ("emotionally disturbed," "other health impaired," "mental retardation").

Table 4.1 Factors Affecting Prevalence of ASD

Year	Event	Comments
1991	U.S. Department of Education, Office of Special Education Programs, requires reporting of autism by the states starting in 1992.	Coincides with implementation of Parts B and H of PL 99-457. The new requirement to serve children from birth to age 5, coupled with the availability of "autism" as a label, results in a huge spike in the number of children identified with autism or PDD-NOS.
1994	*DSM-IV:* Broader menu for diagnosis of autism; first appearance of *Asperger syndrome.*	Six of sixteen milder criteria must be met, such as "lack of spontaneous seeking to share...achievements with other people; [difficulty] sustain[ing] a conversation...lack of varied...social imitative play; persistent preoccupation with parts of objects." Significantly expands scope of children meeting criteria for a spectrum diagnosis.
2000+	Majority of children with ASD now have IQ in nonretarded range (prior to this time, the majority of children with ASD also had mental retardation).	Steady inclusion of milder forms of atypicality under the ASD umbrella leads to inclusion of more children with normal general intelligence.

suddenly develops autism as an adult, or even as a ten-year-old. Furthermore, as we will discuss in Chapter 5, children with ASD improve over time. There's no reason to assume that the severity of ASD in adults should be the same as it is in schoolchildren. If that were the case—if nobody ever improved—what would be the point of early intervention, special education, or therapy?

No one in this country has actually looked to see how many adults with mild ASD (or *autism—residual state,* to use the original *DSM* terminology) really are out there. Unlike the educational system, which compiles a massive amount of information on children, no governmental agency collects any meaningful information about the developmental status of adults. The Census Bureau asks a few questions, as does Social Security, but not enough to generate prevalence estimates of

ASD in adults. In 2009, a British survey of adults living in the community (that is, in noninstitutional settings) reported a prevalence of ASD of 1 percent; most of these individuals were not receiving social or mental health services.

Finally, today's adults grew up at a time when the diagnosis of autism was limited to children with severe disability; there were no such diagnoses as Asperger syndrome or PDD-NOS. Dorothy Bishop, a highly regarded British researcher who has devoted her career to studying language development, recently evaluated thirty-eight adults who had been diagnosed as children with "language disorder." Using a current test for making a diagnosis of ASD, the Autism Diagnostic Observation Schedule (ADOS), she discovered that twelve of these thirty-eight adults (32 percent) met criteria for a diagnosis of ASD. This was a small sample, but her observations suggest that as many as 25 to 30 percent of children diagnosed in the 1970s and 1980s with "language disorder" really had ASD—and still do.

Based on all these facts, I have concluded that the "missing" adults are out there. They are "missing" only in the sense that they may not be receiving necessary mental health services. But they exist.

(i) See the Resource List for additional information on the autism "explosion."

Population Screening for ASD: The Broad End of the Funnel
Up until now, prevalence estimates of ASD have been obtained by counting children who have already been diagnosed. Think back to our example of tall stature. Suppose we just searched endocrine clinics at hospitals. We would find a few very tall people with medical conditions. Taking that as the total number of tall people, and dividing that number by the size of the entire population, we'd come out with a very low prevalence estimate for tall stature. Then suppose we decided to check all NBA players and add them to the total. Our count of tall people would go up, as would our prevalence estimate of tall stature for the entire population. If we station ourselves outside of every "big and tall" clothing store with a tape measure, we'd pick up even more people meeting our criteria for tall, producing a further increase in our prevalence estimate. But we'd still be missing some eligible candidates.

So the ultimate step would be to set up a traffic stop and measure everybody in a large sample of motorists. That way, we'd have a much truer picture of prevalence. The technical term for finding cases is *ascertainment*. Up until quite recently, the ascertainment of children with ASD has been limited to counting the number of children who are already diagnosed (whether by a medical clinic or a school system), but this method misses a lot of children. Within the past couple of years, researchers have finally gotten around to screening entire populations of children for autistic traits, and it turns out that 1 in 75 boys and 1 in 333 girls—double what we get by counting already identified cases—meet criteria for a diagnosis of PDD-NOS. If correct, these numbers put the prevalence of ASD on a par with other developmental disorders. (Mental retardation, for example, affects about 1 child in 30; about 1 child in 20 has some form of learning disability.) This would be sad indeed, but it's no reason to conclude that some unidentified risk factor is driving up the prevalence (or incidence) of ASD. No one is any more atypical than they were the day before, any more than enhancing the ascertainment for tall stature makes anyone taller. Population screening is just the latest step in the process of expanding the definition and ascertainment methods for identifying people with ASD that has been unfolding for over sixty years, and so naturally, it will result in higher prevalence numbers—initially in children, and eventually, as diagnostic criteria become available, in adults. We are getting better and better at finding people with ASD who were there all along but who have been slipping through the cracks up until now. Still, the numbers are breathtaking.

"So," you may ask, "why should I care? This seems like an argument between statisticians, not something that affects *me*." The reason you should care is because many crusaders will try to arouse your fears, and many entrepreneurs will try to sell you their products, by claiming that we are in the middle of an epidemic; therefore, their argument goes, you need to do something to protect your child!—which often means "Blame [fill in the blank]" or "Buy my product." Once we poke a hole in the "fact" that we're in an epidemic, the urgency goes out of the crusade or sales pitch. With that in mind, let's turn to some of the more well-known, but at the moment speculative, "causes" of ASD.

Speculative Causes of ASD

In the last few decades a number of speculative theories about the causes of ASD have gotten a lot of attention. I call them speculative because none of these factors has met the basic tests for known or probable causes we laid out in the previous chapter: Does the supposed cause occur more frequently among children with ASD than among children without ASD? Is there an animal model, in which we can show some type of deleterious changes after exposure to the suspected cause? Or, lacking an animal model, is there some other basis for establishing biological plausibility?

Immunizations

Probably no other factor has been more strongly implicated as a cause of ASD in the mind of the general public than immunizations. The two principal variations on this theme have to do with the MMR (measles-mumps-rubella) vaccine and the use of mercury in the form of thimerosal as a vaccine preservative. Let's take a look at each of these claims.

MMR: A Cause of ASD?

The fear that the measles-mumps-rubella (MMR) vaccine might cause autism is traceable, in large part, to a 1998 publication in the British journal *Lancet* by Andrew Wakefield and his associates (see the Resource List). According to the paper, "12 children were referred to a paediatric gastroenterology unit with a history of normal development followed by loss of acquired skills, including language, together with diarrhoea and abdominal pain.... Onset of behavioural symptoms was associated, by the parents, with measles, mumps, and rubella vaccination in eight of the 12 children.... All 12 children had intestinal abnormalities...which [were] generally associated in time with possible environmental triggers"—the implication being that MMR was the "environmental trigger" that had caused both the children's ASD and their intestinal disease.

This article created a sensation and raised tremendous questions about the safety of the MMR vaccine. Do children who receive the MMR vaccine in fact have an increased frequency of ASD—especially regressive ASD—compared to children who do not receive the MMR?

Has the rate of regressive ASD changed with the introduction of the MMR vaccine? Does regressive ASD occur more commonly right after getting the MMR vaccine than at other times? The way to answer these questions is by means of large, population-based samples. In most developed countries (western Europe, Canada, Japan, etc.), governments maintain a central registry on all citizens, linking their birth records, immunization records, and health and developmental records. (In the United States, some of this information exists, but in separate data sets, making it nearly impossible to obtain a complete population-based sample.) Changes in public health and immunization policies in these countries have provided several natural "experiments" for researchers to look at, comparing the prevalence of ASD in specific birth cohorts of children before and after adoption of the MMR vaccine (as in England), or before, during, and after cessation of using MMR (as in Japan). After looking at millions of children, the answers are in: Neither the prevalence of ASD nor the rate of regressive ASD jumped up following the introduction of the MMR vaccine, nor have they declined following the discontinuation of the MMR vaccine in those countries that have stopped using it. These studies represent one of the few instances in which the incidence of regressive ASD has actually been measured. The data showed no clustering of new ASD cases right after getting the MMR; for every child whose ASD was diagnosed shortly after receiving the MMR, there are many more whose ASD was diagnosed at some other time. Some researchers found an increased frequency of minor bowel complaints (constipation, diarrhea, etc.) among children with regressive ASD, but this has been an inconsistent observation. The biopsy findings described in the article by Wakefield and colleagues (ileal-lymphoid-nodular hyperplasia) have yet to be replicated in a large-scale sample of children with ASD or definitively linked to the receipt of MMR vaccine. So Wakefield's chance observations have not been replicated in large-scale studies, and there is no generally accepted biological mechanism to account for his implied claims of causation.

In 2004, ten of Wakefield's twelve coauthors on the original 1998 paper published a retraction (see the Resource List), seeking to disassociate themselves from the implication that MMR might cause ASD. Referring to the 1998 paper, they wrote, "No causal link was established between MMR vaccine and autism as the data were insufficient." They acknowledged the "major implications for public health" flowing from that paper—the loss of confidence in the MMR. "In view of this," they conclude, " . . . now is the appropriate time that we should together formally retract the interpretation placed upon these findings." And in August 2009 Wakefield and two of his coauthors were charged by the General Medical Council (the British professional licensing board) with acting "dishonestly and irresponsibly in failing to disclose . . . the method by which they recruited patients for inclusion in the research which resulted in a misleading description of the patient population."

It turns out that at least five of Wakefield's twelve subjects were already suing the manufacturer of the MMR vaccine; their attorney had retained Wakefield and provided him with financial support for his work. This in itself is not necessarily damning. But Wakefield kept his legal and financial relationship secret from the editors at the *Lancet* and from the medical center where the work was conducted. This is what has led to the allegation that "Dr Wakefield's conduct in relation to research funds obtained from the Legal Aid Board was dishonest and misleading." Wakefield also faces allegations of ethical misconduct arising from the procedures to which he subjected some of the children (spinal taps, for example) and charges that he "acted unethically and abused his position of trust as a medical practitioner." Win or lose, Wakefield's personal affairs will be newsworthy only for a moment, after the GMC hands down its decision. The larger issue—the implication that the MMR vaccine can cause ASD—has already been addressed by his colleagues' disavowal of the original paper, as well as numerous other studies (Table 4.2). Unfortunately, it's hard to call back misinformation once it's out on the Web. Wakefield implied that the MMR vaccine has a role in causing ASD, and despite the recanting of Wakefield's coauthors and the lack of epidemiologic evidence, the theory has taken on a life of its own.

Mercury: Red Alert or Red Herring?

Mercury is a metal that is liquid at room temperature (its chemical symbol, Hg, comes from its Latin name, *hydrargyrum,* which means "liquid silver"). The level of toxicity from mercury varies tremendously depending on its exact chemical form. A decades-long epidemic of neurologic damage in the populace living along the shores of Minamata Bay, Japan, was traced to the dumping of methyl mercury (one atom of mer-

Table 4.2 MMR-Related Research

Year	Author (Country)	Subjects	Method	Result
1999	Taylor[1] (England)	All children born in 8 London boroughs (approx. 500,000), 1979–98	MMR introduced in England in 1988. Examined long-term trend in prevalence of ASD. For children with regressive ASD, looked at timing of MMR and regression.	No sudden increase in prevalence of ASD following introduction of MMR in 1988; no clustering of regressive ASD cases in the 4 months following receipt of MMR.
2001	Fombonne[2] (England)	262 children with ASD (164 received MMR, 98 did not)	Compared age of onset of regressive ASD in MMR vs. no-MMR groups, and rate of GI symptoms in regressive vs. nonregressive groups.	No difference in rate of regression between MMR and no-MMR groups; no clustering of regression following MMR; no increase in GI symptoms in regressive ASD.
2002	Madsen[3] (Denmark)	All children born in Demark 1991–98 (537,303)	Compared prevalence of ASD between 440,655 children who received MMR and 96,648 who had not received MMR.	No difference in prevalence of ASD between the MMR and no-MMR groups.
2002	Makela[4] (Finland)	535,544 1- to 7-year-old children who received MMR, 1982–86	Examined hospital discharge summaries looking for temporal relationship between receipt of MMR and hospital admission of acute or chronic neurologic problems or bowel problems.	"No clustering of hospitalizations for autism after vaccination. None of the autistic children made hospital visits for inflammatory bowel diseases."
2004	Smeeth[5] (England)	1,294 children with ASD, 1987–2001, and 4,469 children without ASD	Some children in each group received MMR, while others received separate shots for measles, mumps, and rubella.	No difference in prevalence of ASD when comparing MMR recipients and nonrecipients.
2005	Honda[6] (Japan)	300,000 children born in Yokohama, 1986–96	MMR used only 1989–93; compared prevalence of ASD by birth year.	Steadily increasing prevalence of ASD; greatest increase in ASD occurred in 1993, after removal of MMR.
2006	Richler[7] (USA)	351 children with ASD (regressive, 163; nonregressive, 188)	Compared timing of MMR with onset of regression.	Timing of regression did not correlate with receipt of MMR.

Table 4.2 MMR-Related Research (cont'd.)

Year	Author (Country)	Subjects	Method	Result
2006	Fombonne[8] (Canada)	27,749 children born 1987–98	Compared rate of immunization with MMR, vs. prevalence of ASD.	Steadily declining use of MMR; ASD significantly increased as MMR use decreased.
2007	Uchiyama[9] (Japan)	904 children with ASD	MMR used only from 1989–93; compared rate of regressive ASD pre-1989, 1989–93, and post-1993.	No change in rate of regressive autism before, during, or after MMR use.

1. Taylor B et al. Autism and measles, mumps, and rubella vaccine: no epidemiological evidence for a causal association. Lancet. 1999; 353(9169):2026–2029.

2. Fombonne E, Chakrabarti S. No evidence for a new variant of measles-mumps-rubella-induced autism. Pediatrics. 2001; 108(4):E58.

3. Madsen KM et al. A population-based study of measles, mumps, and rubella vaccination and autism. N Engl J Med. 2002; 347(19):1477–1482.

4. Makela A, Nuorti JP, Peltola H. Neurologic disorders after measles-mumps-rubella vaccination. Pediatrics. 2002; 110(5):957–963.

5. Smeeth L. MMR vaccination and pervasive developmental disorders: a case-control study. Lancet. 2004; 364(9438):963–969.

6. Honda H, Shimizu Y, Rutter M. No effect of MMR withdrawal on the incidence of autism: a total population study. J Child Psychol Psychiatry. 2005; 46(6):572–579.

7. Richler J et al. Is there a "regressive phenotype" of autism spectrum disorder associated with the measles-mumps-rubella vaccine? A CPEA study. J Autism Dev Disord. 2006; 36(3): 299–316.

8. Fombonne E et al. Pervasive developmental disorders in Montreal, Quebec, Canada: prevalence and links with immunizations. Pediatrics. 2006; 118(1):e139–e150.

9. Uchiyama T, Kurosawa M, Inaba Y. MMR-vaccine and regression in autism spectrum disorders: negative results presented from Japan. J Autism Dev Disord. 2007; 37(2):210–217.

For additional information, see Doja A, Roberts W. Immunizations and autism: a review of the literature. Can J Neurol Sci. 2006; 33(4):341–346. See also Taylor B. Vaccines and the changing epidemiology of autism. Child Care Health Dev. 2006; 32(5):511–519.

cury plus one atom of carbon) into the bay by a local factory. Today, coal-fired power plants and other forms of industrial pollution rain methyl mercury down on the landscape. Methyl mercury that lands in the water is taken up by microorganisms, which are consumed by plankton, which in turn are consumed by herbivorous fish. Mercury becomes concentrated as it moves up the food chain; the higher up the food chain an animal is, the more mercury in its system. At the top of the aquatic food chain are the large predators, with the highest mercury concentration of all: tuna, swordfish, and shark. The concentration of methyl mercury in these fish has led to warnings from the FDA to limit their consumption, especially by children and pregnant women.

Since the 1930s, ethyl mercury (one atom of mercury plus *two* atoms of carbon) has been used as an ingredient in thimerosal, a preservative added to vaccines. Back in the 1930s, products were not required to meet the safety standards that are in force today. As safety standards rose, thimerosal was simply grandfathered in as a commonly used compound. In 1999, the American Academy of Pediatrics (AAP) and the U.S. Public Health Service (PHS) recommended removing thimerosal from immunizations as a precautionary measure. There were then, and there are now, no studies to establish safety limits for ethyl mercury; rather, the AAP and PHS based their recommendation on the published safety standards for *methyl* mercury. However, methyl and ethyl mercury are about as different as carbon monoxide (one atom of carbon plus one atom of oxygen) and carbon dioxide (one atom of carbon plus two atoms of oxygen); carbon monoxide will kill you in a couple of minutes, while carbon dioxide is part of the air we breathe, and an ingredient in carbonated beverages. There are equally significant differences between methyl and ethyl mercury. Nonetheless, in the absence of safety data for ethyl mercury, the AAP and PHS did the prudent thing, which was to recommend that thimerosal be removed from childhood vaccines. This was effectively accomplished by 2001, with the exception of the influenza vaccine and neonatal hepatitis B.

In the wake of the AAP recommendation and the government's decision, however, the public assumed that if thimerosal was coming out of immunizations, there must be a problem with it. This fear crystallized in 2001 with the publication of a paper by S. Bernard and colleagues asserting that ASD represented a form of mercury poisoning (see the Resource List)—although classical mercury poisoning and ASD actually look very little alike.

As with Wakefield's 1998 paper implicating the MMR vaccine, researchers have responded to public concerns over thimerosal through broad-scale epidemiologic research. To date, properly conducted studies looking at hundreds of thousands of children have found no association between thimerosal and the prevalence of ASD (Table 4.3). Most of these were retrospective studies comparing the prevalence of ASD in specific birth cohorts of children with the calculated dose of thimerosal received by children in that cohort. Since thimerosal was removed from nearly all U.S. vaccines in 2001, the obvious question is: Has the prevalence of ASD gone down? The answer, of course, is no. The prevalence of ASD in the United States continues to rise, even though exposure to thimerosal is negligible. If you refer back to Figure 4.1, you'll see that the biggest jump in cases of ASD occurred in 1992 and onward, *right after thimerosal was removed*. The same phenomenon—continued increase in the prevalence of ASD despite removal of thimerosal—has been reported in Canada, Denmark, and Sweden. It's hard to reconcile Figure 4.1 with the claim that thimerosal causes ASD.

Nonetheless, lawsuits continue. Two highly vocal critics of thimerosal, Mark Geier and David Geier, rest their most alarming claims on biased data: the Vaccine Adverse Event Reporting System (VAERS). VAERS is a hotline that parents or physicians can call if they have even the slightest suspicion that a child may have experienced an adverse reaction following an immunization. To quote from the VAERS website, http://vaers.hhs.gov/vaers.htm: "Q: What if I can't tell if a reaction was caused by a vaccine? A: We encourage you to report any reaction following vaccination to VAERS, regardless of whether or not you can tell if the vaccine or another product caused it." VAERS is intended as an early warning system: If a spike in possible adverse events is detected through VAERS, the way to follow up is with a controlled study. But VAERS by itself was never intended as the way to determine vaccine safety. The biggest problem with using VAERS as a way of estimating vaccine risk in ASD is reporting bias: If you knew your child had received thimerosal, wouldn't you be more likely to call VAERS after getting an ASD diagnosis than if you knew your child never received thimerosal? And what about all the children who got thimerosal-containing shots and did fine, or children who received thimerosal-free shots and still got regressive ASD? VAERS does not collect that information. Therefore, drawing conclusions about the dangers of thimerosal based on VAERS is like announcing half of a baseball score: The number is interesting, but there's no way to tell who won the game. Nonetheless, Geier, Geier, and colleagues continue to rely on VAERS. In one of their papers, they suggest a six-fold increased risk of ASD in children who received immunizations containing thimerosal compared with children who received thimerosal-free immunizations, based on call-ins by parents who were worried that their child's ASD might be due to the shot—certainly not a random sample of all children with

ASD (see the Resource List). No one has been able to replicate the Geiers' findings in an unbiased sample.

The Geiers have come in for judicial as well as scientific criticism. In a 2007 case in which Mark Geier testified on behalf of a child with ASD, a California district court judge ruled, "Dr. Geier is not qualified as a pediatrician, a neurologist, a toxicologist, or an epidemiologist.... While his studies have been 'peer reviewed,' in the sense that they have been published in scientific journals, they have been severely criticized by the IOM [Institute of Medicine], the AAP [American Academy of Pediatrics], and others. In particular, both the AAP and the IOM have pointed out the problems inherent in studies that rely on the VAERS database.... Dr. Geier has been designated as an expert witness in about 100 cases before the Vaccine Court. However, in some of those cases, particularly the more recent ones, his opinion testimony has been excluded or accorded little or no weight beyond a determination that he was testifying beyond his expertise." In three 2009 cases in Federal Vaccine Court, three different Special Masters (judges overhearing the proceedings) conducted their own reviews of the evidence, and likewise concluded that the data did not support the Geiers' theories of causation of ASD by immunizations.

The argument that thimerosal causes ASD lies at the heart of a popular but unproven (and potentially dangerous) form of therapy: chelation, designed to pull metals from the body and—it is claimed—cure ASD. We'll have more to say about chelation in a later chapter, when we discuss sense and nonsense in the treatment of ASD.

Vitamin and Mineral Deficiency

There is no evidence that vitamin or mineral deficiency causes ASD. Nonetheless, megavitamin and megamineral therapy has been used for decades as a "treatment" for ASD, with no convincing evidence of benefit, and occasional cases of nerve damage and even death from vitamin and mineral overdose. (See the Resource List.)

Leaky Gut

The "leaky gut" hypothesis is an offshoot of Wakefield's research. The leaky gut theory speculates that unidentified neurotoxins pass through an abnormally permeable gut lining into the bloodstream, eventually

Table 4.3 Studies Finding No Association Between Thimerosal Exposure and ASD

Year	Author (Country)	Subjects	Method	Result
2003	Madsen[1] (Denmark)	National registry: all children ages 2–10 diagnosed with ASD between 1971 and 2000 (N = 956)	Calculated prevalence of ASD by birth year based on psychiatric diagnoses. Thimerosal was removed from all Danish vaccines in 1992.	Steadily increasing prevalence of ASD, 1971–2000. Steepest increase in prevalence followed the removal of thimerosal, 1992–2000.
2003	Stehr-Green[2] (Denmark and Sweden)	National registry: all children ages 2–10 with ASD (Sweden, 1987–99; Denmark, 1983–2000)	Calculated prevalence of ASD by birth year (thimerosal removed in 1992 in Denmark and in 1993 in Sweden).	Steady increase in prevalence of ASD throughout study period, with continuing increase after discontinuation of thimerosal.
2003	Verstraeten[3] (USA)	140,887 children enrolled in 3 HMOs, born 1991–99	Screened records for neurodevelopmental diagnoses; calculated cumulative dose of thimerosal in first year of life.	No association between dose of thimerosal received and risk of ASD.
2003	Hviid[4] (Denmark)	All children born in Denmark 1990–96 (N = 467,450)	Compared rate of ASD in children vaccinated with thimerosal-containing vs. thimerosal-free vaccine (thimerosal removed in 1992).	No difference in prevalence of ASD between the two groups.
2004	Andrews[5] (England)	109,863 children, born 1988–97 and registered in a national general practice research database	Calculated risk of ASD vs. dose of thimerosal received.	No increased risk of ASD based on dose of thimerosal received.
2004	Heron[6] (England)	14,000 children, born 1990–92	Compared calculated thimerosal exposure with 23 measures of speech, fine motor, and behavioral development.	No significant association between amount of thimerosal received and developmental outcome.
2006	Fombonne[7] (Canada)	27,749 children born 1987–98	Compared thimerosal exposure (removed in Canada in 1995) and prevalence of ASD.	Steady increase in prevalence of ASD from 1987–98; prevalence of ASD was highest in the post-1995 children, who received no thimerosal.

Table 4.3 Studies Finding No Association Between Thimerosal Exposure and ASD

Year	Author (Country)	Subjects	Method	Result
2008	Schechter[8] (USA)	Client data on children ages 3–12, reported to the CA Department of Developmental Services, 1995–2007	Estimated prevalence of ASD by birth year.	Continuous increase in prevalence of ASD by birth year; no decrease in prevalence associated with removal of thimerosal in 2001.
2009	Tozzi[9] (Italy)	1,704 children, 10 years after receiving 2 different levels of thimerosal	Psychometric testing and record review.	No difference in prevalence of neuropsychological abnormalities between groups; 1 case of ASD in the low-thimerosal group, 0 cases in the higher-thimerosal group.

1. Madsen KM et al. Thimerosal and the occurrence of autism: negative ecological evidence from Danish population-based data. *Pediatrics.* 2003; 112(3 Pt 1):604–606.

2. Stehr-Green P et al. Autism and thimerosal-containing vaccines: lack of consistent evidence for an association. *Am J Prev Med.* 2003; 25(2):101–106.

3. Verstraeten T et al. Safety of thimerosal-containing vaccines: a two-phased study of computerized health maintenance organization databases. *Pediatrics.* 2003; 112(5):1039–1048.

4. Hviid A et al. Association between thimerosal-containing vaccine and autism. *JAMA.* 2003; 290(13):1763–1766.

5. Andrews N et al. Thimerosal exposure in infants and developmental disorders: a retrospective cohort study in the United Kingdom does not support a causal association. *Pediatrics.* 2004. 114(3):584–591.

6. Heron J, Golding J. Thimerosal exposure in infants and developmental disorders: a prospective cohort study in the United Kingdom does not support a causal association. *Pediatrics.* 2004; 114(3):577–583.

7. Fombonne E et al. Pervasive developmental disorders in Montreal, Quebec, Canada: prevalence and links with immunizations. *Pediatrics.* 2006; 118(1):e139–e150.

8. Schechter R, Grether JK. Continuing increases in autism reported to California's developmental services system: mercury in retrograde. *Arch Gen Psychiatry.* 2008; 65(1):19–24.

9. Tozzi AE et al. Neuropsychological performance 10 years after immunization in infancy with thimerosal-containing vaccines. *Pediatrics.* 2009; 123(2):475–482.

circulating to the brain and giving rise to ASD. There are a number of competing theories about why the gut might be abnormally permeable. Wakefield's implication was that the MMR vaccine somehow damaged the lining of the gut. Another popular theory is that gluten (a protein found in wheat, rye, and barley) in the diet causes damage to the gut lining, permitting unspecified toxins to gain access to the brain. Although this theory remains unproven, several elements in the chain of speculation are enticing. Gluten intolerance is a bona fide medical disorder. Affected individuals form antibodies to gliadin, a component of gluten. These antibodies attack the lining of the gut, damaging the bowel wall, causing diarrhea, cramps, malabsorption, and poor growth. The medical name for this condition is celiac disease. The only treatment for celiac disease is to remove all wheat products (the source of gluten) from the diet. Increased levels of anti-gliadin antibody, with or without celiac disease, have been found in some adults with brain disorders, including schizophrenia, depression, cerebellar ataxia, and Huntington's disease. We don't know whether celiac disease or anti-gliadin antibodies cause these neurologic disorders, or whether the gut and brain diseases are both due to some underlying factor (an autoimmune process that destroys both gut and brain cells, for example). Gluten-free diet trials in adults with neurologic disorders have yielded inconsistent results. Controlled trials of a gluten-free diet in children with ASD are ongoing at the time of this writing. At present, there simply isn't enough information to make a scientifically based recommendation about the gluten-free diet as a treatment for ASD. My own hunch is that if gluten sensitivity were really a trigger for ASD, we would see an increased prevalence of ASD among children with celiac disease (that is, greater than the 1 in 150 for the general pediatric population). Likewise, we'd find an increase in prevalence of celiac disease among children with ASD compared to children without ASD. However, such associations have not been reported, even though they've been looked for. Some children with ASD have loose stools, but not the severe bowel dysfunction seen in celiac disease. The best I can say for now is that a gluten-free diet is expensive and inconvenient, but it's probably safe. Despite what you hear, there's no proof that it does anything; that will require a large, randomized, controlled trial. Again, I invite you to investigate further on your own. For more information, see the Resource List.

Autoimmune Disease

Autoimmune disorders are conditions in which the body comes under attack by its own immune system—a biological version of mistaken identity. Examples include celiac disease, diabetes, lupus, and rheumatoid arthritis. There have been tantalizing reports of autoimmune abnormalities in children with ASD. It's intriguing to think that there may be a connection to ASD, but there is little in the way of proof at this time. As with the leaky gut theory, I'm skeptical. If autoimmunity really plays a role in ASD, we should see an increased prevalence of autoimmune disorders among children with ASD, or an increased prevalence of ASD among children with autoimmune disorders. Such associations have not been found, nor have studies of autoimmune disorders in women generally revealed an increased risk of ASD in their offspring. But much remains to be learned.

Yeast (Candida)

In 1983 a physician, William G. Crook, published *The Yeast Connection* (see the Resource List), in which he asserted that unspecified "toxins" from yeast in the gut (and in women, the vagina) could cause a variety of disorders. Dr. Crook did not mention autism. Now, however, a legion of holistic practitioners advocate treating children with ASD with antifungal agents to eliminate yeast from the gut, thereby—so it is claimed—improving the child's ASD. (Just enter "yeast + autism" into Google and see for yourself.) The yeast hypothesis is a precursor of the autoimmune and leaky gut arguments. The yeast hypothesis has met none of the most basic tests of plausibility: There are no population data to show that yeast occurs any more frequently in children with ASD than in children with typical development (in fact, yeast is present in the gut of 40 percent of all children), there are no identified yeast "toxins," and there are no controlled trials to show that eliminating yeast from the gut is followed by improvement in atypicality.

Other Environmental Factors

Mercury in dental amalgam (the fillings in our teeth), methyl mercury in the diet or from industrial waste, and other bioactive pollutants in the environment have all been suggested as causes of ASD, but there is no conclusive proof (or disproof) of these theories. This is an area that badly needs to be researched. It's plausible (but unproven), for example, that low-level exposure to heavy metals or a testosterone-like substance in the food chain could nudge the entire population ever so slightly in the direction of increased atypicality, with a resultant increase in the incidence and prevalence of ASD. We have precedent for that sort of thing with IQ and lead exposure: Low-level lead exposure lowers IQ—not enough to cause major disability in most victims, but enough to shift the entire population IQ downward several points. Without careful epidemiologic studies, these kinds of broad, low-level associations will go undetected.

Absence of Proof Is Not Proof of Absence

The foregoing information is reassuring, but still you may ask: *Isn't it possible that some children are uniquely vulnerable to environmental factors, and that these rare children might be missed in large group studies?* The answer, of course, is yes. There is always the chance that an occasional child will be the exception to the rule. Researchers know this, and that is why they have come up with two different ways of studying risk factors: *cohort studies* and *case-control studies* (Figure 4.2). They are both useful, but they serve different purposes.

In medical research, the word *cohort* refers to any defined population—say, all babies born in the United States in 2005, or all children entering kindergarten in the United States in the fall of 2010. The important thing about a cohort is that it includes everyone—those with the disorder we're studying, and those without. The most basic use of

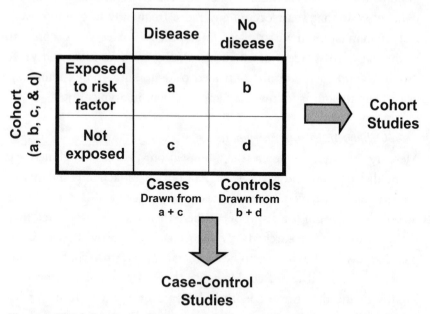

Figure 4.2 Risk Factor Studies *Cohort studies enroll entire populations (a, b, c, and d), regardless of disease state. Case-control studies begin by enrolling "cases"; these are generally people who have come to a medical center for diagnosis and treatment, and they make up an unknown percentage of all persons with the disease (a + c). Then researchers enroll one or more comparison subjects for every case, as controls. The total size of the affected population (a + c) and unaffected population (b + d) is not determined.*

cohort studies is to measure prevalence. To do this, we need to determine whether or not each subject in the cohort has the disorder of interest. (Depending on the particular disorder, this determination may be made on the basis of history, physical examination, a laboratory test, or some other agreed-upon diagnostic standard.) Then we divide the number of subjects having the disorder by the entire number of subjects in the cohort. This fraction is the prevalence of the disorder. If we make our study a bit more sophisticated, then in addition to determining whether each subject has the disorder of interest we can also ask each subject if he or she was exposed to a specific risk factor. Armed with these two facts about every subject, we can construct a two-by-two table, classifying everyone in the sample according to exposure and health status (Figure 4.2). In cell a we record subjects who were exposed to the risk factor and developed the disorder; in cell b we record subjects who were exposed but did not develop the disorder; in cell c we record subjects who were not exposed but still developed the disorder, and in cell d we keep track of subjects who were not exposed and did not develop the disorder. Now we can compare the prevalence of the disorder in subjects who were exposed to the risk factor $[a / (a + b)]$ with the prevalence of the disorder in subjects who where not exposed $[c / (c + d)]$. It's studies like these that enable us to state with confidence that the prevalence of ASD is no higher among children who received the MMR vaccine or vaccines containing thimerosal than it is among children who were not exposed to these agents.

Cohort studies are useful in assessing the likelihood of disease following exposure to a given risk factor, as long as the risk factor and the disease are both common enough that we'll capture a large number of exposed and/or affected individuals in our cohort. But what if the risk factor or the disorder is rare? If either of these is the case, then we might not pick up enough children—even in a large cohort—to be able to detect the problem. In the previous chapter, I described phenylketonuria, a metabolic disorder that occurs about once in every 15,000 live births. In children with PKU, dietary phenylalanine causes mental retardation. But cohort studies are not the best way to study the impact of dietary phenylalanine on IQ. Even if we start out with a cohort of 100,000 children, only 6 or 7 will have PKU. Although those few children might wind up with profound mental retardation due to phenylalanine in the diet, the average IQ for the entire sample of 100,000 children will drop by only a whisker. From these results we might conclude—wrongly—that phenylalanine is safe for all children. A better way to study the relationship between dietary consumption of phenylalanine and IQ is to gather up a population of children with PKU (cases) and look at their IQs on and off a special low-phenylalanine diet, as well as comparing the IQ of each case to one or more controls—children of the same age, gender, ethnicity, economic background, and other relevant characteristics, who do not have PKU. Case-control studies, therefore, begin not with an entire population (most of whom are normal) but with a much smaller group of individuals known to be affected by the disorder of interest. Case-control studies cannot be used to calculate prevalence, since the researcher does not canvass an entire population—just the cases and their matched controls. The value of case-control studies lies in the fact that up to 50 percent of the subjects have the disorder of interest (if there is one control subject per case). Furthermore, the researcher can enroll cases according to whatever criteria he or she wishes: children whose parents claim regression after immunizations, for example. This provides an opportunity to look more closely at specific risk factors—either intrinsic (inborn metabolic errors, immunologic defects, etc.), extrinsic (exposure to specific lots of vaccine, or to formulations such as the MMR vaccine), or historical (history of regression). Unfortunately, although we have quite a few well-conducted cohort studies, there is a general lack of informative case-control research looking for causes of ASD at this time.

This brings us to the case of Hannah Poling. Hannah has a mitochondrial disorder. As we discussed in Chapter 3, mitochondrial disorders are capable of producing neurologic deterioration and death, as well as a host of other neurologic and medical complications. Hannah also has "autistic-like symptoms." Hannah's parents sued for damages in Vaccine Court, alleging that their daughter's symptoms were brought on or aggravated by immunizations. The court sided with the parents, concluding that "the vaccinations [Hannah] received...significantly aggravated an underlying mitochondrial disorder, which predisposed her to deficits in cellular energy metabolism, and manifested as a regressive encephalopathy with features of autism spectrum disorder."

This is a case where the Vaccine Court got ahead of the facts. At the time the judge issued his ruling, and as this book goes to press (2009), there are no studies to show that immunizations can aggravate an underlying mitochondrial disorder, thereby triggering or hastening the onset of ASD—although this is a plausible hypothesis. In the aftermath of the Poling case, the United Mitochondrial Disease Foundation (UMDF)—the largest independent organization dedicated to research on mitochondrial disorders—issued the following statement: "There are no scientific studies documenting that childhood vaccinations... worsen mitochondrial disease symptoms. In the absence of scientific evidence, the UMDF cannot confirm any association between mitochondrial diseases and vaccines." This may change as more facts come to light, but the judge's ruling highlights the discrepancy between legal and scientific standards of proof. In a civil trial, the injured party does not have to prove his or her case beyond a shadow of a doubt—just that there's a 51 percent chance that he or she might be right. In science, the probability has to be greater than 95 percent before a finding is accepted as "statistically significant," and possibly true.

Despite its outcome from a legal standpoint, from a scientific perspective the Poling case leaves us with more questions than answers: Do mitochondrial disorders cause ASD? If they do, is ASD inevitable from the moment the child's genetic makeup is determined, or does there have to be an environmental "hit" to bring on ASD? Can immunization serve as such a stress? We don't have answers to any of these questions. Finally, does the risk of immunization exceed the risk posed by the diseases themselves? Children with mitochondrial disorders are at risk either way, and the fever associated with an immunization may be the lesser of two evils, compared with the fever and metabolic stress associated with getting, say, measles or mumps. Should all children be screened for mitochondrial disorders? This is easier said than done. Some children with mitochondrial disorders can be diagnosed only by muscle biopsy or some other invasive or labor-intensive study.

The Poling case raises a lot of issues. It is not the smoking gun accounting for an unproven epidemic of ASD, or the wholesale condemnation of immunizations, that some people would have you believe. What the Poling case does illustrate, however, is the urgent need for case-control studies of children with regressive ASD, to determine if they are somehow different biologically from children with non-regressive ASD, children with other disabilities, and children with normal development. We also need case-control studies of children with mitochondrial disorders, to see if they are at increased risk for regressive ASD, and to look at the temporal relationship between regression and immunization (as well as other environmental stressors, such as fever from viral infection). Finally, although thimerosal and MMR do not turn up as risks for ASD in cohort studies, that still leaves open the possibility that a small subset of children who regressed following immunization are different from their peers in some way. Earlier, I cited PKU as an example of a disorder that demanded case-control studies in order to unravel the relationship between an environmental risk (dietary phenylalanine) and a bad outcome (mental retardation) in children with a rare genetic disorder. It took the creation of a national PKU registry, but these studies were actually carried out. Similar studies of ASD are long overdue.

Summing Up

Be skeptical of alleged "causes" of ASD that rest on the premise that we're in the midst of an autism epidemic. The *prevalence* of ASD has risen dramatically over the past thirty years, at least in part because of broadening case definition and changes in federal education law, but there is no evidence that the incidence of ASD has changed. So has there been an "explosion" of ASD? Yes. An epidemic? Not as far as we know.

Remember the basic standards for proof of causation: Does the association between ASD and the alleged risk factor occur more often than would be expected on the basis of chance alone? Does the alleged risk factor meet the test of biological plausibility—either via animal models or via "experiments of nature"?

Cohort studies provide a measure of reassurance that alleged risk factors such as MMR and thimerosal are not associated with a detectable increase in prevalence of ASD. (On the contrary, the prevalence of ASD has continued to rise despite the removal of thimerosal and—in the case of Japan—the abandonment of the MMR vaccine.) Despite the lack of evidence of increased risk in cohort studies, however, there is still the possibility that rare children are uniquely susceptible to some environmental agent—whether it's the MMR vaccine, mercury, or something else. In order to investigate these claims, we need case-control studies, comparing children with regressive ASD or specific medical conditions to controls. Although cohort studies are reassuring, they represent only half of the information we need. As this book goes to press, several well-designed case-control studies are getting under way, to round out the research picture.

Chapter 5

What Does the Future Hold?
The Natural History of ASD

Most children with ASD show substantial improvement over time, although the rate and extent of improvement vary. Some of my patients no longer meet criteria for an ASD diagnosis—not many, but enough that you are not crazy to hope for it on behalf of your own child. If I hadn't been the one to write the original reports years earlier, I wouldn't believe the changes in these children myself. (Although, as we shall see, "losing the diagnosis" is not the same as "cure." Even in the best of outcomes, children—and the adults they eventually become—retain some cognitive and behavioral traits as the long-term legacy of their ASD.) For other children, progress of any sort is painfully slow. Why do some children do better than others? That is the question we will explore in this chapter. I can't give you a prediction for your child, sight unseen. But I can give you an overall perspective on the question.

When you hear the term *natural history,* you probably think of big museums, exotic cultures, and tropical rain forests. In medicine, however, the phrase refers to the course of a condition over time, from beginning to end, almost like the "life span" of that condition. Appendicitis, for example, has a natural history: pain starting in the mid-abdomen, shifting to the right lower portion of the abdomen, followed by abdominal rigidity, and so forth. There are many variations on this basic progression of symptoms, but if the doctor has made the correct diagnosis, then he or she can anticipate the potential problems and the range of expected outcomes. Just like appendicitis or any other physical ailment, ASD has a natural history. Although the details are unique in every child, ASD follows a predictable pattern over time.

In this chapter I will paint a picture of the natural history of ASD—still allowing variations on the theme—by creating a 3-D model of ASD that includes your child's *degree of atypicality, level of general intelligence,* and *age.* We will need to look at all three of these factors, and understand how they interact, in order to help your child develop to his or her fullest capacity. Of course, any model is a simplification of reality. It can't show every possible variation on the basic theme, and it can't answer every question. But it provides a useful starting point, giving you a basic framework into which you can place all the information you'll be gathering about your child. I will walk you through the model step by step. If graphs make you nervous, don't worry: I'll explain everything in words as well as pictures.

The Dimension of Atypicality

Remember our train analogy, from Chapter 1? When one or more wheels leave the track, the train has become derailed. To determine the degree of atypicality, we need to know how many wheels are off the track and how far off the track they are. For example, how impaired is your child's eye contact? How rigidly does your son or daughter insist upon adhering to certain routines? How intensely does your child flap his or her arms? How limited is your child's diet? These are all the features we saw in Table 1.2. If we "blenderize" all of these features into one number (a fiction, of course—no child can really be represented by one number), we can describe your child's development along the first dimension of our 3-D model: *degree of atypicality.*

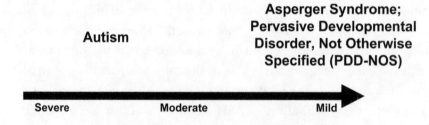

DEGREE OF ATYPICALITY

Figure 5.1 The Dimension of Atypicality *If your child has moderate to severe atypicality, his or her diagnosis is probably autism. If your child has mild to moderate atypicality, normal general intelligence, hyperverbal behavior, and an intense interest in odd topics, his or her diagnosis is probably Asperger syndrome. Children with AS often resemble "little professors," holding forth in a bookish, stilted, pedantic way. If your child has mild to moderate atypicality but fails to meet criteria for either autism or AS, his or her diagnosis is probably pervasive developmental disorder, not otherwise specified. PDD-NOS is a catchall category for children with pronounced atypicality that does not meet criteria for autism or Asperger syndrome.*

THE "SPECIFIED" PERVASIVE DEVELOPMENTAL DISORDERS

By now, you're comfortable with the terms *autism, Asperger syndrome,* and *PDD-NOS.* But the *DSM* lists five types of pervasive developmental disorders. The other two PDDs are Rett syndrome and Heller syndrome. Rett syndrome no longer belongs in the *DSM,* since we have a medical test for the underlying genetic abnormality (the MECP2 gene). Some children with the MECP2 mutation have symptoms of autism at a certain point in their disease; others do not. *Heller syndrome,* also known as childhood disintegrative disorder, is a grab-bag label for children with a variety of degenerative disorders having an onset in early to middle childhood; the term is rarely used, and—like *Rett syndrome*—should probably be abandoned in favor of the specific underlying medical degenerative disorders giving rise to the behavioral changes.

It would be nice if life were so simple. In the real world, the boundaries between autism, AS, and PDD-NOS are not so clearly defined.

Consider Sandy, whose parents brought her to me on her third birthday for evaluation of delayed speech and behavior problems. She had intense difficulty with transitions and was obsessed with one or two preferred television programs. Sandy's speech consisted of moderately unintelligible single words, with occasional echolalia and verbal perseveration ("Blue! Blue! Blue!" she would declare, demanding *Blue's Clues,* one of her fixations.) Yet despite these autistic-like features, she manifested imaginative play (feeding, bathing, and dressing her dolls) and socially aware attention seeking, such as hitting me while watching her parents in order to gauge the impact of her misbehavior on them. (Social awareness and imaginative play are not commonly seen in young children with ASD. I have parents who would give anything if only their child would show social awareness, even if it was during a tantrum.) She had a score of 22 on the Childhood Autism Rating Scale. Where to place Sandy diagnostically? I hedged, and gave her a diagnosis of developmental language disorder with atypical features, and then I sent her to a psychologist for a second opinion. The psychologist's impression was similar to my own: autistic-like in some ways, but not quite on the spectrum.

The classification systems in the *DSM* (and in the *International Classification of Diseases, 10th Edition,* or *ICD-10,* used elsewhere in the world) are useful to the extent that they help physicians and other caregivers communicate more easily with families and with one another about the general outline of the child's needs. However, I try to help parents avoid getting caught up in a debate over boundaries: *Does my child have autism or does he have PDD-NOS?* Autism, PDD-NOS, and AS are not self-contained disorders (like, say, measles, mumps, and chicken pox). Although children with classical cases of autism are easy to distinguish from children with PDD-NOS or AS, the symptoms of these three disorders, as well as disorders at the "borderland" of ASD—nonverbal learning disability and semantic-pragmatic language disorder—blur into one another at the margins. Like Sandy, your child may straddle the lines between diagnostic boundaries. Since there are no biological markers to distinguish these diagnoses from one another, I believe the best approach is for you to focus on your child's unique pattern of strengths and weaknesses, rather than worry about which label to use. (We need to recognize a distinction between clinical care and research, however. If a child is being enrolled in a research project, it is essential that strict diagnostic criteria be met so that other researchers can try to replicate the study elsewhere. Sometimes a child who really has mild ASD may not meet research criteria for an ASD diagnosis even though everyone agrees, clinically, that the child is on the spectrum.)

The Dimension of General Intelligence

Let's go back to our train analogy again. The train can have any number of wheels off the track; that's the degree of atypicality. Separately from that, the train can be late, on time, or even ahead of schedule. If the train has been held up due to a stuck switch, then once it has gotten past the switch it can run a little faster in an effort to make up for lost time. But suppose the train is late because of a problem with the engine. What if the engine is unable to generate enough power and can pull the train at only 30 miles per hour instead of 60? If that's the case, then the train is going to fall further and further behind schedule as time passes. Your child's intelligence is like the power generated by the engine, and your child's rate of development is like the speed at which the engine pulls the train, regardless of how many wheels may be off the track. Like our hypothetical train, we need to consider whether your child's development is advanced, on time, or delayed, in addition to being atypical.

Most of us have a general sense of our abilities and those of others. We tend to think of people as bright, average, or slow, and so we've become used to thinking of intelligence as one uniform entity. In reality, we all perform some mental tasks more easily than others. Maybe you were better at math than at reading, or maybe science came more easily than social studies, although even with those differences, you still knew if you were a good student overall or not.

The discrepancy between different abilities in a child with ASD, on the other hand, can be so big that you sometimes can't believe it until you see it with your own eyes. Severe, disabling deficits can exist side by side with astonishing skills.

I remember one boy I'll call Philip. His mother and father, who had brought Philip in for an evaluation, told me, "Our son is good with letters and numbers, but we can't have a conversation with him." During his first visit, Phillip spent fifteen minutes lying on his back staring at the ceiling, having no interaction with either his parents or with me. Suddenly, he started shouting, "E! X! P! R! E! S! Another S! That's two S!" He had spotted the "Railway Express Agency" sign above the toy trains in the play area. Philip grew more excited as he recited the letters, but he was clearly in his own world, never sharing his excitement with his parents or me. His gaze shifted to a photo of a locomotive on the wall and he shouted, "Susquehanna Railroad!" which was correct. We had no idea if he had recognized the symbol on the front of the engine or if he had been able to read the word *Susquehanna* in tiny letters running down the side of the train. At the time, Philip was two and half years old.

How is this possible? One thing that nearly everyone now agrees about is that intelligence is not a single, uniform trait but a mosaic, with many different components. Since it is so common for a child with ASD to have great strengths alongside great weaknesses, it will help us to get familiar with two schemes psychologists use to divide up intelligence: verbal versus nonverbal intelligence, and crystallized versus fluid intelligence.

- *Verbal versus nonverbal intelligence.* This is the most common way of dividing mental abilities. The verbal portion of an IQ test taps abilities such as vocabulary, verbal analogies, and so on, while the nonverbal portion measures arithmetic, geometry, and other forms of nonverbal ability.
- *Crystallized versus fluid intelligence.* Crystallized intelligence refers to our store of memorized facts, either verbal (*What is the capital of France?*) or nonverbal (2 + 2 = ?). Fluid intelligence, on the other hand, refers to our ability to recognize patterns or relationships, either verbal (*How are a ball and a wheel alike?*) or nonverbal (*Fill in the next number in this series: 2, 4, 8, 16,...*). Fluid intelligence is closely related to central coherence (the ability to see the big picture), as we discussed in Chapter 1.

SAVANT SKILLS: A MIXED BLESSING

You occasionally hear stories of the amazing skills and talents of some people with ASD. These savant skills are mechanical expressions of crystallized knowledge and don't reveal insight or creativity. *Hyperlexia* is the ability to read printed matter with little or no understanding of the text, like a machine. *Calendar savants* can identify the day of the week for any future date. *Artistic savants* can draw a scene in great detail from one glimpse. *Musical savants* can play a composition after hearing it just once (and frequently have perfect pitch). But savant skills do not signify creativity. The child with hyperlexia is not a great author, and the calendar savant is not a historian.

Once you begin to think of intelligence this way, a lot of things your child is doing that seem paradoxical will start to make sense. You are very likely to see a striking difference between your child's crystallized and fluid intelligence. Your son or daughter may be able to memorize an astonishing amount of information (letters, numbers, routes in the car, movie dialogue) but may struggle to see patterns or relationships in all that information. This is why your child may be great at labeling but very poor at small talk. This aspect of ASD may confuse you, especially if your child has demonstrated savant skills. Your child's store of isolated facts can create an impression of superior intellect, but his or her fluid intelligence—the ability to link facts together to draw conclusions or make inferences—may be severely limited.

As we discussed in Chapter 1, theory of mind refers to our ability to attribute thoughts and feelings to others, and so to infer their intentions: If I can formulate an educated guess as to what you are thinking and feeling, then I can formulate an equally good guess as to what you may do next, and why. It is precisely these types of abilities—which rely on fluid rather than crystallized intelligence—that are so hard for people with ASD. We can understand Philip's ability to recite letters, and even perhaps to read, as crystallized intelligence. His ability to make small talk with his parents, on the other hand, is severely limited because of his inability to recognize patterns of human behavior, to draw inferences about others' expectations of him, or to generalize from one setting to another—all skills that depend on fluid intelligence, theory of mind, and central coherence. Memorizing all the locomotives on *Thomas the Tank Engine* is a breeze. Understanding that Mommy is waiting for eye contact is another matter altogether.

Modern intelligence tests also look at other aspects of mental ability, including *processing speed* (the speed at which the subject completes tasks), *attention span,* and *short-term memory.* These are often grouped under the heading of *executive function,* which is just as important as our command of facts, or our ability to analyze, draw inferences, and make connections. Executive function works like the transmission in a car. The transmission connects the engine to the wheels; if it's slipping, you can't harness the power of the engine to move the car forward smoothly and efficiently. Likewise, we rely on executive function to implement our intelligence. People with attention deficit disorder or a head injury typically display deficits of executive function, showing signs of disorganization, inattention, low frustration threshold, forgetfulness, and impaired motor speed. Executive function is often impaired in children with ASD.

Quantifying Intelligence

Intelligence tests (IQ tests) are designed so that the average score is 100. Scores between 85 and 115 constitute average intelligence. A score of 84 to 80 is considered low average, and 79 down to 70 is borderline. Scores below 70 fall in the range of mental retardation (MR): 69 to 55 is mild MR, 54 to 40 is moderate MR, 39 to 29 is severe MR, and under 25 is profound MR. At the other end of the scale, 116 to 130 is bright, while anything above 130 is in the range of superior to genius.

MENTAL RETARDATION

Mental retardation is defined as an IQ score below 70 on a standard intelligence test, plus significantly delayed adaptive (self-care) skills. You can find some examples of adaptive skills in Table 5.1. There are a variety of standardized tests of intelligence and adaptive ability that you are likely to encounter during your child's evaluation (see Appendix III).

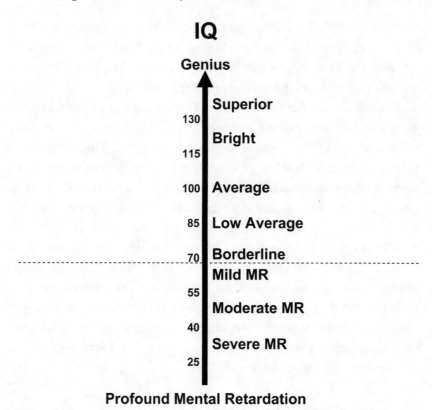

Figure 5.2 The IQ Scale (MR: mental retardation)

Intelligence in ASD

Strictly speaking, no child with ASD has normal intelligence, since ASD disrupts the child's ability to reason, draw inferences, or see patterns in social behavior. However, some children with ASD are clearly brighter than others, and some, sad to say, have mental retardation in addition to ASD. This is like saying that a train is running slower than it should, in addition to having several wheels off the track. Measuring intelligence in a child with ASD takes an examiner who is familiar with how kids on the spectrum behave. Even then, it may be impossible to measure the intelligence of a young child with ASD because of the severity of his or her atypicality.

Let's look at Philip again, the thirty-month-old boy who identified the Susquehanna locomotive in my office. By itself, the ability to decode text or recognize graphic symbols tells me little about Philip's level of general intelligence. These are classical examples of crystallized,

Table 5.1 Adaptive Skills

Age	Skill
7 months	Finger-feeds
10 months	Uses cup (no lid) without help
12 months	Uses spoon without help (may be messy)
24 months	Removes socks, shoes, hat
30 months	Toilet trained
33–36 months	Unbuttons
36 months	Buttons up
48 months	Spreads with knife Starts zippers Opens and closes snaps
5 years	Ties shoes Cuts with knife and fork

catalog-based ability. I am more interested in skills such as tool use: How old was he when he learned to use a spoon to feed himself? How old was he when he started using a crayon as a writing implement rather than a teething object? These skills normally emerge around twelve to fourteen months of age, and I know from experience that ASD by itself does not cause delayed emergence of tool use. If the child's use of a spoon and crayon are delayed, then I have to look elsewhere for an explanation—typically, global cognitive delay (which, in its most pronounced and persistent form, equates to mental retardation) or difficulty with fine motor coordination.

In children with normal development, language competency is usually the best indicator of general intelligence, but this is not true among children with ASD, who are likely to show impairment in complex language production and comprehension regardless of their mental abilities in other areas. If we focus too much on the complex language skills of a child with ASD, we are likely to underestimate the child's true level of intelligence. Conversely, we must not let ourselves be misled by single-word vocabulary, counting, identification of shapes, or other list-based linguistic tasks, which may exceed day-to-day language comprehension skills. Just as we factor out areas of vulnerability specific to ASD, we also must avoid letting these uniquely strong abilities ("inflator scores" or "splinter skills") cloud the findings.

Often our best option when estimating IQ in a child with ASD is to focus on nonverbal problem solving and adaptive skills—such as the use of a spoon and crayon that I discussed above. (We sometimes use tests that are administered nonverbally as well.) When we are unable to engage a child with ASD in formal IQ testing, we can turn our attention to adaptive milestones as a means of estimating general intelligence. Play skills also provide clues to a child's level of cognitive ability.

Among children with ASD, the idea of an IQ score as a single number breaks down completely. A child with autism may have a verbal IQ

Table 5.2 Play Milestones in the Young Child

Age	Play Activities, and Underlying Neurodevelopmental Skills
3 months	Midline hand play (self-awareness)
7–9 months	Banging, shaking, and mouthing objects (awareness of objects)
12 months	Casting—throwing objects over the side of the high chair, then looking for them (object permanence)
14 months	Stacking and dumping; makes marks with crayon (tool use)
14–16 months	Push-button toys (cause and effect)
24 months	Simple imitative play such as "helping" with housework; toy lawnmower or shopping cart; crayon work consists of scribbling (role playing reinforces social awareness)
36 months	Make-believe play; crayon work includes recognizable items such as faces, then stick figures (enhanced ability to manipulate abstract mental concepts)
48 months	Rule-based play, such as simple board games or card games (one-to-one correspondence, counting, sequencing, matching, turn taking)

of 70 (bordering on mental retardation), a nonverbal IQ of 130 (superior), and a full-scale IQ (all subtests considered together) of 100 (average). But none of these three scores would describe such a child very well. Children with Asperger syndrome and nonverbal learning disability commonly display the opposite pattern: high verbal scores and low nonverbal scores. In any case, if there is more than a 20-point split between verbal and nonverbal abilities on IQ testing, the full-scale IQ should not be used as the basis for educational planning or making long-term predictions. This is why I insist on seeing all of the individual subtest scores, not just the full-scale IQ. (See Appendix III for more information on commonly used tests.)

WHEN DOES DEVELOPMENTAL DELAY BECOME MENTAL RETARDATION?

The question of whether and when a diagnosis of developmental delay turns into a diagnosis of mental retardation depends on the child's rate of development. Like a car that leaves the traffic light at 30 miles per hour when all the other cars are going 40, the child with mental retardation falls further behind as time passes. The slower the child's rate of development, the more quickly the gap grows, and the sooner a diagnosis of mental retardation can be made. By age five, a child with mild mental retardation will have reached approximately the three-year-old level; a child with moderate MR will have reached the thirty-month level; and a child with severe MR will have reached the eighteen-to-twenty-four-month level.

In contrast, a premature infant, born at six months' gestation instead of the usual nine, will be three months behind other infants, developmentally, but the gap does not grow as the child gets older, because the child's *rate* of development is normal. At age five, the former premie is still "three months behind," but the gap is so small, relative to the child's age, that it doesn't matter any more.

The Autistic Spectrum in Two Dimensions

Now that we've discussed atypicality and intelligence as separate entities, let's look at the two of them together. Just as our imaginary train can be derailed, delayed, or both, a child can have any degree of atypicality combined with any degree of intelligence. We show this by combining our horizontal scale of atypicality (Figure 5.1) with our vertical scale of intelligence (Figure 5.2), creating a two-dimensional graph (Figure 5.3). If you aren't used to reading this kind of graph, and if the comparison to trains doesn't help, think about atypicality and intelligence as though they were height and weight. A person can have any combination of height and weight: tall and thin like a basketball player, tall and broad like a football player, short and thin like a jockey, short and round like a snowman, or any combination in between. In the same way, a child can have any degree of atypicality from mild to severe, accompanied by any level of intelligence from genius IQ to profound mental retardation.

At this point, it's natural to ask where the different diagnostic labels would show up on such a graph. In Figure 5.4, we've added the *DSM-IV*

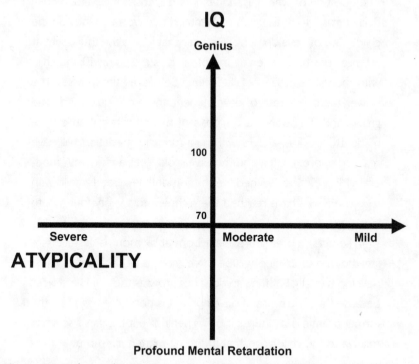

Figure 5.3 Relationship Between Atypicality and Intelligence *An individual can have any degree of atypicality (the horizontal or X axis) in combination with any level of intelligence (the vertical or Y axis).*

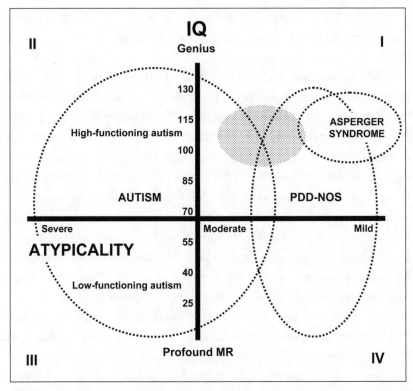

Figure 5.4 Commonly Used Diagnostic Labels *Here the labels are mapped on a graph of atypicality versus IQ. The Roman numerals in the four corners of the graph are for reference only.*

diagnoses we've already discussed, as well as some other labels that are used every day, even though they don't appear in any formal diagnostic handbook: *high-functioning autism* and *low-functioning autism*. For example, you can see that moderate to severe atypicality plus IQ in the normal range commonly add up to a diagnosis of high-functioning autism, whereas the same level of atypicality combined with an IQ below 70 is commonly referred to as low-functioning autism.

Raymond, in the film *Rain Man,* can count six decks of cards at a Las Vegas blackjack table, but he takes the world literally. When the sign at the intersection changes to Don't Walk, he stops in his tracks, even though he's in the middle of the street. He's rigid, insisting that his brother Charlie find a roadside bar so he can stop to watch his favorite TV program, and he has altered sensory processing (he panics when the smoke detector goes off). Raymond has high-functioning autism: severe atypicality plus normal general intelligence (the upper left-hand corner of Figure 5.4).

Mild to moderate atypicality likewise can occur in the presence of either normal IQ or mental retardation. Think of Sean Penn's title role in the film *I Am Sam* (at the very center of the graph, where the X and Y axes cross). Sam has mild to moderate atypicality and low-average to borderline intelligence. He can work setting up tables, meticulously arranging each dispenser of sugar just so, with all the packets right side up and sorted by color (we see a close-up of his hands arranging the sugar packets as the movie opens), but he can't work behind the counter serving the public because the demands are too varied and complex. His daughter Lucy, whom we suspect is brighter than her dad, wants some variety in her bedtime stories, but all Sam wants to read is the Dr. Seuss book *Green Eggs and Ham* (the first line of which, of course, is "I am Sam").

Individuals with mild atypicality, normal general intelligence, hyperverbal behavior, narrow and intense interests, and physical clumsiness have Asperger syndrome (the upper right-hand corner of Figure 5.4). The novel *The Curious Incident of the Dog in the Night-Time* by Mark Haddon, a fictional journal of an unnamed fifteen-year-old boy, depicts the world as seen from the point of view of a teen with Asperger syndrome. As the book opens, the neighbor's dog has been murdered with a pitchfork. The boy sets out to solve the crime. In so doing, he interviews everyone on the street, and meticulously records his findings in his journal. You, the reader, are able to connect the dots, but the boy writing the journal cannot see the patterns that are emerging from the facts he is so diligently recording.

With our two-dimensional model of ASD, we are no longer limited to three rigid diagnostic categories (autism, Asperger syndrome, and PDD-NOS). For example, the shaded area in Figure 5.4 shows the overlap of high-functioning autism, PDD-NOS, and Asperger syndrome. They fall within the same general area on the graph, meaning that children with each of those labels will all have similar needs, making the exact label somewhat irrelevant. There can be other zones of diagnostic overlap as well. Many children fall into the overlap zone between autism and PDD-NOS. Which is the "right" diagnosis? They both are (just as the color orange is neither red nor yellow; it's both). It doesn't matter which label we choose as long as the child receives appropriate services to address his or her developmental needs.

AT THE "BORDERLAND" OF ASD

A great many children and adults occupy an area at the "borderland" of ASD (Figure 5.5). Their social and language skills have the flavor of ASD, but their atypicality is so mild that we hesitate to make an ASD diagnosis. As with the overlap between high-functioning autism, PDD-NOS, and Asperger syndrome, there is no bright line separating these borderland diagnoses from one another, or from AS and PDD-NOS. All of these shades of atypicality pop up in the family members of a child with ASD. It's important to keep these notions of fluidity and overlap in mind.

Nonverbal Learning Disability (NLD)

Children with nonverbal learning disability (NLD) have poor social skills and subtle difficulty with pragmatic language, physical coordination, and right-left discrimination. On IQ testing, they score higher on the verbal portion than the nonverbal portion because of their difficulty with spatial relations and fine motor function. The term *nonverbal learning disability* is actually a misnomer, since the disability affects verbal as well as nonverbal skills. NLD is sometimes also called right hemisphere learning disability, since many spatial and social tasks are influenced by the right hemisphere of the brain. Often children with NLD are objects of derision (the terms *nerd* or *geek* come to mind). Children with NLD differ from kids with "ordinary" learning disabilities, since garden-variety learning disability generally spares social skills. Children with NLD are at increased risk for depression and social isolation. See the Resource List for Chapter 1 for additional information.

Semantic-Pragmatic Language Disorder (SPLD)

Children with semantic-pragmatic language disorder (SPLD) have language issues similar to those of children with NLD, but do not have problems with coordination, and their social issues are less troublesome. However, there is no "bright line" separating these two groups.

Broad Autism Phenotype (BAP)

The term *broad autism phenotype (BAP)* was coined by researchers studying adults to describe individuals manifesting subtle traces of atypical behavior, such as verbal or social awkwardness or a narrow, obsessive interest of some type. As Dorothy Bishop's research (which we described in Chapter 4) has shown, many of these adults were diagnosed with pragmatic language disorder as children and continue to manifest features of mild ASD in adult life. So the exact diagnosis an individual receives is partly a function of how old the individual is when he or she gets a diagnosis: Child diagnosticians are more inclined toward diagnoses such as PDD-NOS and NLD, while adult diagnosticians seem to prefer BAP. (I

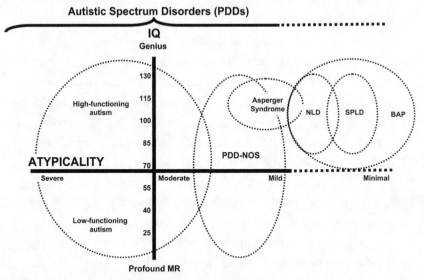

Figure 5.5 At the "Borderland" of ASD *Nonverbal learning disability (NLD), semantic-pragmatic language disorder (SPLD), and the broad autism phenotype (BAP) fall at the "borderland" of ASD; the term BAP is more often applied to adults than to children. As signified by the dashes in the X axis, BAP shades over from symptoms of a disorder to normal cognitive and behavioral traits, with no clear line separating adults with minimal atypicality from the normal adult population.*

have tried—thus far without much success—to use the diagnosis of broad autism phenotype with some of my pediatric patients, in order to secure services for them through their school districts.)

Time: The Third Dimension

Figure 5.1 is a snapshot, showing degree of atypicality. Figure 5.4 adds another dimension, intelligence, but it is still only a snapshot of the relationship between atypicality and intelligence at one moment in time. However, you want to know what will happen to your child in the

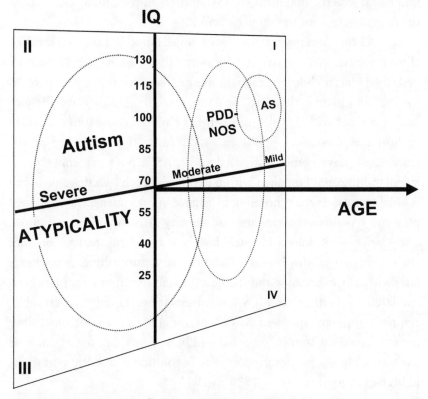

Figure 5.6 Relationship Between Atypicality, IQ, and Age (Time) *Every child starts with a unique combination of atypicality and IQ and then moves forward (to the right) as time passes. The zones for autism, pervasive developmental disorder (PDD-NOS), and Asperger syndrome (AS) are shown. Nonverbal learning disability (NLD), semantic-pragmatic language disorder (SPLD), and broad autism phenotype (BAP) have been omitted for clarity; they would be beyond Asperger syndrome to the right.*

months and years ahead. Therefore, we need to add time as the third dimension of our graph (Figure 5.6). Once we add time, the graph changes from a snapshot to a motion picture, or a map, along which all children with ASD travel as time passes. What path will your child take as he or she crosses this map?

As new therapies have sprung up over the past several decades, too many people have lost sight of the fact that ASD has a natural history of improvement over time. *Wherever your son or daughter begins, either with mild or severe atypicality, the chances are very high that your child will move from that starting point to a place of less impairment.* A lucky few (about 15 percent in most studies) move completely off the graph and lose the diagnosis of ASD entirely (although, again, "losing the diagnosis" is not the same as "cure").

In 1943 the child psychiatrist Leo Kanner published the first modern clinical report on ASD (see the Resource List for Chapter 1). Kanner described eleven children, ranging in age from five to eleven years, as having "an innate inability to form the usual, biologically provided affective contact with people, just as other children come into the world with innate physical or intellectual handicaps." Kanner noted all the features we have come to associate with ASD: poor eye contact, delayed and unusual language with parrotlike speech (what we now call echolalia and delayed echolalia), insistence upon sameness, stereotyped play and repetitive movements, and sensory attractions and aversions. The clarity of Kanner's clinical description and his realization that autism was an inborn biological deficit were astonishing. Sixty years later, virtually everything that he described in that first paper has been validated by further research and observation. Equally remarkable, Kanner's original paper was also a longitudinal study of outcome, since the children on whom he reported had been in his care for as much as five years. Here is his description of the evolution of autistic symptoms in his eleven patients, from 1938 to 1943:

> Between the ages of 5 and 6 years, they gradually abandon the echolalia and learn spontaneously to use personal pronouns with adequate reference. Language becomes more communicative, at first in the sense of a question-and-answer exercise, and then in the sense of greater spontaneity

of sentence formation. Food is accepted without difficulty. Noises and motions are tolerated more than previously. The panic tantrums subside. The repetitiousness assumes the form of obsessive preoccupations. Contact with a limited number of people is established in a twofold way: People are included in the child's world to the extent to which they satisfy his needs, answer his excessive questions, teach him how to read and to do things. Second, though people are still regarded as nuisances, their questions are answered and their commands are obeyed reluctantly, with the implication that it would be best to get these interferences over with, sooner to be able to return to the still much desired aloneness....

Between the ages of 6 and 8 years, the children begin to play in a group, still never *with* the other members of the play group, but at least on the periphery *alongside* the group. Reading skill is acquired quickly, but the children read monotonously, and a story or a moving picture is experienced in unrelated portions rather than in its coherent totality....

Five of our children have by now reached ages between 9 and 11 years.... The basic desire for aloneness and sameness has remained essentially unchanged, but there has been a varying degree of the emergence from solitude, and acceptance of at least some people as being within the child's sphere of consideration.... All of this makes the family feel that, in spite of recognized "difference" from other children, there is progress and improvement.

Kanner's observations have been borne out time and again. None of the children he studied received any specific therapy for ASD, because there was none, yet nearly half of them improved over time—some of them dramatically. In 1971 Kanner published a follow-up paper on his original eleven patients. Several had skilled jobs, and one had obtained a college degree.

So from the moment that ASD was identified and labeled as a specific syndrome, people recognized that, like any other medical condition, it has a natural history, which predicts that some children are destined to improve over time. The next logical question to ask is why some children improve tremendously, shedding most of their autistic features, while other children improve very little, if at all. What conditions make a good outcome more likely, and is there anything we can do to affect that outcome?

My research and that of others indicates that the most significant influence on a child's long-term prognosis, after the severity of the ASD itself, is his or her level of nonverbal intelligence. This includes not just the performance items on an IQ test but also other expressions of nonverbal intelligence such as tool use (age at acquisition of the ability to use a spoon and crayon, for example), adaptive skills (unbuttoning, buttoning up, etc.), and the complexity and degree of imagination reflected in the child's play. Over a dozen research studies, going back thirty years and encompassing more than a thousand children with ASD, have demonstrated that nonverbal skills constitute one of the most important factors predicting outcome (see Appendix II). Up until now, however, no one has combined atypicality, IQ, and the evolution of symptoms over time into one picture. (I realize that it's an oversimplification to equate nonverbal skills with IQ; this is a deliberate simplification for the sake of building a model. This goes back to the dilemma of how to define intelligence in a person with ASD.) The role of intelligence in determining the outcome for a child with ASD is illustrated in Figure 5.7. In a nutshell, *the higher your child's nonverbal IQ, the faster and more completely his or her atypicality will fade over time.*

If you are not comfortable with graphs, imagine a chunk of ice floating in water. A large iceberg corresponds to severe atypicality; a small piece of ice corresponds to mild atypicality. Think of IQ like water temperature: the higher the IQ, the higher the water temperature. Obviously, the warmer the water, the faster and more completely the ice will melt, sometimes disappearing entirely. Likewise, the higher a child's IQ, the faster his or her atypicality will fade over time. My research, as well as the research of others going back thirty years, bears this out (see Appendix II). Thus, having a higher IQ is desirable not just for its own sake; it also hastens the disappearance of atypical features.

Now we also have a partial answer to the question we posed in Chapter 4: Where are all the adults with ASD? Many of them have "lost the diagnosis" of ASD and no longer show up on the radar screen of any

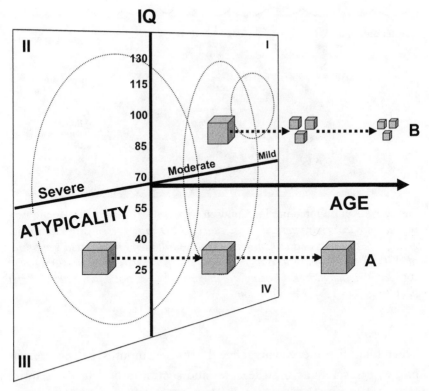

Figure 5.7 Relationship Between Atypicality, IQ, and Improvement over Time
*The courses for two hypothetical children, one with severe atypicality plus
mental retardation (A) and one with mild to moderate atypicality plus normal
intelligence (B), are shown. In both instances, the leftmost cube represents the
child's atypical features at the time of diagnosis. These symptoms remain relatively unchanged in the child with coexisting mental retardation (A) but break
up over time in the child with normal IQ (B). As child B progresses, his or her
diagnosis may change from autism to PDD-NOS to BAP as an adult. Thus, in
addition to shrinking and breaking up into little pieces, child B's cube is also
moving to the right along the X axis.*

human service system, but they still manifest subtle atypical features
(Figure 5.8). Alas, "losing the diagnosis" is not the same as "cure."

Three Young Friends: The Rest of the Story

Let's go back to the three young children I introduced in Chapter 1, to
see how they have progressed over time.

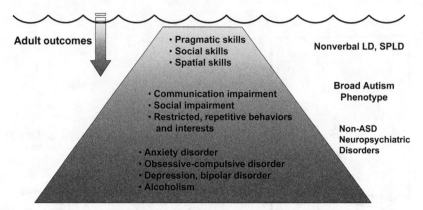

Figure 5.8 Adult Outcomes for Children with ASD *The same underlying neuropsychological characteristics that caused ASD may persist into adulthood, giving rise to the broad autism phenotype. Adults who manifested symptoms of ASD as children are also at increased risk for a variety of non-ASD neuropsychiatric diagnoses. "Losing the diagnosis" does not equal "cure." Refer back to Figure 3.2 for comparison.*

Kevin

When I had first met Kevin, at age thirty-three months, he was nonverbal, with severely atypical features and significantly delayed adaptive skills. I diagnosed autism and developmental delay. At age three and a half, he was still not using a spoon and was not toilet trained, and he remained nonverbal except for rare echolalia. He did not consistently respond to his own name or follow one-step commands. He continued to display classic features of autism, such as poor eye contact, tantrums after minor changes in routine, and a lack of appropriate fear of environmental dangers, such as heights, traffic, and so on. His particular fascination was with rubber bands. He remained in an intensive behaviorally based program (discussed in Chapter 7).

By the time he turned five, Kevin was occasionally using a spoon but still preferred feeding himself with his fingers. He used rare single words and some memorized phrases, inconsistently responded to one-step directions, and had learned to communicate via a picture exchange system plus a limited sign vocabulary (more on communication training in Chapter 9). He was impulsive and often agitated.

We prescribed medication to reduce Kevin's hyperactive and agitated behavior (guanfacine; see Chapter 12). After some initial sleepiness, his attention span improved and he became somewhat calmer on the guanfacine. His parents, better able to take their more composed son out in public, breathed a slight sigh of relief. Shortly thereafter, he transitioned from the preschool special education system into public school, and was enrolled full-time in an autistic support class (more on school placement in Chapter 13).

Kevin was still nonverbal at eight years old. His continued tantrums and outbursts became more problematic as he grew bigger and stronger. He continued to receive behavioral therapies, working on social interaction, household and dressing skills, toilet training, and following one-step commands. His agitation continued, and we tried a different medication (risperidone; Chapter 12) while weaning him off the guanfacine.

Now ten years old, Kevin remains nearly nonverbal and makes poor eye contact. His communication is limited to about a dozen signs, picture cards, and an electronic communication board. He can follow one-step directions with fair reliability and can just about dress and undress himself. He continues to have episodes of agitation, pacing, or "stimmy" behavior, although his parents feel the risperidone helps somewhat. His most recent CARS score was 45 (in the range of severe autism). His nonverbal and adaptive skills are around the three-to-four-year-old level, which translates into a developmental quotient (DQ) of about 30 to 40 (moderate to severe mental retardation). Kevin's course has evolved like that of child A in Figure 5.7.

Darryl

Recall that I first met Darryl at twenty months. At that first visit, he had moderate atypicality and normal adaptive (self-care) skills. I diagnosed Darryl with PDD-NOS. I had no way of knowing his level of intelligence, since he was not engageable in testing, but I was cautiously optimistic based on his normal adaptive skills. At twenty-six months, Darryl's vocalizations remained severely delayed. He was able to follow some simple two-step verbal commands and could indicate desired foods and objects with picture boards. Darryl continued to be obsessed with opening and closing closet doors and with exit signs. He still flapped his arms at the slightest provocation.

At thirty-three months he was still only babbling, but he could communicate "more," "all done," "help," and "eat" with manual signs. Although his eye contact was still erratic, he was more socially interactive, responding appropriately to praise, for example. His hand flapping was less prominent. He could recognize the numerals 1 through 9, at least half of the uppercase alphabet, and various geometric shapes, and had an excellent visual memory and sense of direction. He was repetitious and ritualized about his play, insisting, for example, on following exactly the same sequence when inserting shapes into his shape sorter. He remained obsessed with doors, and the sound of the vacuum cleaner upset him. He was receiving intensive behaviorally based services, speech/language therapy, and occupational therapy (discussed in Chapters 7 to 11).

By age thirty-nine months, Darryl's vocalizations had advanced to multiple syllables and, on rare occasions, sounds that approximated words. He made appropriate use of more than a dozen signs and could lead his parents to desired objects. He began to read facial expressions more readily, and would cry when scolded, showing further improvement in social interaction. Although Darryl still flapped his hands and rocked his body, especially when excited, he now responded to his parents' "no hands" directions. When Darryl turned three, his parents enrolled him in a special education preschool three days per week. He also spent two days per week in a small, highly structured pre-K for children with typical development, under the watchful eye of a seasoned teacher with a knack for getting the best out of children with developmental differences.

Darryl began speaking at three years nine months. His eye contact improved dramatically, although he remained impulsive and distractible. By age five he was speaking in sentences and could answer simple who, what, when, where, and why questions. He still insisted on routines, such as making his mother stand in the driveway with him every evening to await his dad's return home from work, and demanding to be the one who pushed the button on the garage door opener. He remained selective about food, hypersensitive to certain noises, impulsive, and distractible, although our introduction of stimulant medication improved his attention span noticeably.

By age five and a half, this boy who had once been nonverbal had become hyperverbal. His parents' biggest concern now, in fact, was his "incessant questioning, and a huge need to classify everything." His full-scale IQ was 99—perfectly average.

Now six years old, Darryl attends public school in a social communication classroom. He has fair to good eye contact most of the time. He still flaps his arms when excited, and he continues to have prominent verbal scripting—repeating school announcements verbatim when he gets home, reciting the school bus schedule, and so on. He is obsessed with airplanes and airports. Stimulant medication has helped Darryl quite a bit, although he continues to have mild impulsivity. He reads to at least the first-grade level, with some phonetic decoding skills and good comprehension. Darryl's most recent score on CARS was 24—technically no longer in the range of autism on that particular instrument. Nonetheless, Darryl continues to meet *DSM* criteria for autism, based on his persistent difficulties with social relationships, language pragmatics, and repetitive interests and behaviors.

Teddy

Teddy had been referred to me at age seven by his elementary school guidance counselor because of odd behavior. His level of general intelligence was average to above average, but he lacked an awareness of social boundaries or the subtleties of language, and he had an intense interest in trains and the *Titanic;* I diagnosed him with Asperger syndrome. Once Teddy received this diagnosis, his school district modified his educational program to include an instructional "shadow" in the classroom (to keep an eye on him and "bring him back" whenever he began to drift off into inner monologues about the *Titanic* or get stuck on various tasks). He was also enrolled in Lunch Bunch, a social skills program run by the school guidance counselor. (More on social skills in Chapter 10.)

When I saw Teddy at age seven and a half, his fascination with the *Titanic* and trains was still going strong. While waiting for our follow-up visit to start, he tore off three feet of paper from the roll on the examining table and sketched what he described as "the Washington Metro, the Acela, the T in Boston, the tube in London, and the SEPTA," the Philadelphia train and subway. His drawings were precise and accurate, down to the keystone insignia of the Pennsylvania Railroad. He spoke knowledgeably about the Eurostar and French TGV high-speed trains. He continued to have significant impulsivity and distractibility at home and at school, which we treated with stimulant medication.

A year later, Teddy's *Titanic* obsession had begun to interfere with his ability to engage in any type of meaningful play or social activity—when around other children, all he could do was carry on about the *Titanic*. We added a selective serotonin reuptake inhibitor (SSRI; Chapter 12), and over the next two months Teddy's parents saw a dramatic decrease in his obsessive behavior. He continued on the combination of an SSRI and a stimulant, which seemed to help control both his anxious-obsessive behaviors and his impulsivity. At eight years six months, his fixation with the *Titanic* would surface only occasionally, although he remained fascinated by trains and was developing a new interest—space travel. Teddy's IQ was 110—high average.

Teddy was beginning to identify and label his emotions by age ten. His parents described his behavior as "occasionally inappropriate, but not detached." A child psychologist was working with Teddy on his social skills. As for speech, Teddy had minimally flattened inflection and occasionally impaired pragmatics; for example, he would still launch into long monologues without gauging his listener's interest in the subject. At this point, Teddy's family wisely chose to share his diagnosis with him (more information on this in Chapter 15). Armed with this new understanding about himself, Teddy was better able to adjust his behavior in social settings, maintain his self-esteem, and keep his anxiety at a healthy minimum.

By age eleven, Teddy began to have facial and vocal tics. Although these might have been aggravated by the stimulants, Teddy's parents and I chose to continue his medication because of the dramatic improvement in his attention span. When he was twelve, he was attending a mainstream classroom with supplemental support in reading, writing, math, and speech. At the time of our follow-up visit, he had just made a triumphant return from overnight Boy Scout camp, where he had earned a merit badge in, naturally, railroading.

Teddy is now thirteen. He remains on an SSRI and a stimulant. He struggles with social skills but has developed some insight into the fact that he is different from other children. When I asked him what he most wished for in the future, he answered, "I'd like to be able to make friends better, and I wish I wouldn't always get in trouble for things I don't understand."

The stories of these three boys show us quite a lot about the natural history of ASD.

Kevin's delayed adaptive skills (spoon use, toilet training) and delayed play skills (chewing on a crayon rather than writing with it) accurately predicted mental retardation. In the presence of MR, his atypical features—severe to begin with—remained severe, a course similar to that of child A in Figure 5.7, consistent with a diagnosis of low-functioning autism (that is, severe ASD plus MR).

Darryl's adaptive skills emerged at close to their expected times, which helped us correctly predict that his rate of development, and hence his IQ, were normal. His atypical features faded substantially between ages three and six, which is what our research led us to expect in the presence of normal IQ. Darryl's course corresponded to that of child B in Figure 5.7—steady, qualitative improvement over time. Darryl's label of high-functioning autism gradually morphed into PDD-NOS.

Teddy's story is notable for the delay in initial diagnosis of Asperger syndrome, which didn't come to light until his elementary school counselor identified him as "different" at age seven. All through his preschool years, Teddy's parents had simply accepted him as he was and had successfully fostered his self-esteem and development without any outside intervention. He was their only child, so they had no basis for comparison with typically developing children, and had not sought professional assistance. Teddy's pediatrician had not picked up the signs of Asperger syndrome because none of Teddy's atypical features had surfaced during routine office visits (which tend to average about seven minutes). Teddy came to diagnosis with his self-esteem intact.

In all three children we see signs of comorbidity (the simultaneous occurrence of other medical or developmental problems), including mental retardation (Kevin), attention deficit hyperactivity disorder (ADHD) (Darryl and Teddy), dyslexia (Teddy), and tics (Teddy). Darryl and Teddy showed dramatic improvement over time. Ironically, this improvement carries dangers of its own. As their atypical features become less obvious, the risk is that teachers in upper grades who are unfamiliar with the early development of children like Darryl and Teddy will mistakenly label them as disobedient or emotionally disturbed.

Summing Up

ASD has a natural history of improvement over time, regardless of intervention. The single biggest factor influencing the rate of improvement, other than the severity of the ASD itself, is the child's level of general intelligence (best approximated by looking at nonverbal and adaptive skills). Taking these two factors into account gives us the ability to make broadly predictive statements about children on the spectrum, although it may be difficult or impossible to make clear predictions for any individual child, especially at the outset.

Our understanding of the natural history of ASD is critical when we set out to assess each individual child's current situation and then make a reasonable forecast about his or her future. Yet if you are the parent of a child with ASD, you may have mixed reactions to this idea of natural history. On one hand, the concept enables you to orient yourself in a world filled with jargon and conflicting claims and approaches. All the stories you'll hear when you enter the world of ASD will make much more sense, and have greater value, if you are able to place them within the 3-D model I've laid out. If you know the age, degree of atypicality, and level of overall intelligence of the children you hear about, you can determine how relevant their stories are to your own child. On the other hand, this knowledge can come with some pretty scary implications. As one parent told me, "I was prepared to hear that my child was on the autistic spectrum. But the part about possible mental retardation was like being hit over the head with a hammer." I wish there was some way to skirt the issue of IQ, but that isn't the world we've been given.

Remember, however, it can be impossible to actually know your child's IQ early on. Figure 5.7 is based on large numbers of children and lots of hindsight. But there are many times when I have to tell parents, "This is broadly true. But we can't pin down your child's precise location on the map just yet." The first child I ever diagnosed with autism, who was nonverbal and noninteractive at age three, turned out to have an IQ of 150 by the time we were able to test him several years later. He went on to graduate from college, and is now happily living on his own—a perfect example of a "missing" adult with ASD, as we discussed in Chapter 4.

I often feel like the Wizard of Oz, who couldn't give the Scarecrow a brain, the Tin Man a heart, or the Cowardly Lion courage, but could only hand out a diploma, a ticking watch, and a medal—not quite what they had been seeking, but useful nonetheless. In a similar fashion, the natural history of ASD offers you a map of the territory you'll be traveling, but the map alone can't show you the best route to take for your child and your family, nor can I necessarily even tell you exactly where you are on the map at this instant. Like the Wizard, I can't give you exactly what you seek—a complete prescription for your child's future—but I can give you tools to guide you, to help you to evaluate therapy claims critically and choose the appropriate forms of therapy for your child, and to undertake long-range planning with a clear idea of what possibilities may lie beyond the horizon for your child.

PART II

THE WORLD OF
INTERVENTION SERVICES

Chapter 6

What Can I Do? Intervention Basics

In Chapter 1 we detailed the symptoms of ASD. As summarized in Table 1.2, these include problems with social skills, communication, repetitious behavior, and sensorimotor processing. Let's take Table 1.2 and turn it on its head, in order to generate a list of therapy goals.*

- In the social realm, the most basic requirement is that the child acknowledge the presence of other people and reliably respond to social bids for interaction. Once a child has learned to attend to others, the next goal is to foster the child's ability to initiate social interactions with others. Still later, the goal is to enable the child to sustain a back-and-forth interaction and to recognize the feelings of others.
- In the realm of communication, the first goal is to teach the child that there is such a thing as language. That is, we can represent objects and activities with arbitrary sounds (words), gestures (signs), or symbols (picture cards). Initially, this means teaching the child that language has a payoff for him or her—that is, teaching the child how to ask for desired objects. Still later, the goal becomes teaching the child how to sustain a back-and-forth exchange of language with another person (and ultimately how to use language itself as a form of social interaction by sharing feelings with others verbally), and an

* Special thanks to my colleague Judith Watman for suggesting this idea.

ability to appreciate humor, inference, sarcasm, and other nuances of language that go beyond the simple transmission of facts or obtaining desired objects.

• In the realm of behavior, the goal is to alleviate mental and behavioral rigidity, replacing them with more appropriate play activities and increasing the child's tolerance to changes in the environment. Redirecting stereotypies into more socially acceptable forms of behavior may also be a goal. Many of the maladaptive behaviors of children with ASD are biologically driven, in the same way that seizures are biologically driven. In some children, therefore, medication will have a role to play in behavior management, right alongside behavioral techniques.

• Finally, in the realm of sensorimotor processing, the goals include normalizing the child's responses to sensory inputs and working on bodily awareness and coordination. Specific objectives may include reducing food selectivity, increasing tolerance to noise, and so forth, depending on each child's sensory profile.

How to approach these goals is the subject of Part II of this book.

I know you're eager to jump ahead, to get right into the specific therapies. But please stick with me through the next few pages of introductory material. I don't expect you to become a psychologist, educator, or therapist, but it will be useful to know a few key terms and underlying concepts. Even this basic level of understanding will help you to make some sense out of the profusion of therapies, and will also enable you to make informed choices about which therapies will best suit your child at different points in time.

Therapy for children with ASD sits at the confluence of two streams of endeavor: Medicine and Education. Medicine (with a capital M) is evidence-based; Education is not. Before coming to market, new drugs need to meet rigorous standards to demonstrate both safety and effectiveness. Education has no such standards. Where is the research to show how many hours of kindergarten a normally developing five-year-old needs in order to be ready for first grade? Where is the research comparing one kindergarten curriculum with another? Of course, there is no such research. The length of the school year and the content of the curriculum are set by tradition and legislation, not data.

The problem becomes even more difficult when attempting to assess the impact of special education services for a child with developmental issues.

A consensus panel convened by the National Academy of Sciences in 2001 recommended twenty-five hours per week, twelve months a year, of "systematically planned, and developmentally appropriate educational activity" for children with ASD. This recommendation was a consensus, but it was not arrived at in a scientific manner. Why not twenty hours? Why not forty? The panel also bemoaned the absence of comparative studies to help guide decisions between different forms of therapy, and issued a plea for better research on this topic. There are very few controlled studies proving the long-term benefit of any particular therapy, virtually no head-to-head comparisons between competing therapies, and no studies to answer the question "How much therapy is enough?" Nonetheless, the better informed you are, the more effective an advocate you can be for your child.

Patting the Elephant

When I was a child, I learned the legend of the six blind men and the elephant. One man touches the animal's ear and concludes that the elephant is like a fan; another touches a tusk and concludes that the elephant is like a spear; a third grabs the tail and assumes that the elephant is like a rope; and so on. The tale concludes with the warning "Though each of them was partly right, all of them were wrong."

As you sift through the bewildering array of treatment options for your child, you will find yourself confronted by a chorus of recommendations from a wide variety of specialists, each of whom will confidently describe your child's problem using his or her professional jargon. The occupational therapist will stress your child's "sensory integration disorder." The audiologist will focus on your child's "auditory processing disorder." For the speech/language pathologist, it's your child's "pragmatic language disorder." The floor-time practitioner will be concerned with "emotional reciprocity." Conversely, the behavior analyst will focus on "shaping behavior" while studiously disregarding "private mental events" such as emotion, insight, or desire.

(Don't panic. We'll go into each of these therapies chapter by chapter.) Each professional is partly correct—each has something important and useful to offer—but none of them alone can meet all of your child's needs. Your job is to keep your eye on the whole elephant that is ASD, and figure out what is best for your child—something you soon will be able to do better than any individual therapist, no matter how skilled he or she may be in their narrow area of expertise.

In some instances, terms and methods used by one profession can be translated into comparable terms and methods used by another profession. As I will show you, floor time, pivotal response treatment, and natural environment training are all similar; they are just described with different sets of professional jargon. In other instances, trying to compare two types of therapy is like trying to compare apples to oranges. Such therapies differ not just in the jargon employed; they are based on different ideas about the basis of human behavior itself—including ASD. Naturally, they lead to very different therapeutic approaches for ASD. This is not entirely a bad thing, because different models of ASD and their associated therapies are more useful at different stages of your child's development. Let me give you a concrete example of what I'm getting at: If you are driving to the mall, you can pretend the earth is flat. Over such a short distance you can ignore the curvature of the earth; it won't affect your trip. But if you are the commander of the International Space Station, you'd better think of the earth as round, or you'll be in trouble! Each model for the shape of the earth has its usefulness. For driving around town, the flat-earth model is actually the better of the two. You don't need to worry about the longitude and latitude of your destination—you just have to remember where to turn. In a similar way, different models of ASD serve their purpose at different points along the way. For example, applied behavioral analysis (ABA) assumes that all human behavior is the result of conditioning. Like a flat-earth model, ABA is fine—in its place. But as your child progresses, you will need a more complex model—one that takes into account factors such as your child's intentions, insight, and so on—factors that are missing from the ABA model. As I will show you, therapies follow a progression that runs parallel with the natural history of ASD itself. So, rather than trying to equate radically different approaches or rank them as better or worse than one another, you need to understand the role each form of therapy has to play in your child's treatment program and decide which is right for your child *at this time.*

(i) See the Resource List for additional information on intervention basics.

Development Versus Behavior

You will probably hear the words *development* and *behavior* more often than any others as you embark on this journey. They overlap and are in many ways intertwined, but I want you to think of them as separate phenomena. Development is biologically based, long-term (weeks, months, years), and irreversible. Learning to walk, for example, is a developmental process that depends on the maturing of the infant's nervous system over the first twelve months of life. You can't teach a four-month-old to walk, no matter how hard you try. Likewise, once a young child has learned to walk, you can't unteach that skill; it's irreversible.

Behavior, on the other hand, can be either biologically or environmentally based, and if the latter, it is reversible. Imagine a child who throws tantrums whenever he or she wants something. If the tantrums succeed—if the child gets the desired object—the child learns that this is how things work. We would say that the child's tantrum behavior has been *reinforced* by the adults in his or her environment, so the tantrums will continue. However, the adults surrounding the child can put an end to the tantrum behavior if they simply stop rewarding it (in behaviorist terms, the behavior has been *put on extinction*). In this fashion, they can help the child unlearn the behavior. In contrast, biologically based behaviors—tics, for example—cannot be unlearned, although a person might be able to suppress them for a few moments at a time.

Some behaviors can be either biological, environmental, or a combination of the two; self-injurious behavior (SIB) is a case in point. SIB is a severe problem for a small proportion of children with ASD. Some of these children are innately hyperarousable—their fight-or-flight mechanism is on a hair trigger. They can become agitated with minimal or no external provocation, and then direct their agitation against themselves, in the form of face slapping, self-biting, skin picking, or head banging. SIB can also be environmentally based. Let's say a child wants a cookie, and his parent refuses. The child throws a tantrum, but the parent remains firm. Finally the child slaps himself in the face in an act of pure frustration. Horrified, the parent relents. By giving in, the parent unintentionally has reinforced the SIB. Next time around, the child will slap himself a bit earlier in the process, and so on. Eventually, face slapping starts to take on a life of its own as the child learns how powerful a tool he has at his disposal to alter his parents' behavior. Sometimes SIB represents a combination of biological and environmental factors. Many children with ASD have a frustration threshold that is lower than that of a child with normal development, making them more likely to go over the brink during a stressful situation and engage in SIB. The more often the child engages in SIB, the greater the risk that eventually the parent will slip and inadvertently reinforce the behavior (no parent is perfect). Mother Nature has in effect strewn banana peels in the child's path in the form of a reduced frustration threshold, thereby increasing the odds of a secondary, behaviorally based component arising: The more times the child slaps himself in a biologically driven way, the more opportunities he or she has to discover how useful a tool SIB can be. An intervention combining behavior modification plus medication is often required. (More on self-injurious behavior in Chapter 12.)

Why is the distinction between development and behavior so important? Because the process of development continues to unfold even as your child receives therapy. Your child will continue to develop in some way, because that's just how biology works, regardless of the amount or type of therapy he or she may be receiving. As your child's condition improves, you won't always be able to tell whether the improvement is due to naturally occurring developmental changes or to the effects of therapy. Of course, you aren't interested in conducting a science experiment. You just want your child to reach his or her fullest potential. But if I came along and told you, "Use my special therapy program and I'll have your newborn baby walking in just twelve months," you'd know right away that I was pulling a fast one. *Any* child has a 95 percent chance of learning to walk in twelve months, regardless of therapy, because that's just how long it takes for most infants. Yet many therapy programs for children with ASD take credit for all of a child's improvement, including the part that would have occurred due to natural developmental processes.

"Bottom-Up" and "Top-Down"

Psychologists refer to brain activity as either *bottom-up* or *top-down*. These terms reflect a view of the nervous system like a layer cake, with the cerebral cortex of the brain at the top and our muscles and sense organs at the bottom. By *bottom-up,* psychologists mean activity based directly on input from the senses—touch, pain, smell, and so on—and other low-level aspects of nervous system function. High-level activities, such as reasoning, making judgments, or planning for the future, are referred to as *top-down* and originate within the brain—usually the cerebral cortex. When a doctor taps your arm with a hammer and

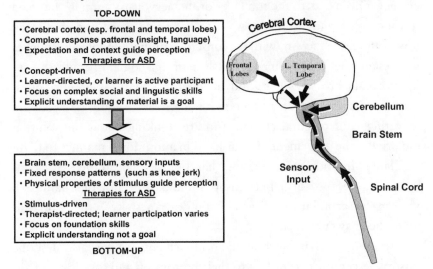

"Top-Down" Versus "Bottom-Up" Therapies

Figure 6.1 Bottom-Up and Top-Down *The cerebral cortex engages in top-down activity (insight, language generation and comprehension, future planning, empathy, etc.), while the sense organs feed information, bottom-up fashion, from below. Therapies for ASD can also be described in terms of their "bottom-up" and "top-down" qualities.*

Figure 6.2 Visual Perception—Bottom-Up *Do you see a square? I hope so! That's because there is a square printed here. The raw data drive your perception.*

causes your wrist muscle to jerk, that's a *bottom-up* stimulus causing a low-level neurologic response. In fact, the reflex causing your wrist to jerk never even gets to the top layer of the nervous system; it's handled in a loop that goes from the wrist to the spinal cord and then back down to the wrist again, with no conscious thought involved. Reflexes are present even when someone is asleep or in a coma. In contrast, *top-down* events involve some kind of mental activity—planning, questioning, imagining. When you work a crossword puzzle, you are activating your cerebral cortex. You are thinking about the solution and driving the movement of your hand in a top-down manner to fill in the blanks. In both instances, your hand moves, but in the first example it was because of a bottom-up stimulus (the doctor's hammer), while in the second it was driven by top-down activity in the brain (filling in the answer to a clue).

Like motor activity such as hand movement, we can also describe sensory perceptions according to their bottom-up and top-down qualities. Bottom-up sensory perceptions depend on the raw data alone. In contrast, top-down perceptions depend on context and our expectations in addition to the raw data. A few examples (Figures 6.2 and 6.3) should make this clear.

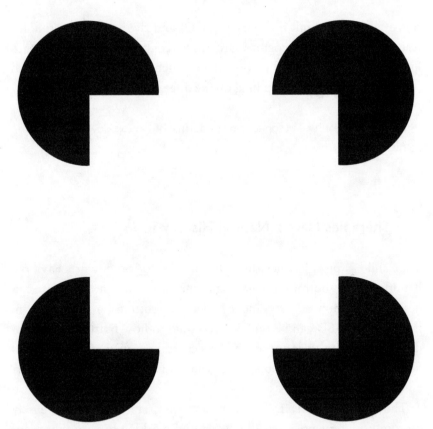

Figure 6.3 Visual Perception—Top-Down *Do you see a square? Most people report seeing a white square, the borders of which are "whiter" than the adjacent page. There is no square, and the entire page is the same shade of white, but your brain "wants" to see a square, based on past experience (the last ten thousand times you saw four corners, they constituted the outer limits of a square). Expectation guides perception, overriding the raw data, causing you to see something that really isn't there. Optical illusions work by creating a conflict between bottom-up and top-down perceptual processing.*

Language also has bottom-up and top-down aspects. If I tell you, "The turkey is ready to eat," you can process the meaning of each word in a bottom-up fashion, retrieving its definition from your mental dictionary. But you still can't tell the meaning of the sentence as a whole unless you know the *context:* Is the turkey in the barnyard, about to peck at a grain of corn, or is it on a platter, steaming hot and ready to be carved? Virtually all complex language tasks—humor, irony, sarcasm, inference, and so on—involve top-down processing. We grasp humor by perceiving the conflict between our top-down expectations (where we think the story is going) and the bottom-up stimulus (the punch line). We recognize sarcasm by contrasting the plain meaning of the words with the context in which they have been uttered ("Isn't that lovely" after spilling one's coffee, for example).

(i) See the Resource List for additional information on top-down and bottom-up processing.

Therapies Have a Natural History Too

Your child is on a journey, from bottom-up to top-down behavior—handflapping is bottom-up; making friends is top-down. Just as we can describe all brain activity and behavior as bottom-up or top-down, therapies for ASD can be ranked according to how bottom-up or top-down they are in their approach. This central organizing principle will help us bring some order out of the chaos of so many competing therapies.

Therapies for ASD follow a progression, starting with intensely bottom-up interventions at the outset and working toward more top-down therapies as the child matures. In general, children who are younger, have more severe atypicality, or have coexisting developmental delay will require more of a bottom-up approach. Children who are older, have milder atypicality, and/or have normal intelligence will be better suited to a top-down approach. (This is where having an accurate developmental diagnosis is key to selecting the right therapies for your child.) A toddler with no eye contact, no speech, and intense self-stimulatory behavior will need a bottom-up approach. A six-year-old with Asperger syndrome who is first diagnosed in kindergarten will never need such intense intervention. Rather, such a child will ease into the sequence somewhere farther along the path, starting out with therapies that are far more top-down in their orientation. Picking the right therapy as your child moves along this path is like hitting a moving target; the answer to your question "What does my child need?" will change as your child makes progress.

Bottom-up therapies focus on the what and how of a task. Top-down therapies focus on the context and the social factors: the when, where, and, most importantly, why. Here are the qualities that distinguish bottom-up from top-down therapies for ASD. Like brain activity itself (which is seldom purely bottom-up or top-down), therapies come in shades of gray rather than just black and white, with a range of options from pure bottom-up to pure top-down.

Initiation

Bottom-up therapies are driven by the therapist. The child is the "target," or passive object, of the therapy; the therapist sets the agenda and does the work. As an example of pure bottom-up intervention, think of a physical therapist stretching a child's limb to increase range of motion. Next along the continuum, the PT might engage the child in active rather than passive exercises by getting the child to flex and extend the affected limb with assistance. Eventually the goal may be for the child to exercise the limb independently, perhaps as the therapist observes. In an educational setting, pure bottom-up learning is exemplified by direct instruction: The adult places a ball on the table and declares, "Touch ball," then praises the child when the child executes the command. Or the adult may guide the child, hand-over-hand, through the desired action (called "prompting" in behavioral terms).

Comprehension

Bottom-up therapies do not require the child to understand or to be able to articulate the goal of the therapy. We require only that the child perform the action. Top-down therapies, on the other hand, are designed to help the child understand the task to be mastered. Going through the motions and merely performing the required task isn't enough. The goal of intervention is achieved in that "Aha!" moment when the child *gets the idea*. Returning to our previous example: Instead of saying, "Touch ball" and praising the child for following the command, the adult might say, "Can you find a ball?" and leave it up to the child to figure out which of several items in the room is actually a ball. At first the child might bring back some other object. "Is this a ball?" the adult might ask in a mildly humorous way. "No, this isn't a ball! Where's the ball?" Sensing that he or she has not solved the problem correctly, the child goes back to find some other object. Rather than simply following a command, now the child is actively engaged in problem solving, trying to figure out what will satisfy the adult's request for a ball. At the next level, the adult might say: "Can you find something that is round and blue?" The skills for solving this problem are a little higher. The process continues, each time involving clues that are a bit more complex or abstract: "Find something we kick," for example. The progression in this example is from nouns to adjectives to functional descriptions (how the object is used). From there, the focus typically moves to social problem solving. To take a common example: If a child has a habit of hugging strangers or other children, a bottom-up approach involves implementing rewards and punishments to extinguish the hugging behavior. Getting the child to understand *why* we don't hug strangers or other children, however, would be the top-down goal. This might involve the use of stories, pictures, role playing in a social skills group, or other techniques that require the child to think before acting.

Skill Level

Bottom-up therapies frequently focus on "foundation skills," in the belief that mastery of these skills will open the door to improved higher-level functioning. The assumption is that the improvement of fine motor skills through occupational therapy, for example, will lead to improved writing and self-care skills, or that work on sensory processing will pay off with enhanced language and social skills. Conversely, top-down approaches usually address the goal directly, such as when a child participates in a social skills group that targets social interaction.

Strategy

Bottom-up tasks don't require strategizing. They are straightforward, mechanical tasks, like memorizing the multiplication tables. Top-down tasks, on the other hand, require us to analyze a situation and decide on the best plan of attack. Solving word problems ("If John earns $2 per day delivering newspapers, how much money does John earn for an entire week?") is a good example. It's not enough to know that $2 \times 7 = 14$. It's necessary to read the text first, figure out how to set up the problem, and only then do the arithmetic. Similarly, com-

Cognitive Orientation and Therapy Attributes

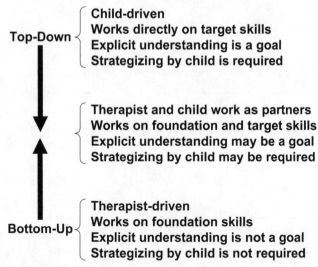

Top-Down
- Child-driven
- Works directly on target skills
- Explicit understanding is a goal
- Strategizing by child is required

- Therapist and child work as partners
- Works on foundation and target skills
- Explicit understanding may be a goal
- Strategizing by child may be required

Bottom-Up
- Therapist-driven
- Works on foundation skills
- Explicit understanding is not a goal
- Strategizing by child is not required

Figure 6.4 General Attributes of Bottom-Up and Top-Down Therapies
Bottom-up therapies require little or no reasoning ability on the part of the child; top-down therapies require active problem solving by the child.

plex social interactions (asking another child over to play, or—later—asking someone for a date) require the child to formulate a workable strategy based on theory of mind skills. This is often challenging. Many children with ASD are good at initiating an interaction based on standard rules of behavior (make eye contact, offer your hand, ask the other person his or her name, etc.) that can be trained in a bottom-up fashion, but they have a harder time sustaining the interaction because of the lack of explicit rules to govern higher-level social behavior. Social skills groups give children with ASD the chance to practice some of these skills.

As your child's symptoms and abilities evolve over time, his or her therapies will also evolve, from bottom-up to top-down approaches. What you need is a way to determine what type of therapy is best for your child *right now*, based on his or her current abilities. Table 6.1 briefly summarizes the progression of social and language skills in ASD. We will use these features as markers to signify when your child is ready to move from one therapeutic level to the next.

Table 6.1 Key Markers of Child's Ability to Advance from Bottom-Up to Top-Down Therapy

| Domain | Decreasing Atypicality ➡ | | |
	Severe	Moderate	Mild
Social	No or rare eye contact; no social reciprocity	Occasional eye contact and social reciprocity	Reliable eye contact and reciprocity; ongoing problems with theory of mind tasks (personal space, social conventions)
Language	Nonverbal or nonfunctional (echolalia and delayed echolalia)	Labeling, requesting; rare or absent initiation (comments, questions) other than to obtain items of interest	Some initiation; ongoing problems with theory of mind tasks (humor, fibbing, etc.)

Next, let's display these two dimensions (level of function and cognitive orientation of therapy) as the axes of a graph (Figure 6.5).

This graph resembles Figure 5.4, in which we laid out atypicality versus IQ. But here, on the vertical axis, we are looking at the cognitive orientation of various therapy programs, and on the horizontal axis we are looking at the improvement in symptoms over time. Right now the graph is empty. Over the next several chapters, we will fill it in with specific programs.

Summing Up

Much time and energy has been wasted arguing about which therapies are "best" for ASD when in reality bottom-up and top-down approaches each have a role to play, but at different points in the natural history of a child's ASD. Having laid out some necessary conceptual groundwork and the goals of therapy, now let's take a closer look at some specific therapies intended to get us there. But before we launch

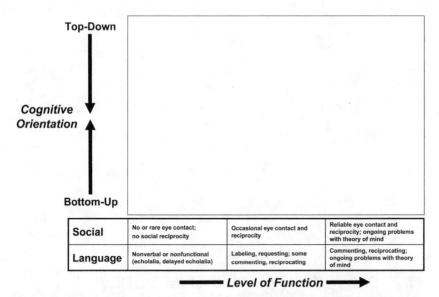

Social	No or rare eye contact; no social reciprocity	Occasional eye contact and reciprocity	Reliable eye contact and reciprocity; ongoing problems with theory of mind
Language	Nonverbal or nonfunctional (echolalia, delayed echolalia)	Labeling, requesting; some commenting, reciprocating	Commenting, reciprocating; ongoing problems with theory of mind

Figure 6.5 Level of Function Versus Cognitive Orientation of Therapy *In general, the more severe a child's atypicality and/or the younger the child's functional level, the greater the need for bottom-up therapies. The older the child, the milder the atypicality, or the more advanced developmentally a child is, the less the need for bottom-up therapies, and the greater the role for top-down interventions.*

into our review of specific therapies, allow me to offer one final word of caution: *Keep your goals reasonable.* Some people will tell you they intend to "cure" your child of ASD. That would be my fondest hope, but there is scant evidence to support any claim of a cure. Therapy can help your child achieve his or her full potential, but no more than that. Anyone who claims otherwise is promising more than they can deliver.

So what's the point of therapy? Think about a car driving on the shoulder of the road. The ride is pretty bumpy on the shoulder. Therapy may not make your child's car go faster, but therapy can get your child's car back on the pavement, where the ride is smoother. Enabling a child who was previously nonverbal to communicate, or providing a child with alternatives to self-injurious behavior, or teaching a child how to play appropriately or eat the same food as his or her siblings—each represents a huge improvement in quality of life for your child, and for you as well. And training in social skills can open doors to a full life as an independent adult—the goal we all have for our children—even if some symptoms of ASD may remain.

Chapter 7

In the Beginning: Intensive Behavioral Intervention

> Applied Behavior Analysis—Discrete Trial Training (ABA-DTT)

A Therapy Session

Remember Kevin? At thirty-three months of age, Kevin was nonverbal, his eye contact was poor, and he did not use pointing as a way of indicating his desires to others. He did not respond to his name or follow any verbal commands. In short, he was cut off from the outside world by his ASD...with one exception: He would guide his parents, hand-over-hand, to desired objects, and he enjoyed being tickled and rough-housed by his dad. So, despite all of his delays and atypical features, physical contact still worked for Kevin—both as a means of communication and as a means of obtaining pleasurable experiences. How could we reach Kevin? Let's take a peek in at one of his first therapy sessions.

We're looking into the therapy room through a two-way mirror. The room contains a low table, an adult-size chair, and on the other side of the table a child's chair. Inside the room, Kevin paces back and forth in front of the glass, gazing at his reflection. He's staring in our direction, but from his side of the glass it's a mirror, so he can't see us. In addition to Kevin, there are two therapists—we'll call them Sue and Jane. Sue is sitting in the adult-size chair. Jane is standing behind Kevin. Sue declares in a firm voice, "Sit!" Kevin gives no response. Three seconds after Kevin fails to respond, Jane gently but firmly places her hands on Kevin's shoulders, guides him to the chair, and gently pushes him into the chair. Kevin becomes agitated and starts to scream. He doesn't have a clue as to what's going on, and besides, Jane has taken him away from a preferred activity—looking at himself in the mirror. At the same time, however, Sue is declaring in a loud, happy voice, "Great job!" while giving Kevin a big tickle on the belly. As soon as the tickle has been delivered, Jane releases Kevin. He jumps up and retreats to a corner of the room. Sue and Jane wait thirty seconds, during which time Kevin calms down and resumes his inspection of the mirror. Then Sue and Jane repeat the same sequence as before, except that this time, instead of the tickle, Sue instantly produces a pretzel stick—one of Kevin's favorite foods—and places it to Kevin's lips while declaring "Great job!" Kevin again cries, but he accepts the pretzel stick. Thirty seconds later, it's the same sequence again: Sue commands "Sit!," Jane guides Kevin into the chair, and Sue immediately presents a reward: some combination of verbal praise, a tickle, or a pretzel stick. Sometimes Sue and Jane switch roles; sometimes they introduce other favorite edibles. Each run-through is termed a "discrete trial," lending this form of therapy the name *discrete trial training*, or DTT.

Over the course of dozens of trials, less and less effort is required to direct Kevin to the chair, and he fusses less. Sue (or Jane, depending on who's in the role of "usher") begins to wait an extra second or two before directing Kevin to the chair. After nearly an hour comes a breakthrough—upon hearing the command "Sit!," Kevin sits down all by himself and looks to the adult's hand for the expected treat! (He's not yet at the point of looking at the adult's face; that comes later.) In less than an hour, Sue and Jane have achieved what Kevin's parents have been unable to achieve in thirty-three months: getting Kevin to follow a verbal command. They have done so through the systematic application of a simple verbal command, followed by physical prompting and the immediate provision of a reward after successful completion of the task. From here on, Sue and Jane (and other therapists) can generalize on this breakthrough, to shape Kevin's behavior to follow essentially an infinite number of one-step verbal commands. And with each new command, Kevin learns a little faster.

Therapy for Kevin at this stage is very bottom-up: The therapist defines the task and provides the physical prompts and the rewards. The goal is to shape Kevin's behavior through the systematic application of external commands and reinforcers. We can't say if Kevin really "understands" the word *sit;* all we know is that he manifests the desired behavior. This emphasis on externally visible behavior gives this particular form of therapy its name: *behaviorism.*

A Bit of History

Behaviorism originated with Edward Thorndike and J. B. Watson in the early twentieth century. In those days, psychology was just beginning to gain respectability; skeptics viewed it as little better than witchcraft. Thorndike and Watson sought to put psychology on the same footing as hard sciences such as physics or chemistry. To accomplish this, they rejected studying anything that wasn't directly observable, including the inner workings of the brain or fuzzy notions such as "thinking" or "understanding." Instead, they concentrated on identifying outwardly visible behaviors and the various environmental factors that increased or decreased the rate at which those behaviors occurred. Although they didn't use the term, Thorndike and Watson were essentially staking out the bottom-up approach to psychology. (Thorndike and Watson's rival, Harvard professor William James, laid claim to the "top-down" approach, asserting that *consciousness* was the proper object of study for psychologists. As you will discover in later chapters, James' point of view is reflected in therapies that seek to enhance the child's theory of mind skills, such as social skills training.)

Thorndike studied the way animals escaped from cages. Over many trials, the animals in his experiments needed less and less time to escape from the cage. He reasoned that since getting out of the cage was attractive to the animal, the experience of getting free reinforced whatever behavior had occurred right before the escape. He called this the *law of effect,* writing in his 1911 book *Animal Intelligence,* "Of several [possible] responses...those which are...closely followed by satisfaction to the animal will...be more likely to recur. Those which are...followed by discomfort to the animal will...be less likely to occur." Thorndike never said anything about the animal thinking its way to a solution, since thinking was not something he could observe or measure. (Thorndike also was interested in seeing if animals escaped more quickly if they had a chance to observe another animal first. For this he studied cats; he found that letting one cat watch another cat escape was no help when the second cat's time came to get out of the cage. This will be important later in our discussion.)

Watson studied children rather than animals. In his 1928 book *Psychological Care of Infant and Child,* Watson denied the existence of inner qualities such as "anger, resentment, sympathy, fear, play, curiosity, sociability, shyness, modesty, jealousy, love, capacity, talent, [or] temperament," declaring that all child behavior was the product of prior conditioning: "We build in at an early age everything that is later to appear." Watson took the education system to task because it was based on the assumption that children could develop from within, if educators could tap each child's creative potential: "I think this doctrine has done serious harm...behaviorists believe that there is *nothing from within to develop*" (emphasis added).

The views of Thorndike and Watson were refined by their most famous student, B. F. Skinner. In one experiment, Skinner pushed a button, causing a food pellet to drop into a pigeon's cage, whenever the bird inadvertently raised its head for a second or two. Before long, the pigeon was keeping its head raised continuously. In Skinner's terms, the pigeon's random behavior (head raising) operated on the environment, resulting in the release of food (with a little behind-the-scenes help from Skinner). Building on Thorndike's law of effect, Skinner described this phenomenon as *operant conditioning.* Just like escaping from the cage, getting a food pellet was a pleasurable experience, which tended to increase the likelihood that the immediately preceding behavior (in this case, head raising) would recur. It wasn't necessary to assume that the pigeon "understood" what was happening. Behaviorists deny the existence of understanding, as we commonly use the word, for humans as well as pigeons. A behaviorist would say that our subjective perception of the "Aha!" phenomenon, when we suddenly seem to get the idea, is just a fiction, a product of successive trials that have reinforced a stimulus-response pattern. Fortunately, we do not need to embrace this belief in order to reap the considerable benefits of behaviorism for your son or daughter.

The ABC's of ABA

Applied behavior analysis (ABA) is the method behaviorists use to describe and manipulate behavior. Practitioners of ABA go to school to become licensed as board-certified behavior analysts. The principles and practices of ABA were refined and promoted by O. Ivar Lovaas, one of Skinner's students. ABA has been used successfully with tens of thousands of children with ASD—as well as children and adults with other developmental and/or behavioral problems—to eliminate unwanted behaviors (self-injury, for example) and to promote desired behaviors, including language, adaptive skills, and at least the outward forms of social behavior.

In approaching any behavior, a behaviorist asks three questions: What immediately precedes the behavior? What precisely is the behavior itself? What immediately follows the behavior? These are the ABC's: the antecedent, the behavior, and the consequence. The behaviorist sets up the child's environment to include an antecedent condition and a consequence that are likely to increase or decrease the likelihood of occurrence of the specified behavior.

In clinical practice, ABA employs specific strategies and techniques, including:

- *Shaping.* Antecedents and consequences are systematically manipulated to increase or decrease the rate of occurrence of specified behaviors.
- *Prompting and fading.* Prompts are verbal or physical clues that increase the chance that the child will produce the desired behavior.

When the child's responses begin trending in the desired direction, the prompts can be systematically decreased, or faded.

• *Chaining and reverse chaining.* Chaining involves breaking down a complex task into smaller units that can be shaped more easily. Depending on circumstances, the therapist may start with the first element in the sequence and work forward, or the last element in the sequence and work backward.

• *Generalization.* A task isn't fully learned until the child can perform it regardless of the setting or the conditions. Prompts and tasks are rotated, presented in different contexts, and presented by different therapists to facilitate generalization.

• *Discrete trials (discrete trial training, DTT).* This includes clearly defined interactions between trainer and subject that follow a typical pattern: The trainer presents a stimulus (a request, task, or behavior to be imitated), the subject responds, and the trainer delivers a consequence. Consequences include:

  • *Positive reinforcement.* Providing a desired consequence, such as food, hugs, tickles, verbal praise, or access to a desired object or activity.

  • *Negative reinforcement.* Removing an undesirable consequence. For example, removing a wet, uncomfortable diaper might be used as a negative reinforcement in a toilet-training program. Negative reinforcement still functions as reinforcement. The word *negative* refers only to something being taken away.

  • *Punishments (aversive stimuli, aversives).* Therapists punish to decrease the likelihood that a behavior will recur. Punishments used to include hitting (in 1981, Lovaas wrote, "Practice on your friends to see how hard you hit"), but are now limited to verbal reprimands, removal of desired objects, and overcorrection. For example, if a child throws his or her cup to the floor during a tantrum, the child might be required not just to wipe up what was spilled but to mop the entire floor. Punishments work in the short term, but they don't accomplish as much as rewards, since they teach the child only what *not* to do, without providing a positive alternative.

  • *Ignoring and time out.* Ignoring includes putting the child's refusals on extinction. As many times as the child turns away from a spoonful of nonpreferred food, the adult just keeps presenting the food. Ignoring also includes tuning out the child's verbal demands. Time out typically involves having the child go to his or her room or sit in a boring spot for a brief period of time. However, time out generally works only if the child is interested in adult attention in the first place. The behavior of a child with severe ASD, who often starts from a position of indifference to adults, may not be readily influenced by time out.

All of this sounds a bit abstract, but in operation it's much simpler. Let's look at a few examples of ways in which behaviorism is used to help children with ASD.

Gerald: Self-Injurious Behavior

Gerald is a four-year-old boy with autism plus self-biting—a behavior we'd obviously like to eliminate. The behavior analyst conducts a series of observations (in behaviorist terms, a *functional behavioral analysis*), recording one hundred episodes of self-biting over a one-week period. What the behavior analyst discovers is that eighty-five episodes of self-biting were immediately preceded by a request from an adult to perform a task; this is the most common antecedent. In the majority of episodes, the adult's response (the consequence) was to terminate the task and offer Gerald a toy in an attempt to calm him down. From these data, the behavior analyst draws two conclusions: (1) the primary function of Gerald's self-biting is escape from a task, and (2) the adults in Gerald's environment are unintentionally reinforcing the self-injurious behavior (SIB). Gerald's SIB is being reinforced two ways: by removal of the task and by provision of a toy. Provision of the toy is easy to understand, and goes by the term *positive reinforcement*, that is, the introduction of a pleasurable experience. Removal of the task is also reinforcing, since Gerald gets out of something he didn't want to do. This is termed *negative reinforcement*, since it involves the *removal* of an unpleasant stimulus. Having analyzed the ABC's, the therapist sets about devising a plan to extinguish Gerald's self-biting. There's not much we can do about the antecedent condition; Gerald needs to learn, and that can occur only if the adults continue to place demands on him. The big opportunity to extinguish Gerald's SIB is to alter the consequences by removing the positive and negative reinforcement he is currently receiving. This means marching Gerald through the task no matter what, while physically blocking his SIB, but with a minimal amount of attention and no rewards such as a toy or other distraction, until after he has completed the task (with hand-over-hand guidance from the therapist if necessary). The therapist explains the new rules to the adults in Gerald's environment and monitors the results. In the first few days Gerald's attempts at self-biting skyrocket. This temporary spike in the unwanted behavior is known as the *extinction burst*. It's almost as if Gerald is saying, "I always got out of the task this way before! Maybe I need to try harder and SIB will work again!" After the extinction burst has peaked, Gerald's SIB suddenly and dramatically declines; the wind has gone out of his sails. He still engages in occasional self-biting, sometimes out of boredom or when he becomes overstimulated. But it's now much easier to engage Gerald in learning tasks.

NEGATIVE REINFORCEMENT: NOT WHAT YOU THINK!

Most people erroneously think that negative reinforcement means punishment. In fact, negative reinforcement and punishment are opposites. Negative reinforcement is the removal of an unpleasant stimulus. All that's negative is that something is being removed; negative reinforcement is still a reinforcer. Punishment, on the other hand, is the application of an unpleasant stimulus—a deterrent to recurrence of the target behavior. Negative reinforcement can be just as powerful as positive reinforcement in sustaining unwanted behavior, but it can be harder to spot and eliminate. Terminating an unpleasant task if the child becomes disruptive is a classic example of negative reinforcement. Another good example takes place at the dinner table: If Johnny has food selectivity, the parents may remove the nonpreferred food from Johnny's plate and provide him with his preferred food instead. Can you figure out which of these is the negative reinforcer? Right. Removing the nonpreferred food. Providing him with his preferred food is a positive reinforcer. It would be better to use "first A, then B" with Johnny: First he has to take one bite of the nonpreferred food; then he can have one bite of his preferred food.

Pablo: Toilet Training

There are many ways to go about toilet training. Here we'll talk about a method first popularized by Nathan Azrin and Richard Foxx, a method that involves manipulating both the antecedent conditions and the consequences in order to achieve urinary continence. (Typically, potty training focuses on either urination or defecation. With luck, once one excretory function has been trained, the other comes along without much fuss.)

Remember Skinner's pigeons? By introducing a food pellet each time a bird randomly raised its head, Skinner soon had them keeping their heads up continuously. Skinner had a big advantage: Head raising is a frequent, naturally occurring pigeon behavior, giving Skinner multiple opportunities over a very short period of time to apply positive reinforcement. If pigeons raised their heads naturally only once or twice a day, it would have taken Skinner years (if ever) to shape the birds' behavior. In other words, *the more frequently the behavior we wish to modify occurs, the more opportunities we have to shape that behavior in the direction we want it to go.* For this reason, it's often easier to work on potty training for urine rather than bowel movements, since children urinate more often than they pass stool. Furthermore, Azrin and Foxx realized they could stack the deck in their favor by providing the child with salty foods and lots of fluid to drink. In this way, the child would need to urinate even more often—thus creating additional opportunities to shape the child's behavior. As with Kevin, who was physically guided to the chair each time Jane or Sue uttered the command "Sit!," Pablo can be physically guided to the potty each time he begins to urinate (training is often done in the bathroom with the child's pants off, so the therapist can spot the moment the child starts to urinate). After Pablo urinates in the potty, he receives verbal praise, tickles, access to a preferred toy, or some other activity that he finds rewarding. Make sure the reinforcers aren't available to the child at other times during the day, so that they remain attractive and effective for toilet training. There are lots of other details to the Azrin and Foxx method; for additional information, see the Resource List. For purposes of this discussion, the main point is that behaviorists can sometimes manipulate the antecedents, as well as the consequences, to speed up the conditioning process. A variation on the theme entails using a water bottle to deliberately soak the child's pants and training the child to pull down his or her pants when they are wet, through a combination of verbal and physical prompting and the provision of rewards. Here again, we see the therapist manipulating the antecedent (wet pants) as well as the consequence (rewards). Regardless of which method is used, the entire sequence can be broken down into individual steps (pants down, underpants off, urinate into potty, underpants on, pants up) and each piece of this sequence can be shaped separately. Then they can all be linked together. This is called *chaining*.

TOILET TRAINING: ANOTHER APPROACH

It's possible to address training for stool first, rather than training for urine. To do so, however, you've got to make one fundamental adjustment in your thinking: Your goal is to train your child to *sit* on the potty at regular intervals, rather than to *have a bowel movement* into the toilet. Your child is ready to be trained for bowel movements when he or she is no longer having BMs in his or her diaper during sleep (pooping while awake in bed is okay). Observe your child over several days to see when he or she usually has a BM so that you can set up a "sitting schedule" to match your child's natural bodily schedule. For example, if your child typically has a BM thirty minutes after eating, then you might set up a schedule whereby your child is required to sit on the potty for five minutes out of every fifteen for the first hour after every meal. Don't pressure your child to "make." Don't even bring it up. Your goal is just to get your child used to sitting on the potty at scheduled times. Provide your child with rewards for sitting—little toys that are available only in the bathroom, for example. Eventually, by luck, your child will poop into the potty, at which point you can provide an additional tangible reward, plus lots of cheering! Slowly but surely, the frequency of pooping on the potty will go up. See the Resource List for additional information.

Sarah: Self-Dressing

Sarah is ten; she has moderate ASD and mild mental retardation. She should be able to dress herself. Yet every morning it's a battle royal.

Sarah eats breakfast in her pajamas. She dawdles at the breakfast table or wanders into the living room to watch cartoons. After much yelling, Sarah's mom eventually gives in and dresses her, otherwise she'll be late for school and Mom will be late for work. What can the behaviorist offer?

Self-dressing is a multistep process. One of the precepts of behaviorism is to make each step so small that success is almost guaranteed. In Sarah's case, this means breaking down the task into the smallest possible units. Another technique is to start at the end and work backward toward the goal—an example of *reverse chaining*. In Sarah's case, this means asking Mom to dress Sarah entirely *except for one shoe*. Manipulating the antecedent conditions also includes having Sarah get dressed before breakfast, not afterward. Now Sarah cannot come downstairs for breakfast or cartoons until she puts on the last shoe (by the way, the program is instituted at the beginning of a ten-day school vacation). On day one of the training program, Sarah protests and attempts to come downstairs with one shoe on and one shoe off. Mom resolutely returns Sarah to her room numerous times, each time explaining, "First your shoe, then breakfast and cartoons," and walks away. Eventually Sarah reappears at the kitchen door, both shoes on. Next day it's the same process, except this time Mom dresses Sarah entirely except for both shoes. The third day it's socks and shoes. Each day Mom leaves a bit more of the task for Sarah. By the end of a week, Sarah is dressing herself entirely! (Be sure to use pullover garments if the child has problems with fasteners. Velcro is better than laces if the child has problems shoe-tying. We're looking for independence here, not buttoning and shoe-tying skills.) Behavioral intervention succeeded through a combination of breaking down the task into manageable units, reverse chaining, and gaining control of the antecedent situation—in this case, heightening Sarah's motivation by placing the demand on her before she could gain access to breakfast and cartoons.

Applied behavior analysis—discrete trial training (ABA-DTT) is most commonly used in children just entering therapy and in older, more severely impacted children whose ability to attend to and imitate adults is limited. ABA-DTT is purely bottom-up: The process is totally con-

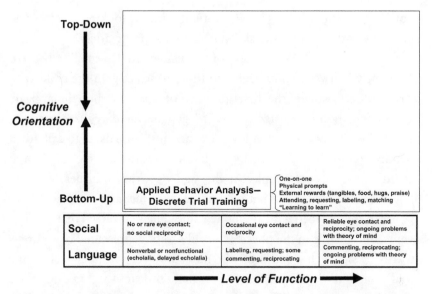

Figure 7.1 Applied Behavior Analysis—Discrete Trial Training *ABA-DTT is purely bottom-up. It is therapist-driven, with little or no expectation that the child will initiate any interactions. This is where we begin with a child who has no or only rare eye contact and social reciprocity.*

trolled by the therapist, and the child responds to physical and verbal inputs. No strategizing is required by the child, and conscious understanding is not the goal. We can now make the first entry on our graph (Figure 7.1).

(i) See the Resource List for additional information on ABA.

ABA: A Cure for ASD?

Behaviorists sometimes claim that ABA can cure ASD, but there are two flaws in their logic. First, behaviorists disregard development, instead attributing all progress to behavioral intervention. But we know that there is such a thing as development, and that development is happening right along with behavioral intervention. The second flaw is tied to behaviorists' disregard of private mental events such as understanding or insight. Brushing these concepts aside, behaviorists permit themselves to define "cure" narrowly, as placement in a normal classroom with normal results on IQ testing, without looking at messy issues such as theory of mind skills or language pragmatics.

We can accept ABA's disregard of "private mental events" only up to the point when your child begins to think abstractly. In the child with normal development, the first glimmer of abstract thought appears around ten months of age. By that age, the child realizes that the sounds "mommy" and "daddy" are not just signals that call forth friendly giants to do the child's bidding. Rather, "mommy" and "daddy" *mean* those people. At this age also, the child begins to respond selectively to his or her own name—not just as a conditioned response, but as a word with symbolic value. The realization that objects, events, and people in the physical world can be represented by symbols (words or signs) that stand for the named object is a huge step in the child's mental development. Other mental leaps are taking place around the same time: The twelve-month-old uses a spoon and crayon to eat and scribble (tools), the fourteen-month-old presses buttons to make things happen (cause and effect). And by eighteen months, a child can learn new behaviors through observation, *exactly what Thorndike's cats could not do.* By age two, children with normal development engage in imitative play, reenacting what they see in the world around them, and by age three, they engage in make-believe, creating fantasy worlds of their own. These skills are light-years beyond the capabilities of Thorndike's cats and Skinner's pigeons. They also lie beyond the realm of purely behaviorally based intervention.

Summing Up

ABA-DTT can be used effectively to extinguish maladaptive behaviors (self-injurious behavior, tantrums, etc.) and to elicit desirable behaviors (attending to an adult, copying, and various self-care skills such as self-dressing and toilet training). Through task analysis and chaining, ABA-DTT can be used to shape surprisingly complex behaviors. In one famous study by M. W. Gold, adults with severe mental retardation were taught to assemble a multipart bicycle brake by training them to respond to the simple verbal prompt "Try another way."

ABA is a crucial first step for many children with ASD, and I recommend it for most of my patients at the outset. The surface goals of ABA-DTT, such as matching geometric shapes or pointing to objects on command, serve a deeper objective: getting your child to reliably sit, attend, and reciprocate, when requested to do so by an adult. In that sense, ABA-DTT is all about learning to learn. Without these basic behaviors, no higher learning can take place. But as soon as a child begins to show a tendency to imitate his or her parents without being prompted to do so, or a tendency to initiate social interaction, it's time to expand the menu of therapies to include something a little more top-down in orientation.

Chapter 8

Next Steps: Playful Sabotage, Watchful Waiting

Natural Environment Training (NET)

Pivotal Response Treatment (PRT)

Developmental–Individual-Differences–Relationship Model (DIR; "Floor Time")

Relationship Development Intervention (RDI)

A Therapy Session

Remember Darryl? When I first met Darryl, at age twenty months, he was nonverbal. He was just beginning to respond to one-step commands, although he was equally likely to disregard adults. He wasn't pointing as a way of indicating his wishes. He was fascinated with exit signs and with opening and closing doors. Let's peek in on Darryl's therapy.

Unlike Kevin, who was in a small, bare room with a table, two chairs, and two therapists, Darryl is in a large playroom with lots of toys scattered about, with one therapist—we'll call him Steve—seated on the floor across from him. At the moment Darryl is playing with a shape sorter, inserting the different shapes through their respective holes. (This is a strong interest for Darryl, who can already name complex shapes, including *hexagon, octagon, trapezoid,* and *ellipse.*) Steve lets Darryl play for a minute or so, then he does an odd thing: Just as Darryl is about to insert a shape into its proper hole, Steve covers the hole with his own hand! Darryl pulls at Steve's fingers, trying to remove the offending hand. Darryl is reacting to Steve's hand as if it were a disembodied object—like a tree branch in the road—but not to Steve himself. "Hand off," Steve says. Darryl pays no attention to Steve and continues to pull at Steve's fingers with mounting frustration. "Hand off," Steve repeats. This time Darryl glances up at Steve, as if to say, *Why are you getting in my way?* The instant Darryl gives eye contact, Steve excitedly declares, "Hand off!," smiles broadly, and removes his hand. Darryl's gaze lingers on Steve's face for a second or two, then he dives back into working the shape sorter. A few minutes later, after Darryl has gotten all of the shapes into the box, he attempts to open the lid to get the pieces out—but Steve has placed his hand over the lid, preventing Darryl from opening the box. "Open box," Steve says in a clear voice. Darryl fusses and pulls at Steve's hand. Steve continues to block Darryl's attempt, each time stating, "Open box." Eventually Darryl looks up at Steve. As before, Steve now declares, "Open box!," smiles, and removes his hand. Over the course of the next several sessions, the amount of time Darryl spends fruitlessly tugging at the offending hand decreases; simultaneously, his eye contact with Steve increases. Slowly but surely, Darryl seems to be getting the idea that in order to get what he wants, he needs to interact not just with Steve's hand as if it were an inert object but with Steve himself. Steve, after all, is the key to Darryl's ability to access his preferred playthings.

Steve's next therapy goal is to elicit not just eye contact from Darryl but speech. On this day Steve has placed all of Darryl's train cars on a high shelf, where Darryl can see them but not reach them. Darryl looks eagerly at the trains. "Want Thomas," Steve says, and then waits until Darryl repeats, "Want Thomas." Only then does Steve reach up and bring down Thomas—but none of the others! Darryl will need to ask, engine by engine: *Want Percy, Want Gordon,* and so on. In this way Steve has productively dragged out the interaction, maximizing adult-child interaction. If Darryl wants to go into another room, Steve might block the door with his body while stating, "Door open," then waiting until Darryl looks up and says, "Door open." Or let's say Darryl is reaching for a glass of juice, Steve might hold Darryl's hands and ask, "What do you want?" This is a more challenging task than repeating a word already modeled by the therapist, and might come after a training session in which Steve has trained Darryl to imitate the word *drink*. Now, to solidify the gain, Darryl needs to produce the word himself, in response to the therapist's question "What do you want?" As soon as Darryl says "drink" or something close to that, Steve hands over the juice.

What we're watching is a lot different from applied behavioral analysis—discrete trial training. In ABA-DTT the therapist dictated the task and doled out a reward (a tickle, a bit of food) after the child completed the task either on his own or after verbal or physical prompting. Here the child is in the lead, choosing an activity of interest to him or her. The adult's job is to figure out what the child finds appealing and how to engineer the environment in a way that will require the child to seek input from the adult as many times as possible in order to gain access to the preferred activity. The direct connection between the child's behavior or speech and the consequence is the natural way that children with typical development learn. There's no need for external rewards such as hugs, tickles, or edibles, because renewed access to the preferred activity constitutes its own reward. With a bit of forethought, the therapist (or parent) can set up the child's environment in such a way as to require the child to continually address the therapist not just in isolated treatment sessions but throughout the day.

The kind of therapy I've just described is available under at least three different names: natural environment training (NET), pivotal response treatment (PRT), and developmental–individual-differences–relationship model (DIR; better known as "floor time"). NET and PRT are direct offshoots of ABA. DIR is the creation of a child psychiatrist, Stanley Greenspan. The biggest differences between NET, PRT, and

DIR are the vocabularies used by the different professionals involved. Behaviorists (NET, PRT) refer to discovering what the child finds rewarding as "establishing operations"; working back-and-forth with the child is called "shared control." Greenspan describes the same activities as "wooing the child," "emotional co-regulation," and "opening and closing circles of communication." This is one place where you could really use a behaviorist-to-psychiatrist bilingual dictionary. But from the child's perspective, all of these programs look remarkably similar—regardless of the differing professional jargon.

Behaviorism in a Natural Setting (NET and PRT)

Board-certified behavior analysts (BCBAs) can administer both ABA-DTT and NET. There is no special training pathway for NET. If you look on the Internet, you will not find a site just for NET or a book about it. Rather, NET is simply one method among many that any properly trained behavior analyst has at his or her disposal. Pivotal response treatment (PRT), on the other hand, is a specific form of behaviorally based therapy that has been developed by Robert and Lynn Koegel and Laura Schreibman at the University of California, Santa Barbara. Pivotal response treatment offers its own training pathway for graduate students. (If you live in Southern California, PRT is probably more readily available than in other parts of the country.)

The Koegels define *pivotal responses* as "behaviors that seem to be central to wide areas of functioning. Positive changes in pivotal behaviors...have wide-spread positive effects on many other behaviors and therefore constitute an efficient way to produce generalized improvements in the behavior of children with autism" (see the Resource List). According to the Koegels, pivotal behaviors include:

- Motivation to engage in social-communicative interaction
- Social initiation, especially shared enjoyment and joint attention
- Self-regulation of behavior

One way in which PRT distinguishes itself from NET is the active role played by parents (and other key individuals in the child's life).

Rather than taking the child for isolated therapy sessions, the Koegels envision PRT as a continuous process, delivered by the child's primary caregivers: "Because PRTs (pivotal response treatments) are highly efficient by nature, and integrated into family routines, they can be implemented with considerable ease, and negligible disruption to everyday life. In fact, when implemented properly, they should considerably improve the quality of life for all family members."

The Koegels provide detailed instructions on ways to set up little scenarios to elicit a pivotal response from a child in a host of ordinary, day-to-day encounters. Using PRT methods is often quite effective at reducing frustration for everyone. In this sense, PRT is truly win-win: The child makes progress, and the parents gain a sense of confidence in their ability to positively impact their child's behavior, often for the first time.

Developmental–Individual-Differences–Relationship Model (DIR; "Floor Time")

DIR (commonly referred to as "floor time," because much of the intervention takes place in play on the floor) is the creation of Stanley Greenspan, MD, a child psychiatrist. As we have seen, behavioral psychologists such as Thorndike, Watson, Skinner, and Lovaas focus on externally visible behaviors while disregarding or denying the existence of the child's inner mental and emotional life. In contrast, Greenspan builds his approach around the belief that *emotions enable all learning* and that the engine of progress lies *within the child* rather than depending on externally applied consequences:

> In working with children's individual differences and developmental levels, we have observed that a critical component of their progress resides in our ability to help them use their own emotions, desires, or intentions to guide first their behavior, and later their thoughts.... Feelings underlie cognitive learning.... Emotion has made storing, organizing, and retrieving...experiences possible.

AFFECT

Affect (pronounced "A-fect," with the accent on the first syllable and the *a* pronounced like in *hat*) is a noun that refers to a person's emotional state—joy, sadness, depression, and so on. Someone who is depressed and speaks in a monotone is described by physicians as having a "flat affect." Don't confuse it with the verb *affect* (accent on the second syllable, "a-FECT," with the *a* pronounced "uh"), as in "Too much coffee can *affect* your ability to sleep." You may have an easier time keeping things straight if you remember that *affect* as a noun is related to the words *affection,* and *affectionate,* which also refer to emotions.

Greenspan believes that the core deficit in ASD is a failure of the affective system to link up with the motor-planning system, leading to verbal and motor stereotypies that lack social meaning. Greenspan argues for engaging a child at the emotional level and then harnessing the child's emotional energy to the child's "sense of purpose and self (i.e. his *self-affect*)." Greenspan's emphasis on internal factors is a complete reversal of Watson's assertion that there is "nothing within to develop."

Like NET and PRT, the goal of DIR is to follow "the child's natural interests and lead in order to mobilize attention, engagement, interaction, communication, and thinking." DIR may begin with the therapist imitating the child's behaviors, including stereotypies, to "turn a self-stimulatory activity into a dance." If the child is flapping his or her arms, the therapist may do likewise. The therapist then "creates... learning challenges for the child to master"—in other words, the therapist playfully sabotages the child's activity in order to provoke a reaction. If the child is hand flapping, the therapist may deliberately get his or her own arm entangled with the child's arm. Now the child is stuck. Until the child acknowledges the therapist, the child cannot continue stimming. From such humble beginnings, DIR works its way up to the kinds of scenarios outlined at the beginning of the chapter.

Greenspan recommends "eight or more 20+-minute floor-time sessions per day," and that "at least a third to half of the child's available time at home should be spent in spontaneous interactions," following the child's lead. But DIR is more than just a set of therapy practices. To Greenspan, it's a philosophy:

> As you work with your child daily, as you engage in millions of little interactions, you strengthen his ability to think logically, creatively, and spontaneously. Each time you hand socks back and forth while dressing, each time you negotiate with gestures about turning on the TV, another little piece is added to his sense of purpose, his sense of who he is, and his ability to be part of true, two-way communication. Through these daily interactions, you help him build the social, emotional, motor and cognitive skills that add up to intelligence, as well as develop his sense of self.

In this statement of principle, we hear echoes of Koegel and Koegel's PRT approach, couched in psychiatric rather than behaviorist terms.

Greenspan postulates six developmental skills that normally developing children use "to carry out emotionally meaningful goals," but that are deficient in children with ASD:

1. *Self-regulation and interest in the world (by three months).* The ability to calm oneself down, and—after calming oneself—the ability to take interest in the sights, sounds, and sensations of the world.
2. *Engagement (by five months).* The ability to engage in two-way relationships with other people. According to Greenspan, "Mastery of this milestone…cements motor, cognitive, and language skills."
3. *Intentional two-way communication (by nine months).* In Greenspan's terminology, "opening and closing circles of communication." "For the first time, the baby becomes a person of volition, someone who can actively choose to do things, knowing that his actions will cause a result."
4. *Complex problem-solving, gestures, preverbal sense of self (by eighteen months).* Greenspan believes that the ability to understand a pattern of behaviors, such as a complex series of gestures

or actions strung together into a deliberate problem-solving sequence, is a prerequisite for speech. For example, looking at a bottle, then looking up at Mommy, then reaching for the bottle while still looking imploringly at Mommy precedes the use of single words to request desired objects.

5. *Emotional ideas—representational capacity and elaboration (by thirty months)*. Greenspan emphasizes the importance of play: "The child's ability to form ideas develops first in play. . . . Later, with help from his parents, he puts names to his range of intentions, wishes and feelings." In play, the child first labels the important elements of his or her world, such as his or her own feelings and the feelings of others: "I feel happy," or "Are you sad, Mommy?"

6. *Emotional thinking—building bridges between ideas (by forty-two to forty-eight months)*. For example, a younger child will have mastered concepts such as anger and sadness as isolated emotional conditions. In stage 6, the child is able to link the two together—for example, "I feel sad when you are angry at me."

Here again, Greenspan's *self-regulation, engagement,* and *intentional two-way communication* are virtually identical to the Koegels' "pivotal responses"—*self-regulation of behavior, motivation to engage in social-communicative interaction,* and *shared enjoyment and joint attention.* Thus, despite the fact that behaviorists and child psychiatrists seem to be worlds apart, they actually focus on the same goals, using—in this case—some of the same terms. The difference, of course, is that psychiatrists focus on the child's internal mental and emotional state, while the behaviorists focus on externally visible behaviors, antecedent conditions, and consequences.

ⓘ See the Resource List for additional information on natural environment training, pivotal response treatment, and DIR.

I use NET/PRT/DIR techniques in the office all the time—not for therapeutic purposes but as part of the evaluation process. For example, if I am testing a child with ASD who is inserting pegs into a pegboard, I deliberately cover the last hole with my fingertip. The child wants to finish the task but can't do so until the obstacle has been dealt with. The child may try to pull my hand away without looking up, as if my hand were just an isolated weight. I persist in holding my finger over the hole until the child gives me eye contact. As soon as the child acknowledges me, I smile and remove my finger. Some children, however, are so impacted by their ASD that they don't look up, no matter how long I obstruct them. If this is the case, or if the child starts to become agitated, I will also remove my hand. In this case, sabotaging their play may have failed to elicit eye contact, but it has yielded important diagnostic information about the severity of the child's ASD.

NET, PRT, and DIR go beyond ABA-DTT by incorporating socially relevant reinforcers in a naturalistic setting. The training experience is still "engineered" by the adult, who stages little scenarios in order to take advantage of the child's interests. The basic goals of NET, PRT, and DIR are to make the child less dependent on prompting, to encourage initiation on the child's part, and finally, to replace therapist-selected rewards (hugs, tickles, edibles, or verbal praise) with natural consequences (access to the child's preferred objects or activities). NET, PRT, and DIR become possible only when the child has reached the stage of acknowledging the presence of others. It would have been premature to use these methods at the outset with Kevin, who was totally self-absorbed. Darryl, on the other hand, made a great candidate: We could capitalize on his newly emerging recognition of the outside world by placing small obstacles in his path—obstacles he could overcome only with the help of the adult. NET, PRT, and DIR are a step higher on the ladder than DTT, moving up from bottom-up to more top-down approaches. Now we can put a second entry on our graph of behavioral therapies (Figure 8.1).

Relationship Development Intervention (RDI)

We are in a living room. Dad is seated cross-legged on the floor. His three-year-old son is darting around the room, flapping his hands and walking on his toes. Dad has a four-piece jigsaw puzzle laid out on the floor. With exaggerated movements he picks up the first piece and ever

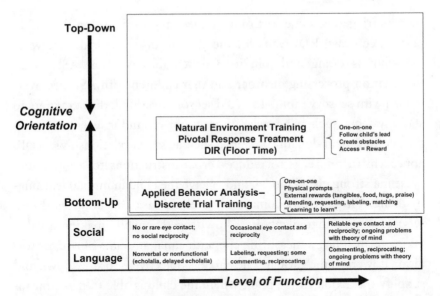

Figure 8.1 NET, PRT, and DIR *These three techniques rely on following the child's lead, then gently sabotaging the child's activity in order to elicit a response. The transition from a purely bottom-up ABA-DTT format to a NET/PRT/DIR format does not happen all at once. Many children start out in a pure ABA-DTT setting and then move into a program that includes DTT for part of the day and a more relaxed, child-centered program the balance of the day. Some children with less severe ASD may never need DTT but may start with NET/PRT/DIR at the outset.*

so slowly moves his arm in a large arc toward the empty frame of the puzzle. He pauses, his hand hovering over the appropriate spot. His son continues to stim, apparently oblivious. Dad makes a soft clucking sound to get his son's attention. Eventually the boy notices his dad's hand suspended in midair. He reaches out and gently pushes his dad's hand downward. Together the two of them insert the puzzle piece. In this fashion, over the course of thirty minutes of patient waiting and subtle nonverbal prompting, Dad has created the opportunity for a socially meaningful interaction between his son and himself.

This is relationship development intervention, or RDI. RDI is the brainchild of Steven Gutstein, PhD, a child psychologist.

RDI is the least intrusive (most "top-down") of all the behavioral interventions. ABA-DTT is wholly therapist-driven. NET, PRT, and DIR follow along with the child, then gently sabotage the child's activities, thereby triggering some sort of awareness and response on the child's part. In contrast, RDI waits for the child to discover or deduce what the adult is doing and join in. Gutstein believes that ASD is an information-processing disorder and that children with ASD are overloaded with sensory input. To avoid sensory overload, they gravitate to static systems, such as perseveration on objects and insistence on routines, rather than dynamic systems, such as social relationships. RDI's approach, therefore, is to reduce verbal instructions to a minimum, present a strong visual model, and engage the child in mutual learning-by-doing. Virtually any common household task can be pressed into service: stirring ingredients in a bowl together while making a cake, taking turns filling a measuring cup with equal amounts of rice, or watering flowers in the garden. The parent's objective is to slow down and simplify the action to the point where the child is able to make meaning out of what the adult is doing. By presenting a calm demeanor, the parent is also affording the chance to develop emotional self-regulation skills. The parent's job, in other words, is to create the physical and emotional conditions that will enable the child to be on the same page as the parent.

One of the keys to RDI's popularity is the centrality of the parents, rather than a cadre of therapists. The parents are given a highly detailed set of goals and instructions, with frequent telephone, videoconference, and online follow-up by an RDI consultant. "RDI parents" are also closely connected to one another. Thus, RDI not only is a therapy approach directed at the child but also serves as a support network for parents.

Like Greenspan, Gutstein has created his own unique set of terms and his own six developmental stages. And despite his disdain for behavioral methods (which he refers to as "scripts" and "faking"), Gutstein acknowledges that children who are "oblivious" to adults will need some "initial behavior modification" to learn "instrumental social skills" such as eye contact and turn taking. This is why the adult must be "firmly in charge of all activities" in Stage 1 of his system. From that point on, Gutstein believes, "curiosity and a desire to share enjoyment will hopefully replace prompting and external reinforcement as the major reason why the child pays attention to you." Stage 2 includes both rule-based play and adult-introduced rule changes (all of a sudden, letting red mean "go" and green mean "stop," for example) to help build cognitive flexibility—highly reminiscent of the playful sabotage of DIR. Stage 3 introduces *metacognitive thinking* (thinking about thinking) by introducing "emotion cards," which enable the child to begin thinking about and describing his or her emotional state (we'll see this method again in the chapter on social skills). Stages 4, 5, and 6 encompass progressively more challenging tasks, such as learning how to lose, making mistakes, evaluating contradictory information, anticipating problems, handling misunderstandings, and describing one's own personality—skills we'd like all our children to acquire.

Now we can make the third entry on our graph (Figure 8.2).

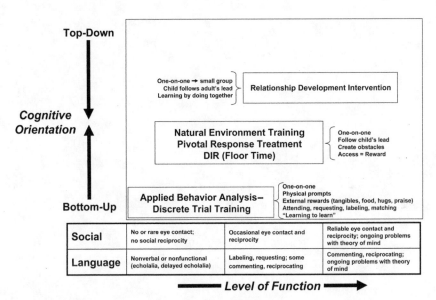

Figure 8.2 RDI *RDI relies on the child's ability to notice the adult and initiate social and verbal interaction.*

(i) See the Resource List for additional information on RDI.

Summing Up

By this point you should be starting to get the idea that there's no one "best" therapy for ASD. Rather, it's a matter of fitting the therapy to your child, based on his or her present level of abilities. Set aside the breathless claims of superiority of one therapy over another (or the dire predictions of disaster if you make the wrong choice). Remember: Your job is to go beyond the confines of any one discipline and see your child's needs in a broader context. It's unfortunate that, along with dealing with your child's ASD, you also have to deal with turf battles. But the sooner you learn to distinguish what's important for your child from such turf issues, the better off you'll be.

Chapter 9

Language Therapies:
Communication First, Speech Second

Does he know that we love him?
—Mother of a nonverbal child with autism

Picture Exchange

Verbal Behavior (VB)

Sign

Pragmatics—Language in a Social Context

Speech/Language Therapy

We use language as a way of bidding for attention ("Hey! Look at me!") and as a way of getting our needs met (whether it's "Cookie!," "Where's the remote?," or "Boss, I think I deserve a raise"). However, communication is not only a means to an end; often it's an end unto itself. That is, for individuals with typical development, the act of communicating is a rewarding behavior in and of itself—think of the teenager who talks on the phone for hours. Children with delayed speech for reasons other than ASD (hearing loss, mental retardation, etc.) likewise retain the *desire* to communicate. This is often not the case for children with ASD. Even after the child with ASD has mastered the ability to use language to secure his or her immediate needs, social language (either small talk or a deep and meaningful conversation) remains challenging.

As we discussed in Chapter 1, some children with ASD are nonverbal, while others actually speak quite well but cannot use language in a functional way. "Our child talks, but he doesn't communicate," one mom told me. Her three-year-old was nonverbal except for the fact that he memorized the Weather Channel's broadcast each morning and went around the house chanting the weather report for the day. Children with ASD who are nonverbal sometimes need help mastering the mechanics of speech production. However, therapy also needs to be directed at helping the child to understand the *purpose* of language. The deeper issue—for verbal as well as nonverbal children with ASD—stems from the child's difficulty with theory of mind. The child with ASD does not understand that other people are "out there," eagerly waiting for him to say something. "If I talk, I'm pretty sure you will listen, and most likely you'll give me what I ask for" is not a lesson we need to teach to a typically developing toddler. But the child with ASD doesn't get it. Furthermore, the child with ASD may not find communication to be an intrinsically enjoyable activity. Therefore, to elicit language from the child with ASD, we need to tie it to tangible reinforcers, at least at the beginning.

A Therapy Session: Picture Exchange

In Chapter 6, we observed Kevin in an ABA-DTT session. The focus of the session was on Kevin's listening behavior: In response to the command "sit," Kevin was physically guided to sit in a chair and then rewarded. Over the course of numerous trials, the physical guidance (prompt) could be faded. ABA-DTT includes a lot of work on tasks of this sort. Today, however, the goal is to enable Kevin to express himself, rather than follow the therapist's commands. This is a challenge, since Kevin is nonverbal and gives no eye contact. What's more, Kevin requires a physical prompt at the beginning of learning any new behavior, and there is no easy way to physically prompt a child to speak.

Peeking through the two-way mirror, we see Kevin seated at a low table. Sue sits across from Kevin, while Jane sits next to Kevin on his side of the table. On the table in front of Kevin is a flash card with a picture of a potato chip. Sue reaches into an unmarked paper bag and produces a chip, which she holds up with one hand to show Kevin while extending her other hand in Kevin's direction, palm up. Kevin starts to reach for the chip, but Jane immediately intervenes, guiding Kevin hand-over-hand to pick up the flash card and place it directly into Sue's open hand. Sue immediately gives Kevin the chip while declaring, "Great job!" Kevin eagerly wolfs down the chip. After pausing for a few seconds, Sue produces another chip, and the cycle repeats. As before, Jane immediately guides Kevin's hand to pick up the flash card, then moves Kevin's arm in the direction of Sue's open hand. Here she pauses and lets go of Kevin's arm an inch short of Sue's hand. Kevin releases the card into Sue's palm on his own. "Great job!" Sue declares, giving him the chip. By the tenth trial, Jane can let go as soon as Kevin has picked up the card and begun to move his arm in Sue's direction. Jane has also been slowly moving her hand back from Kevin's hand, so she is now just guiding him by lightly grasping his elbow. By the twentieth time, she lets go as soon as Kevin's hand has contacted the card. From there, he picks it up and releases it into Sue's palm all by himself. And by the end of the session, Jane does not need to give him any prompting: As soon as Sue pulls out a chip, Kevin reaches for the card, picks it up, places it into Sue's palm, and then takes the chip from her other hand. Instead of just grabbing for the chip or tantruming when Sue does not immediately give it to him, Kevin is now initiating an interaction with an adult to get something. This is a tremendous breakthrough for him.

The next day, Sue and Jane pick up where they left off, but with a twist. After a few warm-up trials, repeating what Kevin mastered the day before, Sue pushes her chair back a few inches from the table.

Now, after picking up the card, Kevin needs to lean across the table in order to reach her. Over successive trials, Sue sits farther and farther back. Eventually, she is sitting across the room. Now, Kevin needs to stand up and walk across the room to bring her the card. (Eventually, Kevin will be trained to bring the card to a therapist in another room or to present a card to receive a reward that is out of sight, rather than visible right in front of him.)

After Kevin has been reliably trained to present the chip card, the setup is changed a bit. No longer is the card just sitting on the table. Now it is stuck to the front cover of a three-ring notebook with Velcro. Kevin needs to unstick the card and bring it to Sue (or Jane; they have been switching roles throughout these sessions to prevent Kevin from becoming dependent on one therapist in particular) in order to get the chip. The goal is to shape Kevin's behavior to exchange the picture card for the corresponding object—this gives the name to this form of therapy: *picture exchange*. The most popular picture exchange program is a proprietary therapy named Picture Exchange Communication System, or PECS. (*PECS* has become almost a generic term, like *Scotch tape* or *Kleenex*. But in fact all three are brand names, and there are competing products in all three categories.)

As time goes along, Kevin's picture exchange repertoire will be broadened to include cards representing many other foods, objects, or activities that he finds rewarding. Each new card will be added to his three-ring notebook. Now Kevin will need to retrieve the appropriate card from an ever-enlarging vocabulary. Also, the therapist will begin modeling the spoken word as he or she presents the item. If fortune smiles on Kevin, he may begin speaking the words for these items in addition to presenting the cards. (Picture exchange was designed as a way to foster communication, not speech. However, in a fair number of cases, once we have gotten the ball rolling with cards, speech follows. It's as if the child needs to grasp the idea of symbolic communication first, via the cards. After that, producing sounds that are the equivalent of what's on the card is relatively simple.)

Next, Kevin will be introduced to the card for the phrase *I want*. In order to get the chip, he will be trained to put together two cards: *I want* + *chip*. Eventually Kevin will be able to request hundreds of items. As Kevin's ability to obtain desired items increases, his tantrum behavior diminishes. Still later he will be introduced to the card *I see,* and will be taught to create sentences such as *I see + ball,* and so forth.

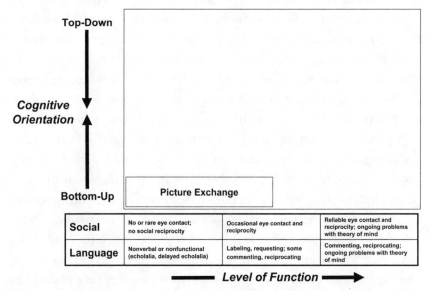

Figure 9.1 Picture Exchange *Picture exchange is the most bottom-up of the language therapies.*

ⓘ See the Resource List for additional information on picture exchange.

ALTERNATIVE COMMUNICATION SYSTEMS

A child who has achieved proficiency with a picture exchange system but has not developed useful speech after several years of intensive therapy may be considered for an alternative communication system. Alternative communication systems range from simple picture boards to laptop-computer-like devices that can speak aloud. A full discussion of alternative communication systems goes beyond the scope of this book. See the Resource List for additional information.

A Therapy Session: Verbal Behavior

Let's take a look at another child; we'll call him Joe. Like Kevin, Joe is thirty-three months old. However, Joe starts out with more skills than Kevin: He gives eye contact, and he looks up about 50 percent of the time when his name is called. He names a few objects, such as Thomas the train, as well as the letters of the alphabet and various geometric shapes (*circle, square, octagon*), although he uses his words mainly for self-talk, rather than to communicate with others. He likes to be bounced, swung, tickled, and chased. He also likes bubbles and chocolate chip cookies. His parents would like him to become more functional verbally.

Joe and his therapist, Mary, are sitting on the floor in a corner of Joe's living room. Mary produces a jar of soap bubbles from her bag. Joe stares eagerly at the jar. "Bubbles," Mary declares slowly and emphatically, pausing for a few seconds to see how Joe responds. Joe continues staring at the jar but does not acknowledge Mary in any way. "Bubbles," Mary declares again. Still no response from Joe. "Bubbles," Mary declares a third time. This time she also gently takes Joe's hands, moving first one of his index fingers and then the other up and down in a pointing-toward-the-ceiling fashion (the sign for *bubbles*). She releases his hands and blows a string of bubbles. Joe laughs happily and chases the bubbles, which rapidly disappear. Mary repeats the cycle, simultaneously saying "bubbles" three times while guiding Joe's hands to produce the sign, pausing a few seconds after each presentation. At first Joe resists a bit. Over successive trials, however, he offers less and less resistance to Mary's guidance. Eventually, in response to Mary's verbal prompt, "Bubbles," Joe begins waving his arms up and down, in a crude approximation of the sign. "Right! Bubbles!" Mary exclaims, blowing a string of bubbles. Joe laughs and produces the sign again, unprompted. Mary rewards him with another stream of bubbles.

After a short break, Mary resumes. This time, she produces a small piece of cookie. "Cookie!" she declares while guiding Joe through the manual sign (thumb and fingertips of the right hand make a twisting movement in the palm of the left hand, as if outlining the shape of a cookie in the left palm). This time Joe catches on fairly quickly. Within half a dozen trials, Joe is making a rough approximation of the sign for *cookie*.

Over the next several sessions, Mary alternates between bubbles and cookies. Slowly but surely Joe's signed responses become more rapid and reliable—and then he begins echoing Mary's verbal prompt! Mary says "bubbles," and Joe echoes "buh," while producing the manual sign. Eventually Joe will acquire the ability to request hundreds of items, initially via signing plus speech and then via speech alone. As with Kevin, Joe's use of sign and spoken words in a social context represents a huge breakthrough.

This form of therapy goes by the name *verbal behavior* (VB). Verbal behavior takes its name from a book of the same title written in 1957 by B. F. Skinner. As a behaviorist, Skinner took the position that speech, like all other human behavior, is *determined solely by prior rewards and punishments*. (Behaviorists reject the "linguistic model," which asserts that certain language skills are genetically programmed, and emerge from within.) Skinner divided verbal behavior into four categories: *manding, tacting, echoic,* and *intraverbals*. *Manding* is basically the same as requesting. (Think of the word *demanding*.) The chances of teaching a child to mand are enhanced by starting out with objects or activities that are highly motivating to the child. *Tacting* is Skinner's term for labeling; *echoic* refers to imitating what someone else has said, and *intraverbals* consist of an exchange of words between two individuals in which the exchanged words do not match (Skinner's definition of a "conversation"). Let's return to Joe and Mary to see how this plays out.

Once Joe is manding successfully, Mary moves on to shaping his behavior to label (tact) objects. Instead of using actual objects, Mary may use pictures of these items, to reduce the likelihood that Joe will get caught up in an interaction with the object itself. It will be easier to separate Joe from a picture of bubbles, than from an actual jar of bubbles, for example.

Mary: "What is this? Dog." [Initially Mary answers her own question, providing Joe with a full verbal prompt.]

Joe: "Dog." [A behaviorist would say that by eliciting imitation of the spoken word *dog* from Joe, Mary has gained control of the echoic function.]

Mary: "Great!...What is this?" [This time Mary asks a question instead of naming the object.]

Joe: "Dog." [The child labels the object without a verbal prompt—tacting.]

Mary: "Great!" [Mary may also provide an edible or tangible reward.]

If Joe does not name the object the second time it's presented, Mary may provide a partial prompt: "What is this? *D*..." fading this partial prompt as quickly as possible. Eventually, Joe will be able to name (tact) dozens or hundreds of pictures and items correctly.

Tacting is followed by intraverbals. This may start with fill-in-the-blank prompts, similar to the method that I've just described for tacting. This works best for material the child has already memorized from prior exposure, for example:

Mary: "Old McDonald had a...?"

Joe: "Farm."

Mary: "Great job! And on that farm, he had a...?"

As Joe's verbal behaviors expand, the program moves on to simple *Wh* questions (what, where, who). The key to this part of the program is the way in which Mary carefully rotates the form of the task.

Mary: "What is this? Bed."

Joe: "Bed."

Mary: "What is this?" [no prompt]

Joe: "Bed." [tact]

Mary: "We sleep in a bed. Where do we sleep? We sleep in a...?" [provides fill-in prompt]

Joe: "Bed." [intraverbal]

Mary: "Where do we sleep?" [no prompt]

Joe: "Bed." [intraverbal]

Mary: "Great job! We sleep in a bed!"

As with manding and tacting, Mary initially provides a full verbal prompt, which is systematically faded. In the example above, also notice that Mary starts with a tact (that is, getting Joe to label the object), then switches gears, to work on getting him to answer a question about the object (intraverbal). The correct response—"bed"—is the same in both cases, but the word is being used differently in each instance (first as a label, then as the answer to a question). The power of VB stems from its ability to analyze the function of words and teach words according to these functions.

THE ECHOIC FUNCTION VERSUS ECHOLALIA

The word *echoic* sounds a lot like *echolalia,* but they are quite different. Echolalia is not under stimulus control. That is, the adult is not able to regulate the child's echolalia by the application of different consequences. Immediate echolalia is reflexive; the child with ASD repeats words automatically as soon as he or she hears them. Delayed echolalia, or "scripting," is equally automatic; repeatedly uttering nonsense syllables or lines of movie dialogue is a form of self-stimulatory behavior. Thus, neither immediate nor delayed echolalia is contingent upon external factors. Skinner's *echoic,* in contrast, refers to the ability to get the child to selectively repeat a target word in response to externally delivered reinforcers. It is essential to gain control of the echoic function in order to shape any of the child's verbal behavior.

I like VB because of its eclectic, do-what-works approach, combining oral instruction and—when necessary—picture exchange or signing. Despite its name—*verbal* behavior—it's the underlying strategy, rather than the specific communication channel (pictures, signs, spoken words), that distinguishes VB from other forms of communication therapy. VB terminology (*mand, tact, intraverbal, echoic, prompting, fading, transfer trials*) takes a bit of getting used to, but once you begin to think about communication in VB terms, you'll see how powerful this method is. There is more to the story than what I've shown you here, but these few examples give you the flavor. For additional information, see the Resource List.

Verbal behavior and picture exchange share some common underlying features, based on a behavioral ABC model. In each case, a highly desired item is presented as the enticement (the antecedent). The child then responds (the behavior), sometimes spontaneously and sometimes with the benefit of prompting by an adult. Prompting can be physical guidance (as we saw with Kevin, where the second adult guided his hand to deliver the picture card, or with Joe, where the adult guided him to form the desired sign), a verbal prompt (again with Joe, where the therapist models the spoken word), or something as subtle as a gesture from the adult. Prompting is faded as quickly as possible over succeeding trials. If the child produces a behavior in the desired direction, the therapist delivers a reward (the consequence). The reward is always something known to be highly desired by the child. Usually the parent or therapist spends several days observing and recording the child's behavior to determine which foods, objects, or activities are most rewarding to a particular child. Items that work best at the beginning are often edibles that can be consumed quickly (individual M&Ms or pieces of cookie rather than a bag of M&Ms or an entire cookie). Soap bubbles are good because they have a short life span and can be delivered over and over without having to be taken away from the child in between times (unlike, say, a spinner toy—once you give it to the child as a reward, it may be hard to get it back without provoking a tantrum).

Another shared behaviorist feature is that of *deprivation* and *satiation*. Simply put, if you deprive the child of an item beforehand, the child's desire to obtain the item will increase. If you give the child unlimited access to the item, then eventually the child will have had his fill of that item, and his desire for more of it will decrease. So if you will be using M&Ms, bubbles, or potato chips as a reward during therapy sessions, your best bet is to restrict or eliminate access to these items at other times. From now on, your child can gain access to them only as a reward for demonstrating the desired behavior. This may seem a bit harsh, but remember that your child with ASD does not intuitively understand the relationship between his or her behavior and the reactions of others. You've got to teach this to your child using signals that he or she can detect. Now is not the time for subtlety! Doling out or withholding highly desired objects is the surest way to shape your child's behavior, at least at the beginning. Later, as your child becomes more interactive, social rewards such as praise will work. But for now, stick with things that your child has already shown are of high value to him or her.

Signing

Signs can be used as part of a VB program, or they can be taught on their own. Signing offers several advantages over speech. First, of course, it is visual, and children with ASD are highly attentive to visual stimuli. Not only are the signs themselves visual stimuli; signing builds eye contact! Second, signing can be taught by the hand-over-hand method. Every time your child with ASD leads you by the hand to a desired object, that's a message straight from your child's brain that hand-over-hand works for him or her as a communication method. Take

---

SIGN, SIGNING, AND AMERICAN SIGN LANGUAGE

Individual hand shapes with defined meanings are signs. Using these hand shapes to communicate is called signing. American Sign Language is a self-contained system of rules of syntax and grammar (word order, verb tense, etc.) that uses signs. ASL is quite different from English or any other spoken language in structure (for example, future tense is marked by producing a sign in front of the body; past tense is shown behind the body; *-ing* verbs are marked by producing the same sign over and over again). When we refer to using sign with a child with ASD, we are not teaching the child ASL. Rather, we are borrowing individual signs from ASL, and using them in English word order (usually, along with the spoken equivalent). As a proper language, ASL is capitalized (just as we capitalize English). Within the hearing-impaired community, *Sign* frequently is also capitalized, when used as a shorthand for ASL. Within this book, however, we are using *sign* with a lowercase s, referring to the individual signs, not ASL the language.

advantage of it. Although many children with ASD have problems with fine motor control, it's okay to accept rough approximations of the target sign; what you're looking for is your child's *intention to communicate,* rather than perfect execution of the hand shapes. Third, and most important of all, signing enhances the development of spoken language. Parents are often fearful that if their child learns to sign, the child will lose the incentive to learn to speak. I understand this concern, but I can assure you that this fear simply does not materialize in the real world. On the contrary, learning to sign is actually a good way to promote the emergence of speech.

One of the first questions you should ask any language therapist should be "Do you know how to sign, and do you ever use signs with your clients with ASD?" If the answers are no and no, then perhaps you should interview another therapist. I'm not saying that all children with ASD need to learn to sign. But I am suggesting that any language therapists who work with young children with ASD should be able to sign, so that they can make a recommendation based on the child's needs rather than on their own limitations. You and your spouse and other children will also need to learn, but it's easy and fun, and you need only stay one step ahead of your child. Your local community college, high school adult education program, or local chapter of the Association for the Hearing Impaired probably offers an introductory Sign Language course. There are also several very nice "Baby and me" learn-to-sign resources on the market.

The simplicity of a picture exchange system, the ability to use full physical prompts to shape the desired behavior, and lack of any requirement that the child imitate (signs or words) enables picture exchange to be used with almost any child. If your child gives little or no eye contact and rarely or never imitates you or initiates any interaction with you, then picture exchange may be the place to begin (along with an ABA-DTT program). Therefore, like ABA-DTT, we can place picture exchange at the base of our bottom-up to top-down graph.

In contrast with picture exchange, both signing and oral imitation via VB depend upon a child's ability to imitate a movement or gesture modeled by another individual. VB shares many commonalities with pivotal response treatment and floor time: VB looks more like play than drill work, and parents are encouraged to incorporate VB methods into their day-to-day communication with the child, so the child is essentially receiving VB instruction during all of his or her waking hours. At its upper levels, VB requires the child to strategize a bit, to come up with the right answers to questions. VB and signing are the place to start if your child has some ability to attend to you, and some ability to imitate you—even if it's only sporadically. VB and signing therefore occupy the next level on our bottom-up to top-down graph (Figure 9.2).

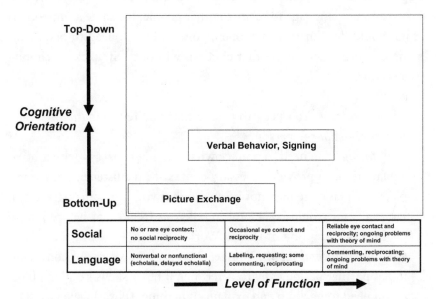

Figure 9.2 Verbal Behavior and Signing *Both VB and signing depend upon the child's ability to imitate behaviors modeled by the adult. This puts these two methods on the next step in the progression from bottom-up to top-down therapies.*

(i) See the Resource List for additional information on VB and signing.

Pragmatics: Language in a Social Context

Up to now we have been talking mainly about the mechanics of communication and the ways in which the child with ASD can use language as an instrument to get what he or she wants (thus the term *instrumen-*

tal language). Instrumental language skills can make a huge difference in quality of life for the child and his or her parents. They also open doors for the child in terms of social and educational options. But contrary to what Skinner would have you believe, language isn't just a tool for obtaining desired objects or the end result of prior conditioning. The long-term goal is for your child to move from requesting or labeling desired objects and providing fill-in-the-blank responses to true two-way communication. Conversation is a social act, just as much as hugging or holding hands. We want your child to ask questions, tell jokes, and use language to relate to other people, the same as any other child would do. For this to happen, your child will need to be taught some linguistic facts of life that children without ASD pick up simply by exposure:

- *Turn taking*. You need to ensure that you're talking *with* someone, not just *at* the person.
- *Framing*. You need to preface what you intend to say with a brief explanation, to provide necessary context to the listener. For example, your playmate may not be aware that you just came back from Florida, so it would be helpful to tell your friend that before jumping into a description of Disney World.
- *Conversational repair*. You need to check in with your conversational partner periodically to determine if he or she is keeping up or if you need to back up and explain something. (Phrases such as "Do you get it?" or "I don't follow you," for example, are ways that we maintain connection with our conversational partner.)
- *Social context matters*. What you say to your parents at home may not be appropriate in public. A bright six-year-old with PDD-NOS once asked me, "Why are you growing a beard in your nose?" His parents were mortified. I was too busy holding back my laughter to help them!
- *Tone of voice matters*. A host of meanings—sarcasm, disbelief, surprise, and so on—are conveyed through tone of voice rather than the words themselves. Children with ASD often can't hear these distinctions and need to learn alternative clues.
- *Words can have more than one meaning*. A greenhouse is not green, and you don't "fix" dinner because it is broken. (The words

I, me, and *you* are tricky, since their meaning varies depending on who is using them. This may explain why children with ASD have such a difficult time with pronouns, sometimes referring to themselves by name rather than *I*.)

Collectively, these aspects of language are grouped under the heading of *pragmatics*—the ability to use the nuances of language to facilitate social interaction. Some of these behaviors can be shaped in a mechanical way: *Stand one arm's length away from your conversational partner. After you have said three things, give the other person a turn,* and so forth. (I've encountered this in the office. A highly verbal child with Asperger syndrome was carrying on about his favorite topic when all of a sudden he stopped, his forehead furrowed in thought, then declared: "Now I've got to give *you* a turn." Clearly, he had absorbed one of his lessons from therapy, although it required a conscious act of recall to execute the lesson in an actual conversation.) Many aspects of pragmatic language are also theory of mind skills, interpreting social and linguistic cues that go beyond the literal meaning of the words (context, tone of voice, body language, etc.): Is the other person serious or joking? Is this person being truthful or trying to deceive me? How do I know if someone is being nice or not nice to me? This is the point at which interventions targeting language and interventions targeting social skills flow together—a topic we will cover at greater length in the next chapter.

Speech/Language Therapy

A speech/language pathologist (SLP) will work on social reciprocity and nonverbal and verbal communication (pointing, labeling, object and picture identification, and answering questions) in roughly the same order as a VB therapist. Initially some of this work will be conducted one-on-one at the table and some in a play setting. Many SLPs are comfortable using signing as an augmentative technique to stimulate speech production at the early stages. As the child's eye contact, joint attention, and imitative skills improve, the SLP will eventually pair the child with ASD with a peer (perhaps another child on the spectrum), and the role of the SLP will be to facilitate communication between them, with an emphasis on turn taking, perspective taking, topic maintenance, and other related pragmatic language skills.

Where do we locate "ordinary" speech/language therapy on our bottom-up to top-down graph? That's tough to say, because there is no one set program for ordinary speech therapy (as there is for picture exchange and VB). At the earliest stages speech/language therapy is never as intensely prompt-driven as picture exchange or VB, while at later stages speech/language therapy draws freely from theory of mind concepts that go beyond the scope of behaviorally based therapies. So we might think of ordinary speech/language therapy something like Figure 9.3.

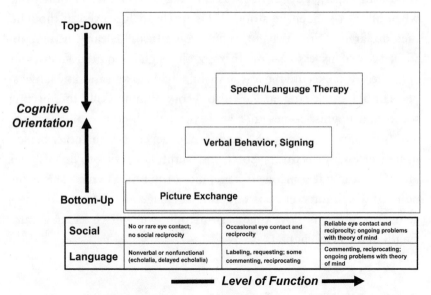

Figure 9.3 Speech/Language Therapy *Traditional speech/language therapy is seldom as prompt-driven as picture exchange or VB, and draws upon social concepts that go beyond these two techniques.*

(i) See the Resource List for additional information on speech/language therapy.

Summing Up

The first goal of language therapy is to get your child communicating as quickly as possible. At the outset, this may mean opting for picture exchange or signing. As disappointing as this may be for you, I assure you that these instructional methods will not harm your child's ability to speak, if speech is in the cards. On the contrary, getting your child to communicate, by whatever means, will actually promote the emergence of speech. As for the choice between traditional speech/language therapy and VB, no one knows which is better, since there have never been any head-to-head comparisons. At the earliest stages of development (acquisition of single words for the purpose of requesting or labeling objects), I would not be surprised to discover that VB holds the advantage, due to its emphasis on behavioral shaping. However, my guess is that the advantage starts to tip in the direction of traditional speech/language therapy as soon as the child reaches theory of mind–related tasks, for the simple reason that VB doesn't have any direct way to talk about the child's inner mental and emotional life. Indeed, VB (and all of behaviorism, for that matter) diligently avoids any mention of such private mental events. It's no surprise that many social skills groups are run by speech/language pathologists, since pragmatic language and social skills are so intertwined. This is where we will turn our attention next.

Chapter 10

Socially Based Therapies

Social Stories

Social Skills Groups

Socially based therapies emphasize social skills over behavioral attributes. The division is somewhat arbitrary, since therapies such as DIR and RDI clearly address social issues. Nonetheless, at a practical level its useful to consider Social Stories and social skills groups as sister therapies that respond to similar needs.

Social Stories

A Social Story is "a short story—defined by specific characteristics—that describes a situation, concept, or social skill using a format that is meaningful for people with ASD. The result is often renewed sensitivity of others to the experience of the person with ASD, and an improvement in the response of the person with ASD." Social Stories have grown in popularity since they were created by Carol Gray in 1991.

Social Stories present the facts, the perspectives of all parties, and a narrative of the child's behavior, written in the first person, all from the child's point of view. The "voice" of the story is what normally would be the child's inner monologue ("Hmmm...what's going on here, and what should I do now?"). Social Stories are written with the intention of becoming part of the child's repertoire through repetition and memorization, giving the child a tool for making sense of events, reminding the child what constitutes proper social behavior, and reassuring the child by helping him or her to remember what to do next. Part of the reason children with ASD insist upon strict routines is not just because the routines are intrinsically appealing but because without their routines, they don't know what to do next. Social Stories acknowledge this trait and turn it to good advantage.

HOW MUCH DO I WEIGH? (A SOCIAL STORY BEFORE GOING TO THE DOCTOR'S OFFICE)

Some things are heavy and some things are light. A big book is heavy. A feather is light. "How much something weighs" tells us how heavy or light it is. My doctor needs to know how much I weigh. This helps my doctor to take care of me. To find out how much I weigh, my doctor will ask me to stand on a scale. The scale is a black square on the floor. It jiggles when I stand on it. This is okay. I will not fall off. I will try to stand quietly on the scale while the doctor finds out how much I weigh. It will not take long. The doctor will be happy to know how much I weigh. This is how I can help my doctor to take good care of me.

Social Stories are fundamentally optimistic. The underlying assumption is that a child with ASD acts strangely because of a knowledge deficit; if we can fill in the missing information for the child, his or her behavior will come around as a result. Thus, the approach is not to fix problematic behaviors using reinforcers and consequences, but rather to give the child access to the big picture, on the assumption that with this greater understanding the child's behaviors will change of their own accord. In other words, rather than teaching a child *how* to act, Social Stories attempt to give the child insight into *why* to act—often based on how the child's behavior will alter the feelings of others, or based on rules of social behavior that usually go unspoken.

The writer of a Social Story must be able to take the perspective of the child. (As Gray perceptively points out, the act of writing a Social Story heightens the author's awareness of the worldview of the person with ASD for whom the story is being written.) The challenge is to figure out which facts to transmit through the story. It's a little like *Jeopardy*, where you know the answer and then have to figure out the question. The "answer" in this case is the child's maladaptive behavior. The "question" is: What social fact does the child not grasp that has led him or her to act this way? We can see the difficulties a child with ASD has, but we don't always know what knowledge gaps exist in the child's mind that lead to inappropriate behavior. The writer has to always ask what information or social convention was so basic that he or she mistakenly assumed the child must already know it. For example, if I'm testing a child with ASD and the child is not looking up at me between items, I have learned to ask the child, "Do you realize that if you look up at me after completing something, I know you're ready for another question?" Many of my patients—even the brightest ones—reply, "No, I didn't know that." If that's their response, I say, "I like it when you look up at me. That's one way I know you've finished, and that I can ask you another question. If it's hard for you to look at me, then say 'Okay,' and I'll know you're ready." I've been amazed at how diligently some of my patients make an effort to look up after that. I can see that their effort to look at me is self-conscious rather than automatic, but their eye contact improves 100 percent—all because I've asked them one simple question and given them one bit of socially relevant information.

Social Stories vary from a few sentences to a page or more, depending on the child's age and level of development. They cover such topics as:

- Why do people brush their teeth?
- Why do dogs bark?
- What is sharing?

Social Stories can also be used in other ways:

- *To memorialize something that the child has done well.* The child with ASD cannot always remember and then build on successes and accomplishments. This gets back to our discussion of central coherence in Chapter 1. Not only is it hard for the child to see the big picture in the external world; it's equally difficult for the child to organize the big picture of his or her own experiences. You can create a "social encyclopedia" for your child by collecting and saving these Social Stories in a binder, to help a child develop his or her "personal autobiographical memory." In fact, this may be the best way to introduce Social Stories to your child. Reading and rereading these stories together will bring pleasure to you and your child, and will get the child used to the idea of verbally replaying a complex social event—something that doesn't come easily to a child with ASD.

- *To prepare your child for something new.* Whether it's an upcoming vacation, a party, starting a new school, or a visit to the doctor, some preparation can ease the anxiety of a new situation or experience for your child. You can break the event down into its smallest component parts. This is a useful technique with normally developing children, not just children with ASD. If, for example, you're about to go on a trip, you can start by breaking it down into how you'll get there ("What does 'airport security' mean?"), where you'll be staying ("What is a hotel?"), whom you'll be seeing, and so on, but even these categories can be broken down: waiting at the gate, the sensations of the airplane, going to the bathroom on the plane, and so forth. Breaking events down into individual steps demystifies the event for a child. The challenge is to apply your intimate knowledge of your child to anticipate any component that may be confusing or upsetting. I wrote the Social Story earlier in this chapter as a way of preparing children for standing on the office scale. If you're going on vacation, the vacuum sound of an airplane toilet—very different from the flush of the toilet in your home— might merit a Social Story. By the way, don't worry about your skill as a writer. It takes a while for anyone to master the art of writing Social Stories, which depends at least as much as on familiarity with the internal mental processes of the child as on literary talent.

SOCIAL STORIES: SIMPLE AND STRAIGHTFORWARD

A good way to think about Social Stories is to think about what they are *not.* They are not allegorical. There are no implied meanings. Everything is spelled out in black and white, in a linear fashion. One of my favorite children's books is *Where the Wild Things Are* by Maurice Sendak. In this tale, a mischievous preschooler named Max is sent to bed without his supper. Max has a dream in which he continues to make mischief with a collection of fantastical creatures—the "wild things" of the title. But then, even in his sleep, Max smells good things to eat, so he "gives up being king of all wild things, to be where someone loves him best of all." He wakes up to find dinner waiting for him. With age-appropriate text and wonderful illustrations, the story speaks to the central challenge of preschool children: relinquishing the gleeful autonomy of toddlerhood to become a more civilized preschool child, ready to do what the grown-up asks. Sendak's story conveys its message through allegory, but children with ASD do not learn by allegory, and would not make the connection between Max's decision to give up being "king of all wild things" and the magical appearance of his supper. If the book had been written as a Social Story, it would contain sentences like, "Mommy is happy when I behave well. If Mommy is happy, she might cancel my punishment." I can't imagine most four-year-olds finding that interesting reading, but this is exactly the form in which the lesson must be presented to children with ASD.

The child with ASD usually needs explicit information about the perspectives of other people ("Mommy feels happy when I use the bathroom") or about social cues ("When Mommy wants me to use the bathroom, she lets me know by saying...."). The analysis needs to precede the writing of the story, so the story can incorporate all the facts, social cues, and perspectives of all the participants, as viewed through the child's eyes. This way, the story can be truly illuminating and open up a new level of understanding, rather than being just a set of step-by-step instructions for the child to memorize.

Even relatively straightforward facts can be confusing, especially for a child whose understanding of the world is literal and whose need for routines is strong. You can use words such as *sometimes* to alert the child to the variable nature of situations, and to clearly explain figures of speech. For example:

> Toilets are in special rooms. Sometimes these rooms are called "bathrooms." Sometimes they have a bathtub in them and sometimes they don't. We can go into a bathroom just to use the toilet, and not to take a bath. Sometimes these special rooms are called "restrooms." We don't use a restroom as a place to take a rest.

Social Stories follow a standard format, including:

- *Descriptive sentences.* The who, what, when, and where facts of a situation.
- *Perspective sentences.* The inner thoughts and emotions of the other people in the story ("Mommy feels happy when..." or "Daddy would like to..."). Usually the child with ASD has trouble understanding the intentions of others; Social Stories try to make these explicit and connect them logically to the child's actions within the framework of the story.
- *Directive sentences.* The desired behavior, or what we would like the child to do. The directive sentence is typically followed by one or more perspective sentences that describe how the child's behavior affects the feelings of others. "I will try to remember to..." is followed by "Mommy is pleased when I..."
- Other common sentence types include:
  - *Affirmative sentences.* These provide reassurance, or help the

child mark something as important: "It is okay if I..." or "It is important to..."

- *Cooperative sentences.* These describe ways in which other individuals in the situation may come to the child's assistance ("My teacher can help me with..."). Lacking theory of mind, the child with ASD may not intuitively understand that other people might recognize his or her plight or that most of the time adults are inclined to help children who are struggling.

Most of the topics addressed by Social Stories are universal, such as using the toilet or washing hands, but you may want to write some that are tailored to your child's unique environment. Perhaps your child with ASD needs one for those Wednesday afternoons when he or she has to go along with you and sit quietly during a sibling's dance class. You should introduce these stories to your child in advance of the situations they address, not during moments of stress. They are intended to be read aloud over and over again. A story about toilet use, for example, can be posted in the bathroom. If your child is going to the dentist, he or she can bring the story along and refer to it as a touchstone during the visit. The repetition, the predictable text, and even the familiarity of the piece of paper are in and of themselves sources of comfort to the child. The actual information and guidance in the story are added bonuses.

The first rung on the developmental and behavioral ladder is attending to others and imitating on demand; these were the focus of ABA-DTT, which I described in Chapter 7. The second rung—whether it goes by the label NET, PRT, or DIR—is play-based interaction, which involved hands-on social reciprocation: *my turn, your turn.* Social Stories ask the child, for the first time, to explicitly recognize his or her own feelings, the feelings of others, their response options in a given situation, and the impact of these choices on the feelings of others. These are the roots of metacognitive thinking, or "thinking about thinking."

Social Stories have been used successfully to enhance peer interaction, teach choice and play skills, and decrease disruptive behavior. The research literature on Social Stories suggests that the technique holds promise, although it's difficult to perform controlled trials in the natu-ralistic settings where the stories are most often used.

(i) See the Resource List for additional information on Social Stories.

Social Skills Groups

A Therapy Session

We're in the waiting room at a therapy center. Will, Eddie, and Alec, all seven- to ten-year-old boys, are waiting for their social skills group to begin. The therapist running the group enters. "Ready?" she asks them. All three look up and eagerly follow the therapist to the occupa-tional therapy gym.

The therapist explains the first activity: Each boy has to listen for his name, and when he hears it, he needs to respond by rolling a ball through a tunnel to the other side of a barricade. There are three tun-nels, three boys, and three therapists (the occupational therapist plus two OT assistants). The game begins—it's pandemonium! The boys and therapists run back and forth from tunnel to tunnel. What looks like organized confusion serves a deeper purpose: Each boy needs to re-main attentive to when his name is called. This is great training for staying focused in a classroom. Indeed, if someone can stay focused during this free-for-all, then staying focused in the classroom almost seems simple by comparison.

After ten minutes of this, the therapist calls all the boys to a mat on the floor. She produces a game that involves drawing cards, exchanging the card for an object, and placing the object inside "Fred's head." The ob-jects are "gross" in an eight-year-old way: plastic vomit, spiders, snakes, and so on. This game is more advanced than the balls and tunnels: Now the object is to learn how to wait one's turn and play cooperatively in a group. Alec wants to draw an item from Fred's head. "You've got to wait to see if you get that card first," the leader explains. Alec understands and waits patiently to see if luck will favor him this evening.

Eddie complains of being "hot," and he retreats to a far corner of the room. The therapist takes Eddie out to get a drink. A few minutes later, Eddie reappears: "Anyone want a drink?" he asks. The therapist has turned Eddie's withdrawal behavior into a teaching moment, to motivate him to communicate with the other children in the group.

After the board game is over, the boys engage in a more physical activity: jumping off a pile of therapy mats. Only this time it's follow-the-leader: Each boy gets to jump in his own unique way, and his peers must imitate what he's done. Again, the hidden agenda of the activity is attending to others, turn taking, and imitation: the bedrock of a successful social interaction.

Social skills groups are just what they sound like: a chance for a child with ASD to practice the social skills involved in interacting with one's peers, in a protected setting. The groups focus on the kinds of theory of mind tasks that baffle children with ASD. Normally developing children learn to ask themselves certain questions in social interactions: *What is the other person thinking? Is the person being friendly or unfriendly? How am I coming across to the other person?* Over time, such questions become second nature, so by the time we reach adulthood, they have become part of our ongoing unconscious inner dialogue. But for the person with ASD, the inability to observe oneself and others in social settings makes it difficult to adapt to life in the adult world.

Interactive play depends on the ability to attend to and engage with one's peers and an interest in doing so. Children with normal development progress from parallel play to interactive play at around three years of age, while the age at which a child with ASD becomes ready for that transition will depend on his or her overall level of development and the degree of atypicality. Social skills groups are available for children of any age, from preschool to high school. What's important is that all the members of a given group are at the same level of language and development. The activities of the group will vary, depending on both the age and the skill level of the children in the group.

The goals of social skills groups include:

- Basic skills for social interaction (eye contact, personal space, voice volume)
- Recognizing and labeling feelings in oneself
- Recognizing feelings in others (facial expressions, vocal inflection, body language)

- Conversational skills (starting, maintaining, and ending conversations; taking turns; asking questions; choosing an appropriate topic)
- Play and friendship skills (understanding what a friend is and how to be one)
- Cognitive flexibility (dealing with the unexpected, changing plans)
- Social problem-solving skills (coping mechanisms, self-control)
- Self-awareness
- Self-esteem

Notice that within these activities there is a progression from bottom-up to top-down thinking, from skills based on concrete stimuli such as eye contact and personal space to skills that entail more abstract goals and purposes. Conversation skills start with the rudimentary: greeting the other person, opening a topic, taking turns, and so on. The eventual goal, however, is to get beyond taking turns to taking *perspectives*—truly listening to another person and seeing the topic from their point of view.

Like Social Stories, social skills groups allow individuals with ASD to learn and get comfortable with explicit rules for social behavior. Instead of telling a child, "Don't stand too close to someone in a conversation," for instance, one might say, "Stand one arm's length away." The goal is to highlight the connection between the child's behavior and some specific outcome: "If you stand too close, other people will avoid you." Understanding cause and effect in this way becomes even more important in adolescence, when self-care skills become crucial: "If you wash and use deodorant, you are more likely to be chosen than if you don't wash and others don't like the way you smell." Social Stories and social skills reinforce each other. They both break down the subtle, unspoken code of social behavior into smaller, more easily learned chunks.

The techniques used in social skills groups will vary but generally include:

- *Teaming the child with one or more partners and emphasizing other-centered thinking.* For example, each child may have to serve a snack to a teammate, rather than to him- or herself. The child may need to find out the teammate's snack preference or other information about the teammate that can be reported at circle time or incorporated into the group's activities.

• *Group-based problem solving.* The teacher might assign a task to a group of children, carefully structuring the task so that the group's success depends on their interacting with one another. (This kind of team-building exercise also is common in military boot camp and at corporate retreats to develop teamwork skills.)

• *Role playing.* Using prepared scripts, taking turns at different roles.

• *Visual prompts and cues.* Cards, signs, critiquing videotapes of the group. Two particularly interesting sources are Carol Gray's *Comic Book Conversations* and Jed Baker's *Social Skills Picture Book.* (See the Resource List.) Both make use of dialogue and thought balloons to reveal the thoughts and emotions of each person in an interaction.

• *Brainstorming.* A brainstorming session led by the therapist is particularly useful for adolescents with strong verbal skills. It can be a good way of learning how to deal with social pressures or exploring feelings of inadequacy when interacting with typically developing peers. The subtle message that comes through in a group setting— that the person isn't alone and that other people have the same kinds of problems—helps build self-esteem and self-acceptance.

• *Homework.* Requiring the child to practice specified skills outside the group.

(i) See the Resource List for additional information on social skills.

We can now complete our graph of behavioral therapies (Figure 10.1), as well as our graph of language therapies (Figure 10.2), adding Social Stories and social skills groups to the upper right-hand corners of both. Social Stories and social skills groups represent the place where these two streams of development (behavioral and language) flow together.

Summing Up

With Social Stories and social skills groups, we've reached the highest rung of the bottom-up to top-down ladder. The ability to infer what

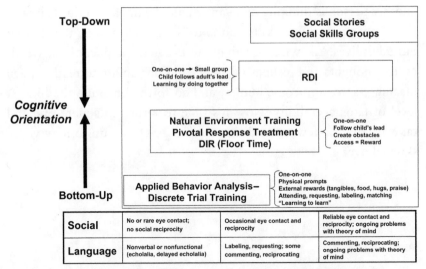

Figure 10.1 Social Stories and Social Skills Groups as Behavioral Therapy *The active reflection required of the child—starting with "What am I supposed to do?" and progressing to "How does my partner feel?"—entail strategizing and perspective taking, placing Social Stories and social skills groups on the highest rung of the behavioral therapies.*

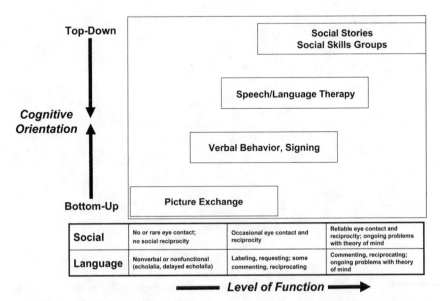

Figure 10.2 Social Stories and Social Skills Groups as Language Therapy *As with the behavioral therapies, Social Stories and social skills groups represent the highest rung of the ladder for language therapy.*

another person is thinking or to anticipate the impact of our behavior on another person are skills you and I continue to hone throughout our adult lives. Likewise, our ability to gauge the impact of our words on the thoughts and feelings of others and our ability to read implied meaning, sarcasm, irony, humor, and so forth constitute the highest level of language ability. Now it's time to return to square one and take a look at a few other dimensions of ASD that up to now we've skipped over.

Chapter 11

Hands-On Therapies

> Cognitive function has its tap root in the spinal cord.
> —*A. Jean Ayres, OT, PhD*

Sensory Dysfunction

Feeding Disorders

A Therapy Session: Sensory Integration

We are in a large, sunny room, about twenty feet on a side. The floor is covered with tumbling mats. Along one wall is a sort of ramp made of foam pads. The end of the ramp drops off two feet into a landing area of beanbag chairs. Nearby is a small trampoline. In the center of the room, a large net, looking like a cross between a hammock and a cargo net, hangs from the ceiling. Rubber balls, ranging from a grapefruit-size ball filled with lead shot (and weighing five pounds) to a large beachball, are scattered about. There are several doors offering access to the therapy space, and to various smaller rooms leading off the central space.

A mom enters, leading her son, Robby, a boy of about four. He's been coming for therapy for several months. Robby doesn't seem to be paying attention to anyone; his eyes are scanning the distance, or so it seems, until he spots his therapist, Joanne. He runs up to Joanne and eagerly holds out his hands, declaring, "Jump, jump!"

"Hi, Robby!" she replies, obligingly leading Robby to the trampoline. But before letting him on the trampoline, Joanne declares, "First your vest, then jump!" Even though Robby's attention is riveted on the trampoline, he obligingly extends his arms as Joanne fastens him into a weighted vest containing two pounds of lead shot sewn into the lining. Then she leads him to the trampoline.

Kneeling next to him, never letting go of his hands, Joanne guides Robby as he rhythmically jumps up and down. In sync with his jumping, she starts singing "The Wheels on the Bus," pausing at the end of each phrase so that Robby can fill in the rest. "The wheels on the . . . ?" she sings.

"Bus!" Robby answers, jumping to lend the word emphasis.

"Right! The wheels on the bus go . . . ?" Joanne prompts.

"Round and round," Robbie responds, in time with his jumping. He and Joanne go through several verses, some of their own invention.

"Okay, Robby," Joanne eventually declares. "Ten more jumps, then we have to stop! One, two, three . . . eight, nine, ten!" And Robby, who ordinarily would become distraught at transitioning away from a preferred activity, readily steps down from the trampoline.

"Ready to swing?" Joanne asks him. Robby eagerly clambers into the cargo net, and once again Robby and Joanne interact. This time, Robby holds up his hands to give Joanne a high-five each time he swings close to her, and she gives him another push with the palms of her hands, as she counts: "One, two, three . . ." When she gets to ten, she stops the swing, and Robby lies prone for another count of ten. Then he sits up as Joanne twirls the net around for another count of ten.

From there they go on to lobbing a weighted ball back and forth. Then Joanne sends Robbie crawling through a tunnel of heavy fabric.

Throughout all of these maneuvers, Robby remains interactive with his therapist, even though his eye contact wanders. "Good work, Robby!" Joanne declares after about forty-five minutes, removing his vest and sending him off with his mom.

Sensory Impairment: The Diagnostic Stepchild

Leo Kanner, the father of all modern care for children with ASD, emphasized sensory behaviors in his landmark 1943 paper: "Loud noises and moving objects…are reacted to with horror. Tricycles, swings, elevators, vacuum cleaners, running water, gas burners, mechanical toys, egg beaters, even the wind could on occasion bring about a major panic." Subsequent research has confirmed Kanner's original insight, and now we have numerous first-person accounts by adults with ASD describing how, as children, they suffered from exaggerated sensations (rough clothing feeling like nails on the skin, for example), or an intense craving for certain forms of sensory input (scrunching into corners or pressing up against people to get deep pressure, licking or sniffing nonfood objects, or even engaging in self-injurious behaviors such as skin picking or head banging as ways to fill their craving for sensory input). Why children with ASD manifest these marked distortions in sensory processing remains unclear.

Amazingly, despite this mountain of information, sensory symptoms play no role in the formal diagnosis of ASD. The *DSM-IV* mentions them, but they do not form part of the diagnostic criteria, and the Autism Diagnostic Observation Schedule (ADOS)—the most widely used tool for enrolling children with ASD into research studies—doesn't mention sensory issues at all. Why not? Partly because sensory symptoms are not unique to ASD. Not all children who over- or underreact to sensory stimuli fall on the autistic spectrum. But the same is true for other symptoms of ASD. Repetitious behaviors, for example, are not unique to ASD (they also occur in children with obsessive-compulsive disorder), yet repetitious behavior is a diagnostic criterion for ASD. So there has to be another reason why sensory issues have been demoted to second-class status when it comes to making the diagnosis of ASD. I suspect it's because most psychiatrists (the *DSM* is written and published by the American Psychiatric Association) and most psychologists are interested in studying mental function rather than something as "low level" as sensory processing. Perhaps with the recent discovery of the mirror neuron system, which ties sensory awareness to higher mental functions such as theory of mind, we will see a reintegration of sensory issues into the core of ASD, as originally proposed by Kanner—who was himself a child psychiatrist.

Sensory Dysfunction: Looking for a Home in the Brain*

In 1972, an occupational therapist named Jean Ayres coined the term *sensory integration.* Ayres believed that the lowermost part of the brain where it exits from the skull and joins the spinal cord (known technically as the *brain stem*—see Figure 3.3 or 6.1) integrates all of the sensory inputs coming up from the body before passing this information to the cerebral cortex. According to Ayres, "sensory integrative processes" in the brain stem "result in perception and other types of syntheses of sensory data that enable man to interact effectively with the environment." She never explained what these processes were other than to say that they involved "organizing sensory information for use."

Ayres believed that sensory input and motor activity during infancy "makes possible meaningful experience for the child." The child learns to move his or her body in space, learns that objects continue to exist even when out of sight, learns how to combine two objects together, and so forth. In her view, these experiences add up to *sensorimotor intelligence,* which she viewed as a prerequisite for *reflective intelligence,* meaning higher cognitive functions, including abstract language.

Ayres observed that many children with mental or physical disability had abnormal responses to sensory input. "When the development of the brain has deviated from the norm," she wrote, "the sense of touch is apt to be diffuse rather than well differentiated, and some children are overly ready with a fight or flight reaction in response to some

* With a tip of the hat to Isabel Rapin: Autism in search of a home in the brain. *Neurology,* 1999, 52(5):902–904.

tactile stimuli." Ayres believed that these abnormal responses were indicative of what she called a *sensory integration disorder* (*SID*), and that SID was due to an abnormality of the brain stem. In her opinion, defective sensory integration in the brain stem was the cause of the abnormal responses to sensory stimuli that she observed in children with disabilities. Ayres and her successors also emphasize the presence of "regulatory and behavior problems," including irregular patterns for sleeping, eating, and elimination, as components of SID.

Ayres then proposed what she called "sensory integration therapy" to train the presumed disorder of the brain stem. Sensory integration therapy, Ayres claimed, would have a beneficial impact not just on brain stem functions such as sensory processing but also on higher cortical functions such as attention and learning. Ayres was interested in applying sensory integration therapy to children with learning disabilities, since she believed learning disabilities were often due to an underlying sensory integration disorder (Ayres did not address autism in her book). Ayres wrote:

> A sensory integrative approach to treating learning disorders differs from many other procedures in that it does not teach specific skills such as matching visual stimuli, learning to remember a sequence of sounds, differentiating one sound from another, drawing lines from one point to another, or even the basic academic material. Rather, the objective is to enhance the brain's ability to learn how to do these things. If the brain develops the capacity to perceive, remember and motor plan, the ability can then be applied toward the mastery of all academic and other tasks, regardless of the specific content. The objective [of sensory integration therapy] is modification of the neurological dysfunction interfering with learning rather than attacking the symptoms of that dysfunction.

As part of sensory integration therapy, Ayres coined the term *sensory diet*—a level of stimulation that was tailored to the particular child. The object of therapy, she believed, was to discover the "just right" level of sensory input for each particular child in each particular sensory domain. If the child is hyperreactive to sensory input, then the goal should be to provide soft, gentle stimulation: rocking, soothing music, and the like. If the child is hyporeactive, then the goal might be to provide sensory-generating activities—bouncing, swinging, and brushing, for example. Weighted vests might be used to heighten sensory input. Play activities are also geared toward providing the child with an optimized sensory diet: Play-Doh, finger painting, sand table, and so on. The therapist also works with the parents to carry over the same approaches to home and school. Modifications such as providing the hypersensitive child with earplugs or headphones to blot out environmental noise, avoidance of rough clothing, removal of clothing tags, replacement of flickering fluorescent lights, and other strategies are common. Occupational therapists believe that many of the symptoms of ASD arise from disordered sensory processing in the brain stem and that if they can fix sensory processing, they can bring about improvement in all the other areas of ASD as well.

In reality, however, we have very little proof that disturbed sensory processing at the level of the brain stem occurs in ASD, and virtually no evidence that disturbances of sensory processing "cause" ASD. No specific neurologic mechanisms or anatomic sites have been identified within the brain stem that might correspond to Ayres' "sensory integration." So, after nearly four decades, the very concept of sensory integration remains unproven, and its home within the brain (if it exists at all) remains a mystery. Uta Frith (a big proponent of central coherence as a core deficit in ASD) theorizes that disordered responses to sensory input are due to abnormalities in the cerebral cortex rather than the brain stem. There is some evidence from EEG and MRI studies to support both points of view. My personal hunch is that the mirror neuron system (situated in the cerebral cortex), the thalamus (situated deep within the brain), and the cerebellum will turn out to be key players, rather than the brain stem. And whether sensory processing "causes" other symptoms such as impaired social skills and language development or simply occurs side by side with them is anybody's guess at this point in time.

Setting aside the theoretical loose ends for a moment, the real question is whether sensory integration therapy works. Perhaps occupational therapists are doing the right things, even though the underlying rationale for their intervention remains to be proven. There is no doubt about the fact that children with ASD have abnormal responses to sensory stimuli—exaggerated at one moment, blunted the next—with sensory-avoidant and sensory-seeking behavior to match. There is also little doubt that kids like Robby definitely seem to be more connected with other people during sensory integration therapy—perhaps because modulated sensory input gets their mirror neurons and theory-of-mind skills temporarily in tune. And sensory integration therapy seems to enhance the quality of life for kids on the spectrum and for their parents—which itself is reason enough to use it. However, despite nearly four decades of use, there are no studies to show that sensory integration therapy brings about the hoped-for long-term changes claimed by Ayres and her successors.

(i) See the Resource List for additional information on sensory integration.

A Therapy Session: Feeding Clinic

We're looking through a two-way mirror into a small room. Inside, we see a child of about three, Rose, seated in a high chair. Sitting opposite Rose is Jen, her feeding specialist. Behind Jen is a counter with a sink, a microwave, and a mini-fridge. Right now Rose is screaming loudly and has turned her head away from Jen. Jen is holding out a small spoon in which there is a tiny bit of vanilla pudding. Jen waits...and waits...and waits, with a look of quiet expectation on her face. Eventually Rose pauses for breath. The instant Rose stops crying, Jen gives her a big smile and says, "Hi, Rose!" (In behaviorist jargon, Jen is doing two things: putting Rose's food refusal on extinction and providing social reinforcement the instant Rose engages in something other than verbal protest—in this case, seizing the instant Rose is not crying to offer her a social smile.) Rose enters another cycle of crying; Jen resumes her passive demeanor, still holding up the spoon. Eventually Rose settles down again. "Good girl, Rose!" Jen exclaims. "First pudding, then chips!" This time Rose leans forward ever so slightly and opens her mouth. Jen gives her the pudding, then immediately offers her a potato chip—one of Rose's preferred foods.

Rose's behavior may seem extreme, but I almost always get a sad smile or a look of utter desperation from parents of a child with ASD when I ask, "What is it like to get your child to try something new to eat?" The majority of children with ASD manifest feeding selectivity, probably due to the combined effects of impaired sensory processing and insistence on sameness. (I think *feeding selectivity* is a better term than the more commonly used *food selectivity,* because some of the contributory factors stem from issues other than the food itself—for example, having to eat from a particular plate, or having the television on.) The child with reduced sensory perception may crave spicy food. The child with heightened sensory perception may reject highly textured foods. Some children eat only starchy food or crunchy food. One of my patients eats only yellow food. Your child may be able to detect incredibly minor variations in the composition of his or her preferred items. One company changed the ingredients for the sauce in their macaroni and cheese, which up until that point had been a staple for one of my patients, and suddenly it was on the child's *no* list.

In addition to demonstrating odd or rigid food preferences, children with ASD frequently have unusual feeding mechanics. The child with oral hyposensitivity may overfill his or her mouth, not sensing that something is already in there. The child with oral hypersensitivity, on the other hand, may refuse to go beyond the softest of pureed foods.

Some children with ASD develop rigid behavioral patterns around eating: not letting different foods on the plate touch, for instance, or rejecting broken items, like crackers with a missing corner. I once made the terrible mistake of breaking a cracker in half in front of such a child—the child reacted first with horror, then with inconsolable crying.

Some children will eat only in a particular location in the house or drink only from a specific cup. Some children gag on nonpreferred foods, for no identifiable anatomic reason. This can become a conditioned reflex, the same way that Pavlov's dogs were conditioned to salivate at the sound of a bell: After enough unpleasant mealtime experiences, the mere sight of the nonpreferred food causes the child to gag.

As my stepmother taught me, an ounce of prevention is worth a pound of cure. In the case of food selectivity, your best strategy is not to let it develop in the first place. Here are some tips to forestall the emergence of food selectivity (although I realize that by the time you read this, it may be too late for preventive measures):

- Despite your child's preference for certain foods, do not get into the habit of serving these items at every meal. Rotate what you serve—then stand back.
- Remain steadfast. If your child turns up his or her nose at what you have offered, do *not* replace your first offering with the child's preferred item. Remember what you learned in the chapter on applied behavior analysis: Removal of the nonpreferred food constitutes *negative reinforcement* and offering the desired food is *positive reinforcement*. Swapping items when your child protests is therefore doubly reinforcing of the refusal behavior and virtually guarantees that the problem will get worse.
- If you don't think you are emotionally able to let your child go hungry through a meal, then put out a *small* portion of your child's preferred foods at the *beginning* of the meal. At least that way you are not directly reinforcing food refusal, and you can quell your anxiety and guilt preemptively.

As difficult as these issues are, I can reassure you on a couple of counts. First, in my thirty years of working with children with ASD, I have seen only a handful of children with clinically significant nutritional issues, where interventions such as the insertion of a feeding tube were necessary. (There have been a handful of case reports of vitamin deficiency in children with ASD and food refusal, but they are so rare as to constitute medical curiosities.) Second, I have yet to see severe food selectivity persist past early childhood. As Leo Kanner pointed out sixty years ago, by the time a child with ASD gets to elementary school age, the most intense of the sensory issues have faded a bit, including food selectivity. On purely medical grounds, therefore, I attach a low priority to the treatment of food selectivity. As the parent of a child with ASD, you have bigger issues to attend to, such as eye contact, social reciprocity, language pragmatics, and play skills.

Mealtimes, however, are a focal point of social interaction. Feeding another person, especially one's family, is an act of love. And, simply at a practical level, tantrums at the meal table are not a lot of fun. Therefore, your child's eating behavior may take on an emotional importance in your mind far beyond its nutritional dimension.

Again, since you are reading this, there is a good chance that you are already past the point of preventive measures. If this is the case, then you may want to seek help from an interdisciplinary feeding team, which is generally composed of an occupational and/or physical therapist, a speech therapist, a registered dietitian, and a behavioral psychologist, all of whom are backed up by a physician (to rule out rare medical causes of feeding problems). Just as the causes of food selectivity are multidimensional, the intervention for food selectivity is also multidimensional. You will probably be asked to complete a questionnaire documenting the amount and range of foods your child eats, their nutritional content, texture, and other characteristics. You will also be asked about the physical context within which your child eats: At the table? In a high chair or regular chair? TV on or off? Rushed or relaxed setting? Other family members present? Spouse present? Whose job is it to feed the children? Parents in agreement with each other or at odds over the child's behavior?

Intervention is based on a blend of nutritional, physical, developmental, and behavioral principles. The team will devise a schedule of progressively more complex foods (texture and flavor) while ensuring adequate caloric intake and nutritional balance. The occupational therapist and speech therapist will look at your child's posture, lip closure, ability to handle silverware, and so forth. All of this takes place within a developmental context. For example, rotary chewing (the way we use our molars, as opposed to biting, which we do with our front teeth) is a twelve-month oromotor skill; the use of a spoon is a twelve-month cognitive and fine motor skill. The feeding goals for any child need to be consistent with his or her current developmental capabilities. An eighteen-month-old with overall developmental delay who is functioning at a six-month level is simply not ready to use a cup and spoon, and may not be ready for items that require chewing. Sitting posture and trunk balance are also important to the mechanics of feeding and swallowing. Does your child depend on his or her arms for sitting balance, for example? If so, a high chair may be preferable to a regular chair. A high chair is also preferred because it gives the adults greater control over the situation from a behavioral standpoint—the meal is over only when the adult says it's over.

This brings us to behavioral considerations. The behaviorist will employ a variety of methods, such as:

- Systematic desensitization
  - At the first session the nonpreferred food may be placed on the table, but not in front of your child. At the next session it is placed directly in front of your child but not on his or her plate; next time, on the plate. The time after that, your child will be expected to handle it, then smell or lick it, then put it in his or her mouth but be permitted to spit it out, and finally to swallow it.
  - Systematic desensitization can also involve giving your child a chance to literally play with the food at times other than meals. (This may not work if your child is also averse to getting sticky fingers.) It is important as well for you to let go of any tendency you may have to be a neat freak during meals—don't wipe your child's mouth after every bite.
- Positive reinforcement and extinction
  - Positive reinforcement requires the child to take a bite of the nonpreferred food *first*; the adult immediately rewards this by offering the child a bite of the preferred food. As part of the behavioral process, it is essential that you refrain from letting the child have the desired food at other times. You've got to keep the desired food in limited supply and dole it out just as a reward for desired eating behavior. This takes willpower on your part.
  - The child is never forced to eat; that is aversive and probably unethical. Rather, the therapist steadfastly presents the nonpreferred item until the child eats it, regardless of the intensity and duration of tantruming on the child's part; this is known in behaviorist jargon as *escape extinction*. The escape behavior—tantruming—is simply ignored, and eventually it recedes.

These methods work, but there are no data to show whether the long-term outcome is any different from what would have been the case with a hands-off approach. To answer this question, one would need to enroll a large group of children with food refusal and randomize them into two subgroups, one of which would receive interdisciplinary intervention for feeding and the other of which would be managed by watchful waiting. I am not aware of anyone having done this, and—given the urgency that most parents attach to feeding—it is unlikely that we will ever see such a study.

Summing Up

Sensory issues are an integral component of ASD, although they have received less than their fair share of attention from the authors of the *DSM,* the creators of the ADOS, and other gold-standard criteria for diagnosing ASD. Research by neuroscientists on the mirror neuron system is tunneling through the mountain from one direction, while the hands-on therapists are tunneling through from the other direction. Someday these two groups will meet in the middle and we will finally reintegrate sensory dysfunction into the diagnostic schema of ASD. At a theoretical level, we will also have a better understanding of how bottom-up processing and top-down processing come together in individuals with ASD. It seems safe to say that sensory integration therapy improves quality of life for children with ASD and their families, but whether it alters long-term outcome remains to be seen. Likewise, feeding therapy can be used to successfully reshape your child's eating behavior, but whether an intensive feeding **program** makes any difference in the long run is also unknown.

Chapter 12

Behavior Management and Psychopharmacology

His autistic behaviors have lessened since his language has developed. However, his behavior has worsened. What is the autism? What is a two-year-old? These lines are blurred for us.

—Parents of a thirty-month-old boy with autism

Behavior problems can make life extremely trying for you and your child with ASD. Even normally simple tasks such as getting your child to sleep each night can be immense challenges if your child is on the spectrum. Often behavioral issues prove to be the key (or the stumbling block) to a child's ultimate success in life. Addressing a child's troublesome behaviors can make a huge difference in quality of life not only for the child but for all the other members of the household.

In this chapter I'll briefly recap the core neurobiological deficits of ASD, and show you how these core deficits give rise to challenging behaviors in children with ASD. Once I have laid this foundation, I'll give you specific advice on how to deal with these behaviors. Sometimes maladaptive behaviors have been learned, so they can be unlearned with the right behavioral techniques. Sometimes maladaptive behaviors are biologically driven and will require medication in addition to behavioral measures. In this chapter we will cover both types of behavior. Often, figuring out what's going on is less clear-cut than the examples I've provided. I hope, however, that the information and examples that follow will give you a way to analyze your child's behavior and respond to it in a thought-out manner.

Not Like Other Children

All children face the need to learn how to fit into the world around them. That task is harder for the child with ASD (and his or her caregivers); social skills easily mastered by the child with typical development are particularly baffling to the child with ASD. Not only are these skills harder for the child to learn, but because they take the child with ASD longer to acquire, parents or other caregivers eventually run into a mismatch between the child's behavioral level and his or her age (and size). Once this happens, behavior management techniques that might have worked in a younger child begin to lose their effectiveness. It's comparatively easy, for example, to deal with disruptive behavior in a toddler—just put the child in his or her crib for a few moments. But what do you do with an agile five-year-old who can easily climb out of a crib, or a twelve-year-old who's bigger, stronger, and faster than his or her parents? Finally, because children with ASD manifest some traits that we simply don't see in children with typical development, some behavioral techniques suitable for dealing with a child with typical development may not work. Ordinarily, for example, providing or withdrawing adult attention is the most powerful tool parents have at their disposal to shape their child's behavior. However, this tool is of limited use in shaping the behavior of a child with ASD who is oblivious to his or her parents in the first place.

So, what can be done? Rest assured: Although it may be more difficult and may take longer, you will still be able to modify your child's behavior. As part of the process, you may benefit from working with a behavior analyst who focuses on the ABC's of your child's behavior: Even though a child on the spectrum may not be responsive to social cues, he or she is still sensitive to other reinforcers. Often, parents are unwittingly reinforcing the very behaviors they find so troubling, such as by dropping a task if the child becomes disruptive; as we've seen in Chapter 7, letting the child use disruptive behavior to escape from a task is a form of negative reinforcement. A behavior analyst can spot these errors and help parents modify their own behavior. Then the child's behavior will usually fall into line.

Sometimes parents will do better working with a child psychologist or family therapist who can help them manage their own feelings and the impact of the child's behavior on other members of the family. Sometimes parents need both: someone to work with them on the mechanics (*When your child does X, you do Y*) as well as someone to work with them on their feelings. This is especially true if the parents have strongly divergent views of behavior management and/or if they are struggling to come to grips with their own emotions. (As we will discuss at greater length in Part III, parents who have not addressed their own needs are frequently unable to manage their child's behavior.) Trusted professionals can offer you a fresh perspective and constructive coaching. It's no shame to seek help. In fact, you're probably going to need it in order to help your child develop to the fullest possible extent.

Unlike the child with typical development, your child with ASD may also need medication to help bring some of his or her behaviors under control. You may be reluctant to think about medication, but ASD is a medical condition, like diabetes. If someone's body isn't making insulin, he or she needs to take insulin. Insulin doesn't cure diabetes, but it can enable the person with diabetes to live nearly a normal life. In a similar fashion, the brain of the child with ASD is not making or responding properly to certain *neurotransmitters*—chemicals within the brain that regulate emotions and behavior. Drug treatment helps to restore the normal action of these neurotransmitters, just as insulin helps the child with diabetes maintain a normal blood sugar level. Psychoactive drugs will not cure your child's ASD, but they may be necessary—just like insulin in a child with diabetes—in order to enable your child with ASD to achieve his or her full potential. Often parents who are the most reluctant to try medication are the same ones who come back and tell me afterward how convinced they are that medicine has made a huge difference in their child's life.

Medications carry risk, but there's also a risk to *not* using medication when it's really needed. Behaviors that begin as biologically driven can take a life of their own, becoming deeply entrenched in your child's behavioral repertoire. Even more concerning, if your child is always being reprimanded or corrected for inappropriate behavior, your child may start to think of him- or herself as "bad" and begin conforming to that role. If your child's teachers tell you that your child's behavior is getting in the way of his or her ability to learn despite appropriate classroom supports, that's one sign that a medication trial may be in order. If you and your partner have been working with a behavioral or mental health specialist and things still aren't getting better, that's another clue that medication may have a role to play. Often the combination of medication plus behavioral intervention is more successful than either approach by itself. (In my practice, I require parents to sign a consent form agreeing to behavioral or family therapy if I feel these are warranted, before I will prescribe psychoactive medication for their child.)

Common Scenarios

Do any of these children sound familiar to you?

Nate: Inflexible

Nate's parents brought him to me at age three for evaluation of delayed speech, hyperactivity, and obsessive behavior. He had a handful of socially appropriate single words and short phrases, which he used mainly to convey his own needs; otherwise, his speech was limited to echolalia and scripting. His eye contact was poor. He needed everything to be on his terms or he would become upset. Once when Nate was an infant, his mother was holding him in her arms while dusting the living room furniture. She inadvertently rearranged the framed photographs on the mantelpiece, sending Nate into a fit of tears. He remained inconsolable until Mom discovered the problem; as soon as she put the pictures back in their original order, his crying stopped. As a toddler, his play consisted chiefly of lining up his toys; he became frantic if one was missing or if anyone disturbed the arrangement. He had intense body rocking, hand flapping, and toe walking, and he repeatedly ran around the house in a defined path. He also mouthed, licked, and sniffed nonfood items, and he seemed to have an increased pain threshold; he could take a big fall, then get up and keep going without a whimper. Over the next several years, Nate's mouthing and licking behaviors disappeared; he continued to take a little sniff of his crayons before using them. His physical stereotypies faded somewhat (although they reemerged whenever he became excited), but his repetitious behaviors showed no sign of abating: His parents had to park in a certain lot at the mall or Nate would be inconsolable. Once inside the mall, they had to go from store to store in a prescribed order (regardless of whether they needed to buy anything) or Nate would have a full-scale meltdown. And if they went into a restaurant, Nate insisted on going from table to table, collecting every ketchup bottle in sight. When Nate was three, the other diners had smiled benignly. By age six, it was no longer cute. Much to their own dismay, the parents had started taking turns going out with the other children, leaving one parent behind with Nate: no more family trips to the mall or dinners at the local restaurant. At school, Nate was inconsolable if he could not do something perfectly, and he could not let go of one task to move on to the next until he had finished the first task to his own satisfaction. If the teacher unwisely pressed the issue, Nate's behavior deteriorated to a full-scale meltdown, with screaming and hitting. "Nate's obsessions are taking over his life—and ours," his parents mourned.

Isabel: Blowing Hot and Cold

Like Nate, Isabel has her rigid side. She will wear only purple shirts and purple hair clips. Her diet consists of six exact things—no substitutions. Her drawings consist of endless, stereotyped variations on the same Webkinz character. Her parents have read the same three storybooks with her at bedtime a thousand times (at least it feels that way to them). But whenever Isabel is not glued to the computer or her Webkinz toys, she is darting all over the place. "Our daughter has only two speeds: stop and full steam ahead," her parents wrote in the preevaluation questionnaire. And sure enough, when I meet her, that's exactly the case. Isabel presents as a very active five-year-old, darting around the play area of the waiting room, playing intensely but briefly with a variety of objects: first the wooden Thomas trains, which she happily crashes off the end of the track; then the dollhouse, where she attempts in a haphazard way to arrange the furniture; then the puzzles, which she dumps onto the floor. Testing Isabel is a challenge. Throughout the session, she alternates between perseverative behavior (drawing a page full of circles instead of just one, stacking all twelve blocks instead of building a three-block tower in imitation of the examiner, insistently pointing to all four pictures on every page during a vocabulary test instead of just the one picture I ask her to point to), and impulsive, hyperactive behavior (running in circles around the exam table, grabbing items out of my medical bag, climbing on top of the trash container and jumping off). Throughout all of these behaviors, she seems willing to work with me, but she seems driven by forces beyond her control. By the end of the session, my office is in shambles, and I am exhausted. "Now you understand what our day is like," the parents say, trying to console me as I stare at the wreckage that was once my examining room.

Calvin: Explosive

My receptionist buzzes me on the intercom: "It's Mrs. Brown. She says it's an emergency. Will you speak with her?"

Mom is on a cell phone. "Dr. Coplan, you've got to help me!" she sobs. In the background, I hear her five-year-old son, Calvin—my patient—shrieking at the top of his lungs. I also hear Calvin's two-year-old sister, Marie, crying, and behind all three of them I hear cars and trucks zooming by.

"Are you driving?" I ask.

"No," Mrs. Brown replies, her voice trembling. "I've pulled over onto the shoulder of the road. Calvin is having a total meltdown—he's going after Marie with his fingernails, and he's biting himself. I don't know what to do! You've got to help me!" She bursts into tears again as Calvin shrieks, his sister wails, and traffic whizzes past.

I'm dismayed but not surprised to get this call. Calvin was a handful from the day his parents first brought him home from the hospital: He was colicky, he slept poorly, and when awake he screamed at the least provocation. I first evaluated Calvin at age thirty months. He was an easily agitated little boy, with poor eye contact. His vocalizations consisted of shrieking and rare single words. I was unable to engage him in any type of developmental testing. I recommended intensive ABA-DTT, advancing to more socially based interventions as his ability to imitate and initiate social interaction improved. Thereafter, I had been following Calvin's progress every six months, most recently at age four and a half. His eye contact and speech had slowly improved. His agitated behavior, however, had not. In fact, he had gone from shrieking to throwing objects, flopping to the floor, and most recently biting and scratching himself, as well as anyone within arm's reach. These behaviors were usually preceded by some type of frustration: not getting access to a desired toy, for example, or being told *no*. And now it has come to this: Mom parked on the shoulder of the highway, Calvin in a full-scale meltdown, biting or digging at himself, and his younger sister cowering in her car seat, trying to keep out of her brother's reach.

Marc: Sleepless

I diagnosed Marc with PDD-NOS at age three. Now he's six. He's made nice progress in terms of his language; he's independent for most self-care skills except shoe tying, and his play, once dominated by rigid, repetitious behaviors such as studying the wheels of his toy trains or lining up the letters of the alphabet across the living room floor, has become more age-appropriate, with him starting to take an interest in his siblings and peers and now engaging in some simple make-believe. The problem is Marc's sleep: He takes at least an hour to fall asleep each evening, and when he does finally fall asleep, he's a very restless sleeper. How do the parents know? Because he sleeps with them in the master bedroom. The parents have tried putting him back in his room, but somehow he's always in their bed again in the morning. Marc's parents would be thankful if Marc actually slept through the night, even if it's in their bed. But more often than not, Marc wakes up around before dawn, ready to go for the day. Meanwhile, his parents, bleary-eyed, can barely drag themselves around.

Looking Beneath the Surface

In order to remedy maladaptive behavior in a child with ASD, we need to look beyond the behaviors themselves to the core deficits that lie beneath the surface. At the simplest level, we can link the core deficits of ASD and the resulting outward behavioral symptoms as follows (Figure 12.1):

Core Deficits	Symptoms
Cognitive rigidity Abnormal regulation of attention Abnormal regulation of arousal Abnormal regulation of sleep Abnormal sensory processing	Routines, stereotypies Perseveration / inattention Agitation / lethargy Insomnia Sensory-seeking / avoidance

Figure 12.1 Relationship Between Core Deficits and Outward Behaviors in ASD

In order to think critically about maladaptive behavior in children with ASD, however, we need to dig a little deeper. First, let's arrange the core deficits like numbers on the dial of a clock (Figure 12.2). Starting at twelve o'clock we have cognitive rigidity. At three o'clock we have abnormal regulation of attention. The tendency to become overfocused (perseveration) is represented by the upward-pointing arrow, to signify excessive attention. Difficulty maintaining focus (inattention) is represented by a downward-pointing arrow. At six o'clock, notice a similar

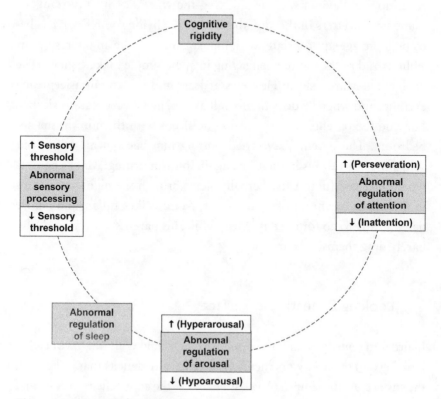

Figure 12.2 Core Deficits in ASD

situation for regulation of arousal: hyperarousability (a hair trigger on the fight-or-flight mechanism), contrasted with hypoarousability. Disorders of arousal and disorders of sleep are genetically linked; I've placed abnormal regulation of sleep at seven, because of the close relationship between these two mechanisms. Sensory processing, at nine o'clock, also reflects two opposing states: increased (upward-pointing arrow) and decreased (downward-pointing arrow) sensory threshold. By arranging all of these features around the perimeter of a circle, we will be able to see not only how each individual core trait leads to maladaptive behavior but also how these different core traits interact with one another. That's what makes the problem so challenging. This will get a little complicated—after all, ASD itself is a little complicated—but we'll take it one step at a time. You don't need to memorize this material. Instead, think of the next few pages as navigational charts that you may need to refer to over the years ahead.

Cognitive Rigidity

During the preschool years, cognitive rigidity shows up as insistence on sameness, difficulty with transitions, and fascination with specific objects or activities. When the child with ASD enters school, cognitive rigidity frequently expresses itself as perfectionism (the inability to let go of an assignment until the child has completed the task to his or her self-imposed level of perfection) and anxiety (since the child is never able to achieve the elusive perfection his or her brain demands). Paradoxically, the same rigid, perfectionistic trait may also trigger task refusal: The child may refuse to try something unfamiliar or refuse to attempt a task that the child knows he or she will not be able to complete perfectly. *Better not to get involved in the first place!* seems to be the child's operating principle. Often children with cognitive rigidity are also anxious or fearful as well: *What will happen if a burglar comes? Or a storm? What if the school catches fire?*

If a child with cognitive rigidity is prevented from completing some ritualistic behavior or task, or if there is a break in the child's routine, the child may become quite agitated, progressing to combative or self-injurious behavior. The child isn't intrinsically violent (few children on the spectrum are). Rather, the child has "lost it" because he or she was prevented from completing his or her routine (Figure 12.3).

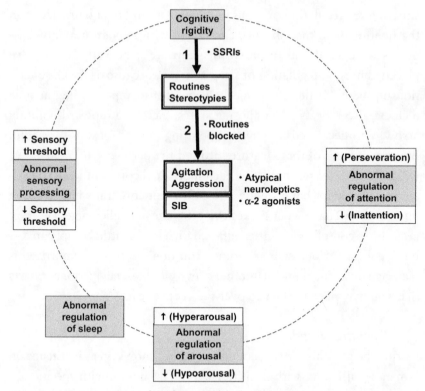

Figure 12.3 Interaction of Deficits and Behaviors in ASD, Part I: Cognitive Rigidity *At step 1 in the diagram, cognitive rigidity leads to insistence on routines, difficulty with transitions, perfectionism, and performance anxiety. If the child's rigid expectations cannot be met and the child is given no way of dissipating his or her stress, then the child's behavior may escalate to step 2: agitation, aggression, and self-injurious behavior (SIB). Medication (one of the selective serotonin reuptake inhibitors, SSRIs) is sometimes used as one component of treatment, along with behavioral measures.*

Sometimes anxiety produces symptoms that mimic attention deficit hyperactivity disorder (ADHD). The child may fidget not because of impulsivity but because he or she is anxious. The child may be inattentive to the teacher not because of short attention span but because he or she is preoccupied with some perseverative thought. In cases like this, treating the child for anxiety sometimes results in a marked reduction in fidgety behavior and reduces the amount of time the child spends inwardly perseverating. Inattentive behavior is not always due to attention deficit hyperactivity disorder—especially if the child has ASD.

Abnormal Regulation of Attention

Regulation of attention is a balancing act. We need to focus our attention on whatever we are doing at the moment but be able to break that focus to attend to something else when necessary. When driving, we have to be able to pay attention to the road ahead but remain prepared at any instant to shift our attention to an ambulance coming in from a side street. Individuals with obsessive-compulsive disorder have difficulty letting go; they get stuck on one thing and have trouble moving on to something else. Conversely, individuals with attention deficit hyperactivity disorder have a hard time maintaining focus; their brains are always shifting from one thing to another. Children with ASD frequently veer to the obsessive/perseverative side of the road (Figure 12.4, pathway 3). The father of one overfocused child with ASD

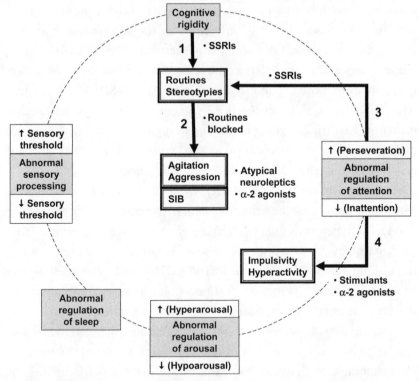

Figure 12.4 Interaction of Deficits and Behaviors in ASD, Part II: Abnormal Regulation of Attention *Many children with ASD alternate between perseveration (3) and inattention (4). Perseveration (3) and cognitive rigidity (1) reinforce each other, magnifying the child's stress level if things do not go according to the child's plan.*

quipped, "My child has *overattention* deficit disorder." In this situation, cognitive rigidity (pathway 1) and hyperfocused attention (pathway 3) reinforce each other. We saw this with Nate in the first vignette. Some children with ASD, such as Isabel in the second vignette, swing wildly back and forth, perseverative one minute and inattentive (Figure 12.4, pathway 4) the next.

Abnormal Regulation of Emotional State (Arousal)

When danger approaches, we instinctively get ready to fight or run. Our bodies pump out adrenaline: our heart rates go up; we begin to tremble; we take deeper breaths; we become keenly aware of every detail in our immediate environment. This is the fight-or-flight response, which is deeply wired into our brains. Like our attentional mechanism, which is delicately balanced between maintaining focus and breaking away, our emotional state is also poised between two conditions: calm and aroused. There are vast differences in the threshold for arousal among people in general: Some people remain calm no matter what, while others go into red alert at the least sign of trouble. These differences are even more pronounced in children with ASD: Many children with ASD (like Calvin, in the third vignette) have an arousal mechanism on a hair trigger, going from calm to highly agitated with minimal provocation—or no provocation at all (Figure 12.5, pathway 6). Others seem chronically underaroused, almost lethargic.

As we saw in the case of anxiety, dysregulation of emotional state can also masquerade as attention deficit hyperactivity disorder. The child with hyperarousability is frequently on the go all the time (Figure 12.5, pathway 5). The presence of severe agitation, however, is a distinguishing feature between ordinary ADHD and emotional hyperarousability. The distinction is important because stimulants—the mainstay of treatment for ADHD—will make agitation worse.

Some children, however, have both dysregulation of attention *and* dysregulation of emotional state (Figure 12.6). In this scenario, the impulsivity attributable to dysregulation of attention (pathway 4) amplifies the hyperarousability attributable to dysregulation of the fight-or-flight mechanism (pathway 5), and vice versa. What's more, because of the linkage between the arousal mechanism and the regulation of sleep, children with this combination of issues typically are hyperactive and agitated by

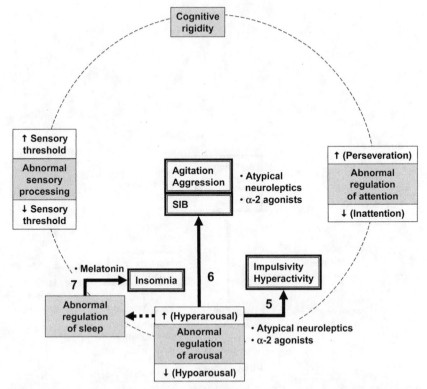

Figure 12.5 Interaction of Deficits and Behaviors in ASD, Part III: Abnormal Regulation of Arousal *Decreased threshold for emotional arousal leads to hyperactive behavior (5) and frequent episodes of agitation (6). Regulation of arousal and regulation of sleep are biologically linked; children with hyperarousability often have poor sleep as well (7).*

day, and poor sleepers by night (Figures 12.5 and 12.6, pathway 7). We saw this with Calvin. This is a particularly challenging combination.

Abnormal Regulation of Sleep

Children with typical development often resist going to bed, but once they fall asleep, their sleep pattern itself is normal. Children with ASD may resist going to bed for behavioral reasons too. But many children with ASD also have a biological defect in the regulation of their sleep/wake cycle, resulting in difficulty falling asleep and shorter periods of sleep, with frequent night wakenings. This is because children with ASD do not make melatonin in the normal fashion. Melatonin is a hormone produced by the brain; it's what tells your body, "You're

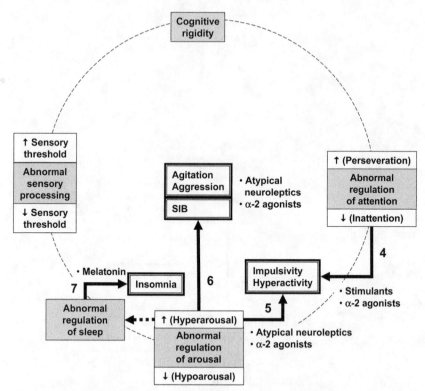

Figure 12.6 Interaction of Deficits and Behaviors in ASD, Part IV: Inattention Plus Hyperarousal *Inattention (4) and hyperarousal (5) both feed into impulsivity and hyperactivity.*

tired now." Normally, the body's production of melatonin follows a twenty-four-hour cycle—less melatonin production in the daytime, and a surge in melatonin production in the evening, when the sun goes down. Unfortunately, many children with ASD do not show a spike in melatonin production in the evening. As a result, they simply don't feel sleepy in the evening, they have shorter periods of sleep with frequent night waking, and they may wake up before dawn, ready to face the new day. We saw this with Marc in the fourth vignette.

Disordered sleep is an integral part of ASD, right along with social impairment, language delay, repetitive behavior, and abnormal sensory processing—another example of how ASD rewrites the rules of engagement for child rearing: Simply putting the child back to bed and letting him cry it out, as you might do with a normally developing toddler, isn't going to work. The exact percentage of children with ASD who have disordered sleep is unknown. But many adults with ASD have similar problems, which suggests that we are looking at a lifelong situation for some individuals. Sleep disorders also run in families of children with ASD—another clue to the shared genetics of sleep and atypicality.

Abnormal Sensory Processing

Like attention and arousal, sensory processing also alternates between two "settings": sensory-seeking and sensory-avoidant (Figure 12.7). Whether a person is sensory-seeking or sensory-avoidant seems to be related to his or her threshold for perception. Think of having an increased sensory threshold, like being hard of hearing—not just for

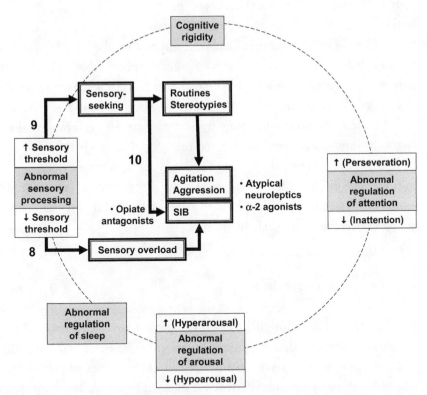

Figure 12.7 Interaction of Deficits and Behaviors in ASD, Part V: Dysregulation of Sensory Perception *The child with a decreased sensory threshold is prone to sensory overload (8), which can trigger agitation and self-injury (as a form of stress reduction). An increased threshold (pathway 9) leads directly to sensory-seeking behavior—including, in the extreme case, self-injury (10).*

sounds but for all kinds of sensory input. The person with an increased threshold doesn't perceive ordinary inputs as being very exciting—they are dim, distant, and blunted. Children who are blind sometimes put pressure on their eyeballs in order to stimulate the eyes when light cannot. In a similar way, children with ASD and blunted sensory perception may engage in sensory-seeking behaviors such as staring at lights, sniffing or licking objects, flapping and spinning, or in extreme cases self-injurious behavior—anything to supply the brain with detectable input that rises above the child's elevated threshold for perception.

In addition to satisfying a craving for sensory input, stereotypies such as flapping or spinning can also reduce stress. We all "jump for joy" when happy, or "bang our heads against the wall" when frustrated. Research has shown that these types of behavior actually reduce heart rate. Some children with ASD take sensory-seeking to extremes, to the point of producing significant self-injury. One theory is that such extreme behavior serves as a releaser of endorphins (the body's own narcotics), creating a pleasurable sensation similar to a runner's high.

Conversely, a child with a *decreased* sensory threshold is predisposed to sensory overload. Ordinary stimuli may be perceived as unbearably intense. A woolen sweater may feel like a cloak of nails. Children with hypersensitivity to sound may panic during fire drills or refuse to use public toilets because the flush is too loud. Taking a child with a decreased sensory threshold to the mall or a loud party can trigger agitation and a full-scale meltdown.

Tying It All Together

As you can see, the same behavioral symptom often can be traced to different underlying deficits or combination of deficits (Figure 12.8). The objective is to help your child stay out of the center of the circle, where the worst symptoms (destructive and self-injurious behavior) lie.

Now that I've shown you the big picture, let's go back to the children I described at the beginning of this chapter, to try to figure out what went wrong and how we can help.

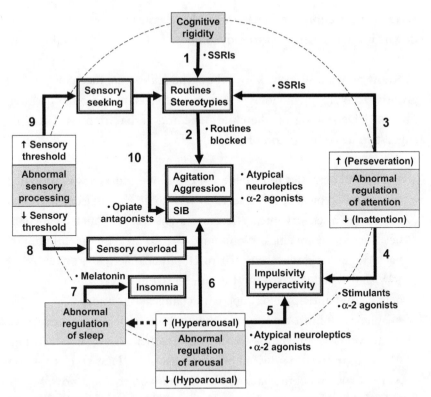

Figure 12.8 Interaction of Deficits and Behaviors in ASD, Part VI: Overview
Different underlying deficits, or combinations of deficits, frequently give rise to behaviors that outwardly appear the same. It's important to reason backward from the observed behavior to try to deduce the underlying factors that gave rise to it.

Routines and Stereotypies

Let's go back and look at Nate, in the first vignette. As a toddler, Nate's cognitive rigidity (path 1), hyperfocused behavior (path 3), and increased sensory threshold (path 9) gave rise to a behavior pattern characterized by insistence on routines, sensory-seeking behaviors, and physical stereotypies. As Nate transitioned from preschool to elementary school, many of his outwardly visible symptoms, such as mouthing and licking of nonfood items or spontaneous flapping and running in circles, slowly faded. However, his underlying neurobiological patterns continued to express themselves in new and more complex ways—starting with hoarding ketchup bottles and moving on from there to perfectionistic behavior in the classroom and intense melt-downs if the teacher tried to move him on before he was ready (pathway 2).

Knowing what we now know about the underlying mechanisms that give rise to Nate's behavior, what can we offer Nate and other children like him? Depending on the child's age and verbal abilities, I usually suggest some combination of the following:

- Physical activities to provide sensory input and as a way of letting off steam. Typically, these services will come through occupational therapy, in a sensory integration format, as well as nonmedical channels such as gymnastics, swimming, martial arts, therapeutic horseback riding, or similar semistructured physical activities.
- Visual schedules (see the Resource List) and verbal warnings, to help a child anticipate or cope with changes in routine.
- When you must transition a child before he or she is ready, place your emphasis on what is coming next, rather than simply insisting, "You've got to stop now." If possible, also say, "First you have to do X, then you can come back to finish what you're doing now."
- Social Stories on the theme of what to do when something unexpected occurs (or how to handle the disappointment when an eagerly anticipated event fails to occur). As part of this process, I suggest that parents prepare three "Surprise" cards for the child. One side can have a broken dish, lightning bolts, or some other visual metaphor. On the other side, the parent or child can draw a picture or write a few words to describe what the surprise was and how the child handled it. The child gets three Surprise cards each day and "plays" one whenever an unexpected event occurs. In this way, the parents have actually created a new ritual: the break in daily routine (missing the bus, spilling one's milk, cancellation of a trip to the zoo, or whatever) is enclosed inside another, larger routine (filling out the card). Filling out the Surprise card partially defuses the stress of the break in routine itself. The completed cards go into a three-ring notebook and become part of the child's library of past events that he or she can refer to in the future. Often it's not the surprise itself that's the problem. Rather, it's not knowing what to do next. So keeping a library of events on file serves as a way to prepare the child

for the next surprise. It also serves as a way of helping the child to relive his or her past successes.

• Cognitive-behavioral techniques (deep breathing, counting to ten, mental imagery) to help a child cope with stress in the moment.

• Teach the child how to identify his or her own stress level, label it, and ask for a break. I especially like the Incredible 5-Point Scale for this purpose (see the Resource List), accompanied by giving the child three "Take a Break" cards each morning. If the child senses that he or she is only one step away from a red alert, then the child can play a Take a Break card, for access to the occupational therapy gym or some other area where he or she can let off steam, instead of having a meltdown. Like the Surprise cards, these Take a Break cards can be saved in a book to help the child begin to anticipate what will give him or her stress the next time. Your goal is to enable your child to express his or her feelings with words, particularly in times of stress. There are several nice books for children with anxiety (see the Resource List for references on anxiety, visual schedules, and Social Stories).

• Medication. If you saw the movie *Aviator,* you have an idea of what obsessive-compulsive disorder (OCD) looks like. Howard Hughes (played by Leonardo DiCaprio in the film) struggles with intrusive thoughts and repetitive behaviors, which he is powerless to control—even though he wants to stop. Children with ASD also have repetitive thoughts and behaviors, but—unlike people with OCD—they don't seem to be particularly bothered by these thoughts and behaviors, and have no apparent desire to stop. Even though Nate doesn't know any better, however, you and I can see that his perfectionism, anxiety, and inflexibility are preventing him from reaching his full potential. This rigidity is part of Nate's basic biology. Social Stories and visual schedules can be of some help, but adding medication to the mix can be a godsend for Nate and other children in his situation. The medication of choice is a selective serotonin reuptake inhibitor (SSRI).* In brief, the SSRIs magnify the effect of the body's own serotonin on those portions of the brain that are regulated by this neurotransmitter. The oldest of all the SSRIs is fluoxetine (the

---

* However, two recent studies have cast doubt on the utility of SSRIs in children on the spectrum. Additional research will be needed to clarify this issue, since many clinicians—myself among them—continue to rely on these agents.

original brand was Prozac; it's now available as a generic, which works equally well). There are several SSRIs on the market. Sometimes a child will respond to one SSRI better than another, but there are virtually no head-to-head studies of one SSRI against another in children with ASD to guide us. Rather, it's a matter of clinical experience. SSRIs loosen the grip of cognitive rigidity (pathway 1) and hyperattentive behavior (pathway 3). Unexpected breaks in routine or being prevented from completing a ritual, which previously would have triggered a full-scale meltdown, are now tolerated with less stress. Perfectionism becomes less of a problem. Nathan responded dramatically to fluoxetine; his hoarding behavior, anxiety, and perfectionism dwindled to manageable proportions, and he was overall a happier little boy. "Doctor, you have given our child his life back," Nathan's mom and dad reported.

Impulsivity Plus Compulsivity

If Nate's "hour hand" is pointed to twelve on our hypothetical clock, then Isabel's is pointed squarely at the three. Her regulatory mechanism for attention is off-kilter—at times she's overfocused and compulsive, just like Nate. At other times, she's underfocused hyperactive, and impulsive, like a child with ADHD. Like going from fever to chills during a bout of the flu, Isabel's attention span is veering between two extremes. We can help Isabel by simplifying her immediate environment so that she does not become either distracted by or overfocused on irrelevant details. We can also give her short, clear verbal instructions, augmented by a visual schedule. But that still leaves her wasting a lot of time and energy that could be better spent on more productive activities. If all she had was impulsivity, we'd be tempted to try a stimulant such as methylphenidate or dextroamphetamine (the mainstays of treatment for children with ADHD), and in fact, stimulants can probably help Isabel. However, stimulants can make compulsive behavior worse. So I generally start an SSRI first in children like Isabel, to put a "safety net" under them and keep their compulsive behaviors from getting out of control; *then* I add a stimulant to control the hyperactivity. It's not an FDA-studied or -approved combination, but my colleagues and I use it regularly to address the combination of impulsive and compulsive behavior often seen in children on the spectrum. As an alternative to stimulants, I often use guanfacine, which works by a different biological pathway, and does not aggravate anxiety or cognitive rigidity. (See Appendix IV.)

Agitation, Aggression, and Self-Injurious Behavior

This triad of behavior, at the center of Figures 12.4–12.8, is probably the most fearsome aspect of ASD—and, as you can see, there are lots of pathways by which a child might reach this unfortunate bull's-eye. Figuring out why a given child is experiencing agitated or self-injurious behavior, therefore, can take a bit of sleuthing.

We've already discussed one path: the child with rigid, compulsive behaviors, who becomes agitated when prevented from completing his or her rituals. Far more challenging are children like Calvin, whose fight-or-flight mechanism is on a hair trigger. Children who are innately hyperarousable can suddenly switch from calm to agitated after minimal external provocation. "We feel like we're walking on eggs," the parents of such children often say. And the child's siblings often retreat in fear, never knowing when their brother or sister with ASD and hyperarousability is going to lash out at them next.

Sometimes aggression and self-injurious behavior are learned behaviors. We touched on this in our discussion of ABA. Suppose the parent places a demand on the child, and—purely out of frustration—the child slaps himself in the face. Horrified, the parent backs off. Unfortunately, the parent has just reinforced a behavior—self-hitting—that started out as a purely reflexive response on the child's part. If the parent does this enough times, the child's self-injurious behavior will take on a life of its own, escalating in frequency and intensity as the child discovers how useful it is as a way to avoid demands. Likewise, if the child engages in SIB after being told no or after being denied access to a preferred object (say, the TV remote) and the parent caves in, rescinding the no or giving the child the desired object, the parent has just increased the likelihood that the child will engage in SIB again in the future.

Much of the time, however, aggression and self-injurious behavior do not fall cleanly into just one category (biologically driven or learned). The child with an intrinsically defective arousal mechanism is more likely to manifest disruptive behavior than a child whose ability to regulate his or her emotional state is intact. The more often a child with defective regulation of arousal manifests disruptive behavior, the greater the likelihood that—sooner or later—his or her parents will inadvertently reinforce that behavior. It doesn't take long under such circumstances for disruptive behavior to become routine—as a means of escaping tasks or gaining access to preferred objects—on top of its original, purely biological foundation.

The way to deal disruptive and self-injurious behavior is to identify any consistent antecedents (demands being placed on the child, desire for an object, being told no, etc.) and document the consequences that follow. Does the child succeed in getting what he wants or escaping from the task? Working with a behavior analyst, it should be possible to answer these questions, and stop unwittingly reinforcing the child's disruptive behaviors. Often, however, there is an irreducible minimum of disruptive behavior that just can't be made to go away through behavioral measures. Remember, you may be in this predicament in the first place because your child is intrinsically hyperarousable. Once you reach this conclusion, medication becomes a reasonable consideration. The first-line medications for disruptive, agitated behavior are the atypical neuroleptics (so named because they differ in certain ways from older neuroleptic drugs). Risperidone is the first atypical neuroleptic to be approved specifically for the treatment of disruptive behavior in children with ASD. Atypical neuroleptics have significant side effects, including weight gain and the risk of triggering diabetes or involuntary movements. For this reason, I often try guanfacine first. However, for children whose agitation, aggression, and self-injurious behavior are severe, atypical neuroleptics are a necessary fact of life— at least until something better comes along.

Insomnia

If your child takes more than thirty minutes to fall asleep, or if your child has frequent night wakings, he or she may have a biologically based sleep disorder. The treatment of choice is a trial of melatonin. In the United States, melatonin is classified as a supplement rather than a drug, so it falls outside of FDA regulations for safety and efficacy. However, there is a reasonable base of well-conducted scientific research in support of melatonin, typically at a dose of 1 to 3 mg thirty minutes before bedtime. Melatonin comes as tablets, capsules, and drops (flavored and unflavored). It's probably okay to repeat a dose if your child wakes up in the middle of the night (there's also a long-acting form available). If your child does not have a melatonin deficiency, then giving melatonin probably won't make any difference, and you can stop. (It's not a sedative; it just signals the body that it's time to go to sleep.)

If melatonin doesn't work, I sometimes use clonidine because of its mildly sedating properties. Like guanfacine (which we mentioned earlier), clonidine also down-regulates hyperactivity and agitation, so it may be particularly helpful in the child with insomnia plus these daytime behaviors. See Appendix IV for details on both of these drugs.

Understandably, a child who cannot fall asleep may not stay in bed. A toddler can be confined to a crib, but an agile three-year-old is harder to restrain. For the sake of their child's safety as well as for household quiet, parents often choose to bring the child into bed with them. Unfortunately, "just this one time" soon becomes the norm. We saw this with Marc. Now the child's biologically disordered sleep pattern has been compounded by well-intentioned but ultimately self-defeating parental behavior. Sometimes Mom and child are in the master bed and Dad is sleeping in another room or on the living room sofa. There are some marital dimensions to this, which we'll talk about in Part III. For now, let's just talk about the behavioral piece of things.

- First, you may need to revise your expectations. You cannot make your child sleep. Instead of trying to have your child asleep by a particular hour, set a more realistic goal of having your child *stay in his or her room no matter what,* after a certain hour of the evening.
- Establish a pre-bedtime ritual that includes calming activities such as a bath, stories, or a snack, just as you might do for a child with typical development. Avoid highly stimulating activities such as roughhousing or video games. Stick to a schedule so that the entire sequence of activities, culminating with going to bed, becomes fixed in the child's mind as a nightly ritual. If your child is old enough to understand visual schedules, record the routine in a series of photographs and create a storyboard or a book of picture cards. As you go through the routine each night, check off each event with a pencil or sticker. The next-to-last picture might be of your child asleep in his

or her own bed, and the very last one might show everyone else in the family asleep in their own beds. This not only provides an image of how things are supposed to be but also assures the child that the other family members are still present, each in their own bed. (The children's classic *Goodnight Moon* by Margaret Wise Brown does a wonderful job at this.)

• Install an alarm on your child's bedroom door (search the Web for "door alarms," or purchase one through a travel supply store). If your child triggers the alarm, return him or her to bed with little or no conversation. Get as loud an alarm as you can stand. In addition to alerting you, the noise may serve as an aversive stimulus to your child. One of my families had the inspired idea of hanging a large red STOP sign on the inside of their child's bedroom door (you can buy genuine Department of Transportation–approved highway signs, just like the real ones, on the Web; just search on "DOT-approved highway signs"). Being visually oriented and very attentive to rules, the child obeyed the sign and learned to remain in his room.

• Consider giving your child low-stimulus toys in bed, such as storybooks or quiet toys—not electronic action games. Remember, your goal is to get your child to stay in bed, not make him or her sleep. Access to quiet toys will probably not interfere with sleep and will certainly make staying in bed easier. Isn't this what you would want for yourself if you had insomnia?

• At first you may need to continue sleeping with your child, but do so *in the child's bedroom*. Put a mattress for yourself on the floor next to the child's bed. Provide a parental presence but as little attention as possible. Minimize your interaction with the child, even turning your back and trying to go to sleep. If you have a spouse or partner, take turns sleeping in the child's bedroom. Both parents need to be involved in order to make the program work. This may also be a chance for both parents to start getting used to having their own bedroom back. Over a period of several nights, move your mattress farther away from the child's bed until it's just inside the doorway to the child's room. The next step is to move into the hall right outside your child's room. Continue using the door alarm. If the child tries to leave the room, put him or her back in bed immediately. Keep this up until the child stops trying to leave the room.

Hang in there; your child will try very hard to draw you back into your old behavior pattern. Remember what we said in an earlier chapter about the extinction burst.

Even for parents of typically developing children with sleep problems, this can be a trying period, with conflict arising out of differences in expectations and management styles combining with fatigue, anger, anxiety, and depression. You might want to get some professional help from a family or behavior therapist who can work to harmonize your efforts while helping you deal with your own stress.

Finally, be prepared for the fact that even after you have gotten your child to stay in his or her room after a certain hour, your child may still wake up at all hours of the night. Address this using the same tactics and principles that I've outlined above, gradually reducing your presence and involvement over time. You can't make your child sleep, but you can avoid reinforcing the undesired behaviors caused by disordered sleep.

Sensory-Seeking/Sensory-Avoidant Behavior

There is no drug available at this time capable of modifying a child's sensory threshold in the way that we can modify attention, cognitive rigidity, or arousability. Intervention, therefore, is strictly symptomatic, and leans heavily on occupational therapy's premise of finding the "just right" level of sensory input for any given child, as we discussed in Chapter 11. This may mean devising a sensory diet that includes stimuli that the child finds enjoyable while at the same time redirecting the child's sensory-seeking activity into socially acceptable forms (using a safe toy to chew on, for example, rather than chewing on other people). If sensory seeking serves as a stress reliever, then the child's school program may build in "movement breaks," permitting the child to go to the gym or occupational therapy room for multiple brief periods during the school day. Drugs such as naltrexone that block the action of narcotics (including endorphins) have been used to treat children with severe self-injurious behavior, with mixed results. "Response blocking" sometimes helps. For example, head banging, face slapping, or eye poking may be prevented by a helmet, with a face guard if necessary. One teenage girl I treated many years ago simply could not stop her self-injurious behavior. When we took off her helmet for the physical exam, she plaintively insisted, "Helmet on! Helmet on!" She was aware of her involuntary face slapping and head banging, and wanted the helmet for her own protection.

Alternatively, if a child with a very low sensory threshold (that is, exaggerated perception of sensory input) is placed into a highly stimulating environment, the level of overstimulation can also trigger agitation and in extreme cases SIB. The solution here is to avoid the antecedent. You don't want to take such a child to a loud party, for example. And if you have to go to the mall, give your child a set of noise-canceling earphones so that he or she can block out the excess noise. Soft clothing, low lights, limited stimuli in the classroom, and gentle sensory inputs from an occupational therapist may all help.

Not So Different from Other Children After All

Up to now, we have been focused on the differences between children on the spectrum and children who are neurotypical. As we have seen, children with ASD don't always respond to ordinary behavior management techniques. A child with ASD who is oblivious to the adults in his environment is incapable of noncompliance since he doesn't know what's expected of him in the first place. For similar reasons, time out may have no effect. Happily, as we discussed in Chapter 5, there is a good chance that your child's atypicality will gradually fade. Stereotypies often diminish or disappear, eye contact and speech usually improve, and social skills begin to appear. Eventually the child with ASD begins to manifest some garden-variety behaviors that look just like those of a normally developing but younger child. I've seen many five-year-olds with ASD who are finally developing an awareness of others and suddenly discover the wonderful pleasures of willful disobedience. This is cause for celebration. I'm delighted when a previously nonverbal, disengaged child stares me in the eye and loudly declares, "No!" or when such a child gleefully runs away from me, laughing and looking back to see if I am in pursuit. These behaviors tell me that the child has finally begun to experience the pleasures of normal toddlerhood—even though these behaviors are appearing a couple of years behind schedule. Once the child reaches this stage, it becomes possible to start using the same behavioral techniques that would apply with any other toddler.

Time Out

Recall what I said at the beginning of this chapter: Under normal circumstances, the single most powerful behavior management tool parents have at their disposal is providing or withdrawing their own attention. This is the premise behind time out (TO). After years of hard work to elicit eye contact and social engagement from a child with ASD, it is often difficult for parents to do an about-face and begin using TO as a behavior management tool. All I can say is trust me: In thirty years I've never seen a child with ASD retreat back into his or her shell when parents start using TO. On the contrary, children with ASD become a bit more civilized—just like any other child.

TIME OUT: WHY IT WORKS AND HOW TO DO IT

The essence of time out is withdrawal of your attention. Follow these simple steps:

- Identify a concrete behavior you'd like to end.
- Use a consistent verbal warning ("That's one. That's two. That's three. Time out").
- Don't explain or reprimand. These constitute attention. Attention only reinforces the very behavior you are trying to extinguish. Above all else, don't fall into the habit of saying, "Do you want a time out?" Just count: "One. Two. Three."
- Designate a special location where the child must spend the TO.
- Use a timer (an inexpensive kitchen timer is fine) and train the child to remain in TO until the timer beeps. Multiple brief episodes of TO work best.
- If the child is using disruptive behavior to escape a task, march the child through the task first; *then* put the child into TO. Don't let the child use TO as an escape mechanism.

ⓘ See the Resource List for additional information on time out.

Token Economy

Time out is great for children who need immediate consequences. Eventually, however, the object of life shifts to working for deferred rather than immediate gratification. Once your child understands the elements of rule-based play, such as simple board games, it's time to think about moving on from TO to a token economy as a way of shaping his or her behavior.

A token economy consists of a chart of clearly defined behaviors—desirable and undesirable—for which the child earns or loses points. The behaviors need to be defined in a very concrete way. "Being good" is too vague. "Going five minutes without hitting your sister" is very specific. The child earns and loses points according to the system (the "economy") you have set up—for example, one smiley face for every five-minute interval with no hitting. Notice that we've defined the behavior as "no hitting" rather than "hitting." That way you and your child will focus on what we want him to do (not hit) rather than what we want him not to do (hit). After the child accumulates a specified number of points (stars, stickers, smiley faces) for no hitting, he or she can cash them in for the specified reward (time on the computer, for example).

- The rate of exchange should be very simple at the beginning. For example, if "time on the computer" is the reward the child is working toward, then a one-for-one exchange (five minutes on the computer for every five minutes of no hitting) is a good place to start. Provide the reward as soon as your child has succeeded at not hitting for five minutes. Remember, we're transitioning from the immediate consequences of TO to the deferred framework of a token economy; keep each step in that transition process small. Later, you might show a pie divided into three wedges; now the child would have to earn three smiley faces—one for each wedge—before gaining access to the computer. Eventually, you could lengthen the no-hitting interval to fifteen or thirty minutes, and so on. But we want the child (and you too) to experience some immediate success.

- Be sure to limit access to the reinforcer (the reward) to just what the child has earned via the token economy. That keeps the child motivated. If the reinforcer is access to the computer, then the child should only be granted access to the computer according to how many points he or she has earned. This is probably the single biggest stumbling block for parents. Giving the child extra time on the computer isn't going to work. Rather, the child needs to refrain from hitting (or whatever the defined behavior is) for five minutes; then he or she gets five minutes on the computer. After that, the computer is off limits until the child has earned more time.

• At the beginning, notice that there's no provision for losing points. All we want is to teach the child how the game is played: no hitting for five minutes and the child is rewarded with five minutes of computer time. Once the child has got this under his or her belt, then you need to add "sad face" stickers for hitting. Every time the child hits, you put up a sad face sticker. If the child has already earned a smiley, then put the sad face over the smiley, or some other visual cue to indicate that the child has just lost the time he or she had already earned. One therapist I know uses puzzle pieces instead of stars or tokens: As the child earns points, he or she gets to slowly fill in the puzzle. If the child loses a point, the therapist removes a puzzle piece. When the puzzle is complete, the child gets the reward shown on the puzzle (a trip to the zoo, a toy train, etc.).

• At first, use the chart on a daily basis. Later, as your child becomes more able to defer gratification, you will increase the time frame to a week.

Children with ASD usually respond well to token economy systems: The chart itself is visual, and the rules for earning and losing points are explicit—two features that appeal to children with ASD.

See the Resource List for additional information on token economies. Go to the Internet and enter "custom jigsaw puzzle" for sites where you can order your own puzzles, customized to show your child's favorite objects or activities.

Summing Up

It's impossible in one chapter, or even an entire book, to give you a complete summary of behavior management and psychopharmacology for children with ASD. What I've tried to do is give you a brief overview of the relationship between the underlying biological deficits and the most common and most troublesome behaviors expressed by children on the spectrum. Even though this treatment has necessarily been limited, I hope you have a basic grasp of the fundamentals, so you will be able to look beneath the surface of any particular behavior and try to analyze where that behavior is coming from.

If only my patients—your children—could tell me what's bothering them! So often, they can't; all they know how to do is act out. I hope some of the insights I've provided in this chapter will enable you to become a bit better at deciphering your child's behavior and at helping your child up the social learning curve to achieve his or her full potential. Be sure to see the Resource List and Appendix IV for additional information on behavior management and psychoactive medications.

Chapter 13

Going to School

Services from birth to age thirty-six months are provided through Early Intervention, and from three to five by preschool special education. At five, children age out of these services and transition to public school. Placement varies—either a self-contained autistic support classroom, a "blended" program (spending part of each day with typically developing peers and the rest in a special-needs setting), or a regular education setting with their typically developing peers. Classroom variables include class size (smaller is better), staff-to-pupil ratio (higher is better), and communication methods within the classroom (oral, picture exchange, signing), as well as intangibles such as the eagerness of the staff to take on a child with challenges and the skill level of the staff. Child variables include the degree of atypicality, intellectual abilities, communication skills, and the presence of complicating behaviors, such as anxiety, agitation, impulsivity, or self-injury. There are three additional factors for parents to consider that don't always make it into the discussion: self-esteem, neurologic maturation, and behavior management.

Self-Esteem

Self-esteem is the emotional "fuel" that enables a child to achieve his or her best. Self-esteem, in turn, comes from the experience of overcoming modest hurdles; there's nothing quite so good for one's self esteem as being able to say, "Look! I did it!" The parents' job is to identify a classroom where their child can compete successfully with the other children in the room. Everyone can't be in the middle of the pack. Someone is always going to be first, and someone is always going to be bringing up the rear. But no one should be so far ahead or so far behind that he or she is *always* first or *always* last. Putting a child in a situation where insufficient demands are made and putting a child in a situation where the demands are impossibly high are both destructive to a child's self-esteem.

Neurologic Maturation

Recall our discussion in Chapter 5 of the natural history of ASD. With each passing year, some of your child's atypicality is going to fade. Social challenges that may be insurmountable one year become achievable the next—not just because of therapy services but also because of neurologic maturation. This is why I often suggest that parents consider giving their child with ASD an extra year in the preschool special education setting before stepping onto the escalator of the public school system. Your five-year-old with ASD may be great at rote tasks such as reading and arithmetic, but I don't want to see your son or daughter "fail" playground, cafeteria, bathroom, and school bus. Although not listed on your child's report card, these unofficial "classes" will determine how well your child does in the long run. I'm also thinking about high school, and the academic and social demands your child will face at that time. Sight-word reading and answering concrete *wh* questions are one matter; reading for inference and being able to converse with peers are something else altogether. It may be hard to imagine your five-year-old as a high school freshman, but part of my job is to help you take the long view. Remember what I said earlier: Your job is to see the whole elephant, not just the problems of the moment. The child study team advising you on your child's readiness for kindergarten does not think about what will happen when your child reaches high school. But you need to. Even though your five-year-old may pass all the academic readiness tests for kindergarten, giving your child an extra year of neurologic maturation before moving into public school will pay huge dividends ten years from now.

Behavior Management

Every single child with ASD needs a behavior management plan. Unfortunately, many school systems seem to write behavior management plans just for children with disruptive behavior, such as aggression, self-injury, property destruction, and tantrums (collectively referred to as *externalizing behaviors,* because they are externally visible). Equally important is to have a behavior management plan to address anxiety, perfectionism, and cognitive rigidity (internalizing behaviors, which, as the name suggests, are not always visible on the outside). Children with internalizing behavior are not disruptive to classroom routine, which is why they often do not get the behavioral supports they need until they become so stressed that they begin to manifest externalizing behavior. It would be much better to provide assistance early on, before that threshold is crossed. (My hunch is that girls on the spectrum are at greater risk than boys for having unaddressed internalizing behavior.)

Your child's classroom needs to provide appropriate guidance for your child, at an appropriate stimulus level, with immediate, appropriate responses from staff. If your child is exhibiting disruptive, noncompliant, or agitated behavior, is this because the classroom is too stimulating, because the demands on your child exceed his or her abilities, or perhaps because your child has mastered the art of using disruptive behavior as an escape mechanism? If your child is anxious, perfectionistic, or rigid about routines, do the staff take this into account, giving your child advance notice of transitions and reassuring your child that mistakes are just another part of learning? Does your child's individualized education program (IEP) include the option for your child to take "stress breaks"? I often suggest that children with ASD be issued three Take a Break cards each day and that they be permitted to play these one at a time over the course of the day. A Take a Break card would entitle the child access to a quiet area, or perhaps the occupational therapy gym. The flip side of the coin is that the child is expected to remain in class and toe the line at other times. Giving the child some ownership over when he or she can take a break is one step toward enabling the child to regulate his or her own behavior. The Incredible 5-Point Scale (see the Resource List for Chapter 12) or a similar technique is useful as an adjunct to the Take a Break cards, since it teaches the child how to recognize and label his or her stress level.

We can't describe all possible classroom variations here. Instead, we'll look at two settings: a self-contained autistic support program based on the TEACCH model, and a "split" program, part-time in a typical setting with supports and part-time in a special-needs environment. These will give you a flavor of some of the options that may be available when your child gets to school. For additional information, see the Resource List.

Treatment and Education of Autistic and Related Communication-Handicapped Children (TEACCH)

Kevin

Kevin was the most severely impacted of the three children you met in Chapter 1, with both autism and mental retardation. When Kevin transitioned into public school, he was enrolled full-time in an autistic support class. Each area of Kevin's classroom is color-coded (the sink area is blue, the play area is green, etc.), there are pathways laid out as brightly colored footprints painted on the floor, and there is a large picture schedule up on the wall, with symbols for different activities (cubby, circle time, break, etc.). Each child has a desk, but instead of facing forward in the middle of the room, the desks are arranged around the perimeter of the room, turned toward the wall, and set off from one another by cubicle dividers. This is done to reduce visual distraction. To the left of each desk is a plastic bin, of the type used to store laundry or children's toys.

When we enter the room, we see Kevin plus five other children, a teacher, and two assistant teachers—a two-to-one student-teacher ratio and a total class size of six. The teacher has all of the children seated at a semicircular table at the front of the room, assembling a Halloween skeleton. One at a time, each child picks up a cardboard bone. "Kevin," the teacher calls out enthusiastically, "you got the *leg*. Can you show me your *leg*?" Kevin gives no response, so one of the aides guides him, hand-over-hand, to point to his leg. Then the aide guides Kevin to the front of the room, where he pins the leg onto the slowly growing skeleton. The game goes around the circle until all the children have had a turn and all the pieces are used up. "Okay! Work time!" the teacher calls out. Each child returns to his or her desk. Kevin checks the bin to the left of his desk, where he finds colored paper marked with geometric shapes, child's scissors, a square of heavy cardboard, and paste, which his teacher has placed in the bin as a visual prompt. He proceeds to cut out the shapes and paste them to the cardboard. As Kevin is working on his art project, the teacher places a washcloth in his bin; this will serve as Kevin's next prompt. When Kevin finishes his art work, he deposits the completed cardboard into the bin and takes the washcloth to the sink, where he washes his hands. After washing his hands, he returns to his desk and checks the bin a third time. He finds a toy locomotive waiting for him. He brings the locomotive to the train table and takes a well-earned break.

Darryl

Darryl's classroom is down the hall. Darryl's ASD is not quite as severe as Kevin's (as you will recall, Darryl's developmental diagnosis is PDD-NOS), and his level of general intelligence is higher than Kevin's (Kevin has mental retardation in addition to autism). The first thing we notice is that Darryl's classroom is slightly bigger. (Kevin's room is small by design, since too much space leads the children to wander.) As in Kevin's room, each child's desk is facing the wall. In contrast to Kevin's class, where the tasks are usually in a bin right next to each child's desk, in Darryl's classroom, the work areas are spread out. And instead of using objects (washcloths, construction paper, etc.) as prompts, the children in Darryl's classroom rely on pictures, symbols, or printed cues. Taped to the wall over Darryl's desk is a vertical strip of Velcro, with half a dozen small square cards attached. Each card displays a stick-figure illustration and the corresponding printed text: *Work with Teacher, Work Alone, Lunch, Group, Break, Playground, Speech, Goodbye* (dismissal for the day). (As children get older, the symbols or pictures get smaller and the printed words get bigger. In the higher grades, printed word lists alone will suffice, and the child often prints out his or her list for the day on the computer. In keeping with the children's improved social and attending skills, the desks in the upper grades are oriented in the traditional fashion, facing the front of the room.)

Darryl peels off the first card; it's a capital letter *H*. He takes the square over to a rack of cubbies, removes a plastic box from the cubby labeled *H,* takes the box back to his desk, opens it up, and starts working on the word-matching worksheet inside. When he's done, he returns the box to its cubby, goes back to his desk, and peels off the second card: a picture of his language teacher. He walks across the room to the language area, presents his teacher with the card, and sits down. The two of them work for fifteen minutes on a new vocabulary word. When done, Darryl returns to his desk for the third card: *snack*. Over the course of the day, he works through his task list in this fashion. All of the other children are equally busy. What's amazing to watch, in fact, is half a dozen children each quietly moving about the room, completing their assignments. If a child does go off-task, a teacher merely has to say "Go check your schedule," and the child is back on track.

Another difference between Darryl's room and Kevin's: In Darryl's room, the pathways on the floor are laid out with strips of tape rather than painted footprints—a subtle indication of the greater ability of the children in Darryl's class to appreciate the abstract meaning of a line, rather than requiring a concrete representation of footprints.

Most of the aspects of Kevin's and Darryl's classrooms are based on the TEACCH curriculum. TEACCH was devised in the late 1960s by Eric Schopler, PhD, a developmental psychologist at the University of North Carolina. TEACCH incorporates methods from many different theoretical orientations. In younger or more severely impacted children, TEACCH uses ABA techniques (antecedent, behavior, and consequence). In a break from pure behaviorism, however, TEACCH is also guided by *cognitive–social learning theory*. According to cognitive–social learning theory, the *meaning* a child attaches to a given behavior is just as important as the antecedents and consequences of that behavior: Simply shaping the child's behavior by manipulating the consequences of that behavior is not enough. How the child *feels* and what the child *thinks* are also important: "One's understanding of a situation [has] as much of an impact on behavior as rewards or punishments," Schopler wrote. TEACCH incorporates bits and pieces from a range of therapeutic methods, including elements of natural environment training, pivotal response training, DIR (floor time), and social skills groups. (Actually, it would be more correct to say that NET, PRT, DIR, and social skills groups each incorporate bits of TEACCH, since TEACCH pioneered most of these other methods.)

TEACCH is mercifully free of the doctrinaire or inflated claims of "cure" that mark so many other therapy programs. TEACCH acknowledges the biological basis of ASD, the "tremendous individual differences" among individuals with ASD, and the central role that IQ plays in these differences. Schopler and his colleagues concluded early on that most children with autism would not recover. These assumptions—that autism has a biological cause, that it is not curable, and that IQ can affect outcome—lie at the core of the TEACCH program. While these assumptions may at first seem defeatist, they are actually liberating, since goals can now be stated in terms of what is best for the child rather than in terms of measuring up to some societal standard or adhering strictly to the "party line" of one particular therapy approach. As Schopler and colleagues wrote in 2006:

> Because the organically-based problems that define ASD are not totally reversible, we do not take "being normal" as the goal of our educational and therapeutic efforts. Rather, the long-term goal of the TEACCH program is for the individual with ASD to fit as comfortably and effectively as possible into our culture as an adult...given their individual circumstances.

Bear in mind that Schopler created TEACCH at a time when the definition of autism was restricted to children with severe disability. Thus, much of TEACCH applies to what we would today refer to as children with low-functioning ASD: moderate to severe atypicality, plus some degree of global cognitive delay. As we discussed in Chapter 5, the long-term prognosis for children with these characteristics is generally for lifelong expression of atypicality and significant functional limitation.

Since TEACCH is flexible enough to adapt to different ages and levels of ability, there is no one "TEACCH method," but there are certain qualities that characterize every TEACCH program:

- *Structured therapy environment.* The physical layout of the classroom and the teacher's instructional method should enable the child always to know where to be and what to do for how long, and it should also provide cues for the child as to what comes next.
  - Based on the assumption that children with ASD are much stronger as visual learners than as auditory learners, TEACCH makes heavy use of visual cues to make the environment more comprehensible to the child. Charts, lists, color-coded materials, colored floor mats, and tape on the floor marking areas for specific activities can help the adult guide the child's behavior. The child can learn, for example, to start each day at his or her cubby and return to the cubby after completing each task, where there might be color-coded items linked to upcoming tasks displayed on a chart.
  - Regular routines incorporate daily schedules of assigned tasks at assigned locations—a "work/activity system," in Schopler's terminology.
  - Multimodal language intervention emphasizes visual modalities in addition to orally based methods. For example, with the youngest or most severely affected children, objects are used to signify activities. The washcloth in Kevin's cubby, for instance, functioned as his signal to go wash his hands. Once a child masters the direct connection between an object and an activity, the object is replaced with a picture and ultimately the printed word, all aided by verbal prompting.
- *Capitalize on each child's strengths and interests.*
  - With younger or more severely atypical children who are obsessed with a particular activity, the adult makes that activity the focus of the therapeutic interaction, as would happen in NET, PRT, or DIR. Similarly, the adult may also playfully sabotage the child's stereotypical behavior in order to engage the child's attention.

- With older or less severely affected children, social skills training focuses on "making play and socializing enjoyable...rather than teaching specific social behaviors that might make an individual appear more 'normal.' If this important goal is accomplished, then specific behaviors such as eye contact and smiling may follow, if they are truly essential for meaningful interactions." Here we see the TEACCH philosophy in action: The goal of TEACCH is not to get the child to "pass" as normal by society's standards. Rather, the goal is to teach the child how to enjoy social interaction.

In 1978, the legislature of North Carolina adopted TEACCH as the official form of publicly funded education for children with ASD statewide. Unless you live in North Carolina, you may be hard-pressed to find an official TEACCH classroom for your child. However, most of the techniques developed by TEACCH have percolated out to autistic support classes across the country.

(i) See the Resource List for additional information on educational approaches in ASD.

Split Programming

Remember Teddy, whom we met in Chapter 1 and saw again in Chapter 5? He was referred to me by his first-grade guidance counselor because of unusual behaviors, including perseveration on odd topics, variable eye contact, odd speech inflection, and limited social awareness. He was genuinely eager to please his teachers, and he wanted to engage with peers, but he struggled with the unwritten rules of social interaction, going off on monologues about the Pennsylvania Railroad or the *Titanic*, with no inkling that he was losing his conversational partner. (This is what I meant earlier in this chapter when I referred to "failing playground.") We diagnosed Teddy with Asperger syndrome. He had normal general intelligence, and excellent powers of memorization, which enabled him to attend math and reading class with his typically developing peers. In the regular classroom, Teddy received a variety of modifications and supports: He was seated in the front row, close to the teacher but away from the window (to minimize distraction); his teacher also made frequent use of visual and verbal cueing to keep Teddy on task. Initially daily, and then weekly, Teddy received a visual schedule for all anticipated activities, with verbal and pictorial explanations of any anticipated breaks in routine (special assemblies, field trips, etc.). He also had a stress and behavior management plan in place, with three Take a Break cards that he was allowed to use each day for access to a quiet room or the occupational therapy gym when he became overly anxious. He was permitted to take tests in a quiet room. Finally, a spiral-bound notebook went back and forth from teacher to parents every day, with notes on Teddy's day. In addition to these supports in the regular classroom, Teddy went for speech/language therapy (addressing pragmatic skills such as eye contact, topic maintenance, and expressing interest in what the other child has to say) and social skills training (cooperation, turn taking, perspective taking, winning and losing, etc.). Finally, he was scheduled for monthly meetings with the school guidance counselor to monitor his self-esteem, stress level, and coping strategies proactively, instead of waiting for some kind of problem to erupt. Teddy has done well with this combination of supports in both a mainstreamed and a special-ed setting. He looks forward to school eagerly, and is proud of his accomplishments.

Summing Up

The single most important objective when mapping your child's educational path is his or her self-esteem, which comes from surmounting reasonable challenges.

More likely than not, your child will have significant discrepancies across, and sometimes within, skill areas. Your challenge, and that of your child's educators, is to find the right mix of services that mesh with your child's range of cognitive, social, and physical skills. It's not that one setting is "better" than another in an absolute sense. Rather, it depends upon the "fit" between the program and the child—how well the program sets up reasonable challenges for your child and helps him or her surmount them. If your child is eager to go to school each day—not bored because the work is too easy, and not frustrated and acting out or anxious because the work is too hard—that's a good litmus test of the appropriateness of your child's classroom placement.

All children with ASD need a behavior management plan. Children with externalizing behaviors are hard to ignore; they're literally in the teacher's face, and are usually provided with some kind of behavioral intervention. Internalizing behaviors can be just as limiting to your child's progress as externalizing behaviors but may be harder to spot.

Do not be in a hurry to get your child into first grade. When deciding about that extra twelve months in preschool or kindergarten, place at least as much weight on your child's social skills as on his or her academic abilities. An extra twelve months for neurologic maturation at the outset of your child's educational career will pay handsome dividends ten or twenty years from now.

Chapter 14

Sense and Nonsense in the Treatment of ASD

I know I have not made all the best choices for our loved one with autism over the years, but at least I can pass on some words of advice based on trial and error and years of observation to you who are just starting out. Has anyone ever reported a child "recovering" completely from autism using extreme and dangerous methods such as chelation and transdermal whatever? All I have ever heard of is families dosing their children with chemicals they would never take themselves, and that there is slight improvement. Of course, we all see improvement over time with many types of interventions and attention paid to our children and their needs. Please stop doing this to your kids! These methods wouldn't be allowed on prisoners! You are using doctors who are biased towards finding the results you want in order to perpetuate this system and keep themselves in business.... Autism can make you feel desperate at times, but don't get so desperate to "fix" the situation that you end up treating a human child as a test tube. Please take a deep breath and realize what you are doing.

—*Parent of an adult child with ASD*

Right now you may be swimming in information—from friends, relatives, and most of all the Internet. Everywhere you turn, you read about some wonderful form of therapy that has cured someone's lucky child of autism. Your job is to take a hard look at these therapies and prioritize your resources. Every dollar that you spend on one therapy is a dollar less that you can spend somewhere else. Even if money is no object, there are still only twenty-four hours in the day and seven days in the week. Sooner or later you will reach a point where you cannot squeeze anything else into your child's schedule. What's worth keeping, and what can you drop—or avoid in the first place?

Protecting Your Child, and Your Pocketbook

Apply the following guidelines to *all* of your child's therapies, including traditional as well as complementary and alternative therapies. By holding all therapies to the same standard, you will be able to form your own conclusions about which therapies are worth trying and which are too risky or just too far out to impose on your child.

Follow the Money
Who is promoting the therapy you are considering, other than the people who make their living selling it and parents who have already spent a lot of money on it for their own child? The answer to this one question is as informative as all the scientific ways of evaluating a therapy combined. Legitimate therapies are promoted by a wide range of professionals—including many who don't make a nickel from providing such therapies themselves. There's nothing wrong with making money by providing a service. But if the *only* people promoting a particular form of therapy are the providers and consumers of that therapy, I'd be extremely cautious if I were you.

Examine the Evidence
Don't be satisfied until you've seen hard facts to confirm that the improvement claimed on behalf of a therapy is not due to the natural history of ASD, luck, observer bias, or the placebo effect—any of which can make worthless "treatments" look like miracle cures.

Before talking about what evidence *is,* let's be clear about what evidence *isn't*:

- *Chance observations are not evidence.* As we pointed out in Chapters 3 and 4, chance observations are useful as the basis for future research, to see if they hold up to scrutiny, but they do not constitute evidence in and of themselves. The stampede to treat ASD with injections of secretin (a pancreatic hormone) was launched by a chance observation in three children. Properly performed research involving hundreds of children has failed to confirm the original chance observation.
- *Testimonials are not evidence.* Don't be swayed by heartwarming stories—you want hard facts. For example: Many parents swear by the gluten-free/casein-free (GF/CF) diet, but as of this moment there are no randomized controlled trials to show that children on the GF/CF diet improve faster or more often than children on a regular diet.
- *Sworn testimony in a court of law is not evidence in the scientific sense.* Testimony under oath is still just one person's assertion as to what is true.
- *Court rulings are not evidence.* In a civil trial (for example, in Vaccine Court), the aggrieved party needs only to establish that a preponderance of evidence (50 percent plus a feather, as the saying goes) is in their favor. Suppose the pilot of the next plane you boarded told you that your chances of landing safely were 50 percent plus a feather. I'd want a little more assurance of safe outcome than that, wouldn't you? The law accepts this standard in civil trials because of society's need to reach closure; it is not the same as establishing scientific truth. (The legal standard in criminal cases is "beyond a shadow of a doubt," but that's not where most autism cases are heard.)
- *Coincidence is not evidence.* The fact that a child got better after being in therapy does not prove that he or she got better *because of* therapy. Put a child with ASD into *any* long-term therapy, and—measured over a time span of months to years—some degree of improvement is almost bound to occur, simply because of the natural history of ASD (Figure 5.7). Sixty years ago—in an era when there were no treatments for ASD—Leo Kanner observed dramatic im-

provement as his patients passed through early and middle childhood. "All of this," Kanner wrote, "makes the family feel that, in spite of recognized 'difference' from other children, there is progress and improvement."

So what *is* evidence, scientifically speaking? Scientific evidence consists of *observations or measurements that have been gathered by*

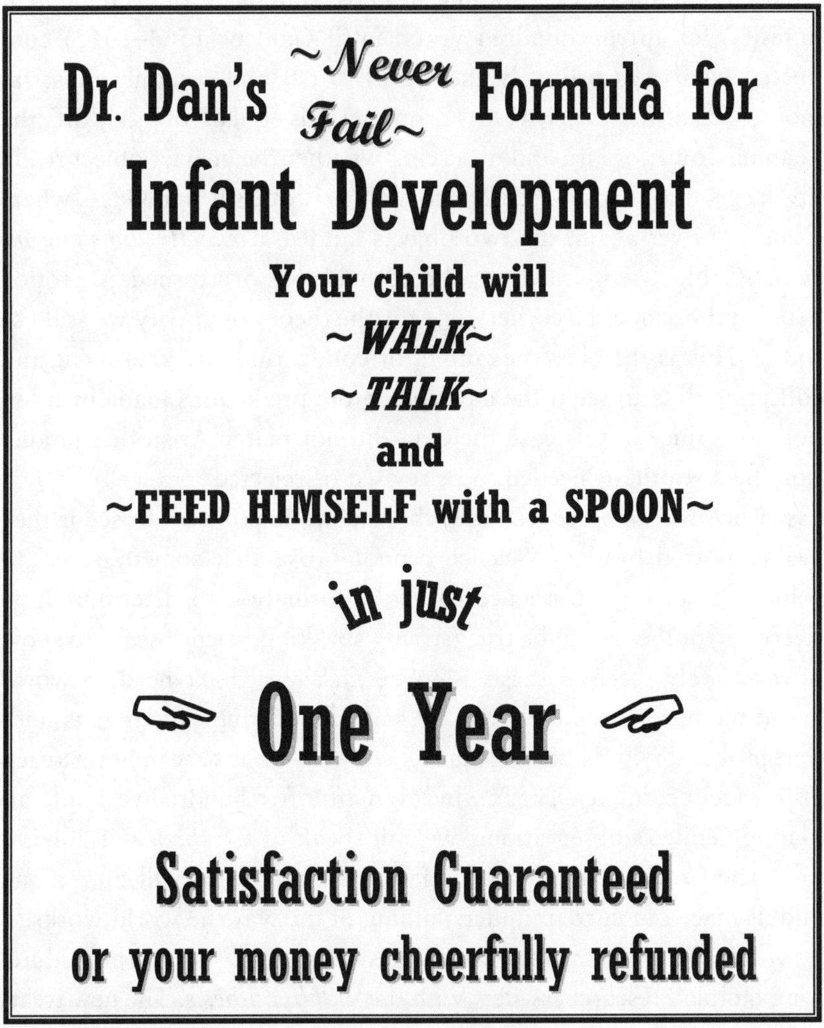

Dr. Dan's ~*Never Fail*~ Formula for Infant Development

Your child will

~*WALK*~

~*TALK*~

and

~FEED HIMSELF with a SPOON~

in just

☞ One Year ☜

Satisfaction Guaranteed or your money cheerfully refunded

Figure 14.1 The Healing Powers of Time *"Wouldn't all these children learn to walk and talk in twelve months on their own anyway?" you might ask. Of course they would. Many claims of "cure" for ASD are equally dubious.*

standardized, repeatable methods, then subjected to appropriate analysis to determine the validity of a hypothesis. A hypothesis is simply a statement about how we think the world works. A good hypothesis has predictive value; experiments are conducted to determine whether the results predicted by the hypothesis actually occur. Let me give you an example. Aristotle (384–322 B.C.E.) believed that heavy objects fall faster than lighter objects. Aristotle's assumption was accepted unquestioningly; he was a revered figure, and besides, his belief makes common sense, doesn't it? His statement of "fact" went untested for fifteen hundred years, until Galileo (1564–1642) conducted what was probably the world's first, and certainly most famous, scientific experiment: dropping dissimilar objects off the Leaning Tower of Pisa and observing whether the heavier object really hit the ground first, in accordance with Aristotle's belief. Guess what? Over and over again, the two objects landed at *exactly the same instant.* Galileo's empirically gathered evidence overturned Aristotle's belief and became the cornerstone for the theory of gravity we still use today. This is the classic example of conducting an experiment and collecting data to see if the data match the predictions made by a hypothesis. Since in this case the data did not match Aristotle's prediction, his hypothesis needed to be revised or rejected.

Science works by continually challenging hypotheses to see if they are supported by data. Science cannot prove that something is absolutely true. Rather, science gathers information to determine how *likely* a hypothesis is to be true (strictly speaking, science seeks to show how *unlikely* the hypothesis is to be *false*; we don't need to worry about the difference here). We can keep conducting experiments until that probability is as big or small as we wish—but we can never reach 100 percent certainty. That's why, even after five hundred years of validating Galileo's observations, we still speak of the *theory* of gravitation. There's always the chance that a better hypothesis will come along and displace our current understanding of the way the world works.

When evaluating a treatment (a new drug or a surgical procedure, for example), researchers start with the *null hypothesis:* The new treatment is no better than the old one (or no better than no treatment at all). Then the researcher conducts controlled trials that compare two groups of subjects—one group gets the new treatment and the other group gets the old treatment (or a placebo, depending on study design)—and looks for differences in outcome between the two groups. If there is a difference in outcome between the two groups and if the degree of difference that was found would occur less than 5 percent of the time by chance alone, then the researcher rejects the null hypothesis of no difference between treatments. In other words, it's very likely that there *is* a valid difference between the treatments.

Another study design, termed a *crossover* design, enables each subject to participate in both arms of the study, in randomized order (each subject crosses over from one group to the other). Most of the studies of secretin were done this way: Each child received either secretin or saltwater placebo in the first round, and the opposite substance in the second round. In study after study, in a blind, randomized crossover format, parents have been unable to tell the effects of secretin from placebo.

Researchers and patients alike are vulnerable to self-deception. Researchers are tempted to see a pattern in the data that supports their theory. Patients want to get better and may be inclined to report improvement (or side effects) if they think they are receiving a powerful new treatment. Good research uses random assignment to treatment group, blinding (concealment of group membership), and sham treatment (placebo) to keep all participants honest and objective.

Randomization guards against some difference creeping into the makeup of the two groups. Once someone agrees to participate in a study, he or she is randomly assigned to one group or another. (Part of the consent form to join the study in the first place includes an agreement to be randomized.) If the researcher or the participants got to pick who went into which group, this could alter the composition of the groups, affecting the outcome even before the study gets going. If you pick your subjects right, you can make any therapy look good!

THE POWER OF RANDOMIZED CONTROLLED TRIALS

Forty years ago, as a freshman in medical school, I worked in a pediatric hematology clinic, helping care for children with acute lymphoblastic leukemia (ALL). Treatment for ALL in those days was primitive and fraught with complications; by the time I graduated four years later, most of those children had already died. At the same time, however, there were a variety of randomized controlled trials (RCTs) under way. Parents of children with newly diagnosed ALL were offered a choice: take the best available therapy of the day (knowing that their child would probably die within a few years) or, if they agreed to participate in an RCT, have their child randomly assigned to receive either the best available therapy or some newer, experimental treatment. Whichever treatment turned out to have the better outcome became the new "best available" therapy for the next round of RCTs. Parents knew their children were soldiers in a war and that children randomized to the less effective treatment would have poorer survival rates. But nobody knew, at the beginning of each round of RCTs, which treatment would turn out to be the "wrong" one. Today, rather than dying within five years, a child with newly diagnosed ALL has a better than 95 percent chance of going into complete remission after one course of treatment.

Blinding minimizes the tendency to see changes where there are none. In order for blinding to be effective, subjects in both groups must receive therapy that looks the same (or as close as possible), otherwise they will guess which group they are in; that's why good studies include a placebo, or sham-treatment group. The strictest studies are double-blind: Neither the researcher nor the subjects know who has been assigned to which group. If only the subjects are in the dark, the study is single-blind. If neither the researcher nor the subjects is in the dark, it is a nonblinded or open-label study. The persons evaluating outcome also need to be blind to group assignment. (Even in strict, double-blind studies, there is always a research monitor who knows the code; if a significant difference in outcome between the two groups emerges while the study is ongoing, the monitor halts the study.)

A placebo is a treatment whose only active ingredient is faith. Good research includes a sham-treatment arm to cancel out the placebo effect. The sham treatment can be sugar pills, saltwater injections, or even sham surgery—whatever it takes to prevent subjects from figuring out which arm of the study they are in. There was once a surgical procedure in which an artery in the chest would be sewn onto the surface of the heart to reduce cardiac pain. Patients reported reduced pain after the procedure, but researchers were skeptical, so they conducted a randomized, placebo-controlled trial. Half of the subjects got the real surgery, and the other half underwent general anesthesia and received a small incision in the skin, which was then sewn up, so it looked like they might have had the actual procedure. The two groups reported identical reduction in chest pain. Both groups expected to feel better—so they did. Needless to say, that particular form of heart surgery is no longer performed, because it was no better than placebo. The moral to the tale is that we see what we expect to see.

Placebo effects are notoriously powerful in studies of human behavior. One famous example was discovered at the Hawthorne Works of the Western Electric Company (hence its name, the Hawthorne effect). Wanting to improve worker productivity, factory managers increased lighting on the production line. Sure enough, productivity went up. But productivity also went up when management *decreased* the lighting. Puzzled, they called in some industrial psychologists, who proceeded to manipulate various aspects of the workers' environment: longer breaks, shorter breaks, and so on. Even as the workers grumbled about some of the changes, their productivity continued to go up. Conclusion: As long as the workers felt that management was interested in their welfare (and therefore expected that all the changes management was putting in place were for their benefit), they worked harder and productivity rose.

In the Hawthorne example, the workers' expectations influenced *their own* behavior (they worked harder). Sometimes our expectations can also influence *other people's* behavior. A researcher named Robert Rosenthal wanted to find out whether teachers' expectations of their students could influence the children's performance. With the permission of the school board, Rosenthal set up an experiment at an elementary school. At the beginning of the school year, he circulated a list to all the teachers at the school, identifying 10 percent of the incoming students as gifted. In fact, Rosenthal had pulled the "gifted" children's names out of a hat. But by the following spring, those children tested 10 to 15 points higher than their classmates on a standardized IQ test. The teachers' expectations alone had been enough to raise the children's IQ scores. Notice that even though the initial belief was false—

the children did not start out gifted—the outcome was real: Their scores really went up. The Rosenthal effect (also known as the Pygmalion effect, for the mythical sculptor who fell in love with his own creation) is one more twist on the placebo effect. I urge you to read *Pygmalion in the Classroom* (cited in the Resource List), which describes Rosenthal's experiment in detail. This book should be on the required reading list for all diagnosticians, therapists, and parents. The moral for diagnosticians (myself included) is that we need to guard against creating self-fulfilling negative prophecies about children. The moral for parents is that if you believe strongly enough in a therapy— *any* therapy—your child is likely to improve, not necessarily from the therapy but from the impact of your expectation of improvement. So be careful what you put your faith into.

Let's see how some of these principles play out in real life. We'll look at developmental therapies first.

Developmental Therapy: Three Cautionary Tales

ABA: Not a 47 Percent Cure for ASD

In 1987, Ivar Lovaas published a paper stating that 47 percent of children with ASD whom he had treated with ABA had a normal outcome (see the Resource List for citations to this and the several articles that follow). However, subjects were not randomly assigned to the two treatment groups. As a result, subjects in the ABA group were younger and brighter than the non-ABA group *prior to the start of treatment.* Furthermore, there was no sham treatment for the subjects in the non-ABA group, making it obvious to all participants who was getting the active therapy. These design flaws seriously undermine the conclusions of his paper. One of Lovaas' trainees, named Smith, subsequently conducted his own study, which remedied these design flaws, and in that study only 13 percent of subjects achieved what Lovaas had defined as "normal functioning." Additional research by Sallows and Graupner has confirmed the importance of pretreatment IQ as a major factor influencing outcome. These papers, and others like them, have led critics including Gresham and MacMillan to conclude that Lovaas' claim of a 47 percent cure rate should be viewed with "an attitude of healthy skepticism." Does this mean that I reject ABA? Not at all. But it does mean that I am very modest in the claims I make on behalf of ABA: It works to shape behavior, but claims of a 47 percent cure rate are not supported by the data.

Therapeutic Listening: Listen to the Evidence

Glowing testimonials for auditory integration training (AIT) abound on the Internet, but when you read the fine print, you will see that very few of them include random assignment of children to treatment groups or a blinded assessment of outcome (that is, evaluations performed by examiners who don't know which children received actual therapy and which were controls). Most reports do not involve the use of control groups at all, just the administration of AIT, and claims of subsequent improvement. In contrast to these heartwarming anecdotes, children in randomized controlled trials of AIT have done no better than—and occasionally have performed *worse* than—subjects in the sham-treatment group. In one study, children listened either to ordinary music or to a specially prepared set of "therapeutic" listening materials. Subjects in both groups improved by exactly the same amount. The simplest explanation, of course, is that passage of time and the placebo effect had a hand. The authors of that paper tried to salvage therapeutic listening in spite of the absence of difference between therapeutic listening and the control condition, expressing the view that "some aspect of both auditory training and listening to selected unmodified music may have a beneficial effect on children with autism and sound sensitivity." That may be true. But why spend thousands of dollars on a therapy that appears to work no better than giving your child an iPod?

Facilitated Communication: The Power of Self-Deception

Perhaps the most egregious example of seeing what we expect to see is the sad story of facilitated communication (FC). FC is a technique in which the adult (the facilitator) assists the person with disability at a keyboard. FC was originally devised for persons with physical disability but was soon adopted for use among children with ASD. The facilitator would support the child's hand while the child typed at a keyboard. The theory was that children with ASD had impaired fine motor praxis (apraxia), which they were able to overcome with the support of the facilitator. FC caught on like wildfire. Soon, however, reports of sexual abuse made by children via facilitated communication began to surface. Typically, the allegations were against the child's father, and the communications were facilitated by the child's teacher or therapist. The alleged perpetrators fell under suspicion; families were torn apart and men's lives were destroyed. In the wake of these events, some carefully controlled trials were performed in which the facilitator and the child with ASD were fed different information (via headphones, a visual display, or other means). What the researchers found was that the facilitated output frequently reflected information that *only the facilitator had received*, not what the child had seen or heard. In other words, under controlled conditions, the typed output was actually the result of unconscious facilitator control of the typing process. Far from merely supporting the child's hand, the facilitator was unconsciously guiding it. FC is a cautionary tale of an unproven and apparently benign therapy that did great harm. Think twice whenever someone tells you that their therapy for ASD is "perfectly safe."

Now let's turn our attention to medical therapies.

Spotting Quackery

Quackery is medical self-promotion that goes beyond the evidence. For the most part, quackery is not intentional fraud; most quacks sincerely believe in the products they promote. You can recognize quackery by certain nearly universal themes. One hundred years ago, patent medicine salesmen traveled from town to town, hawking their wares. If you look through advertisements for their products, you will notice five themes: The treatment is always *simple yet mysterious*. It is always *completely safe*. It can cure *multiple different problems*. It is supported by heartfelt *testimonials*. And the promoters frequently take pride in their role as *challengers to (or victims of) the mainstream medical establishment*. Let's take a look at each of these elements a bit more closely. Once you develop an ear for them, you can pick them out as easily on the Internet as from a nineteenth-century pamphlet.

Collier's for October 7 1905

THE GREAT AMERICAN FRAUD

By SAMUEL HOPKINS ADAMS

Figure 14.2 Frontispiece to Samuel Hopkins Adams' 1905 Series on Quack Medicine *Publication of this exposé assisted in generating public support for the creation of the Food and Drug Administration (FDA).*

Simple yet Mysterious

Quack remedies invoke forces that have a simplistic appeal, but without any of the messy details as to exactly how these forces work within the body. These mysterious forces break down into two types: back-to-nature and high-tech.

Back-to-nature cures seek to restore the body's balance in some way that is harmonious with nature, free of anything artificial. One hundred years ago, the back-to-nature group extolled the curative properties of herbs, roots, bark, and rattlesnake oil (actually, it was mineral oil with flavorings). Not much has changed in a century except that snake oil has gone off the menu.

High-tech practitioners, on the other hand, exploit the legitimate scientific achievements of their time, capitalizing on the gee-whiz aspect of technology. Samuel Morse invented the telegraph—an electromagnetic device—in 1840; quack treatments of that era touted magnetism as a cure-all. Electricity emerged as a power source in the late nineteenth and early twentieth century; quack therapy devices followed right along, with various "electric belts" and other electrical appliances. In 1903, the Nobel Prize in physics went to Antoine Becquerel and the husband-and-wife team of Marie and Pierre Curie for their work on radioactivity; medical quacks immediately jumped on the bandwagon and began selling radioactive tablets and radioactive water as "cures." This finally came to a halt in 1932, when the FDA outlawed such products after the death by radiation poisoning of a prominent public figure. Not to be deterred, quacks took one look at the glowing vacuum tubes inside radios, and moved on to selling "purple ray" devices that emanated ozone (a lung irritant) for inhalation!

Complementary and alternative medicine (CAM) therapies for ASD also break down into back-to-nature and high-tech varieties: megavitamins, herbal remedies, and homeopathy are good examples of the former, while hyperbaric oxygen and chelation are good examples of the latter. It's up to you to decide whether the similarity to nineteenth-century quack medicine is more than skin-deep.

All-Powerful yet Safe

Common sense should tell you that anything powerful enough to cure also has the power to do harm. In his 1905 exposé of the patent medicine industry, Samuel Hopkins Adams pointedly observed: "The ignorant drug-taker, returning to health from some disease which he has overcome by the natural resistant powers of his body, dips his pen in gratitude and writes his testimonial. The man who dies in spite of the patent medicine—or perhaps because of it—doesn't bear witness to what it did for him. We see recorded only the favorable results: the unfavorable lie silent." Next time you are listening to someone pitch a product, just ask, "What are the potential side effects?" and listen carefully to the response. If they try to convince you there are no side effects, my advice is to thank them politely, then walk away—while keeping a firm grip on your pocketbook.

Cures Multiple Diseases

Quack remedies of the nineteenth century claimed the power to cure broad swaths of disorders, including cancer, tuberculosis, asthma, emphysema, "female problems," depression, pain, and sexual dysfunction. A popular therapy for ASD currently advertised on the Web claims that it can help children with "heavy metal damage, autoimmune damage, intestinal inflammation, yeast, viral and bacterial infections, and cellular energy dysfunction." Notice the similarity?

Reliance on Heartfelt Testimonials

In his series on patent medicine, Adams had this to say about testimonials: "While many of the printed testimonials are genuine enough, they represent not the average evidence, but the most glowing opinions which the nostrum vender can obtain. But the innocent public regards them as the type, not the exception."

Here is a testimonial from 1882 for Dr. Scott's Electric Flesh Brush (a brush with a magnet hidden inside the handle): "My sister had suffered a great amount from Chronic Rheumatism for MANY YEARS and could find no relief from medicines or applications. She has been using your Electric Flesh Brush for a short time, and is RELIEVED FROM ALL PAIN, and is perfectly cured." Here is a testimonial on the Web for a popular autism treatment: "Our son started talking after just ONE treatment with [product name]. . . . He is set to start kindergarten in the fall, and his teachers say he is going to be just fine. Thank you for being there when we needed you. We tell all our friends about you." Notice any similarities?

Supporters Claim the Role of Underdog or Challenger to Conventional Medicine

Americans love the underdog. The dream of overcoming adversity and rising to fame and fortune against all odds is woven into American popular culture. Quacks play on this theme, depicting themselves as noble victims, weaving a cloak of legitimacy for themselves out of the very criticisms directed at them by the mainstream medical community. In addition, quacks depict mainstream medicine as stubbornly obstructing curative therapy, or—at its most extreme expression— actually causing the problems for which the quack claims to have a cure. "It is pardonable in you to want to know these formulas, for they are good. But you must not ask us to reveal these valuable secrets, to do what you would not do yourselves." So said W. A. Talbot, owner of Piso's Consumption Cure and president of the Proprietary Medicine Association, speaking out against the American Medical Association's support of pure food and drug legislation in 1905. The idea that doctors have caused an autism epidemic by unleashing immunizations on hapless children plays directly to these sentiments.

Today you can go on the Internet and see the same medicine show that made the rounds of country fairs a hundred years ago. Now, as then, the pitch contains the same five elements: simple yet mysterious; all-powerful yet safe; cures multiple disorders; supported by testimonials from the cured; proponents revel in their role as the underdog. Look for these five elements in whatever therapy you are contemplating for your child. If it looks like a duck, sounds like a duck, and walks like a duck, it may be a duck—or, in this case, quackery.

Biomedical Therapies for ASD

Chelation

As we discussed in Chapter 4, there are scant valid data to incriminate mercury as a cause of ASD. Nonetheless, large numbers of parents administer chelating agents to their children in the hopes of "pulling" mercury and other metals from the body. There are no controlled studies of chelation to support the hypothesis that chelation improves outcome for children with ASD, and there are unlikely ever to be any. Why not? Because research has shown that succimer, the most popular oral chelating agent, causes brain damage.

This is a tragic tale, because parents continue to give succimer a try in the erroneous belief that "it can't hurt." The lid was blown off this assumption in a 2007 paper by Diane Stangle and colleagues (see the Resource List) that looked at the risks and benefits of succimer in the treatment of lead poisoning in rats (the study used lead rather than mercury because of the public health implications of low-level lead exposure in children and the frequent necessity of chelating children with proven lead poisoning). The authors set up two groups: rats that were exposed to neurotoxic levels of lead and a comparable group of nonexposed rats. Then they administered succimer to both groups. As succimer removed lead from the lead-poisoned rats, their learning ability returned to normal. This observation is in keeping with the hypothesis that lead in the brain is bad for brain function, and came as no surprise. The researchers were surprised to discover, however, that when the non-lead-exposed rats were treated with succimer, *their test scores went down*. After treatment with succimer, they were doing about as badly as the lead-exposed rats had been doing before treatment with succimer (that is, when they were lead-poisoned). It seems as if, finding no lead to pull from the lead-free rats' brains, the succimer had started attacking the brain cells themselves! As a result of this study, in 2008 the National Institutes of Health canceled a controlled trial of succimer treatment in children with ASD because of the risk of brain damage from succimer.

Even if the claims that mercury causes ASD and that chelation helps are both true (and at present there are very few data to support either of these hypotheses), somewhere there has to be a tipping point between the risks of mercury exposure and the risk of brain damage from succimer itself. If the child's mercury level is not high enough, the succimer will go after the child's brain instead. Where exactly is that tipping point? Nobody knows. How much of your child's IQ are you prepared to put at risk in order to gamble on the unproven benefit of succimer as a "treatment" for your child's ASD?

Hyperbaric Oxygen

Proponents of hyperbaric oxygen as a treatment for ASD apparently go by the adage "If some is good, then more is better." Unfortunately, in the case of oxygen, it's not true. Suppose you're relaxing in front of a warm cozy fireplace, and I come along and tell you, "You're having such a nice time in front of the fire; wouldn't you like me to set your sofa and curtains on fire too?" I think you'd show me to the nearest exit. Yet this is just about what we'd be doing if we subjected someone's brain to excess oxygen.

Increased level of oxygen in the tissues can be achieved in either of two ways: increasing the percentage of oxygen in the air someone breathes (ordinary air is about 21 percent oxygen; we can boost that to 25 percent, 30 percent, or even 100 percent) or increasing the pressure. Hyperbaric oxygen is oxygen at greater than normal atmospheric pressure. Either way, the outcome is an increased level of oxygen in the tissues of the body (hyperoxia). Hyperoxia has some narrowly defined medical uses (for example, to protect heart muscle following a heart attack, or to promote wound healing). But hyperoxia generally is not a good idea, any more than setting your sofa and curtains on fire would be. There are several reasons why this is so:

- Hyperoxia *increases oxidative stress* and the release of reactive oxygen species (which we discussed in Chapter 3).

- Exposing mice to increased levels of oxygen causes brain damage, via oxidative stress.
- As many as one in fifteen children with ASD may have mitochondrial disorders, which are already associated with increased oxidative stress. Subjecting children with an underlying mitochondrial disorder to excess oxygen is therefore likely to be especially damaging.
- Hyperoxia triggers cell death by a process known as apoptosis.
- Hyperoxia leads to Alzheimer's disease–related changes in the brain. Wouldn't it be tragic if ten, twenty, or thirty years from now we discover that hyperbaric oxygen in childhood leads to Alzheimer's disease? The evidence so far is preliminary but consistent with that hypothesis. And the history of medicine is full of similar, delayed-reaction horror stories (thyroid cancer in adults following irradiation in childhood, for example).

In animal studies, the damaging effects of excess oxygen are most prominent in mouse pups—the developmental equivalent of human children from birth to thirty-six months of age. I've included several citations in the Resource List. They are all highly technical, but here's one title anyone should be able to understand: *"Oxygen causes cell death in the developing brain."*

Given all that we know about the dangers of hyperoxia, it boggles my mind to think that anyone would deliberately risk increasing the level of oxidative stress in their child's brain. Nonetheless, a small but ardent group of practitioners, as well as parents who have sunk large sums of money into such therapy already, advocate hyperbaric oxygen therapy (HBOT) as a treatment for ASD. In the first randomized controlled trial of HBOT (see the Resource List) sixty-two children received either HBOT or placebo treatment (slightly compressed room air). The authors used three scales—the Aberrant Behavior Checklist (ABC), the Autism Treatment Evaluation Checklist (ATEC), and the Clinical Global Impression (CGI)—as outcome measures. They found differences in favor of the HBOT group for one of six subscales on the ABC, one of five subscales on the ATEC, and three of eighteen subscales on the CGI, but even these few beneficial results were inconsistent. For example, while *eye contact* and *receptive language* were improved on the CGI following HBOT, *social awareness, social inter-*

action, and *speech/language*—which tap similar skills—were not. The authors completely disregard the research showing oxygen toxicity to the developing brain, asserting that "hyperbaric treatment for children is generally regarded as safe" on the basis of a single paper pertaining to the use of HBOT as a treatment for bone damage after radiation therapy.

Even if you are persuaded that exposure to increased oxygen levels is effective in the treatment of ASD, and that the risks of brain damage from oxygen have been overblown, you may be surprised to learn that breathing oxygen from a mask can achieve the same increase in brain oxygen levels as going into a tank. (I'm not advocating doing this. My personal view is that unnecessarily exposing a child's brain to excess oxygen is the biological equivalent of setting the child's brain on fire— or, at the very least, blowing on the embers. The coals may burn brighter for a moment, but will burn out faster in the long run.) Obviously, delivery of oxygen by mask could be done at a tiny fraction of the cost of hard-tank HBOT. Remember rule number one when diagnosing quackery: *Follow the money.*

Finally, the advocates of any treatment have an ethical obligation to seek the safest way of achieving therapeutic results. In 2009, a four-year-old boy undergoing HBOT for cerebral palsy and his grandmother were burned to death when the tank in which they were confined burst into flames. I can hear the counter-argument already: The fire occurred during a treatment using 100 percent oxygen, while HBOT for ASD uses much lower concentrations. That's true, but the larger issue— always seek the least invasive technique to achieve one's therapeutic goals—is still paramount. HBOT for cerebral palsy was also advertised as "extremely safe," but as we all know, accidents happen.

Omega-3 Fatty Acids

Omega-3 fatty acids (found in, among other sources, fish oil) are antioxidants. As I explained in Chapter 3, antioxidants are essential to minimize oxidative stress. Biochemical markers for increased oxidative stress have been reported in a host of psychiatric and neurodevelopmental disorders, including mental retardation, Rett syndrome, ADHD, schizophrenia, anxiety disorders, and ASD, among others. It is a reasonable hypothesis, therefore, that anything that alleviates oxidative stress might be beneficial in treating these conditions. There are numerous published reports of omega-3 fatty acids used as treatment in various disorders and at least two placebo-controlled trials showing behavioral improvement in children with ASD. The assumption is that the observed improvement is due to reduced oxidative stress, but it's also possible that there may be some other direct effect on nerve transmission. Not all studies have shown benefit, however, and experts still disagree as to whether omega-3 fatty acids really work. At present, we do not have enough data to state with certainty that they work, and we have no long-term data on their safety when used in large doses in young children.

Of all the complementary and alternative treatments parents may be

Table 14.1 Trials of Omega-3 Fatty Acids

Year	Author (Country)	Subjects	Method	Result
2006	Schultz (USA)	Online parent survey; 861 children with autistic spectrum disorder and 123 control children	Compared rate of ASD according to method of infant feeding: breast (rich in omega-3s), non-omega-3 and omega-3-supplemented formula	Infant formula without omega-3s vs. 100 percent breastfeeding: risk of ASD quadruples with non-omega-3 formula
2005	Richardson (England)	117 children, ages 5–12, with developmental coordination disorder	Randomized controlled trial of omega-3 and omega-6 fatty acids vs. placebo	No effect on motor skills, but significant improvements for fatty acid group in reading, spelling, and behavior
2007	Amminger (Canada)	13 children, ages 5–17 years, with ASD plus severe behavior disorders (tantrums, self-injury, aggression)	Six-week double-blind randomized control trial with 1.5 g daily omega-3 supplementation or placebo; behaviors scored on Aberrant Behavior Checklist at 6 weeks	Omega-3 fatty acids superior to placebo for hyperactivity and stereotypy
2008	Meguid (England)	30 children with ASD ages 3–11 years and 30 healthy subjects	Oral supplementation with Efalex (evening primrose oil and tuna oil)	Two-thirds of children with ASD showed clinical and biochemical improvement
2008	Politi (Italy)	19 adults with severe ASD, ages 18–40 years	Open-label trial of omega-3 supplementation for 6 weeks	No observed improvement on behavioral rating scale

tempted to try, this is the one I'm most comfortable with. The risks (as far as we know) appear small, there is a plausible biological mechanism that has been verified in animal models and human subjects with other disorders, and there are some data to suggest benefits in children with ASD. Thus—unlike the GF/CF diet, chelation, or hyperbaric oxygen therapy—the omega-3 fatty acids meet the tests for possible causation and possible benefit (I wouldn't yet say probable). These are hot topics for research, with exciting developments imminent.

Keeping an Open Mind

Occasionally, established wisdom is wrong and the revolutionary is right. One hundred sixty years ago a Hungarian physician by the name of Ignaz Semmelweis claimed that fever and death could be caused by invisible animals living in the patient's blood. Everyone thought he was crazy, but his only mistake was to be ahead of his time. Louis Pasteur (who invented the process of heating milk to kill the tuberculosis bacteria it frequently contained), Robert Koch (who transferred body fluid from sick mice to healthy ones, proving that infection was in the fluid), and Joseph Lister (inventor of sterile surgical technique) would not arrive on the scene and vindicate Semmelweis' theory for another decade.

Yet even though Semmelweis was regarded as a madman in his own lifetime, if you had been around in 1847 you would have been able to separate his germ theory of disease from the quackery of his day, using the principles I've outlined in this chapter: First, Semmelweis was not motivated by financial gain. On the contrary, his adherence to his germ theory cost him dearly, since he was shunned by most of his colleagues. Second, he had hard evidence to back up his theory: The death rate from "childbed fever" (what today we call sepsis) among new mothers on the physician-run obstetrical ward at his hospital was *triple* the death rate on the midwife-run ward—a deviation from chance that far exceeded the null hypothesis of no difference between groups. Semmelweis theorized that childbed fever was caused by physicians infecting their patients with bacteria by performing pelvic exams straight after coming from the autopsy laboratory, without first washing their hands. Midwives, in contrast, did not perform autopsies. This, he reasoned, was why the death rate from childbed fever on the midwife-run ward was so much lower. Third, manipulating the suspected risk factor by requiring the doctors to wash their hands produced results—a dramatic reduction in maternal deaths—that supported his hypothesis.

Summing Up

It's hard to maintain two states of mind—hope and healthy skepticism—at the same time; it's the emotional equivalent of patting your head while rubbing your stomach. Yet this is what you need to do when evaluating possible treatments for your child. Check out all leads, but don't let your hopes for your child color your thinking. When considering a therapy—especially any form of biomedical intervention—ask to see the data. Ask about side effects. Find out if anyone other than parties with a financial stake are also promoting the therapy. Don't be pulled in by the emotional undertow of testimonials, and most important of all, use your common sense. There is no such thing as a treatment that is all-powerful yet perfectly safe; the history of medicine is littered with therapies that turned out to have unexpected consequences. If something sounds too good to be true, it usually is. I've provided supplemental readings on all of the topics we've covered in this chapter in the Resource List.

Your job is not to subject your child to every unproven therapy out there in the hope that he or she will represent the one chance in a million of cure. Rather, your job is to make a judgment as to what's safe and reasonably likely to help. There are, in fact, some stones that are better left unturned.

PART III

THE WORLD
OF THE FAMILY

Chapter 15

Family Matters

> Your child with special needs is a *member* of the family, but
> should not become the *center* of the family.
> —*Ruby Moye Salazar, LCSW, BCD*

We Have a Diagnosis. Now What?

Immediate Reactions

You are at a doctor's office. The doctor just informed you that your son
or daughter has ASD. If you were not expecting the diagnosis, your
first reaction will probably be one of shock or disbelief: *How could this
be true? How can the doctor be so sure?* Shock is often followed by
anger: *Why did this happen? Why didn't our child's pediatrician or
teachers tell us sooner?* These initial reactions serve as necessary emotional defenses. Bad news puts some people into fight-or-flight mode;
after the initial shock, they are ready to fight. But who is the enemy?
There is no enemy—although, as the bearer of bad news, I have occasionally been the target of parents' anger, and some parents transfer
their anger to the health care system or the educational system.

More likely, however, you had some inkling of the diagnosis before the doctor said the words. With all the publicity about ASD in the media, I find that fewer and fewer parents come to me totally unprepared for an autism diagnosis. If that's the case, your initial reaction may have been one of relief as much as grief—relief because finally you've found someone who listens to you and sees the things that have been worrying you, and grief because now it's official. No matter how much you may have tried to prepare yourself for the diagnosis, hearing the words spoken out loud is still devastating. Now it's no longer just a fear or a suspicion; now it's a reality. But if you are like most parents, your overriding urge—almost before your tears have dried—will be to translate your grief into action: *What services does my child need, and how do I get them?* The sadness is still there (it never totally goes away, no matter how well you adjust), but now you are able to bob back to the surface, emotionally speaking, and resume the business of making the most out of life—whatever that means under these irrevocably altered circumstances.

What Do I Tell Our Other Children?

Tell them the truth—at a level they can understand. It's useless to try to keep it from them. Children have radar, and they sense that you are unhappy. If you don't tell them the truth, they will fill in the blank with something worse, like the mapmakers in Columbus' time who sketched in sea monsters at the edges of the known world.

For young children, something like this may be enough: "Mommy and Daddy are very sad because your brother has trouble learning how to talk or do other things like you. It's not his fault, it's not Mommy and Daddy's fault, and it's not your fault either." Especially for preschool or elementary school children, it's important to reassure them that it's nobody's fault. This may sound strange, but stop and think for a minute: Haven't you been blaming yourself, or perhaps looked for someone or something to blame (the obstetrician, immunizations, etc.)? Preschool children do the same thing. They are naturally egocentric—that's why they can be so demanding. Likewise, if something bad happens, their natural tendency is to blame themselves, as illogical as that may seem to you by adult standards. For older children, it's appropriate to talk about genetics or other causes (if the cause of their sibling's ASD is known). It's also appropriate to address their concern (spoken or not) about whether this could happen to you again or to them when they become parents.

What Do I Tell My Parents/In-Laws?

There is nothing quite so maddening as well-intended but misguided grandparents: "Everything's fine. What are you worried about? He's just a boy. His father was just the same at this age." Or, even more damaging, "We never had anything like this on *our* side of the family before." If your relationship with your parents or in-laws up until now has been founded on mutual trust and respect, new challenges will bring you closer together. If, on the other hand, your relationship with them has been conflicted, it's not going to magically get better now. Still, it's important for your own peace of mind and mental health to be candid with them: "This is the way it is. I'm sorry if you can't see the problem," or "I'm sorry if you think I'm handling things all wrong, but I'm the parent now, and I need to make the best decisions I can for my own children—just like you did for me when I was little." Support from grandparents can be a blessing, but beware if your parents or in-laws start undercutting your efforts at imposing discipline. If your child has a star chart for positive and negative behaviors, make sure a copy of it goes along with him to Grandma's house!

What Do I Tell My Friends or Coworkers?

Tell them as much or as little as you like. You may discover that some of your friends will have a hard time hearing your story. Conversely, some acquaintances, whom you may know only peripherally at the moment, will turn out to have a better ear for what's burdening you, and you will find yourself becoming closer to them. You may discover parents just like yourself—parents of a child with ASD, who can say, "I know how you feel," and you know they really do.

Next Steps

Adaptation

After receiving the diagnosis of ASD, many parents initially experience angry thoughts such as "Why my child?" and feelings of deep despair.

Although those feelings may never disappear altogether, eventually they cease to be the focus of parents' day-to-day existence. Over the next several months after receiving a diagnosis, most parents go through a painful but healthy period of readjustment. Then, as with the parent of any child, parents of a child with ASD rededicate themselves to helping their child to reach his or her full potential. What that potential may be, and the means required to get the child there, will differ from what would have been the case if the child's development were normal. But the parents' underlying goals and priorities will be the same. Many parents find a way to redirect their anger and grief, channeling the energy from those emotions into activities that will benefit their child—forming a local support group, joining the local school committee, working to raise awareness or money on behalf of children with ASD or to pass legislation, and so forth. None of this may be on your mind as you leave the doctor's or psychologist's office with an ASD diagnosis on that first day; but eventually the adaptive process should begin to take over.

THE MYTH OF "GETTING OVER IT"

As far as I can tell, parents never really "get over" having a child with special needs. There are too many reminders of how things might have been if only circumstances had turned out as they were supposed to. This happens to siblings too. I'm sixty-one, and I still wonder what our family would have been like if my sister didn't have mental retardation. Do I love my sister for who she is? Sure. And in a weird way, if she didn't have mental retardation, she wouldn't be my sister; she'd be somebody else. But I still wonder, "What if…?"

As you go through this process of adaptation, give yourself permission to feel angry and disappointed as well as sad. Years ago, I conducted an interview with the parents of a child I had been treating during my fellowship training. Zach had been a premature infant with multiple complications that left him with cerebral palsy, deafness, seizures, and mental retardation. During the interview, Zach's mom was reflecting on how far she had come in the three years since her son had been born:

I used to look into the mirror and think, *What kind of a terrible person am I, to reject my own child?* Then I realized that it was okay to wish I didn't have to change his smelly diapers anymore, to wish that I didn't have to handle his drool anymore or to deal with his tantrums anymore. It was okay to wish that he'd never been born. All of those feelings were okay.

As she spoke, she sat up straighter in her chair; I could almost see an invisible weight lifting from her shoulders as she let go of her self-imposed guilt and shame. The same may be true for you: Whatever feelings you have, even the unpleasant ones (*especially* the unpleasant ones), are okay. You may consider some of your feelings shameful by society's standards, but remember two things: First, those whose judgment you fear haven't spent time walking in your shoes. And second, your harshest critic and severest judge is probably you. You need to get your feelings out. Unexpressed feelings—especially guilt, shame, and anger—do not go away. Instead, like corrosive poisons seeping from a buried oil drum, unexpressed negative feelings have the potential to contaminate all aspects of your life.

RISK FACTORS THAT MAY GET IN THE WAY OF MAKING A HEALTHY ADAPTATION

Anger and grief are unpleasant feelings, but they are not *problems*, in the sense of needing to be "fixed." True problems arise when a parent is unable to move on, even after months or years. Here are some factors that put parents at risk for getting "stuck" in the adaptation process:

How Were You Raised as a Child?

Were you ridiculed or shamed when you made mistakes? If so, you may have internalized those behaviors, and you may be inflicting them on yourself, even if your parents are no longer around to do so. Did you grow up in a blaming household, where everything that went wrong was always someone's fault? If so, you may be stuck with anger directed either against yourself or—more likely—against others as being "to blame" for your child's ASD.

Is Your Child with ASD a "Special Child"?

The following situations can make it particularly difficult for parents to adapt to the presence of disability:

- *Child conceived after prolonged infertility.* If a woman has had a hard time getting pregnant, especially if she or her partner have undergone arduous fertility treatments, then when she does eventually give birth, the baby is super-precious. If there turns out to be something wrong with this child, the emotional blow can be particularly devastating.
- *Older first-time parents.* Parents who have put off childbearing until their mid-thirties or beyond seem to have a harder time adapting to the birth of a child with special needs. I don't know exactly why; probably it's due to a combination of factors. If you find yourself in this position, be especially sure to look after your own needs. Depression is a significant risk, in my experience.
- *A child who's a Jr., II, III, etc.* Dads tend to have a really hard time with this one. Not only are parents grieving the disability in *this* child, but they are also dealing with the loss of a family tradition. Who will carry on the family name?
- *Unwanted pregnancy.* The parents' ambivalence or anger about having the child in the first place become taboo topics (in the parents' minds). Since they are never able to ventilate these feelings, they remain permanently stuck in an early phase of the grieving process.

Do You or Your Partner Have Mental Health Issues?

As we discussed in Chapter 4, the frequency of anxiety disorders, depression, and OCD is very high among the parents of children with ASD.

If any of these risk factors applies to you, you may benefit from working with a mental health professional (psychologist, family therapist, social worker) to help you through the adaptation process.

Take Care of Yourself

Remember what we are instructed to do on an airplane if the aircraft loses cabin pressure: Put the oxygen mask over your own nose and mouth first, then help the person sitting next to you. It's the same thing here: Take care of yourself first. At the very least, be sure to reserve 5 percent of your total energy for yourself. Don't become so overfocused on your child that you push everything and everyone else right off your plate. Make time for hobbies, physical exercise, time with your friends, or attendance at your house of worship or social group. (You may need to convince yourself, repeatedly telling yourself, "I'm doing this so that I can reenergize myself to go right out there and advocate for my child.") Otherwise, you run the risk of alienating your partner, your other children, and all those around you who might be able to help you in your efforts on behalf of your child with ASD. You also run the risk of burnout (mental and physical exhaustion). Who will see to it that all your plans are carried out if that happens?

If you are employed, your job may provide some relief and support for your sagging morale. Parents who have a life of their own outside of the home make better parents when they are at home, compared to parents who have nothing else to live for besides caring for their child with special needs. It may be necessary for you to take a temporary leave from work to get your child's therapies set up, but it's in your child's long-term best interests (as well as your own) for you to remain involved in some type of out-of-home activity. As much as you love your child with ASD, it's not healthy for your life to revolve around him or her. You need human companionship and ways to fill your life with meaning besides just meeting the needs of your child with ASD.

The urge to be alone when under stress is a worrisome trait. If you recognize this trait in yourself, make a conscious effort to counteract it: Spend twenty minutes a day of private time with your partner, make a date to have lunch with friends, see a counselor, join a group, go back to your day job—whatever reconnects you with humanity.

Take Care of Your Partner

I have just uttered the fateful words: *"I'm sorry to tell you this, but your son has autism."* Mom bursts into tears. In the same moment, Dad readies his pencil and starts asking me questions about educational services. Six months later, the roles are reversed: Dad is despondent that things will "never be right" with his son, while Mom has regained a bit of energy and optimism. She calmly holds her husband's hand as he weeps during the interview.

Everyone reacts to things in their own way and at their own pace. This can be a problem if one member of the team is still in the denial phase while the other has moved on to "What do we do next?" On the other hand, having partners at different stages is also a potential source of strength: Precisely because they *are* out-of-sync, each partner can be there for the other as the other falls apart. Whether you are the giver or receiver of support at any given moment depends on your emotional makeup and the inner workings of your relationship with your partner. The best advice I can give you is to check in with your significant other—ask what he or she is feeling and thinking, and then *just listen.* This means not trying to argue your partner out of their feelings (and in some cases it may also mean not going on the defensive if your partner seems to be blaming you). If your partner says, "This is awful!," don't try to prove why it's not so bad. Just listen and let your partner vent. Sooner or later you may find yourself on the other side of the same conversation. And if your partner says, "You're doing X all wrong," don't angrily snap back, "No, you're the one who's all wrong!" Instead, just listen, then say, "I know we have different approaches. Maybe we can talk with someone about how to reach a consensus." That's what family therapists are for. If your partner is unwilling to go, it may be necessary for you to go alone—at least at the beginning.

Both partners should attend any meeting in which information will be provided or decisions will be made about their child's future. It's not fair to place on one partner the burden of going home and having to tell the other what the doctor or school said. Therapists often unwittingly weaken the bonds between husband and wife by becoming the primary emotional support to Mom, inadvertently displacing Dad from this role. Physicians often do the same by giving important news when Mom alone is present. In my practice, I insist that both parents attend the evaluation even if they are divorced. Sometimes parents don't take me seriously; on rare occasions I have had to send Mom home with instructions to return on another day with her husband. This angers some people in the short run but in the long run strengthens family bonds. The alternative is that one parent slowly assumes a more dominant role in caring for their child with ASD and the other partner drifts, or is nudged, further into the periphery.

Take Care of Your Relationship with Your Partner

Isn't this what we just discussed in the preceding paragraph? No, not really. The previous paragraph was talking about two individuals. Here we're talking about the couple. My wife and I use a little verbal cue to remind ourselves of the importance of our relationship: Rather than saying "We need a vacation," one of us will say "*Us* needs a vacation." "Us," in other words, is a separate entity, with a life of its own. It's not the same as "we," which is composed of two unitary individuals: "I" + "I" = "we." "Us," on the other hand, is a creation all its own; I think that's what people are driving at when they talk about matrimony as the union of two individuals into one entity. "Us" needs to be nurtured and cared for as if it were a separate member of the family, or (somewhat humorously) a pet or a plant—"us" needs feeding and watering from time to time. Sad to say, lots of married couples seem to forget about their "us."

What can you do to take care of your relationship? You and your partner need to take time away from the grind (and it can be a grind) of all your day-to-day responsibilities. Occasionally I actually write out a prescription—*Dinner for two. Refill six times. Take as directed*—and hand it to the parents along with tongue-in-cheek instructions to come back with the credit card receipts at the next office visit. This is my way of helping parents give themselves permission to take time for themselves as a couple. Even if your date is a trip to the supermarket together and a cup of coffee somewhere on the way home, be sure to make time for these little outings. Otherwise, "us" will slowly wear away.

BABYSITTERS AND HOW TO FIND THEM

Years ago, when I worked in Syracuse, New York, there was an organization known as Take a Break. Take a Break was a group of parents of children with special needs who took turns babysitting for one another's kids. The idea was that parents of a child with special needs were the people best suited to babysit for someone else's child with special needs. If you want to do something constructive to make meaning out of the fact that you have a child with ASD, organize a babysitting circle composed of parents of children in your community with ASD. It should be a simple task to complete with e-mail. "I can't find a sitter" should not be an excuse. If you can't find a sitter, maybe the real problem is that you are anxious about letting go and find it hard to trust someone else to take care of your child. This is a valid concern. But other parents who have walked in shoes just like yours should be up to the task.

Another suggestion, if you are lucky enough to live in a community with a college, is to advertise for a graduate student in child psychology or special education.

Take Care of Your Other Children

Selma Fraiberg, a wise and beloved child psychiatrist, once wrote, "Children want not just the love of their parents; they want the *exclusive* love of their parents." Not only is a young child jealous of his or her siblings; the child is even jealous of his or her parents! Have you ever seen a toddler get in between Mommy and Daddy and try to push them apart when they are hugging? *Your love is just for me—not for each other!* the toddler seems to be saying. Sibling rivalry is therefore perfectly normal—even among siblings who are developmentally intact and whose parents' treatment of their children is equitable. Imagine how much more intense these feelings can become if the parent is objectively favoring one child over the others.

Try to spend a few minutes per day with each child separately, doing something that represents a special bond between you and that child. It could even be a simple household chore, such as folding and putting away the clothes together, as long as you make it your special chore to do together. A surprising amount of pleasant chitchat can go back and forth between parent and child during the twenty minutes it takes to fold the laundry. The key is that each child should have some regular, uninterrupted time with each parent. No cell phone, no TV, no doorbell. And no intrusion by your child with ASD. So you may need to time your special moments around conflicting school or therapy schedules. I know it can be hectic—daunting, even—but in the end it is time well spent.

Give your typically developing children permission to feel angry and cheated as well as sad. Your child with ASD probably is not as much fun to be around as a sibling with typical development. You probably *are* spending more time with your child with ASD than is "fair." And you probably *do* let your child with ASD get away with certain things that you don't tolerate in your other children—not because you intend to show favoritism toward your child with ASD, but because you need to pick your battles. It's better to be honest with the other kids than to pretend the inequities don't exist: "I wish it wasn't that way, and I feel bad about it myself" is a far better response than trying to talk your other children out of their feelings with arguments such as "But look at all the things you know how to do that your brother can't do"; this is true, but it misses the point. Your child with typical development feels cheated; your job is to convey to them that their feelings are okay, just as you need to be able to look into the mirror and tell yourself that *your own* feelings are okay (like Zach's mom earlier in this chapter). Even more destructive than parents' efforts to dissuade siblings from expressions of disappointment is an angry parental response, along these lines: "Can't you see your sister has a problem? You're just jealous of all the attention we give her! All you want is more for yourself!" Parents who talk this way are caught up with their own anger, guilt, and grief. Children who are the target of this type of treatment are at risk for internalizing their parents' criticisms (that is, coming to believe that what their parents say in anger must be true, which imposes a tremendous cost to their own development).

Your other children don't need you to make the world a perfect place to live, and they can see right through any attempt on your part to convince them that things are great when they're really not. What they need is the same thing you need: someone to listen to them in a compassionate, nonjudgmental fashion, someone to tell them that their feelings are okay. Obviously you won't be able to do this until you have had a chance to ventilate your own feelings. If you are consumed by anger or weighed down by depression or guilt, you can't be emotionally available to your other children. Take care of yourself. Then take care of your family obligations.

Besides making special times to spend with each child and listening in a nonjudgemental way to their complaints, another way to bond with your other children and make them feel valued is to explain their sibling's ASD to them, at a level they can understand. There are many excellent books for siblings of the child with ASD (see the Resource List). These books accomplish several objectives. First, the very existence of such books conveys an unspoken message: "You are not alone—other kids just like you have siblings with ASD too." (I wish there had been books like that when I was a kid. I felt like I was the only child in the world to have a sister with special needs.) Second, it is usually easier to talk with your kids about difficult topics when describing characters in a book, rather than speaking about ourselves: "How do you think the mommy in the story feels?" is less threatening than asking "How do you think I feel?" Third, such books enable your typically developing children to see the world through the eyes of their sibling with ASD. "Oh, so *that's* why my brother is like that!" Rather than simply feeling frustrated, annoyed, or—sometimes—mystified and frightened by their sibling with ASD, now your other children can approach their sibling with understanding and compassion.

You don't need to cover everything the first time. Just read a couple of these books once or twice, then leave them lying out somewhere. Eventually your child with typical development will probably express an interest in going back to them, or you can refer to them at the appropriate moment: "Remember the book we read about...?" Buying and reading such books with your typically developing children signals them that you are an approachable, "askable" parent. Ultimately, reading such books together with your typically developing children is a great way to enlist them as members of the team.

SIBLING GROUPS

Sibling groups can help your child to feel less alone with his or her feelings. Just as no one but another parent can truthfully say to you, "I know how you feel," no one but another sibling of a child with ASD can say to your other kids, "I know how you feel." *Not even you.*

You can obtain more information about sibling support groups at www.siblingsupport.org, a national organization created to support the siblings of people with special needs. Additional resources available from this site include books, DVDs, and Web links through which your typically developing children can connect online with other siblings of children with ASD.

Family Mental Health

Just like individuals, families can be healthy or dysfunctional. Healthy families are a rich stew of shifting roles and allegiances: Sometimes Jack is the hero, and his sister Taylor is in the doghouse; sometimes it's the other way around. Sometimes Maddy is center stage; sometimes she takes a backseat to her brother. The same applies to parental roles: Sometimes Mom is the enforcer and Dad is the softie; sometimes it's the other way around.

Another sign of resiliency is that all legitimate combinations of family members arise from time to time: Sometimes Mom and Dad take all the kids out to the movies; sometimes Mommy and big sister go out shopping while Daddy stays home to watch Matthew and the baby. Each combination of family members has its own special chemistry. As part of this healthy variation, there are times when it's okay to leave your child with ASD at home with a sitter and take the other children somewhere. Going to a water park may include your child with ASD. Going to a Broadway show may not. You may feel sad and guilty about leaving your child with ASD behind, but there are times when your other children have equal claim on your undivided attention and you need to balance one good thing against another. This is an area where you may find it hard to give yourself permission to deviate from some self-imposed standard of proper behavior. But insisting that everyone go everywhere together, in lockstep, is neither logical nor healthy for anyone.

Is one of your children always in the doghouse, rebellious, or moody? Is one parent always the disciplinarian? Is one parent always working late or out of town on business? Has one parent taken over all responsibility for managing the child with ASD? If you answered yes to any of these questions, it may be time to consider intervention centered on family function. Here are a couple of examples.

The Workaholic Dad

Bryan S. is a six-year-old-boy with PDD-NOS, borderline intelligence, and impulsivity. I've been monitoring his progress for the past three years. Today is a scheduled follow-up visit. Bryan waits in the playroom with his grandmother. Mr. and Mrs. S. enter my office and take seats on the sofa. I can tell there's a problem before either of them has said a word: Dad sits all the way over to the left, reclining against the arm of the sofa, and Mom sits all the way over to the right, hands folded across her chest, knees pressed together. The space between them on the sofa is clearly no-man's-land.

"How are things going?" I ask cautiously, glancing back and forth, then letting my gaze come to rest on an imaginary spot on the wall, midway between the two of them.

There's a moment of awkward silence before Mrs. S. speaks up—cautiously at first, then with a slowly rising tone. "We've got a few problems, I'm afraid. Bryan's tantrums have been getting worse. He's still coming into bed with us. And just getting him to get up and dressed and onto the school bus each morning is nearly impossible!"

I turn to Dad: "What do you think about what your wife has just said, Mr. S.?"

Dad has a somewhat detached look. "Well, I guess my wife is really the best one to answer those questions—"

Before he can finish his sentence, his wife explodes: "That's right! Because you're never around! That's really the problem!" Then, turning to me, she continues: "Either he's always at the office or when he's home he's such a pushover that Bryan walks all over us." Then she starts to cry. Dad stares off into the distance, but his eyes redden, and he seems to be fighting back tears himself.

The Perfect Mom

Mr. and Mrs. J. are back with Noah for his regular six-month check. Noah is eight. He has autism, mild mental retardation, and intermittent agitated behavior. I've known Noah since he was three. Noah waits in the playroom with his teenage sister, whom the parents have brought to mind him during the parent interview. Mrs. J. enters my office clutching a large three-ring notebook overflowing with papers and carrying a brown cardboard accordion folder, also filled to near capacity. She sits down, carefully arranging the notebook and folder on the seat cushion next to her. Her husband sits at the far end of the sofa, separated from his wife by the notebook and folder. Before I have a chance to open my mouth, Mrs. J. begins to give me a detailed and somewhat negative account of Noah's school experience over the past six months. Nothing, it seems, is going right. Barely pausing for breath, she switches to a detailed narrative of Noah's various after-school activities, each of which she religiously attends: swimming, gymnastics, therapeutic horseback riding, and more. Her narrative is interrupted by the sound of Noah crying from the waiting room. Mom interrupts her narrative and rushes out to see what the matter might be. Dad glances at me, shrugs, and sighs in resignation.

What has gone wrong in these families?

At my urging, Mr. and Mrs. S. go for family therapy. After a few sessions, Mr. S. reveals that he is overwhelmed, not just by grief but by a sense of failure and shame because he can't make things all better for his son. Eventually, in response to further questions from the therapist, Mr. S. blurts out that as a child, he was repeatedly humiliated by his own father for minor mistakes and beaten for anything more serious. In essence, Mr. S. has picked up where his own father left off, inflicting shame on himself just as his father used to do to him. So Mr. S. has been burying himself in his work as his way of shielding himself from his feelings. At least when he is at the office, he can conquer the obstacles in his path; at home, no matter how hard he tries, he can't defeat his child's ASD. And when he is home, Mr. S. is so weighted down by his own issues that he is unable to apply discipline to Bryan. "He works so hard in therapy," says Mr. S., handing Bryan the toy he has been tantruming for, over his wife's objections. "Why do we have to make his life any harder?"

Just recognizing the connection between his upbringing and his present misery is a huge step forward for Mr. S. We'd like Mr. S. to be able to look in the mirror and say, "I can't fix my son's autism, but I'm still a good person. And it's okay for me to cause my son a little frustration now and then—it's what he needs in order to grow. It's not the same as what my father did to me." Fortunately, Mrs. S. is sympathetic, and once she realizes what her husband is dealing with, she is able to support him in his efforts to change.

The S. family illustrates the benefit of therapy, the extent to which previously unsuspected factors (in this case Dad's upbringing) can play a role, and the progress that can be made when both partners are willing to work something through. The S. family also illustrates why I often delay prescribing medication for disruptive behavior until the parents are working with a mental health professional and/or behavior specialist. In fact, as Mr. and Mrs. S. became more supportive of each other, they also became better at shaping Bryan's behavior to the point where his tantrums and cosleeping have been reduced to manageable proportions without medication.

What about the J. family? On the surface, Noah's mother looks like the perfect, dedicated mom, but when you look beneath the surface, she's not so different from Mr. S. She too is carrying a self-imposed burden, only instead of escaping to the office she has martyred herself to the "cause" of her child with disabilities. She and her husband have not been out to dinner or a movie—much less a weekend away from home—in years. She's just too busy: There's always a committee meeting, or an IEP to rewrite, or a therapy session. Besides, she protests, "There's no one else I can trust to take care of him!" Meanwhile, she slowly alienates her husband, her other children, and everyone else who might be able to help her share responsibility for Noah. In therapy, it comes out that Mrs. J. was raised in a very strict household with a black-and-white moral code and the belief that sin leads to punishment. Mrs. J.'s quest to cure her child is, at times, her way of trying to avert the guilt she would experience if she were ever to fully accept the reality of her son's disability; at other times it serves as her penance—a way of working off her self-perceived sin ("I must have sinned; otherwise why does my child have autism?"). It also comes out that Mrs. J.—like her mother and sister—suffers from anxiety, and that she has a brother with OCD. Unfortunately, Mrs. J. has become so tightly bonded to her self-appointed mission that she perceives any bid to share that burden with her as a threat. She resists medication and terminates therapy. Within twelve months she and Mr. J. separate.

The preceding examples may seem extreme or contrived, but they are fairly common variations on a theme I see in my office all the time. We all carry baggage from our childhoods into our adult lives, which colors our perception of the present and the meaning we ascribe to events. As we discussed earlier when I talked about "special children," it's not only the fact that your child has ASD that's causing you pain. It's also *whatever meaning you attach to that fact* that's causing pain. Did you set yourself up to be the perfect parent? Does your child carry the family name (John Smith IV, for example)? Was this a very badly wanted child, conceived after prolonged delay? Or perhaps a "surprise" baby, conceived after contraceptive failure or when Mom thought she was menopausal? Any of these circumstances can increase the pain of having a child with a disability, beyond the objective fact of the disability itself. Are you inflicting shame or guilt on yourself because of some supposed failure or defect on your part? Such unspoken (and frequently unconscious) meanings can become roadblocks to moving forward through the stages of grieving. If you or your partner seem to be stuck at one stage of the adaptation process (disbelief, anger, grief), then it's probably a wise idea to sit down with a mental health professional to explore why that might be so. It's no shame to get help; going for therapy to address unending sorrow is no different from taking someone to the operating room to locate and remove a foreign body, so healing can occur.

MAKING MEANING

The noted psychiatrist and philosopher Viktor Frankl credited his ability to survive imprisonment in a Nazi concentration camp to his ability to make meaning out of his existence, even in the midst of suffering and injustice. Our search for meaning, Frankl believes, is the highest expression of the human spirit. Right now you may be struggling to make meaning out of your own life, and the fact of your child's disability. I have no answers, but Frankl's book, *Man's Search for Meaning*, has been a source of strength to me in troubled times; you may find it helpful as well.

All families run into bumps from time to time. If you are interested in working on family relationship issues, I highly recommend *Married with*

Special-Needs Children: A Couples' Guide to Keeping Connected by Laura Marshak and Fran P. Prezant as a source of very readable and practical advice (see the Resource List). You and your partner may also benefit from reading the essays in *Voices from the Spectrum*, a collection of essays by parents, siblings, grandparents, and persons with high-functioning ASD, edited by Cindy Ariel and Robert Naseef. If, however, you feel that your relationship is potentially endangered, you should probably seek professional help. The American Association of Marriage and Family Therapists (AAMFT) is an excellent resource (see below). Psychologists with a grounding in family systems theory can also be helpful.

WHAT IS MARRIAGE AND FAMILY THERAPY?*

A family's patterns of behavior influence the individual and therefore may need to be a part of the treatment plan. In marriage and family therapy, the unit of treatment isn't just the person, even if only a single person is interviewed; it is the set of relationships in which the person is embedded. Marriage and family therapy is:

- Brief
- Solution focused
- Specific, with attainable therapeutic goals
- Designed with the end in mind.

Marriage and family therapists treat a wide range of serious clinical problems, including depression, marital problems, anxiety, individual psychological problems, and child-parent problems. The website of the American Association of Marriage and Family Therapists (www.aamft.org) contains a therapist locator utility to enable you to find a family therapist near you.

*From the AAMFT website

What Do I Tell My Child with ASD?

Brianna

Brianna is a bright seven-year-old with PDD-NOS. She's here for her regular follow-up. As part of my evaluation, I often ask children to draw me a picture of anything they like. Ugly, ugly, ugly, *Brianna has scrawled across the top of the page; under these words she has drawn a stick figure with a sad face. On the other side of the paper she has drawn a smiling girl with pigtails and a party dress;* Beautiful, *Brianna has labeled this one.* "Can you tell me about these pictures, Brianna?" *I ask. She hesitates for a moment, unsure of herself.* "This one is me," *she says, pointing to the ugly one.* "The other one," *she says, turning the page over,* "is my sister."

Malcolm

Malcolm came to me for the first time as an adolescent, on a referral from his guidance counselor. He had Asperger syndrome, but his parents had steadfastly avoided sharing his diagnosis with him, and had also prohibited school personnel from doing so. Malcolm was suffering from crippling anxiety and depression. He had been rebuffed by a girl whom he had invited to the prom, and thereafter had retreated into his own private world of computer gaming. His grades, previously A's and B's, were now C's and D's. His grooming had slipped. "I'm a terrible person," *he had told his guidance counselor;* "I would be better off dead." *That statement had prompted the consultation with me. Malcolm's parents wanted me to prescribe an antidepressant—but not to discuss his diagnosis with him.*

Over time, through a combination of hard work and neurologic maturation, many of your child's atypical features will fade. Eye contact, once so difficult to elicit, will improve. Social isolation, once so troublesome, will be replaced by a desire to participate—although your child may have difficulty figuring out all of the unwritten rules of how to go about making and keeping friends. All the while, a slow-motion race is going on between your child's atypicality and his or her level of self-awareness. At the beginning, atypicality is way out in front; self-awareness is not even in the running. If your child is lucky, however, he or she will develop the ability to understand humor, tell fibs, and engage in verbal make-believe, role playing, and turn taking. As these skills develop, self-awareness is slowly gaining on atypicality. Finally, self-awareness draws abreast of atypicality. This is progress! But this is also the moment when your child will realize that he or she is *different from other children.* You have worked hard up to this point to give your son or daughter all of the necessary social skills; now you need to face the bittersweet moment of explaining ASD to your child. I've saved this topic for last, because it's undoubtedly the most difficult. Your ability to attend to this task depends on how well you and your partner have been able to deal with your own issues, as we've discussed above.

As much as you want to protect your child—"I don't want my child to see himself as different, or as damaged goods"—you really can't avoid the topic. Eventually, children with ASD plus normal IQ will catch on to their own differences. It's up to you to make that transition as smooth as possible. But one way or another, it's going to happen. Either you tell the child the truth in a way that is empowering or you try to evade the topic. If you go the latter route, your child will fill in the blank with dire speculations—like Brianna or Malcolm in the previous vignettes. Or, worse, your child will come home in tears some day, having been teased and called "weird" by the playground bully. Your best bet is to get ahead of the curve and arm your child with the information he or she will need to fend off bullies and preserve his or her self-esteem.

When and how should you tell your child about his or her ASD? It's not so different from informing a child who has been adopted: The rule of thumb there is that the child who is adopted should never be able to look back and remember the day he or she was first told. So begin using terms like *ASD* (or *PDD-NOS* or *Asperger syndrome*) even before your child understands what you are talking about. You can even do your best to make light of it: "Oh, Ethan, I know you're a sweet boy and you didn't mean to get so upset about that missing toy. That was your ASD getting in the way again!" In this way, you and your child form a partnership, and ASD is your *shared adversary.* I realize that this walks a thin line of sounding like you don't fully accept your child for exactly who he or she is—but such is the split reality in which you now live. There's also the risk that your child may learn to manipulate the system: "I couldn't help it! My autism made me do it!" But there are going to be lots of times when this is really true, and your child needs to have a chance to say so. If your child becomes inconsolably anxious because his favorite blue spoon is missing, he should know that it's okay for him to feel bad, and that he himself is not to blame for the anxiety—any more than a child with diabetes is to blame for having an insulin reaction.

Just as there are books for siblings of the child with ASD, there are books for children with ASD themselves, to teach them about their own situation. These books start very young, and work all the way through to adolescence and adulthood (see the Resource List). You want to frame the information in a way that is reaffirming for your child. One book, for example, talks about famous people in history who might have been on the spectrum. There's something very cool about sharing a place in history with Einstein, Mozart, or van Gogh. Many of my families wisely decide to work with a psychologist or family therapist to help them and their child through the informing process. The same resources we discussed earlier, such as the AAMFT, are applicable here. In addition, for adolescents and adults with high-functioning autism or Asperger syndrome, there are self-support groups (some face-to-face and some online). There are even resources for spouses of adults with high-functioning autism.

Now let's see what happened with the children you met at the beginning of this section.

Brianna's parents had already been considering how to inform their daughter of her diagnosis but had felt that it was not necessary—yet. "She doesn't seem to be aware of her differences," they had told me on their previous visit. One look at her pictures, however, told another story. Brianna was not specifically focused on her ASD, but she was clearly starting to compare herself unfavorably to her sister. At my recommendation, the parents enrolled Brianna in play therapy. Over the course of several months, Brianna astonished her parents with the depth of feelings revealed in her artwork. Slowly the parents began to introduce Brianna to terms such as PDD, explaining to her that kids with PDD weren't "ugly," "dumb," or "lazy," that it wasn't fair that she had PDD, and that it was okay for her to be angry about it. Brianna's mood brightened considerably. She still flaps, spins, and perseverates on Polly Pocket dolls, but overall she seems happier with herself. And her parents have made a chart titled "Brianna's PDD," on which they have listed behaviors for Brianna to work on as part of a token economy.

I explained to Malcolm's parents that what they wanted—a prescription, while keeping their son in the dark regarding his condition—was not good medical practice, and not good for Malcolm. Malcolm was bright enough to go to college, but we needed to give him insight into his own situation so that he could survive away from home. Eventually, after several lengthy discussions with me and my social worker, the parents consented to seeing a child psychologist with Malcolm and, with the psychologist's help, to revealing Malcolm's diagnosis to him, along with various support materials. With this plan in place, I agreed to write a prescription for fluoxetine. The combination of information, counseling, and pharmacotherapy led to substantial improvement in Malcolm's outlook on life. His grades returned to their previous level, and he again began talking optimistically about his intention to become a computer programmer for NASA.

Summing Up

My not-so-hidden agenda throughout this chapter has been to reassure you that your feelings—whatever they are—are okay. What I hope to avert is a situation where you are inflicting additional pain on yourself, over and above the objective realities of your child's situation. Look within yourself to see what additional meaning you may have attached to the fact that your child has a disability. Stay engaged with life; the urge to be alone when under stress is a red flag. Make time for yourself, and for your relationship with your partner if you are in a committed relationship. Find—or make—meaning from your experience. Keep a sense of humor. Get help when you need it. There's no shame in doing so, and burnout is not an option.

Chapter 16

Practical Concerns

In this chapter we will discuss some of the legal and financial concerns you face as part of your effort to secure the best possible future for your child with ASD. I will have to paint the picture with broad strokes—partly because these are areas that go beyond my scope of expertise (see the Resource List for additional information), and partly because the range of potential outcomes for any given child is so broad. Some aspects of your long-term blueprint will be more in the vein of contingency planning, rather than cast in stone. Like a landscape painter, we can depict foreground items in detail, but the farther the eye moves to the horizon, the hazier the picture becomes. In the immediate foreground of the picture is your child's current developmental status and therapy or educational program. A path into the hills leads into the middle distance. And in the background, fittingly, are what might be called the "blue-sky" issues: your vision of your child's future twenty, thirty, or fifty years from now. Although the general composition of the picture has been laid out, vast areas of the canvas are still blank. I'll sketch in what I can, and direct you to experts in other fields who can help work on the rest.

Special Education: Your Rights Under the Law

Ignore your rights... and they'll go away.

—Anonymous

Free and Appropriate Public Education
In the 1954 landmark case *Brown v. Board of Education of Topeka, Kansas,* the U.S. Supreme Court overturned racial segregation in the public schools, establishing the principle that separate educational facilities for nonwhite children were "inherently unequal." It took another two decades, several lawsuits, and an act of Congress to get these principles extended to cover children with developmental disabilities, but in 1975 Congress finally enacted the Education of All Handicapped Children Act (EAHCA). Patterned directly on the principles articulated by the Supreme Court in *Brown,* EAHCA mandated that

> all handicapped children have available to them... a free appropriate public education [FAPE] which emphasizes special education and related services designed to meet their unique needs.... To the maximum extent appropriate, children with disabilities... should be educated with children who are not disabled.... Special classes, separate schooling, or other removal of children with disabilities from the regular educational environment should occur only when the nature or severity of the disability is such that education in regular classes with the use of supplementary aids and services cannot be achieved satisfactorily [and] to assure that the rights of handicapped children and their parents or guardians are protected.

Least Restrictive Environment
Under the principle of least restrictive environment (LRE), each child is to be educated in the least restrictive setting possible. Toward this end, schools are required to provide "related services," defined as "transportation, and such developmental, corrective and other supportive services... as may be required to assist a handicapped child to benefit from special education." Many of these "related services" include what

had previously been regarded as medical services such as occupational therapy and physical therapy, modifications of the environment (say, a wheelchair ramp), and other services not traditionally viewed as part of the standard educational framework.

Due Process

Due process is the principle of fair play and having to follow the rules, with checks and balances to ensure a level playing field. Prior to EAHCA, parents had no due process rights when seeking services or challenging a school's decisions vis-à-vis their child's placement. Congress and the courts realized that the rights conferred to children would amount to nothing but a hollow gesture unless parents were also given due process rights, including the right to review all of their child's educational records, the right to advance notice of all meetings pertaining to their child, the right to attend such meetings, the right to an independent outside evaluation, and a requirement that service providers obtain the parents' signed approval before implementing an Individualized Family Service Plan (IFSP) or Individualized Education Program (IEP). There is also a due process mechanism that grants parents the right to challenge the proposed plan, as well as the right to be represented by an attorney and to present evidence before an impartial hearing officer. Exactly what constitutes an appropriate intervention program, the least restrictive environment, or a related service are common bones of contention between parents and service providers. This is a shifting boundary, and precedent-setting cases frequently go all the way up to the U.S. Supreme Court. For the latest and best guidance, consult an attorney who specializes in education law.

Individuals with Disabilities Education Act

The principles of FAPE, LRE, related services, and due process were reaffirmed and extended in the Individuals with Disabilities Education Act (IDEA), which superseded EAHCA in 1990. IDEA itself has been amended several times since then, and remains the basis in federal law for all education rights for children with special needs.

IDEA is broken into various parts; we need only to concern ourselves with Parts C and B. Part C mandates the provision of early intervention (EI) services for children from birth up to three. (In some places, EI is described as "birth to two." In other places, you will see "birth to three." Just remember that Part C covers children from birth to two years and 364 days of age.) Part C of IDEA requires each state to designate or provide:

- A "lead agency" that takes responsibility for EI-related activity and reports directly to the governor. In many states, the Department of Health is the designated lead agency. In others, it may be the Department of Education or some other human-service agency.
- A statewide "child find system" to detect children with special needs.
- "A timely, comprehensive, multidisciplinary evaluation of the functioning of each infant or toddler with a disability...and a family-directed identification of the needs of each family of such an infant or toddler, to assist appropriately in the development of the infant or toddler."
- An Individualized Family Service Plan (IFSP) for each infant or toddler with a disability.

Notice the emphasis on "family-centered" and "family-directed." The IFSP is intended to meet the needs of *the family* as the family seeks to optimize the development of their child.

EI services are paid for partly with public funds, but you may be asked to come up with a copay. Each state is different. EI services can be provided in your home or in whatever setting your child may be in (day care, preschool). The scope of services typically includes an infant special education teacher, speech therapist, occupational therapist, and physical therapist. To access EI, contact your state Department of Health or state Department of Education. They, in turn, will put you in touch with the "child find" agency in your state, to get the ball rolling.

Part B of IDEA mandates special education services from the child's third birthday to age twenty-one. The lead agency for Part B is the state Department of Education. Typically, children from three to five are served by a dedicated component of the Department of Education (preschool special ed). Part B requires the preparation of an Individualized Education Program (IEP), based on a comprehensive assessment with standardized instruments, which delineates the child's needs, and the proposed educational and related services (transportation, various therapies) intended to address these needs. These special education services are supported by tax dollars.

Working with the School District

• *Keep good records.* This includes written documentation of all communication with the school, as well as copies of all your child's test reports. Buy a three-ring notebook each year and divide it by sections. (Keep records by academic year September to August, not calendar year.) It's also helpful to have a separate notebook that can go back and forth with your child to school so that you and your child's teachers can stay in touch.

• *Learn to negotiate.* There's an expression in the business world: You don't get what you deserve; you get what you negotiate for. Things usually aren't that cutthroat in education, but you need to be prepared to negotiate. Remember that *negotiate* means give and take: Do not meekly accept only what the system offers, but do not rigidly demand everything that you would like either. To become a successful negotiator, you need to become an informed consumer of services, and you need to be knowledgeable about how the system works. An excellent place to begin is the Wrightslaw website: www.wrightslaw .com. I've put additional references in the Resource List.

• *Don't go it alone.* Of course, you are your child's advocate. Often, however, your wisest course is to bring in an outside advocate. This may be a private psychologist or educational consultant. Such a person can review the test data generated by the school, generate additional data if needed, and make unbiased recommendations to you about your child's needs, using the technical language a school district will understand. Or the advocate may be someone versed in education law who will be able to help you gently but firmly press for your rights—and at the same time work to keep the level of reactivity down on both sides. Backing someone into a corner or putting them on the defensive should be your very last option.

• *Don't fire unless fired upon.* If you have a serious disagreement with your service provider, try to work it out through mediation rather than confrontation, if at all possible. Most educational professionals really do have your child's welfare in mind. But don't be afraid to stand your ground. The only reason you and your child enjoy the rights you have today is because parents of earlier generations fought for them. See the Resource List for additional information.

Following the Money

Medical Assistance

Medical Assistance (MA, Medicaid) was established in 1965 under Title XIX of the Social Security Act. MA covers health care costs for people with low income. People with disabilities, including children, are also potentially eligible for MA if they have a severe, long-lasting (longer than twelve months) disabling condition. MA serves as the child's backup insurance after his or her parents' private health insurance (if any) has picked up whatever the parents' policy would normally cover. MA is a godsend for families whose children incur extraordinary medical expenses. In some states, MA will also pay for some behavioral health services, which can be especially useful for families of children with ASD.

Depending on the state of residence, there may or may not be a financial criterion for children with disability. In Pennsylvania, where I practice, only the child's income (typically, zero) is counted; if the child meets disability criteria, based on severity and duration of the disability itself, then issuance of an MA card is essentially automatic. In Massachusetts, to pick another example, family income is an additional criterion, but families whose income exceeds the threshold for MA eligibility are allowed to "buy in" to MA on behalf of their child, according to a sliding scale. In other states, if the family income exceeds a certain limit, the child is out of luck. The Kaiser Foundation has put together an informative publication on the role of Medicaid in funding services for children with disabilities (see the Resource List).

Supplemental Security Income

Supplemental Security Income (SSI) is another component of the Social Security Act. Unlike Medicaid, which covers health care costs directly,

SSI provides cash payments to children with disabilities whose parents' income and household assets fall below defined levels. Children who qualify for SSI automatically qualify for MA, but the reverse is not true. For additional information, see the Resource List.

Long-Term Planning

Predictive Value of Developmental Testing

The 3-D model I presented in Chapter 5 is based on the averaged experience of lots of children. However, just as we can't predict which way a coin will land on any one flip—even though we know that it will come up heads about half the time over a large number of flips—predicting the long-term outcome for a particular child is difficult. Prediction is not an idle exercise, to prove how good the doctor is at crystal ball gazing. Rather, it is a response to parents' urgent need for a best-guess picture of the future, so they can address decisions that need to be made today: *How shall we apportion our assets in our will, taking into account the future needs of our child with ASD? Shall we have more children? Should we consider moving to another county or state where services might be better?* I cannot tell parents how to divide their assets or whether to enlarge their families. But I do have an obligation to give them my assessment of the most likely range of outcomes for their child. We've touched on some of this in Chapter 5, but it's a good idea to briefly recap.

A developmental quotient (DQ) of less than 50 percent at age three is strongly suggestive of a diagnosis of mental retardation. This turned out to be the case for Kevin, whom you met in Chapter 1 and saw again in Chapters 5, 7, and 13. Even before Kevin reached elementary school, it was possible to predict, with a fair degree of certainty, that he would require some level of support and supervision as an adult. Does this mean that developmental specialists can predict, at age five, whether a given child will learn to speak or read? No. But we usually can advise parents—in broad outline—on their child's likely needs as an adult. Three-year-olds with a DQ over 70 are probably safely in the range of normal intelligence. Likewise, it was fairly easy to make reasonably certain predictions about Teddy, who was referred by his first-grade guidance counselor for evaluation of atypical behavior. Teddy had above-average intelligence on formal IQ testing, normal academic skills, and Asperger syndrome. We can safely predict that Teddy will be able to compete in the marketplace and live on his own as an adult, even if he retains some atypical behaviors. Will he go to college, marry, or raise a family? It's too soon to say. But—as with Kevin—I can be reasonably certain on the question of Teddy's ability to function independently as an adult. Preschool children with a DQ between 50 and 70 are tough to call. Over time some of them pull things together and eventually fall into the normal IQ range. Others, however, struggle even harder, as life's challenges become increasingly more complex. Their IQ scores may even decline somewhat—not because they are deteriorating neurologically, but because the tasks become more abstract. Early on, a child's excellent rote memory and generally well-preserved visual-spatial skills may be enough to carry the day. Gradually, however, the emphasis shifts to tasks requiring fluid intelligence. This brings us to Darryl. Darryl falls somewhere in between Kevin and Teddy, developmentally speaking, and for now (elementary school), it's not possible to peer over the horizon. Will Darryl be able to live on his own and hold down a job? It's simply too soon to say.

There's another big caveat to consider when estimating the future abilities of a young child with ASD: Frequently the child's ASD gets in the way of tapping his or her true level of ability during testing. In a sense, the atypicality serves as an extenuating circumstance and gives us reason to hope that there's more going on than we can presently see—unlike, say, a child with across-the-board delay without atypicality. In that instance, the examiner can be pretty confident of having elicited the child's best.

The Life Care Plan

The purpose of a life care plan is to ensure your child a secure existence after you are no longer here. Normally, this is not a subject that parents of a young child sit around thinking about. If parents do think about their children's future, they imagine all sorts of wonderful things like college or weddings—not the possibility that their child may still be dependent on others decades from now. In some respects, planning for your child's welfare after you're no longer here is even more stressful than dealing with the here and now. The subject evokes one's own mortality as well as the vulnerability of the child. And the reality is that you will need to draw up some long-term plans now, before your child's prognosis is clear, with the understanding that you should revisit and revise your plans annually as your child's future slowly reveals itself. Fortunately, there are good people—attorneys, life care planners—you can turn to, to help you tackle this task (see the Resource List), and you will feel better once you've taken care of it.

First, you need an advance medical directive and a will for yourself and your spouse. These documents instruct others how to care for you if and when you are no longer able to speak on your own behalf, and how to distribute your assets after you are gone. Your need to identify guardians for your children—a process that requires more thought and commitment than usual, due to the special circumstances of your child with ASD. Not only does your child with ASD require extraordinary care right now, but it's conceivable that he or she will continue to require oversight and assistance as an adult. You may want to think about naming an adult family member or close friend as guardian for the moment, but building in a provision to transfer guardianship to one of your other children once they reach a certain age. Stipulating a future guardian for a child with ASD, especially after he or she has reached eighteen or twenty-one, can be tricky and may require a court order, declaring the child with ASD legally incompetent. I can't imagine many things that would be harder for a parent to do, but this may be the only way to protect your child from falling into some legal limbo, or being exploited by unscrupulous individuals who would see your adult child with ASD as an easy target for financial exploitation. You probably want to place your child's inheritance into a special-needs trust, with a trustee who will administer the trust on your child's behalf, rather than leaving the money to your child directly. A trust will avoid the necessity of spending down all of your assets before your child can receive public benefits. As with guardianship, you will need to decide whom to name as trustee.

You need to develop a financial plan based upon factors such as your child's projected life expectancy, earning potential, care requirements, and so forth. Then you will have to figure out where the money will come from. Some of it will come from you, some from insurance, some from federal programs such as SSI. As mentioned above, a trust can provide financial protection.

Don't put this off. You are probably decades away from your own demise. But it's possible that you and your partner may die in a motor vehicle accident tomorrow. Without a will, a trust, and guardians, your estate could be nibbled away by taxes and legal fees, and your child could wind up in foster care or reared by someone who doesn't share your values and your vision of your child's future.

(i) See the Resource List for additional information on legal and financial planning.

Transition to Adulthood

When I was a boy of fourteen, my father was so ignorant I could hardly stand to have the old man around. But when I got to be twenty-one, I was astonished at how much the old man had learned in seven years.

—*Mark Twain*

Right now, you may have no idea of your child's long-term potential, but whatever it is, I want you to contemplate the future with the assumption that when adulthood arrives, your child with ASD will be leaving home. As Mark Twain knew, Mother Nature intends all children to leave the nest. It may be to go to college, enlist in the armed forces, or take a job in another city. There are lots of good resources to guide you on subjects such as careers and higher education, as well as typical teen issues such as the physical, psychological, and hormonal changes that come with puberty, written in a way that will be meaningful to a young person with atypicality (the importance of good grooming, for example, which may not be self-evident to a teen on the spectrum).

(i) See the Resource List for additional information on puberty and post–high school education and career planning.

If your child has severe atypicality and/or mental retardation in addition to ASD, leaving the nest may mean moving in to a group home or a residential living facility. But, just as with higher-functioning children who may go off to college alone, atypicality and all, your child with more significant issues also needs to leave home. Why do I say that? Don't you know how to care for your child better than anyone else? Can't you anticipate his or her needs better than anyone else? Well...yes and no. You probably know the ins and outs of your child's day-to-day care better than anyone else, but everyone needs a peer group, and your child with ASD is no exception. Feelings of self-worth come from membership in a group. No matter how carefully you tend to your children's needs, you cannot provide the external validation that comes from being accepted as part of a group by individuals similar to oneself. Your child with ASD is no different from his or her typically developing peers in this regard. And hanging on for too long—even for the best of reasons—carries significant risks.

Why am I bringing up this subject now, when your child may still be in preschool? Because transition to adulthood is a *process,* rather than an event at one moment in time. (And because it's *you,* as much as your child, who needs to start transitioning.) The transition process began the day your son or daughter was born. Steps along the way include the first time you leave your child with a sitter, the first time you leave your child overnight with grandparents, or the first time you send your child to sleepaway camp. For your child with ASD, steps in transition to adulthood may include in-home or out-of-home respite care (overnight or for a weekend), a trial stay at a group home, or working in a supported employment setting. Each of these moments entails letting go and trusting both your child and his or her temporary caregivers or supervisors. This is not easy. But it's an essential part of your child's process of becoming a competent adult. It's far better to ease your child into transition at a time when you are still around to check in on him or her in the new setting than to put matters off until there's a crisis of some kind.

Leo

Leo, fourteen, provides an example of the kind of crisis that may arise. Leo has autism, moderate mental retardation, and agitated behavior. He lives at home with his parents and two younger siblings: Jared, age nine, and Jenny, age seven. His mom used to work as a medical secretary but has been a full-time stay-at-home mom since Leo's ASD was diagnosed at age three. Over the past twelve months, puberty has transformed Leo into a husky fellow who towers over his mother. Leo is now physically uncontrollable. He terrorizes his siblings, especially Jenny. Usually she is able to stay out of harm's way. Today, however, with better aim than usual, Leo throws a vase at her, striking her in the eye. No amount of medication can offset the fact that Leo is out of control at home. Fortunately, his parents have already been investigating several residential programs, "just in case." They hadn't planned to take this step so soon, but their physical inability to restrain their son has forced their hand.

Frank

Forty-seven-year-old Frank has autism and mental retardation. He lives at home with his parents, who are in their sixties. His father is a retired university professor. His mother is a retired schoolteacher, on partial disability because of a herniated disk. Frank is their only child. They have never felt comfortable entrusting his care to third parties. One day, while the family is in the garden picking flowers, Frank's father suddenly clutches his chest, and collapses with a fatal heart attack. Frank's mother is now a widow, and her infirmities make it impossible for her to care for Frank unassisted. But she and Frank's father had no plans in place. One option would be to hire a home health aide. Another would be to consider out-of-home placement for Frank. A third option would be to look for some type of assisted-living program where both she and Frank could live. This might be the best option under the circumstances, rather than inflicting a second loss by separating them in the immediate aftermath of Frank's father's death. Good programs, however, typically have waiting lists, so their options may be limited.

If you have other children, what role will they play in the long-term care of your child with ASD? Many parents find it gratifying to include their other children in planning meetings on behalf of their sibling with ASD. Especially as your other children approach adolescence, think about including them as "nonvoting members of the board." Including your typically abled children in the planning process is a wonderful way to strengthen the family and convey a sense of trust in your other children. The greater the trust you show in your other children, the more ownership they will feel of their special sibling's needs. You may hope that your other children will look after your child with ASD after you are gone, and if they volunteer to do so, that's great. Remember, however, that they will be starting lives of their own—spouses, babies, jobs, moves, unforeseen health problems. The only way you can be sure they are really volunteering is by creating a viable alternative.

In summary, your child with ASD will probably outlive you. And you may not simply die. You may have a stroke or develop some other physical infirmity that prevents you from caring for either yourself or your adult child with ASD. Suddenly having to leave home in the aftermath of your death or incapacitation will be a double blow for him or her. It is far better for your child to go through the transition process when you are alive and well and able to ease the transition by visiting your child in his or her new setting. (And is it fair to mention that maybe you are also entitled to some respite, after all the years you will have spent caring for your child?)

Expecting one of your other children to take in your child with ASD does nothing to meet your child with ASD's need for a peer group or to address potential safety issues (do you want your adult child with ASD living in the same household as your two-year-old grandchild?). Your other children may be willing and able to take on the responsibility, but give them the chance to do so electively, rather than out of necessity. Another option, one that is sometimes better for all parties, might be for your child with ASD to live in an assisted community setting, in as close an approximation to normal as his or her abilities will allow, with your other children functioning as guardian angels somewhere nearby.

Summing Up

None of the topics we've covered in this chapter is easy. Even something as innocent as planning for the next IEP meeting taps into your unspoken hopes and fears about your child's long-term outlook. Life planning explicitly thrusts these issues onto center stage at a time when most parents are more focused on their child's next soccer game. I know it's not fair. But if you are able to deal with these issues, you will feel a sense of liberation and accomplishment. I hope that in the process of working through the issues I have laid out in this chapter, you will develop a healthy outlook and a secure future for your child with ASD, your other children, your partner, and yourself. More than that, no parent can provide or expect of him- or herself.

Epilogue

We have come to the end of our time together. Over the course of this book, we have surveyed a vast amount of information, from the earliest reports of what we now call autistic spectrum disorder to the latest research on molecular biology. At this point, I hope you have developed a working knowledge of:

- The medical underpinnings of ASD
- The underlying cognitive deficits that go into ASD
- The difference between atypicality and global developmental delay
- The theoretical basis for and practical application of various educational therapies for ASD
- Fundamentals of behavior management and the role of medication
- Ways to recognize medical quackery
- Ways to take care of yourself and the significant others in your life
- Ways to face the future with confidence and equanimity as well as hope

One hundred and fifty years ago, Sir William Osler warned the graduating class at Johns Hopkins University School of Medicine: "Unfortunately I must inform you that half of what we have taught you is wrong. Even more unfortunately, we cannot tell you which half." Likewise, some of what you have read here is doubtless wrong, or at least would be disputed by others in the field. Some of it is true only for now and will become outdated as medical science pushes back the frontiers of our knowledge of ASD.

Some of the advances I hope to see, and that will surely occur in your child's lifetime, include:

- *The ability to map specific cognitive and behavioral patterns to specific areas of the brain.* Why do some children with ASD sniff objects, and others do not? Why are some clumsy and others not? What is the relationship between mirror neurons and theory of mind? The questions posed by ASD are very deep: What is the neural basis of empathy? Where does the sense of self reside?

- *The ability to test for specific genes, and combinations of genes, that give rise to the behaviors we lump together today as ASD.* One hundred years ago, all forms of kidney failure were lumped together under the term *Bright's disease.* It didn't really matter, though, because there were no treatments available anyway. Glancing through old medical textbooks gives me an anticipatory feeling of déjà vu: In fifty years, or even ten or twenty, physicians will look back bemused at how little we knew about ASD at the turn of the twenty-first century.

- *New knowledge of environmental cofactors.* As yet there are few smoking guns. Thalidomide and valproic acid, certainly. What about male hormones, either in the food chain or in the environment? Or neurotoxins such as mercury or polychlorinated biphenyls (PCBs)? Are there subsets of children with ASD (those with mitochondrial disorders, perhaps) who are uniquely vulnerable to specific environmental agents? At this point we just don't know.

- *A deeper understanding of the neurochemistry of ASD.* Present-day psychopharmacology is a form of educated trial and error, based entirely on the outward expression of symptoms. Someday soon we will be able to view images of chemical receptors in the brain, which will allow us to know exactly where the deficit is and what drugs will work the best for any particular child. We will also be able to identify genetic factors that give rise to neurotransmitter deficits or that lead to drug responsivity.

• *A fundamental shift in our view of ASD, along the same lines as we now think about intelligence and mental retardation.* Most children with mild mental retardation (IQ 55 to 70) are simply on the lower end of the statistical curve. There is nothing medically wrong with them. Virtually all children with an IQ of less than 55 have a medical disorder as the reason for their low IQ. Between 55 and 70, it's a mix of the two groups: the lower tail of the normal population, and the upper tail of those with medical conditions. The same will turn out to be the case, I predict, for ASD: The majority of people with mild atypicality will eventually be recognized as simply expressing a variation of normal development—no missing or extra genetic material, no other biological impairment, just normal folks whose theory of mind skills are at the lower end of the normal curve. Those with extreme atypicality—like those with IQs less than 55—will all turn out to have identifiable medical conditions. In between, we will find a mixture of people, some with medical conditions and some who are just normal for themselves. This will be a fundamental sea change in the way we view ASD, and in my opinion this will explain the so-called explosion in ASD—we will come to recognize the prevalence of what I will call "normal ASD" in the population at large.

Some things will not change. Parents will continue to want the best for their children, and will remain willing to do whatever it takes to get it for them. And legitimate professionals will continue to apply their skills to try to mend the little bit of the universe they know something about. Sad to say, however, there will also be self-styled experts who will be eager to sell parents hope in a bottle, in the form of a promised cure for their child's ASD. Remember to ask: "Is it safe? Does it work?" For answers to these questions, look to controlled trials performed by people who do not have a financial or emotional stake in the outcome. As a parent, your overriding question is: "Might it work?" Of course, phrased that way, the question is a lot harder to answer. However, if you apply the standards I've outlined in earlier chapters, you'll be able to recognize therapies that rest primarily on unverified testimonials rather than facts.

Francis Bacon was right: Knowledge is power. Throughout this book, I've tried to give you not just information but sufficient context so you can convert that information into usable knowledge. At times I have run the risk of speaking to you as if you were medical students, rather than parents of a child with ASD. My editors have done their best to tone me down, but I've still deluged you with facts, often rather technical or obscure. Raising a child with ASD is an immense challenge. You did not sign up to take this class, but the dean of students upstairs decided to enroll you anyway, and here you are.

I had a classmate in medical school who was more than a little bit arrogant. "Professor Rodin," he asked our beloved neuroanatomy professor, who was giving us a lecture on the intricacies of the brain, "will this be relevant to me in my practice of medicine?" Without missing a beat, our professor gently replied, "Everything you remember from medical school will be relevant to you in your practice of medicine. Whatever you do *not* remember will *not* be relevant to you." I hope that most of what we have covered in this book will someday be relevant to you in your care of your child. You do not need to memorize it. Just know that it's here to look up. Armed with knowledge, you can go forth and begin the task of sorting through the mass of information and misinformation, eventually coming to peace with whatever decisions you make on behalf of your child with ASD. No one is in a better position to make these choices than you.

Finally, it has been my intention to give you hope. First, of course, there is hope embedded in the concept of the natural history of ASD. ASD improves over time. Sometimes the progress may seem painfully slow, but it happens nonetheless, and you would be powerless to hold it back even if you wished to try. I can't tell you exactly how quickly your child will make progress. As we have seen, that depends on your child's degree of atypicality and his or her level of general intelligence. It also depends, to some degree, on the type and intensity of his or her intervention program.

Children of an earlier era stricken with leukemia were foot soldiers in a war they did not seek. Without their sacrifices as participants in randomized controlled trials, children of today would still face a 95 percent death rate. Instead, a child newly diagnosed with leukemia today has a 95 percent chance of achieving long-term survival. In order to beat back ASD, parents of children on the spectrum need to face and accept the same challenge, and place their hope in the same promise—that through controlled research, autism's mysteries can be unlocked and remedied. This progress will come about through a partnership between parents and researchers. Research is badly needed on both the medical and developmental fronts. We need randomized, controlled studies of developmental and biomedical interventions in order to figure out which therapies are best for which children at which points in their development and which are useless or even harmful. Until parents and clinicians are mutually prepared to undertake such research, blind men will go on arguing about the nature of the elephant, quackery will thrive, and parents will go on pouring time and money into dubious therapies, while better treatments lie unused or undiscovered.

Keep your sense of humor. Families with a sense of humor tend to be resilient in the face of setbacks. If you can find at least one thing a day to laugh about, your chances of surviving all the tribulations you face rise immensely.

Be kind to yourself. If, at the end of the day, you have only accomplished 99 percent of the tasks on your mental clipboard (or 90 percent or 50 percent), it's not a calamity. Just think about the U.S. Navy's construction battalion, the Seabees, who have a motto: *The difficult we do immediately. The impossible takes a little longer.*

Don't be thrown into a panic by those who would have you believe that some magic window is closing. That's a scare tactic. Don't fall for it. Your child is not going to suddenly encounter a big crack in the earth that prevents further progress.

Be patient with others, but only up to a point. All of the laws and services we have today for people with special needs, from curb cuts for wheelchairs to EI, have come about because someone somewhere stood up and fought for them.

Keep up hope. Nowhere is this more true today than in the field of ASD. When I entered medical school nearly forty years ago, we were taught that cold, rejecting mothers (so-called refrigerator mothers) caused autism. DNA had barely been discovered, and no one had heard of fragile X. The SSRIs had not been invented. People with special needs were ridiculed and shut off from society in giant institutions. Today, society is more tolerant of differences than it was when I was a child. Resources are available. Topics that were taboo fifty years ago can now be openly discussed. Disability research is a thriving enterprise. We need to guard and preserve these resources and values. The way in which a society treats its least able members is a measure of that society's worth. You are now the bearer of that torch—it's a role you didn't seek, but it is yours nonetheless.

Pace yourself. Remember, this is a marathon, not a sprint.

Good luck on your journey.

Resource List

Part I: The World of the Child

Chapter 1: Patterns of Development

Autism
- Kanner L. Autistic disturbances of affective contact. *Nervous Child.* 1943; 2:217–250. The original paper on autism, and still one of the best descriptions of ASD. Available online at www.neurodiversity.com/library_kanner_1943.pdf.
- **Autism Society of America:** The oldest national organization for individuals with ASD and their families, www.autism-society.org.

PDD-NOS
- **Commonly asked questions regarding PDD:** National Dissemination Center for Children with Disabilities, www.nichcy.org/pubs/factshe/fs20txt.htm.

Asperger Syndrome
- **OASIS:** Online Asperger Syndrome Information and Support, www.udel.edu/bkirby/asperger.

Nonverbal Learning Disability
- **NLD on the Web:** www.nldontheweb.org.
- **Nonverbal Learning Disorders Association:** www.nlda.org.
- **NLDline:** www.nldline.com.

Chapter 2: Getting a Diagnosis

If You Suspect ASD
- **First Signs:** Dedicated to educating parents and pediatric professionals about the early warning signs of autism, www.firstsigns.org.
- **Centers for Disease Control and Prevention—Autism Information Center:** Basic information and resource links, www.cdc.gov/autism.
- **National Institutes of Health:** www.ninds.nih.gov/disorders/autism/autism.htm, www.nimh.nih.gov/publicat/autism.cfm, and www.nlm.nih.gov/medlineplus/autism.html#cat3.

What to Expect in a Medical Evaluation
Look for a physician who adheres to the practices outlined below. Although written for physicians, most of this material will be understandable by the average lay reader.
- **American Academy of Pediatrics:** www.medicalhomeinfo.org/health/autism.html.
    - Caring for Children with Autism Spectrum Disorders: A Resource Toolkit for Clinicians (CD available for purchase).
    - Identification and Evaluation of Children with Autism Spectrum Disorders.
    - Management of Children with Autism Spectrum Disorders.

Chapter 3: Why My Child? A Medical Primer

Causes of ASD—Reviews
- Cohen D et al. Specific genetic disorders and autism: clinical contribution towards their identification. *J Autism Dev Disord.* 2005; 35(1):103–116.
- DiCicco-Bloom E et al. The developmental neurobiology of autism spectrum disorder. *J Neuroscience.* 2006; 26(26):6897–6906.

- Tuchman R, Rapin I. *Autism: A Neurological Disorder of Early Brain Development.* London: MacKeith Press, 2006. Written by and for child neurologists; provides a detailed discussion of the current state of the medical science of ASD.

Mitochondrial disorders

- Pons R et al. Mitochondrial DNA abnormalities and autistic spectrum disorders. *J Pediatr.* 2004; 144(1):81–85.
- Oliveira G et al. Mitochondrial dysfunction in autism spectrum disorders: a population-based study. *Dev Med Child Neurol.* 2005; 47(3):185–189.
- Tsao CY, Mendell JR. Autistic disorder in 2 children with mitochondrial disorders. *J Child Neurol.* 2007; 22(9):1121–1123.
- Weissman JR et al. Mitochondrial disease in autism spectrum disorder patients: a cohort analysis. *PLoS ONE.* 2008; 3(11):e3815.
- Smith M, Spence MA, Flodman P. Nuclear and mitochondrial genome defects in autisms. *Ann N Y Acad Sci.* 2009; 1151: 102–132.

Endocrine effects ("super male" brain)

- Baron-Cohen S, Knickmeyer RC, Belmonte MK. Sex differences in the brain: implications for explaining autism. *Science.* 2005; 310(5749):819–823.

Parental age, infertility

- Croen LA et al. Maternal and paternal age and risk of autism spectrum disorders. *Arch Ped Adol Med.* 2007; 161(4):334–340.
- Knoester M et al. Matched follow-up study of 58 year-old ICSI singletons: child behaviour, parenting stress and child (health-related) quality of life. *Hum Reprod.* 2007; 22(12):3098–3107.

Home movies, onset of symptoms

- Palomo R, Belinchon M, Ozonoff S. Autism and family home movies: a comprehensive review. *J Dev Behav Pediatr.* 2006; 27(2 suppl):S59–68.

Autistic regression

- Fombonne E, Chakrabarti S. No evidence for a new variant of measles-mumps-rubella-induced autism. *Pediatrics.* 2001; 108(4):E58.

- Lord C, Shulman C, DiLavore P. Regression and word loss in autistic spectrum disorders. *J Child Psychol Psychiatry.* 2004; 45(5):936–955.
- Richler J et al. Is there a "regressive phenotype" of autism spectrum disorder associated with the measles-mumps-rubella vaccine? A CPEA study. *J Autism Dev Disord.* 2006; 36(3):299–316.

Seizures
- Canitano R. Epilepsy in autism spectrum disorders. *Eur Child Adolesc Psychiatry.* 2007; 16(1):61–66.

Perinatal events
- Schendel D, Bhasin TX. Birth weight and gestational age characteristics of children with autism, including a comparison with other developmental disabilities. *Pediatrics.* 2008; 121(6):1155–64.
- Limperopoulos C et al. Positive screening for autism in ex-preterm infants: prevalence and risk factors. *Pediatrics.* 2008; 121(4):758–765.

Current Autism Research

- **National Institutes of Health (NIH):** http://ndar.nih.gov/ndarpublicweb.
- **IAN, the Interactive Autism Network:** www.ianproject.org.
- Another federal government site: http://clinicaltrials.gov/ct2/home.
- **Autism Speaks:** Dedicated to funding global biomedical research into the causes, prevention, treatments, and cure for autism, www.autismspeaks.org.

Where Is Autism?

- Rapin I. Autism in search of a home in the brain. *Neurology.* 1999; 52(5):902–904.
- Frith C. What do imaging studies tell us about the neural basis of autism? *Novartis Found Symp.* 2003; 251:149–166; discussion 166–176, 281–297.
- Iacoboni M. *Mirroring People: The New Science of How We Connect with Others.* New York: Farrar, Straus and Giroux, 2008.
- Rodier PM. Converging evidence for brain stem injury in autism. *Dev Psychopathol.* 2002; 14(3):537–557.

Chapter 4: Speculative Causes of ASD, and the ASD "Explosion"

- Houston R, Frith U. *Autism in History: The Case of Hugh Blair of Borgue.* Oxford: Blackwell Publishers, 2000.
- Grinker R. *Unstrange Minds: Remapping the World of Autism.* New York: Basic Books, 2007. Includes a good discussion by the parent of a child with ASD of the so-called autism epidemic.
- Memoirs by adults on the spectrum:
  - Grandin T. *Thinking in Pictures and Other Reports from My Life with Autism.* New York: Random House, 1995.
  - Williams D. *Somebody Somewhere: Breaking Free from the World of Autism.* New York: Three Rivers Press, 1994.
  - Willey LH. *Pretending to Be Normal: Living with Asperger's Syndrome.* Philadelphia: Jessica Kingsley Publishers, 1999.
  - Robinson JE. *Look Me in the Eye: My Life with Asperger's.* New York: Three Rivers Press, 2007.

Diagnostic Substitution
- Bishop DV et al. Autism and diagnostic substitution: evidence from a study of adults with a history of developmental language disorder. *Dev Med Child Neurol.* 2008; 50(5):341–345.
- Coo H et al. Trends in autism prevalence: diagnostic substitution revisited. *J Autism Dev Disord.* 2008; 38(6):1036–1046.

Population Screening
- Constantino JN, Todd RD. Autistic traits in the general population: a twin study. *Arch Gen Psychiatry.* 2003; 60(5):524–530.
- Autistic spectrum disorder in adults living in households throughout England, 2007: Report from the Adult Psychiatric Morbidity Survey, 2007. www.ic.nhs.uk/pubs/asdpsychiatricmorbidity07.

Speculative Causes of ASD
Immunizations
- Wakefield AJ et al. Ileal-lymphoid-nodular hyperplasia, nonspecific colitis, and pervasive developmental disorder in children. *Lancet.* 1998; 351(9103):637–641.

- Murch SH et al. Retraction of an interpretation. *Lancet*. 2004; 363(9411):750.

Mercury

- Bernard S et al. Autism: a novel form of mercury poisoning. *Med Hypotheses*. 2001; 56(4):462–471.
- Geier MR, Geier DA. Neurodevelopmental disorders after thimerosal-containing vaccines: a brief communication. *Exp Biol Med (Maywood)*. 2003; 228(6):660–664.
- Ng DK et al. Low-level chronic mercury exposure in children and adolescents: meta-analysis. *Pediatr Int*. 2007; 49(1):80–87.
- U.S. Court of Federal Claims, Office of Special Masters No. 98-916v (Filed: February 12, 2009); *Theresa Cedillo and Michael Cedillo vs. Secretary of Health and Human Services*. ftp://autism.uscfc.uscourts.gov/autism/vaccine/Hastings-Cedillo.pdf.
- U.S. Court of Federal Claims Office of Special Masters No. 03-654v (E-Filed: February 12, 2009), *Rolf and Angela Hazlehurst vs. Secretary of the Department of Health and Human Services*. ftp://autism.uscfc.uscourts.gov/autism/vaccine/Campbell-Smith %20Hazlehurst%20Decision.pdf.
- U.S. Court of Federal Claims Office of Special Masters, No. 01-162v (Filed: February 12, 2009), *Colten Snyder vs. Secretary of the Department of Health and Human Services*. ftp://autism.uscfc.uscourts.gov/autism/vaccine/Vowell.Snyder.pdf.

Vitamin/mineral deficiency and supplementation

- McGuire JK, Kulkarni MS, Baden HP. Fatal hypermagnesemia in a child treated with megavitamin/megamineral therapy. *Pediatrics*. 2000; 105(2):E18.
- Nye C, Brice A. Combined vitamin B_6-magnesium treatment in autism spectrum disorder. *Cochrane Database Syst Rev*. 2005(4):CD003497.

Gluten

- Erickson CA et al. Gastrointestinal factors in autistic disorder: a critical review. *J Autism Dev Disord*. 2005; 35(6):713–727.
- Christison GW, Ivany K. Elimination diets in autism spectrum disorders: any wheat amidst the chaff? *J Dev Behav Pediatr*. 2006; 27(2 suppl):S162–171.

Yeast
- Crook W. *The Yeast Connection: A Medical Breakthrough*. New York: Knopf, 1986.

Chapter 5: What Does the Future Hold? The Natural History of ASD

- Binet A. New methods for the diagnosis of intellectual subnormals. *L'Année Psychologique*. 1905; 12:191–244. Available from http://psychclassics.yorku.ca/Binet/binet1.htm.
- We cited Kanner's landmark 1943 paper in the references to Chapter 1. Nearly thirty years later, Kanner managed to trace most of his original patients; here is his follow-up paper: www.neurodiversity.com/library_kanner_1971.html.
- Howlin P, Udwin O. *Outcomes in Neurodevelopmental and Genetic Disorders*. Chapter 6: Autistic disorders. New York: Cambridge University Press, 2002.
- Howlin P et al. Adult outcome for children with autism. *J Child Psychol Psychiatry*. 2004; 45(2):212–229.

Part II: The World of Intervention Services

Chapter 6: What Can I Do? Intervention Basics

- Patting the elephant: For more on this delightful tale, go here: http://en.wikipedia.org/wiki/Blind_Men_and_an_Elephant, or enter *Saxe + Elephant* into Google for citations to the best-known version of the tale, by the nineteenth-century humorist and poet John Godfrey Saxe.
- **General guides:** I like these sources because they provide a broad overview of services, and they are free of the claims frequently made by champions of any one specific therapy.
  - *Educating Children with Autism*. Washington, DC: Committee on Educational Interventions for Children with Autism, National Research Council, National Academy Press: 2001. Available online at www.nap.edu/catalog.php?record_id=10017#toc.

- **Autism Society of America:** www.autism-society.org. Enter "therapy" as your search term and you will be taken to a review of therapies. www.autism-society.org/site/PageServer ?pagename=about_treatment_learning.
- Seigel B. *Helping Children with Autism Learn: Treatment Approaches for Parents and Professionals.* New York: Oxford University Press, 2003. Good discussion of ABA and TEACCH.
- Quill KA. *Do-Watch-Listen-Say.* Baltimore: Paul H. Brookes, 2000. Side-by-side comparison of different therapies for ASD.
- Bashe P, Kirby BL. *The OASIS Guide to Asperger Syndrome, Revised.* New York: Crown Publishers, 2005.
- Klin A, Volkmar F, Sparrow S (Eds.). *Asperger Syndrome.* New York: Guilford Press, 2000.
- Klin A, Volkmar F. *Asperger Syndrome: Treatment and Intervention. Some Guidelines for Parents.* Includes an excellent generic IEP for children with AS. Go to http://info.med .yale.edu/chldstdy/autism/aspergers.html. Then, at the bottom of the page, click on the link that says "PDF File" for this article.
- Stewart K. *Helping a Child with Nonverbal Learning Disorder or Asperger's Syndrome.* Oakland (CA): New Harbinger Publications, 2002.

Top-Down Versus Bottom-Up

- Missiuna C, Malloy-Miller T, Mandich A. "Cognitive, or 'Top-Down': Approaches to Intervention." Go to the CanChild Centre for Childhood Disability Research: http://canchild.ca/en/index.asp, and enter the search term "top down." Or go to http://canchild .icreate3.esolutionsgroup.ca/en/ourresearch/cognitiveapproaches.asp.

Chapter 7: In the Beginning: Intensive Behavioral Intervention

- Lovaas OI. *Teaching Developmentally Disabled Children: The ME Book.* Austin: PRO-ED, 1981. This is where it all began. Although badly dated in some respects (refers to children with ASD as "atavistic"; recommends hitting), this book is still widely read and lays out the basics of ABA.

- Lovaas OI. *Teaching Individuals with Developmental Delays: Basic Intervention Techniques.* Austin: PRO-ED, 2003.
- Harris SL, Weiss MJ. *Right from the Start: Behavioral Interventions for Young Children with Autism, 2nd Edition.* Bethesda (MD): Woodbine House, 2007.
- Maurice C, Green G, Foxx RM (Eds.). *Making a Difference: Behavioral Intervention for Autism.* Austin: PRO-ED, 2001.
- **Association for Behavior Analysis International:** www.abainternational.org. National professional organization of ABA practitioners; go to the "Special Interest" link on their home page, and click on "Autism."
- A list of board-certified behavior analysts is available at the **Behavior Analyst Certification Board:** www.bacb.com.
- Gold MW. Stimulus factors in skill training of retarded adolescents on a complex assembly task: acquisition, transfer, and retention. *Am J Ment Defic.* 1972; 76(5):517–526. One of the first papers to show that task analysis and proper behavioral intervention can lift the capability of persons previously believed to be "sub-trainable."

Toilet Training

- Foxx RM, Azrin NH. *Toilet Training Persons with Developmental Disabilities: A Rapid Program for Day and Nighttime Independent Toileting, or Toilet Training the Retarded.* Champaign: Research Press, 1973. Everything that follows is a variation on the methods outlined here. Out of print, but available via used-book sellers.
- Azrin NH, Foxx RM. *Toilet Training in Less Than a Day.* New York: Pocket Books, 1974. Similar methods, for children with typical development.
- Lovaas OI. *Teaching Individuals with Developmental Delays: Basic Intervention Techniques.* Chapter 21. Austin: PRO-ED, 2003.
- **Koegel and Koegel:** www.education.ucsb.edu/autism. Click on the link for "Training Manuals" for the toilet training manual.
- Wheeler M (Ed.). *Toilet Training for Individuals with Autism and Related Disorders.* Arlington (TX): Future Horizons, 2004.

- **TEACCH: Applying Structured Teaching Principles to Toilet Training:** Excellent discussion and charts, www.teacch.com/toilet.html.
- **Toilet training tips:** www.personal.kent.edu/~depeters/data/toilet/toilet.htm.
- **Toilet training. BBB autism support network:** Chatty, informative, very readable. www.bbbautism.com/pdf/article_25_toilet_training.pdf.
- American Academy of Pediatrics. *Guide to Toilet Training.* New York: Bantam Books, 2003. Not written with ASD in mind, but still contains many useful tips, especially for first-time parents.

Chapter 8: Next Steps: Playful Sabotage, Watchful Waiting

Pivotal Response Treatment
- Koegel RL, Koegel LK. *Pivotal Response Treatments for Autism.* Baltimore: Paul H. Brookes, 2006.
- www.education.ucsb.edu/autism. Click on the link "Training Manuals," which cover topics ranging from fundamentals of self-care to social skills.
- http://psy.ucsd.edu/autism/prttraining.html.

Floor Time
- Greenspan S, Wieder S. *The Child with Special Needs.* New York: DaCapo Press, 1998.
- Greenspan S, Lewis D. *The Affect-Based Language Curriculum (ABLC): An Intensive Program for Families, Therapists and Teachers, 2nd Edition.* Bethesda: Interdisciplinary Council on Developmental and Learning Disorders, 2005.
- **Floortime Foundation:** www.floortime.org.

RDI
- Gutstein S, Sheely R. *Relationship Development Intervention with Young Children.* New York: Jessica Kingsley Publishers, 2002. Or visit the website: www.rdiconnect.com.
- Gutstein SE. *The RDI Book: Forging New Pathways for Autism,*

Asperger's and PDD with the Relationship Development Intervention Program. Houston: Center Publishing, 2009.

Chapter 9: Language Therapies: Communication First, Speech Second

Picture Exchange

- **Pyramid Educational Consultants, creators of PECS (Picture Exchange Communication System):** www.pecs.com.
- **Augmentative resources:** "Low tech" AAC, www.augresources.com.
- **Mayer-Johnson Corporation:** This link is to their research articles, www.mayer-johnson.com/ResearchArticles.aspx. Visit their home page for information on their product line.
- **Poppin:** Creator of DynaSyms (another popular symbol system) as well as other AAC materials, www.poppinandcompany.com/index .shtml.
- **Bliss:** www.blissymbolics.us.
- **www.difflearn.com:** A commercial site providing various low-tech materials (for example, Sign and Say Verbal Language Flashcards, which have clear photos of common objects on one side, with the corresponding manual sign on the reverse).

Verbal Behavior

- Barbera M. *The Verbal Behavior Approach. How to Teach Children with Autism and Related Disorders.* Philadelphia: Jessica Kingsley Publishers, 2007. An excellent introduction to VB. www.verbalbehaviorapproach.com.
- **Vincent Carbone** is another leading practitioner of VB, www.drcarbone.net.
- **Establishing Operations, Inc.:** Provides training materials to enable parents to implement VB. www.establishingoperationsinc.com.
- www.christinaburkaba.com/GettingStarted.htm.
- Sundberg M, Partington J. *Teaching Language to Children with Autism or Other Developmental Disabilities.* Pleasant Hill, (CA): Behavior Analysts, 1998. The bible in the field, but daunting as a first read.

Signing

- Good discussions here of the rationale for using sign language in children with normal hearing:
    - www.behavior-consultant.com/asl-pecs.htm.
    - www.nas.org.uk/nas/jsp/polopoly.jsp?d=364&a=2186 (from the National Autistic Society).
- Commercial **"Baby and me" signing programs** developed for normally developing children, adaptable for children with ASD (teach hand-over-hand):
    - www.signwithme.com.
    - www.signingtime.com.
    - www.sign2me.com.
    - www.babysigns.com.
    - www.babyseensign.com/index.htm.
- **University of Michigan:** Brief discussion of signing and picture exchange: http://sitemaker.umich.edu/356.kobza/home.
- **CESA7:** Implementation of Alternative and Augmentative Communication (AAC) in the school setting. Browse the site for other information of interest (IDEA, IEP planning, etc.). Lots of good, practical information. www.cesa7.k12.wi.us/sped/autism/index2.htm.

Speech/Language Therapy

- **American Speech-Language and Hearing Association (ASHA): Guidelines for Speech-Language Pathologists in Diagnosis, Assessment, and Treatment of Autism Spectrum Disorders Across the Life Span.** Well-referenced, nonbiased discussion of the goals and methods of language enhancement for children with ASD, from the perspective of traditional speech/language pathology: www.asha.org/docs/html/GL2006-00049.html#sec1.10. Go to their home page to search for additional documents on ASD.

Augmentative Communication

- Look for the nearest **University Center of Excellence in Developmental Disabilities (UCEDD)** or **Leadership Education in Neurodevelopmental Disabilities (LEND)**, and inquire whether they have an augmentative communication program. Go to the Association of University Centers on Disabilities for information on UCEDDs and LENDs: www.aucd.org/template/index.cfm.

- **Abledata:** A comprehensive noncommercial site that functions as a clearinghouse of information on technology resources for persons with disabilities, www.abledata.com.
- Beukelman DR, Mirenda P. *Supporting Children and Adults with Complex Communication Needs, 3rd Edition.* Baltimore: Paul H. Brookes, 2005.

Chapter 10: Socially Based Therapies

Social Stories

- **Social Stories:** The Gray Center, www.thegraycenter.org. From the home page, select "Store," then "Social Stories."
- Howley M, Arnold E. *Revealing the Hidden Social Code.* Philadelphia: Jessica Kingsley Publishers, 2005. Teaches you how see the world through the eyes of a child with ASD, and how to use that insight to write Social Stories.
- **For an excellent review of the research literature on social stories:** Reynhout G, Carter M. Social Stories for children with disabilities. *J Autism Dev Disord.* 2006; 36(4):445–469.

Social Skills (Arranged Roughly in Developmental Order)

- Bellini S. *Building Social Relationships.* Shawnee Mission (KS): Autism Asperger Publishing, 2006. Excellent overview of various methods, plus suggestions as to which methods may be best for your child at any given point in his or her development.
- Baker J. *The Social Skills Picture Book: Teaching Play, Emotion, and Communication to Children with Autism.* Arlington (TX): Future Horizons, 2001. Photographs with dialog balloons and "thought bubbles."
- **Sandbox Learning:** Additional materials for social skills training (picture cards, Success Stories, monitoring sheets, etc.), www.sandbox-learning.com.
- **Center for Social Thinking:** www.socialthinking.com/default.asp.
- McAfee J. *Navigating the Social World: A Curriculum for Individuals with Asperger's Syndrome, High Functioning Autism and*

Related Disorders. Arlington (TX): Future Horizons, 2001.
www.futurehorizons-autism.com.

- Sohn A, Grayson C. *Parenting Your Asperger Child: Individualized Solutions for Teaching Your Child Practical Skills*. New York: Perigee, 2005.
- Heinrichs R. *Perfect Targets: Asperger Syndrome and Bullying: Practical Solutions for Surviving the Social World.* Shawnee Mission (KS): Autism Asperger Publishing, 2003. www.aspergerinformation.org.
- **Coulter Video:** Social skills, with an emphasis on Asperger Syndrome, http://home.att.net/~coultervideo.

Chapter 11: Hands-On Therapies

Sensory Integration Therapy

- Ayers A. *Sensory Integration and Learning Disorders*. Los Angeles: Western Psychological Services, 1972. In 2005, a twenty-fifth anniversary edition was also published. Both editions are out of print but available online through used-book sellers.
- Miller-Kuhaneck H (Ed.). *Autism: A Comprehensive Occupational Therapy Approach, 2nd Edition*. Bethesda: American Occupational Therapy Association Press, 2004.
- Schaaf RC, Miller LJ. Occupational therapy using a sensory integrative approach for children with developmental disabilities. *Mental Retard Dev D R*. 2005; 11(2):143–148.
- *American Journal of Occupational Therapy*. 2007; 61(2): Special issue: "Conceptualizing and Identifying Sensory Processing Issues; Sensory Integration Treatment."
- Parham LD et al. Fidelity in sensory integration intervention research. *Am J Occup Ther*. 2007; 61(2):216–227.
- Kranowitz C. *The Out-of-Sync Child*. New York: Penguin, 2005. Also by her, *The Out-of-Sync Child Has Fun*. New York: Perigee, 2003.
- Kurckinka M. *Raising Your Spirited Child*. New York: Harper, 2006.
- Tomchek SD, Dunn W. Sensory processing in children with and without autism: a comparative study using the short sensory profile. *Am J Occup Ther*. 2007; 61(2):190–200.

- Williams JH et al. Neural mechanisms of imitation and "mirror neuron" functioning in autistic spectrum disorder. *Neuropsychologia.* 2006; 44(4):610–621.

Food Selectivity and Eating Behavior

- Lovaas OI. *Teaching Individuals with Developmental Delays: Basic Intervention Techniques.* Chapter 21. Austin: PRO-ED, 2003.
- Help! My son eats only macaroni and cheese. Dealing with feeding problems in children with autism. In: Maurice C, Green G, Foxx RM, eds. *Making a Difference. Behavioral Intervention for Autism.* Austin: PRO-ED, 2001: 51–74.
- Ernsperger L, Stegen-Hanson T. *Just Take a Bite: Easy, Effective Answers to Food Aversions and Eating Challenges.* Arlington (TX): Future Horizons, 2004.
- Legge B. *Can't Eat, Won't Eat: Dietary Difficulties and the Autism Spectrum.* London: Jessica Kingsley Publishers, 2002.

Chapter 12: Behavior Management and Psychopharmacology

General

- Phelan T. *1-2-3-Magic: Effective Discipline for Children 2–12, 3rd Edition.* Glen Ellyn (IL): Child Management Inc., 2003. Probably one of the most widely read books on behavior management in young children; complete explanation of time out, and much more. From ParentMagic, www.parentmagic.com.
- Phelan, T. *1-2-3-Magic: Managing Difficult Behavior in Children 2–12.* Glen Ellyn (IL): Child Management, Inc., 2003. A companion CD, also from www.parentmagic.com.
- Parker HC. *Behavior Management at Home: A Token Economy Program for Children and Teens.* Plantation (FL): Specialty Press, 1995. The next step beyond time out.

Anxiety, Stress

- Buron KD. *When My Worries Get Too Big.* Shawnee Mission (KS): Autism Asperger Publishing, 2006. A good introductory book about feelings for young children.

- Buron KD, Curtis M. *The Incredible 5-Point Scale. Assisting Students with Autistic Spectrum Disorders in Understanding Social Interactions and Controlling Their Emotions.* Shawnee Mission (KS): Autism Asperger Publishing, 2003. Companion to *When My Worries Get Too Big.* Enhances child's awareness of his or her stress level and helps child to avert meltdowns.
- Wagner A. *Worried No More: Help and Hope for Anxious Children, 2nd Edition.* Rochester (NY): Lighthouse Press, 2005. For addressing anxiety that frequently accompanies ASD. www.lighthouse-press.com.
- **Anxiety Disorder Association of America:** The tab on "Anxiety Disorders in Children and Teens" contains much useful advice about anxiety management (although no specific mention of ASD). www.adaa.org/GettingHelp/FocusOn/Children&Adolescents.asp.

Visual Schedules
- Cohen MJ, Sloan DL. *Visual Supports for People with Autism: A Guide for Parents and Professionals.* Bethesda: Woodbine House, 2007.
- **Why schedules work**
  - www.setbc.org/projects/vss/default.html.
  - www.specialed.us/autism/structure/str11.htm.
- **Where to get them**
  - TEACCH: www.teacch.com.
  - www.leapsandbounds.com. Enter "Daily Planner" as your search term.
  - "Make a schedule" computer software: www.dotolearn.com.

Agitation, Anger, Tantrums
- Greene RW. *The Explosive Child.* New York: Harper, 2005.
- **Koegel and Koegel:** www.education.ucsb.edu/autism. Click on the link for "Training Manuals" for the problem behavior manual.
- Lovaas OI. *Teaching Individuals with Developmental Delays: Basic Intervention Techniques.* Austin: PRO-ED, 2003.
- Harris SL, Weiss MJ. *Right from the Start: Behavioral Interventions for Young Children with Autism, 2nd Edition.* Bethesda: Woodbine House, 2007.

- Maurice C, Green G, Foxx RM (Eds.). *Making a Difference: Behavioral Intervention for Autism.* Austin: PRO-ED, 2001.

Sleep Disorders

- Durand VM. *Sleep Better! Guide to Improving Sleep for Children with Special Needs.* Baltimore: Paul H. Brookes, 1998. A practical guide written by a professional who is also the parent of a child with special needs.
- Stores G, Wiggs L. *Sleep Disturbance in Children and Adolescents with Disorders of Development: Its Significance and Management.* London: Mac Keith Press, 2001. Although written with the professional in mind, it contains much information that will be useful to parents.
- **National Autistic Society (England).** *Sleep and Autism: Helping Your Child.* A good review and many practical suggestions. www.nas.org.uk/nas/jsp/polopoly.jsp?a=3376&d=1071.
- **General information about sleep, sleep disorders, melatonin, and current research:** www.nlm.nih.gov/medlineplus/sleepdisorders .html.

Psychopharmacology
Beginners

- **National Institute of Mental Health (NIMH):** A good "first read" on drug treatment. www.nimh.nih.gov/publicat/autism.cfm #treatment.
- **Medline Plus:** www.nlm.nih.gov/medlineplus/autism.html#cat3. General resource with links to information on drug treatment.
- **Epocrates** is a popular reference site for physicians. This is their open-access link: https://online.epocrates.com/front_porch.

Advanced

- Stahl S. *Essential Psychopharmacology: The Prescriber's Guide. Revised and Updated.* New York: Cambridge University Press, 2006. Excellent reference. Although written for professionals, the layout and manner of presentation make this book relatively accessible to the lay reader.
- Stahl S. *Essential Psychopharmacology: Neuroscientific Basis and*

Practical Applications, 2nd Edition. New York: Cambridge University Press, 2000.

Chapter 13: Going to School

Classroom Techniques
- **TEACCH** (Treatment and Education of Autistic and Communication Handicapped Children).
  - The TEACCH website: www.teacch.com.
  - Mesibov G, Shea V, Schopler E. *The TEACCH Approach to Autism Spectrum Disorders.* New York: Springer, 2006.
- Seigel B. *Helping Children with Autism Learn: Treatment Approaches for Parents and Professionals.* New York: Oxford University Press, 2003. More on TEACCH.
- **Yale Child Study Center:** "Asperger's Syndrome," excellent review of the features of AS, www.med.yale.edu/chldstdy/autism/aspergers .html. Be sure to click on the links to download the two associated PDF files: "Asperger's Syndrome: Guidelines for Assessment and Diagnosis" and "Asperger's Syndrome: Guidelines for Treatment and Intervention." Many of the suggestions in the second article are also applicable to children with mild autism or PDD-NOS.
- **www.behavioradvisor.com:** A general site on behavior management in the classroom. Although oriented primarily toward classroom teachers, there is much useful information here for parents. Specific sections on ASD are very helpful.

Chapter 14: Sense and Nonsense in the Treatment of ASD

Quackery and How to Spot It
- **Quackwatch:** "A nonprofit corporation whose purpose is to combat health-related frauds, fads, and fallacies." Informative and readable. www.quackwatch.com.
- On the **history of quack medicine:** Young JH. *The Toadstool Millionaires: A Social History of Patent Medicines in America Before Federal Regulation.* Princeton: Princeton University Press, 1961. Available free online at www.quackwatch.org/13Hx/TM/00.html.

- For a sobering reminder of how the **themes of medical quackery** never change, read *The Great American Fraud,* a series of articles on patent medicines originally published in *Collier's Magazine* (1905–06). The first installment is available online at Wikipedia: http://en.wikipedia.org/wiki/Quackery.
- For a chilling account of the **death by radiation poisoning** of Eben Byers from radithor, a quack medicine containing radium and thorium: Macklis R. The Great Radium Scandal. *Scientific American.* August 1993; 269(2):94–99.
- Schriebman L. *The Science and Fiction of Autism.* Cambridge (MA): Harvard University Press, 2005. Excellent discussion of the core deficits of ASD and therapies, reputable and not-so-reputable.

The Placebo Effect
- Rosenthal R, Jacobson L. *Pygmalion in the Classroom: Teacher Expectation and Pupils' Intellectual Development.* Norwalk (CT): Crown House, 1992.

ABA: Not a Cure for Autism
- Lovaas OI. Behavioral treatment and normal educational and intellectual functioning in young autistic children. *J Consult Clin Psychol.* 1987; 55(1):3–9.
- Smith T, Groen AD, Wynn JW. Randomized trial of intensive early intervention for children with pervasive developmental disorder. *Am J Ment Retard.* 2000; 105(4):269–285.
- Sallows GO, Graupner TD. Intensive behavioral treatment for children with autism: four-year outcome and predictors. *Am J Ment Retard.* 2005; 110(6):417–438.
- Gresham FM, MacMillan DL. Early Intervention Project: can its claims be substantiated and its effects replicated? *J Autism Dev Disord.* 1998; 28(1):5–13.

Listening Therapies ("Auditory Integration Training")
- Goldstein H. Commentary: Interventions to facilitate auditory, visual, and motor integration: "show me the data." *J Autism Dev Disord.* 2000; 30(5):423–425.

- Sinha Y et al. Auditory integration training and other sound therapies for autism spectrum disorders: a systematic review. *Arch Dis Child.* 2006; 91(12):1018–1022.
- Sinha Y et al. Auditory integration training and other sound therapies for autism spectrum disorders. *Cochrane Database Syst Rev.* 2004; 1:CD003681.
- Mudford OC et al. Auditory integration training for children with autism: no behavioral benefits detected. *Am J Ment Retard.* 2000; 105(2):118–129.
- Bettison S. The long-term effects of auditory training on children with autism. *J Autism Dev Disord.* 1996; 26(3):361–374.
- Dawson G, Watling R. Interventions to facilitate auditory, visual, and motor integration in autism: a review of the evidence. *J Autism Dev Disord.* 2000; 30(5):415–421.
- American Academy of Pediatrics. Committee on Children with Disabilities. Auditory integration training and facilitated communication for autism. *Pediatrics.* 1998; 102(2 Pt 1):431–433.

Facilitated Communication

- Twachman-Cullen D. *A Passion to Believe: Autism and the Facilitated Communication Phenomenon.* Boulder: Westview Press, 1997. The power of self-deception in the treatment of children with autism.
- Mostert MP. Facilitated communication since 1995: a review of published studies. *J Autism Dev Disord.* 2001; 31(3):287–313.

Megavitamins, Megaminerals

- McGuire JK, Kulkarni MS, Baden HP. Fatal hypermagnesemia in a child treated with megavitamin/megamineral therapy. *Pediatrics.* 2000; 105(2):E18.

Chelation, Succimer

- Deaths associated with hypocalcemia from chelation therapy— Texas, Pennsylvania, and Oregon, 2003–2005. *MMWR.* 2006; 55(8):204–207.
- Stangle DE et al. Succimer chelation improves learning, attention, and arousal regulation in lead-exposed rats but produces lasting

cognitive impairment in the absence of lead exposure. *Environ Health Perspect.* 2007; 115(2):201–209.

Hyperoxia

- Fukui K et al. Impairment of learning and memory in rats caused by oxidative stress and aging, and changes in antioxidative defense systems. *Ann N Y Acad Sci.* 2001; 928:168–175.
- Panayiotidis MI et al. Hyperoxia-induced DNA damage causes decreased DNA methylation in human lung epithelial-like A549 cells. *Antioxid Redox Signal.* 2004; 6(1):129–136.
- Watson NA et al. The effect of hyperoxia on cerebral blood flow: a study in healthy volunteers using magnetic resonance phase-contrast angiography. *Eur J Anaesthesiol.* 2000; 17(3):152–159.
- Zheng L et al. Oxidative stress induces intralysosomal accumulation of Alzheimer amyloid beta-protein in cultured neuroblastoma cells. *Ann N Y Acad Sci.* 2006; 1067:248–251.
- Torbati D et al. Multiple-organ effect of normobaric hyperoxia in neonatal rats. *J Crit Care.* 2006; 21(1):85–93; discussion 93–94.
- Felderhoff-Mueser U et al. Oxygen causes cell death in the developing brain. *Neurobiol Dis.* 2004; 17(2):273–282.
- Dean JB et al. Neuronal sensitivity to hyperoxia, hypercapnia, and inert gases at hyperbaric pressures. *J Appl Physiol.* 2003; 95(3):883–909.
- Conconi MT et al. Effects of hyperbaric oxygen on proliferative and apoptotic activities and reactive oxygen species generation in mouse fibroblast 3T3/J2 cell line. *J Investig Med.* 2003; 51(4):227–232.
- Rossignol D et al. Hyperbaric treatment for children with autism: a multicenter, randomized, double-blind, controlled trial. *BMC Pediatr.* 2009; 9:21. www.biomedcentral.com.

Omega-3 Fatty Acids

- Schultz ST et al. Breastfeeding, infant formula supplementation, and autistic disorder: the results of a parent survey. *Int Breastfeed J.* 2006; 1:16.
- Richardson AJ, Montgomery P. The Oxford-Durham study: a randomized, controlled trial of dietary supplementation with fatty

acids in children with developmental coordination disorder. *Pediatrics.* 2005; 115(5):1360–1366.

- Amminger GP et al. Omega-3 fatty acids supplementation in children with autism: a double-blind randomized, placebo-controlled pilot study. *Biol Psychiatry.* 2007; 61(4):551–553.
- Meguid NA et al. Role of polyunsaturated fatty acids in the management of Egyptian children with autism. *Clin Biochem.* 2008; 41(13):1044–1048.
- Politi P et al. Behavioral effects of omega-3 fatty acid supplementation in young adults with severe autism: an open label study. *Arch Med Res.* 2008; 39(7):682–685.
- Bent S, Bertoglio K, Hendren RL. Omega-3 fatty acids for autistic spectrum disorder: a systematic review. *J Autism Dev Disord.* 2009; 39(8):1145–1154.

Leaky Gut

- For more on gluten-free diets, see www.clinicaltrials.gov/ct/show/nct00090428?order=%20; www.ucdmc.ucdavis.edu/mindinstitute/research/clinicalstudies.html; www.uclid.org:8080/uclid/re_autism.html.

Part III: The World of the Family

Chapter 15: Family Matters

Taking Care of Yourself, Your Marriage, or Other Significant Relationships

- Marshak L, Prezant FP. *Married with Special Needs Children: A Couples' Guide to Keeping Connected.* Bethesda: Woodbine House, 2006.
- Ariel C, Naseef R (Eds.). *Voices from the Spectrum: Parents, Grandparents, Siblings, People with Autism, and Professionals Share Their Wisdom.* Philadelphia: Jessica Kingsley Publishers, 2006.
- **American Association of Marriage and Family Therapy:** www.aamft.org/index_nm.asp.
- Frank VE. *Man's Search for Meaning.* New York: Washington Square Press, 1984.

Self-Awareness

Younger Children

- Vermeulen P. *I Am Special: Introducing Children and Young People to Their Autism Spectrum Disorder.* Philadelphia: Jessica Kingsley Publishers, 2000.
- Elder J. *Different Like Me: My Book of Autism Heroes.* Philadelphia: Jessica Kingsley Publishers, 2005.
- Faherty C. *Asperger's... What Does It Mean to Me? A Workbook Explaining Awareness and Life Lessons to the Child or Youth with High Functioning Autism or Asperger's.* Arlington (TX): Future Horizons, 2000. Numerous other titles also available at www.fhautism.com/index.htm.

Older Children and Adolescents

- Wrobel M. *Taking Care of Myself: A Hygiene, Puberty and Personal Curriculum for Young People with Autism.* Arlington (TX): Future Horizons, 2003.

Books for Siblings

- Bishop B. *My Friend with Autism: A Coloring Book for Peers and Siblings.* Arlington (TX): Future Horizons, 2005.
- Peralta S. *All About My Brother: An Eight-Year-Old Sister's Introduction to Her Brother Who Has Autism.* Shawnee Mission (KS): Autism Asperger Publishing, 2002.
- Thompson M. *Andy and His Yellow Frisbee.* Bethesda: Woodbine House, 1996.
- Ogaz N. *Buster and the Amazing Daisy.* Philadelphia: Jessica Kingsley Publishers, 2002.
- Bleach F. *Everybody Is Different: A Book for Young People Who Have Brothers or Sisters with Autism.* Shawnee Mission (KS): Autism Asperger Publishing, 2005.
- Lears L. *Ian's Walk: A Story About Autism.* Morton Grove (IL): Albert Whitman, 2003.
- Amenta CA. *Russell Is Extra Special: A Book About Autism for Children.* Washington, DC: American Psychological Association, 1992.
- Healy A. *Sometimes My Brother: Helping Kids Understand Autism Through a Sibling's Eyes.* Arlington (TX): Future Horizons, 1998.

- Edwards A. *Taking Autism to School.* Woodbury (NY): JayJo Books, 2001. www.jayjo.com.
- *Understanding Brothers and Sisters on the Autism Spectrum,* and *Brothers and Sisters with Asperger Syndrome.* Each DVD contains four programs—three for siblings of different ages and developmental levels, and one for their parents. The sibling programs are for children ages 4–7, ages 7–12, and ages 12–adult. Available from Coulter Video, 1428 Pinecroft Drive, Winston-Salem, NC 27104, 336–794–0298, www.coultervideo.com.
- **Autism Society of America:** The ASA website has excellent info on sibling issues: www.autism-society.org/site/PageServer?pagename =about_lwa_siblings.
- Researchers at the Waisman Center in Madison, Wisconsin, have published a booklet that describes the experiences of now-adult siblings of persons with ASD. You may find the section "Advice from Adult Siblings to Parents of a Child with ASD" helpful as you struggle to find ways of speaking to your other children about their brother or sister with ASD. www.strengthforcaring.com. daily-care/caring-for-someone-with-autism/reflections-from-adult -siblings-who-have-a-brother-or-sister-with-an-autism-spectrum -disorder.
- **Sibling support groups:** www.siblingsupport.org.

Support Groups (Information for Parents and the Adolescent or Adult with AS or High-Functioning Autism)

- **Online Asperger Syndrome Information & Support (OASIS):** The granddaddy of AS web support, www.udel.edu/bkirby/asperger.
- **Asperger Association of New England (AANE):** Provides comprehensive and up-to-date information and support on Asperger syndrome. Although technically a regional organization, they have become national leaders in areas such as support, education, and advocacy. www.aane.org.
- **Global and Regional Asperger Syndrome Partnership (GRASP):** Serving individuals on the autism spectrum, and run by those individuals. The basic philosophy of the GRASP organization is to educate and empower persons with AS. www.grasp.org.
- **MAAP Services for Autism and Asperger Syndrome:** Support

to families and individuals with Asperger syndrome and other high-functioning autism spectrum disorders. www.maapservices .org.

Partners/Spouses of an Adult with AS or High-Functioning Autism

- Stanford A, Willey LH. *Asperger Syndrome and Long-Term Relationships.* Philadelphia: Jessica Kingsley Publishers, 2002.
- Gaus VL. *Cognitive-Behavioral Therapy for Adult Asperger Syndrome.* New York: Guilford Press, 2007. Although written for clinicians, this book may appeal to adults with AS because of its factual style.

Chapter 16: Practical Concerns

Special Education: Your Rights Under the Law

- **IDEA:** The official government website: http://idea.ed.gov.
- **Scope of the law and your rights:** Excellent series of fact sheets published by the ARC (formerly the Association for Retarded Citizens): www.thearc.org/NetCommunity/Page.aspx?&pid=1646 &srcid=1433.
- **FAPE:** Another clearinghouse of information about IDEA: www.fape.org.
- **National Early Childhood Education Technical Assistance Center (NECTAC):** Their mission is to strengthen service systems to ensure that children with disabilities (birth through five years) and their families receive and benefit from high-quality, culturally appropriate, and family-centered supports and services: www.nectac.org/idea/idea.asp.
- **Wrightslaw:** Information about special education law, education law, and advocacy for children with disabilities: www.wrightslaw.com.
- **Education Law Association:** www.educationlaw.org/index.php.
- Sherman DA. *Autism: Asserting Your Child's Right to a Special Education.* 2007. A very readable, step-by-step book by a special education attorney, with lots of concrete guidance, including sample forms, form letters, etc. www.aboutautismlaw.com.

Following the Money
Medical Assistance (Medicaid) and Medicare
- Navigating Medicare and Medicaid: Resource Guides for People with Disabilities, Their Families, and Their Advocates, www.kff .org/medicare.
Supplemental Security Income
- www.ssa.gov/pubs/10026.html.
- www.disabilityinfo.gov/digov-public/public/DisplayPage.do ?parentFolderId=171.
- www.ssa.gov/disability/disability_starter_kits_child_eng.htm.
- www.socialsecurity.gov/kids/index.htm.
- www.buzzle.com/editorials/2-21-2006-89457.asp.
Other
- **DisabilityInfo.gov:** The federal government's one-stop website for people with disabilities: http://disabilityinfo.gov.

Long-Term Planning
Developing a Life Care Plan
- Russell LM, Grant AE. *Planning for the Future: Providing a Meaningful Life for a Child with a Disability After Your Death, 6th Edition.* 2006. Planning for the Future, Inc., 86 W. King Henry Ct, Palatine, IL 60067; www.specialneedslegal.com.
- *Family Resource Guides,* published by the ARC: www.thearc.org/ NetCommunity/Page.aspx?&pid=1400&srcid=183.
- *Future Planning: Making Financial Arrangements with a Trust.* Also published by the ARC. www.thearc.org/NetCommunity/ Document.Doc?&id=156.

Transition to Adulthood
General
- Wehman P, Smith MD, Schall S. *Autism and the Transition to Adulthood: Success Beyond the Classroom.* Baltimore: Paul H. Brookes, 2009.
Puberty and Sexuality
- Sicile-Kira C, Grandin T. *Adolescents on the Autism Spectrum: A Parent's Guide to the Cognitive, Social, Physical, and Transition*

Needs of Teenagers with Autism Spectrum Disorders. New York: Berkley, 2006.
- Hénault I. *Asperger's Syndrome and Sexuality: From Adolescence Through Adulthood.* Philadelphia: Jessica Kingsley Publishers, 2006.
- Nichols S, Moravcik GM, Tetenbaum SP. *Girls Growing Up on the Autism Spectrum: What Parents and Professionals Should Know About the Pre-Teen and Teenage Years.* Philadelphia: Jessica Kingsley Publishers, 2009.

Careers
- Grandin T, Duffy K. *Developing Talents: Careers for Individuals with Asperger Syndrome and High-Functioning Autism.* Shawnee Mission (KS): Autism Asperger Publishing, 2004.

Other
- **Life span issues for families that include a person with special needs:** www.waisman.wisc.edu/family/index.html.
- **Family Village:** www.familyvillage.wisc.edu. Excellent general resource for people with special needs and their families.

Glossary

- **5-HT:** 5-Hydroxytryptamine, the technical name for serotonin.
- **AAC (Augmentative and Alternative Communication):** Augmentative communication methods are used in conjunction with speech, or with the goal of leading to speech; alternative communication methods are intended to be used instead of speech.
- **ABA (Applied Behavior Analysis):** *see* Behaviorism.
- **ABLC (Affect-Based Language Curriculum):** *see* Floor Time.
- **ABLLS (Assessment of Basic Language and Learning Skills):** The evaluation procedure for verbal behavior analysis (VBA).
- **Adaptive Skills:** Self-care skills (feeding, clothing, grooming), also referred to as ADL ("activity of daily living") skills.
- **AEDs:** Antiepileptic drugs (anticonvulsants); also function as mood stabilizers.
- **Agonist:** A drug that activates or accentuates the action of a particular pathway (*see* Antagonist). Example: Dextroamphetamine is an adrenergic *agonist*, since it mimics the action of adrenaline.
- **AIT:** Auditory integration training.
- **Alpha-2 Agonists:** Drugs that activate the alpha (α)-2 system; include clonidine and guanfacine.

- **Antagonist:** A drug that works in opposition to a particular pathway (*see* Agonist). Risperidone works in part as a dopamine antagonist, since it blocks dopamine receptor sites.
- **Applied Behavior Analysis:** *see* Behaviorism.
- **ASD:** *see* Autistic Spectrum Disorder.
- **ASL:** American Sign Language.
- **Asperger Syndrome:** An autistic spectrum disorder characterized by pedantic, hyperverbal speech with an intense focus on one or more odd topics, difficulty with fine motor tasks, and impaired theory of mind skills.
- **Atypical/Atypicality:** Developmental features that would be considered abnormal at any age (as opposed to developmental delay, which signifies developmental features that would be normal in a younger child). Atypical development is the hallmark of autistic spectrum disorder.
- **Atypical Neuroleptics:** *see* Neuroleptic.
- **Autistic Spectrum Disorder (ASD):** A neurologically based developmental disorder encompassing atypical development in four domains: relating to others, language, repetitive behaviors, and sensory processing. ASD varies in expression from mild to profound and may be accompanied by any degree of intelligence from genius IQ to profound mental retardation.
- **Aversives:** Punishment. Reduces the frequency of recurrence of the immediately preceding behavior.
- **Behaviorism:** A branch of psychology that views behavior as the consequence of prior rewards and punishments. Applied behavior analysis (ABA) is the technical component of behaviorism. ABA begins by performing a functional behavioral analysis (FBA) to determine what function any given behavior serves (in particular, what are the antecedents to, and the consequences of, a given behavior?), and proceeds from the FBA to a systematic application of pleasant and unpleasant stimuli in order to reinforce or extinguish selected behaviors. Shaping of behavior relies on the method of operant conditioning: The subject's behavior "operates" on the environment, following which the subject receives either a reward or an aversive stimulus from the therapist. Starts with discrete trial train-

ing (DTT), which is tightly controlled by the therapist, and moves on to natural environment training (NET), which is done in a more naturalistic setting.

- **Bottom-Up and Top-Down:** A way of viewing the nervous system with sensory input at the lowest level and cerebral cortical activity at the highest level.
- **Brain Stem:** The portion of the brain that joins to the upper spinal cord.
- **Central Coherence:** The brain's ability to pull all the little pieces together into one big picture.
- **Cerebellum:** Literally, the "little brain." Located beneath the cerebral cortex and behind the brain stem. Abnormalities of the cerebellum are common in ASD.
- **Cerebral Cortex:** The upper, outer surface of the brain; the highest level of the nervous system.
- **Childhood Disintegrative Disorder:** Refers to children with autistic-like regression, occurring after age three to four.
- **Clonidine:** *see* Alpha-2 Agonists.
- **Concordance:** Identical findings in twins. If both twins share a particular trait, they are concordant; if one twin has the trait and the other doesn't, they are discordant for that trait.
- **DA:** Dopamine.
- **Delayed Echolalia:** *see* Echolalia.
- **Developmental Delay:** Development is delayed but qualitatively normal and would be unremarkable if observed in a younger child (*contra*: atypical/atypicality). For example, a twenty-four-month-old with babbling is demonstrating delayed (but typical) language milestones.
- **Dextroamphetamine:** *see* Stimulants.
- **DIR (Developmental–Individual-Difference–Relationship Model):** *see* Floor Time.
- **Discordance:** *see* Concordance.
- **Discrete Trial Training:** *see* Behaviorism.
- **DSM:** *Diagnostic and Statistical Manual of the American Psychiatric Association.* Presently in its fourth edition, with text revision (*DSM-IV-TR*).
- **Echolalia:** Echoed speech. May be immediate or delayed. The per-

son with immediate echolalia repeats back what is said to him or her, word for word (often the last few words of what the adult said, rather than all of it). The person with delayed echolalia memorizes words, phrases, or entire chunks of speech, and produces this material hours or days later. Delayed echolalia is sometimes referred to as "scripting."

- **EI:** Early intervention. Federally mandated special education services for children birth to three. EI is home-based (therapists come to your child). Typically, EI is administered locally by the county health department.
- **-ergic:** Suffix meaning "energized by." Serotoninergic neurons are driven by serotonin; dopaminergic neurons are driven by dopamine, etc.
- **Externalizing Behavior:** Outwardly directed, aggressive or antisocial behavior (hitting, biting, tantrums, property destruction). Even self-injury is classified as "externalizing" behavior. *Cf.* Internalizing Behavior.
- **Extinction:** The disappearance of a behavior as a result of cessation of rewards, and/or the imposition of aversive consequences for that behavior. Just before a previously rewarded behavior goes away, it may temporarily increase in intensity (the extinction burst).
- **Extinction Burst:** *see* Extinction.
- **FAPE:** Free and appropriate public education. Mandated by the Education for All Handicapped Law (Public Law 94-142), which came into effect in 1975 and has been revised several times since, most recently as IDEA (Individuals with Disabilities Education Act).
- **Floor Time:** A proprietary form of intervention for children with autistic spectrum disorder, created by Stanly Greenspan, MD, a child psychiatrist. Includes DIR and the Affect-Based Language Curriculum (ABLC).
- **Functional Behavioral Analysis:** *see* Behaviorism.
- **Guanfacine:** *see* Alpha-2 Agonists.
- **Heller Syndrome:** *see* Childhood Disintegrative Disorder.
- **Hyperlexia:** The ability to decode printed material far above one's level of reading comprehension.
- **Idiot Savant:** Term coined by Langdon Down in 1887 to refer to

individuals with profound delay in most cognitive areas—"idiots" (the technical term at that time, not a term of derision) who had isolated areas of extreme ability. *See* Savant Skill.

- **Incidence:** The number of new cases of a particular disorder occurring over a specified length of time. Epidemics are defined as a sudden increase in incidence (for example, if a given county typically sees one new case of hepatitis per week and then suddenly begins to see ten new cases per week).
- **Internalizing Behavior:** Inwardly directed negative behavior, including anxiety, depression, withdrawal. *Cf.* Externalizing Behavior.
- **Kanner, Leo:** First modern author to describe autism. *Kanner-type autism* refers to the clinical profile of his original patients—what we would refer to as severe ASD.
- **Lytic:** A drug that blocks a naturally occurring neurotransmitter; an antagonist.
- **Manipulables:** Items used in the course of developmental or psychological testing, typically consisting of wooden cubes, shape sorters, formboards, pegboards, etc.
- **Mental Retardation:** Significantly subaverage general intelligence, accompanied by delayed adaptive skills, arising during the first five years of life.
- **Methylphenidate:** *see* Stimulants.
- **Mimetic:** A drug that mimics a naturally occurring neurotransmitter; an agonist.
- **Mitochondria:** Structures inside cells where oxidation and energy production take place.
- **Mood Stabilizer:** Drug used to treat changes in mood (agitation, depression, mania). Includes neuroleptics and antiepileptic drugs (AEDs).
- **Natural Environment Training:** *see* Behaviorism.
- **Negative Reinforcement:** Removal of, or avoidance of, an undesired stimulus. We drive within the speed limit in order to not receive a traffic ticket. Not getting the ticket is a form of negative reinforcement. Not to be confused with punishment.
- **NE:** Norepinephrine.
- **NET:** Natural environment training. *See* Behaviorism.
- **Neuroleptic:** Literally, a drug that "seizes the brain." Antiquated

term used to cover drugs such as risperidone and aripiprazole, which function as mood stabilizers.

- **Omega-3 Fatty Acids:** Also known as essential fatty acids, since they are required for health, but cannot be manufactured by the human body. Dietary sources include fish, certain plants, and nuts. The name derives from the fact that all carbon atoms in a fatty acid are numbered, like links in a chain; the third carbon atom occupies the omega-3 position. All omega-3s have a double bond (unsaturated) at the omega-3 position. Omega-3 supplementation may have a beneficial role in neurodevelopment.

- **Operant Conditioning:** The technique by which behaviorism shapes behavior.

- **Overcorrection:** A form of punishment or aversive stimulus in which the child is required to overcorrect his or her behavior. For example, if the child spills a glass of milk, the child may be required not just to wipe up the spill, but to mop the entire kitchen floor.

- **PDD-NOS (Pervasive Developmental Disorder, Not Otherwise Specified):** The remainder category in the *DSM* for children with atypical development who do not meet criteria for a specified PDD (autism or Asperger syndrome).

- **PECS:** Picture Exchange Communication System.

- **Perseveration:** Inability to shift focus of attention from current activity, in order to move on to something else.

- **Positive Reinforcement:** Any pleasant stimulus that results in an increased likelihood that the immediately preceding behavior will recur; a reward.

- **Pragmatics:** The use of language as a tool for social interchange.

- **Prevalence:** The proportion of individuals in the population who manifest a particular trait at any one moment in time. For example, the *prevalence* of male gender in the United States is approximately 50 percent.

- **Prosody:** Inflection.

- **PRT (Pivotal Response Treatment):** A variant of ABA that closely resembles natural environment training (NET) and floor time. All three are based on the strategy of following the child's lead, then gently sabotaging the child's activity in order to require the child to interact with the adult.

- **Punishment:** *see* Aversives. Not to be confused with Negative Reinforcement.
- **RAS:** Reticular activating system. Located in the brain stem, the RAS is responsible for level of attention. Underactive RAS is treated with stimulants.
- **RDI:** Relationship development intervention. A proprietary form of intervention for ASD emphasizing language and social interaction.
- **Rett Syndrome:** A slowly degenerative, ultimately fatal disorder in females, due to mutation of the MECP2 gene. Early during the course of the disease, the girl has symptoms of autism. Now that the gene has been discovered, we know that the MECP2 mutation can cause a broader array of clinical disorders than classical Rett syndrome; it can also occur in boys.
- **Savant Skill:** Isolated skill that does not translate into generalized cognitive ability—for example, calendar savant (able to tell days of the week for past and future dates), musical savant (able to play a piece of music by heart after one or two hearings), hyperlexia (able to decode printed matter at a level far above day-to-day use of language).
- **Scripting:** *see* Echolalia.
- **Selective Serotonin Reuptake Inhibitor:** Enhances the action of serotonin by preventing its reuptake from the synapse (the junction between the nerve cells).
- **Sensory Diet:** *see* Sensory Integration.
- **Sensory Integration:** Term coined by A. Jean Ayres, PhD, as a process that "result(s) in perception and other types of syntheses of sensory data that enable man to interact effectively with the environment." Ayres also postulated that disordered "sensory integration" at the level of the brain stem would lead to disruption of higher neurologic functions, such as academic learning. Finally, she postulated that providing specific forms of stimulation (a sensory diet under the rubric of sensory integration therapy") would repair the brain stem deficit and would also lead to improvement in learning and other higher neurologic functions. These concepts remain largely unproven.
- **Sensory Integration Disorder (SID):** *see* Sensory Integration.
- **Sensory Integration Therapy:** *see* Sensory Integration.

- **Sensory Processing Disorder (SPD):** *see* Sensory Integration.
- **Serotonin:** 5-Hydroxytryptamine; 5-HT. A master neurotransmitter within the brain that has a host of direct and indirect effects. Deficiency of serotoninergic pathways is probably a core biological component of ASD.
- **SSRI:** *see* Selective Serotonin Reuptake Inhibitor.
- **Stereotypy:** Repetitive, stereotyped movement, with no identifiable external purpose.
- **Stim/Stimming:** Repetitious, stereotyped movements that serve as self-stimulation (for example, twiddling an object in front of one's face to study the visual pattern).
- **Stimulants:** Drugs that enhance the action of adrenergic neurotransmitters within the reticular activating system. Includes dextroamphetamine and methylphenidate.
- **Syndrome:** A group of symptoms that regularly occur together (for example, Down syndrome; toxic shock syndrome). Sometimes the underlying cause of the syndrome is known, sometimes it is not.
- **TEACCH (Treatment and Education of Autistic and Related Communication-Handicapped Children):** Method of instruction for children with ASD created by the late Eric Schopler and his colleagues in Chapel Hill, North Carolina.
- **Theory of Mind:** The realization that other people have their own thoughts and feelings, and the ability to make an educated guess as to what other people are thinking and feeling.
- **TO (Time Out):** Withdrawal of adult attention. Used as a form of mild punishment to decrease attention-seeking and tantrum behavior. Should not be used if the object of the child's tantrum is to escape from a task.
- **Top-Down:** *see* Bottom-Up and Top-Down.
- **VBA (Verbal Behavior Analysis):** An offshoot of ABA that uses operant conditioning techniques to shape verbal behavior and speech.

Appendix I: The *DSM*—Not Carved in Stone

It makes interesting reading to see how the *Diagnostic and Statistical Manual of the American Psychiatric Association* (*DSM*), the benchmark for making a diagnosis of autism, has evolved over the past twenty-four years. The *DSM-IV* codes individual symptoms as either present or absent but doesn't allow for grading the severity of any one symptom. However, each successive edition of the *DSM* has broadened the criteria themselves, leading to an increase in the number of people eligible for an autism diagnosis.

DSM-III (1984)

The *DSM-III* marked the first appearance "Infantile Autism" as a diagnostic category. Prior to the *DSM-III*, psychiatrists had lumped autism and childhood schizophrenia together, even though Leo Kanner—a child psychiatrist—had described autism forty years earlier. (We see the effort to separate autism from schizophrenia in criterion VI.) *DSM-III* criteria for Infantile Autism selected for children with severe autism, excluding children whom we would recognize today as having mild autism, PDD-NOS, or Asperger Syndrome.

Infantile Autism
I. Onset below 30 months of age II. Pervasive lack of responsiveness to other people III. Gross impairment in communication skills IV. Peculiar speech patterns if speech is present V. Bizarre response to the environment VI. Absence of delusions, hallucinations, loosening of associations, and incoherence

The *DSM-III* also contained diagnoses of Childhood Onset Pervasive Developmental Disorder and Atypical Pervasive Developmental Disorder for children with onset of symptoms over thirty months and children whose atypical features were not severe enough to warrant a diagnosis of Infantile Autism (although Childhood Onset PDD also required "gross and sustained disturbance of social relations"). Today, we would describe many of these children as having PDD-NOS, Asperger Syndrome, or one of the "borderland" diagnoses (Nonverbal Learning Disability or Semantic-Pragmatic Language Disorder).

Childhood Onset Pervasive Developmental Disorder
Gross and sustained disturbance of social relations Multiple oddities of behavior Development of symptoms after 30 months and before 12 years of age Absence of psychotic features

Atypical Pervasive Developmental Disorder
This category is reserved for cases in which classification precludes Infantile Autism or Childhood Onset PDD.

DSM-III-R (Revised) (1987)

Infantile Autism was replaced by *Autistic Disorder*. Criteria for a diagnosis of Autistic Disorder encompass a broader range of symptoms than Infantile Autism. Representative behaviors were arranged roughly according to developmental stages, so that a child might qualify for a diagnosis of Autistic Disorder even if behavior was not "bizarre" or "grossly disturbed," as long as it deviated from age-appropriate norms. The qualifier "at times" was added for many behaviors, and the age cutoff (onset below thirty months) was dropped. All of these changes significantly broadened the scope of children meeting criteria for Autistic Disorder, as opposed to Infantile Autism.

The *DSM-III-R* listed sensory attractions as an optional diagnostic feature but placed them under the heading of "restricted interests" (a cognitively based interpretation) rather than elevating them to the same rank as impaired social interaction and communication. Perhaps this is because psychiatry views itself as concerned with "things of the mind," rather than mere sensory processing. Sensory aversions were not listed, despite the fact that they figured prominently in Kanner's 1943 description.

Diagnostic Criteria for Autistic Disorder

At least eight of the following sixteen items, including at least two from Category A, one from Category B, and one from Category C:

A. Qualitative impairment in reciprocal social interaction as manifested by the following:

   1. Marked lack of awareness of the existence or feelings of others (e.g., treats a person as if he or she were a piece of furniture; does not notice another person's distress; apparently has no concept of the need of others for privacy)

   2. No, or abnormal seeking of comfort at times of distress (e.g., does not come for comfort even when ill, hurt, or tired; seeks comfort in a stereotyped way, e.g., says "cheese, cheese, cheese" whenever hurt)

   3. No, or impaired imitation (e.g., does not wave bye-bye; does not copy mother's domestic activities; mechanical imitation of others' actions out of context)

   4. No, or abnormal social play (e.g., does not actively participate in simple games; prefers solitary play activities; involves other children in play only as "mechanical aids")

   5. Gross impairment in ability to make peer friendships (e.g., no interest in making peer friendships; despite interest in making friends, demonstrates lack of understanding of conventions of social interaction, e.g., reads phone book to uninterested peer)

B. Qualitative impairment in verbal and nonverbal communication, and in imaginative activity, as manifested by the following:

   1. No mode of communication, such as communicative babbling, facial expression, gesture, mime, or spoken language

2. Markedly abnormal nonverbal communication, as in the use of eye-to-eye gaze, facial expression, body posture, or gestures to initiate or modulate social interaction (e.g., does not anticipate being held, stiffens when held, does not look at the person or smile when making a social approach, does not greet parents or visitors, has a fixed stare in social situations)

3. Absence of imaginative activity such as playacting of adult roles, fantasy characters, or animals; lack of interest in stories about imaginary events

4. Marked abnormalities in the production of speech, including volume, pitch, stress, rate, rhythm, and intonation (e.g., monotonous tone, questionlike melody, or high pitch)

5. Marked abnormalities in the form or content of speech, including stereotyped and repetitive use of speech (e.g., immediate echolalia or mechanical repetition of television commercials); use of "you" when "I" is meant (e.g., using "You want cookie?" to mean "I want a cookie"); idiosyncratic use of words or phrases (e.g., "Go on greed riding" to mean "I want to go on the swing"); or frequent irrelevant remarks (e.g., starts talking about train schedules during a conversation about sports)

6. Marked impairment in the ability to initiate or sustain a conversation with others, despite adequate speech (e.g., indulging in lengthy monologues on one subject regardless of interjections from others)

C. Markedly restricted repertoire of activities and interests, as manifested by:

1. Stereotyped body movements (e.g., hand-flicking or -twisting, spinning, head-banging, complex whole-body movements)

2. Persistent preoccupation with parts of objects (e.g., sniffing or smelling objects, repetitive feeling of texture of materials, spinning wheels of toy cars), or attachment to unusual objects (e.g., insists on carrying around a piece of string)

3. Marked distress over changes in trivial aspects of environment (e.g., when a vase is moved from usual position)

4. Unreasonable insistence upon following routines in precise detail (e.g., insisting that exactly the same route always be followed when shopping)

5. Markedly restricted range of interests and a preoccupation with one narrow interest (e.g., interested only in lining up objects, in amassing facts about meteorology, or in pretending to be a fantasy character)

D. Onset during infancy or childhood
   Specify if childhood onset (after 36 months of age)

PDD-NOS appears for the first time, as a catch-all category: "Cases that meet the general description of a PDD but not the specific criteria for Autistic Disorder are diagnosed as PDD, Not Otherwise Specified

(PDD-NOS)."* The lingering struggle to differentiate PDD-NOS from mental illness is also reflected in the definition.

Pervasive Developmental Disorder, Not Otherwise Specified

This category should be used when there is a qualitative impairment in the development or reciprocal social interaction and of verbal and nonverbal communication skills, but the criteria are not met for Autistic Disorder, Schizophrenia, or Schizotypal or Schizoid Personality Disorder. Some people with this diagnosis will exhibit a markedly restricted repertoire of activities and interests, but others will not.

DSM-IV (1994)

The *DSM-IV* lists five Pervasive Developmental Disorders:† Autistic Disorder, Rett's Disorder, Childhood Disintegrative Disorder, Asperger Syndrome (appearing for the first time), and the old standby, PDD-NOS. As in the *DSM-III-R,* the *DSM-IV* offers menu options for a diagnosis of Autistic Disorder. Item descriptions have been simplified and broadened compared to the *DSM-III-R.* The *DSM-IV,* for example, explicitly recognizes Autistic Disorder in individuals with "adequate speech" but qualitative impairments in the use of language.

In a backward move, the *DSM-IV* drops the sensory-seeking behaviors listed in the *DSM-III-R,* such as sniffing, or attraction to textures as diagnostic criteria, although they are mentioned in the narrative text that accompanies the checklist of diagnostic symptoms.

---

* In my opinion, it would be better to call the overarching category Autistic Spectrum Disorders (ASDs) rather than PDDs, and replace PDD-NOS with Autistic Spectrum Disorder, Not Otherwise Specified (ASD-NOS). Perhaps we will see these changes in the *DSM-V.* The term *Autistic Spectrum Disorder* is not, at this time, a *DSM* category.

† Rett's Disorder doesn't belong in the *DSM,* since it represents a specific medical—rather than psychiatric—diagnosis. Likewise, Childhood Disintegrative Disorder, also known by the archaic term Heller's Syndrome, almost certainly represents a collection of disparate degenerative disorders that have been lumped together and given a psychiatric label.

Autistic Disorder

A. A total of six (or more) items from 1, 2, and 3, with at least two from (1) and one each from (2) and (3)

  1) Qualitative Impairment in social interaction, as manifested by at least two of the following:

    a) Marked impairment in the use of multiple nonverbal behaviors such as eye-to-eye gaze, facial expression, body postures, and gestures to regulate social interaction

    b) Failure to develop peer relationships appropriate to developmental level

    c) Lack of spontaneous seeking to share enjoyment, interests, or achievements with other people (e.g., by a lack of showing, bringing, or pointing out objects of interest)

    d) Lack of social or emotional reciprocity

  2) Qualitative impairments in communication as manifested by at least one of the following:

    a) Delay in, or total lack of, the development of spoken language (not accompanied by an attempt to compensate through alternative modes of communication such as gesture or mime)

    b) In individuals with adequate speech, marked impairment in the ability to initiate or sustain a conversation with others

    c) Stereotyped and repetitive use of language or idiosyncratic language

    d) Lack of varied, spontaneous make-believe play or social imitative play appropriate to developmental level

  3) Restricted repetitive and stereotyped patterns of behavior, interests, and activities, as manifested by at least one of the following:

    a) Encompassing preoccupation with one or more stereotyped and restricted patterns of interest that is abnormal either in intensity or focus

    b) Apparently inflexible adherence to specific, nonfunctional routines or rituals

    c) Stereotyped and repetitive motor mannerisms (e.g., hand or finger flapping or twisting, or complex whole-body movements)

    d) Persistent preoccupation with parts of objects

AND:

B. Delays or abnormal functioning in at least one of the following areas, with onset prior to age 3 years: (1) Social interaction, (2) Language as used in social communication, or (3) Symbolic or imaginative play

C. The disturbance is not better accounted for by Rett's Disorder or Childhood Disintegrative Disorder

Asperger's Disorder (commonly referred to as Asperger Syndrome; AS)* appears for the first time. The pedantic nature of speech, hyper-verbal behavior, and physical clumsiness commonly seen in AS, and as originally described by Asperger himself, do not receive adequate emphasis in the *DSM*. (Children with autism are typically hypoverbal rather than hyperverbal, and may be very physically adept.) It is possible to go back and forth between the diagnosis of AS and Autistic Disorder as given in the *DSM-IV*, scratching one's head, trying to identify a "bright line" that distinguishes these two conditions. (For a good discussion of the difficulties stemming from the current *DSM* definition of AS, see Klin A et al. Three diagnostic approaches to Asperger syndrome: implications for research. *Autism Dev Disord*. 2005; 35(2):221–234.)

Asperger's Disorder

A. Qualitative impairment in social interaction, as manifested by at least two of the following:

1. Marked impairment in the use of multiple non-verbal behaviors such as eye-to-eye gaze, facial expression, body postures, and gestures to regulate social interaction
2. Failure to develop peer relationships appropriate to developmental level
3. Lack of spontaneous seeking to share enjoyment, interests or achievements with other people (e.g., by a lack of showing, bringing, or pointing out objects of interest to other people)
4. Lack of social or emotional reciprocity

B. Restricted repetitive and stereotyped patterns of behavior, interests, and activities, as manifested by at least one of the following:

1. Encompassing preoccupation with one or more stereotyped and restricted patterns of interest that is abnormal either in intensity or focus
2. Apparently inflexible adherence to specific, nonfunctional routines or rituals
3. Stereotyped and repetitive motor mannerisms (e.g., hand or finger flapping or twisting, or complex whole-body movements)
4. Persistent preoccupation with parts of objects

---

* Standard medical usage avoids the apostrophe: We speak of Down Syndrome, Kawasaki Syndrome, etc., without the possessive. Psychiatrists and nonphysicians, however, retain the apostrophe.

C. The disturbance causes clinically significant impairment in social, occupational, or other important areas of functioning

D. There is no clinically significant general delay in language (e.g., single words used by age 2 years, communicative phrases used by age 3 years)

E. There is no clinically significant delay in cognitive development or in the development of age-appropriate self-help skills, adaptive behavior (other than social interaction), and curiosity about the environment in childhood

F. Criteria are not met for another specific Pervasive Developmental Disorder or Schizophrenia

PDD-NOS is retained and broadened to include children with "subthreshold symptomatology," thus further enlarging the scope of this diagnostic term. (The so-called explosion in prevalence of autistic disorders followed the publication of these criteria.)

Pervasive Developmental Disorder, Not Otherwise Specified (including Atypical Autism)

This category should be used when there is a severe and pervasive impairment in the development of reciprocal social interaction or verbal and nonverbal communication skills, or when stereotyped behavior, interests, and activities are present, but the criteria are not met for a specific Pervasive Developmental Disorder, Schizophrenia, Schizotypal Personality Disorder, or Avoidant Personality Disorder. For example, this category includes "atypical autism"—presentations that do not meet the criteria for Autistic Disorder because of late age at onset, atypical symptomatology, or subthreshold symptomatology, or all of these.

DSM-IV-TR (Text Revision) (2003)

The *DSM-IV-TR* continues to list five conditions: Autistic Disorder, Rett's Disorder, Childhood Disintegrative Disorder, Asperger's Disorder, and Pervasive Developmental Disorder, Not Otherwise Specified. There are no significant changes in the diagnostic criteria.

Comments

Autism and its variants have been a moving target, insofar as the *DSM* is concerned. Boundaries and categories have shifted over time. Up to now, these disorders have been defined in purely behavioral terms. Sixty years after Kanner's original paper, however, we know that Kanner was right: ASDs are biological disorders with behavioral symptoms—in Kanner's words, "an inborn disturbance of affective contact." And at some point, as our ability to unlock the biological basis for behavior improves, we will start to redraw the boundaries of ASD and its various subtypes along biological, rather than purely behavioral, lines.

Appendix II: Outcome Studies of ASD

I became personally familiar with the natural history of ASD early in my career. For eighteen years, I was the only university-hospital-based neurodevelopmental pediatrician in central upstate New York. In that position, I had the chance to evaluate an enormous variety of children all across the spectrum, and to watch them grow and develop. I struggled to account for the fact that some of my patients did much better than others. I was also responsible for training pediatric interns, residents, and fellows, and I struggled to help them make sense out of the *DSM* definitions, which seemed to blur into one another.

My "Aha!" moment came while reading a paper by another researcher, Deborah Fein (Fein D et al. Cognitive subtypes in developmentally disabled children: a pilot study. *J Autism Dev Disord.* 1985; 15(1):77–95). Fein had studied children with autism plus mental retardation. She reported that "manifestations of autistic aloofness and tendency to sameness may be relatively independent of cognitive skill patterns ... [and] orthogonal to cognitive ... level." In other words, the degree of atypicality and the level of intelligence—at least among children with autism plus mental retardation—were separate from each other. *Orthogonal* means "at right angles," which got me to thinking in terms of two axes on a graph. There was no graph in Fein's paper, but, translated into pictures, what she was suggesting was this:

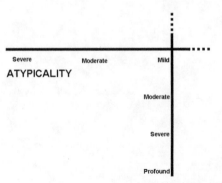

Degree of Mental Retardation

I asked myself what would happen if I extended her two axes to include children with normal intelligence? Doing so gave me the 2-D graph we have already seen (Figure 5.3). Fein also noted that her subjects with ASD would need to be observed over time—what researchers call "longitudinal follow-up"—to confirm her observations. Since I tend to think in pictures, it was only another short step for me to add the Z axis, representing time, coming out from the point where the X and Y axes intersect. This, of course, is the fully developed 3-D model we have discussed in Chapter 5. All that remained was for me to put the model to the test. Fortunately, it seems to be holding up nicely.

In 1997 I moved from upstate New York to The Children's Hospital of Philadelphia. There, a colleague and I set out to study the natural history of ASD (Coplan J, Jawad AF. Modeling clinical outcome of children with autistic spectrum disorders. *Pediatrics*. 2005; 116(1):117–122). We watched ninety-one children over seven years, periodically measuring their degree of atypicality and level of nonverbal intelligence. We used the Childhood Autism Rating Scale to measure the degree of atypicality (recall that the best possible CARS score is 15 and the worst is 60) and a variety of nonverbal IQ and adaptive measures to measure general intelligence. We divided the children into two groups, those with an IQ or developmental quotient (DQ)* of 70 or above at the time of the first

---

* *Developmental quotient*, a similar measure to IQ, based on clinical examination rather than a formal IQ test. See Chapter 5.

visit, and those with an initial IQ or DQ below 70 (i.e., in the range of mental retardation). What we found was that over time, CARS scores steadily improved in children whose initial IQ or DQ was 70 or greater. In contrast, CARS scores did not improve in children whose initial IQ or DQ was less than 70. In other words, *the natural history of ASD differs according to the child's IQ.* Our data matched the findings of previous researchers, and now, for the first time, we were actually able to predict the outcome for each group, based on the child's IQ at the time of initial diagnosis. The 3-D model gives us a way to think about this information and a way to "map" a child's progress over time.

Here I have pulled together several studies of factors affecting outcome. Bartak (1976) hit the nail on the head: Any given child's IQ will be as influential as the child's degree of child's atypicality, in determining outcome.

Table A.1

Author(s); Year	Subjects	Methods	Results
DeMyer, 1973[1]	120 children with "infantile autism"; average age at diagnosis 5½ years	Average length of follow-up: 6 years (range 2–16 years)	Performance IQ at initial evaluation predicted work/school status at follow-up.
Bartak, 1976[2]	45 boys with "infantile autism," onset below 30 months of age	Reassessed at 10–17 years of age by a variety of nonverbal IQ measures	"In terms of scholastic progress, social competence, and work opportunities, the child's IQ level is as influential as the presence of autism. These findings suggest that there may be differences in the origin of autism according to the presence or absence of mental retardation."
Lotter, 1978[3]	8 studies totaling 474 children with autism	Followed for 4–15 years	• "Good" outcome (attending normal school, or employed) in about 15 percent • Nonverbal IQ at the time of diagnosis, and acquisition of some functional speech by age 5 were the best predictors of outcome.

Table A.1 (cont'd.)

Author(s); Year	Subjects	Methods	Results
Gillberg & Steffenburg, 1978[4]	46 young adults who had been diagnosed with "infantile autism and other childhood psychoses" as children	Age at follow-up 16–23 years	"IQ at diagnosis and communicative speech development before 6 years were the most important prognostic factors."
Szatmari, 1989[5]	16 adults who had been diagnosed with autism plus normal intelligence (mean IQ 92) during childhood	Followed for 11–27 years	"Four [25%] had a very good outcome and might be considered recovered.... Neuropsychologic measures of nonverbal problem solving were highly correlated with outcomes."
Venter, 1992[6]	58 high-functioning autistic children enrolled in preschool or elementary school	Assessed during preschool/elementary school and followed for 8 years	Verbal skills and nonverbal IQ showed a positive relationship with outcome.
Piven, 1996[7]	38 high-IQ adolescent and adult autistic individuals, age 13–28, diagnosed with autism below 5 years of age	Comparison of current status with status at age 5	"Five of 38 subjects who met DSM-IV criteria for autistic disorder at age 5 years no longer met criteria... although all five continued to have substantial impairment... The study of patterns of behavioral change over time in autism has practical implications for both diagnosis and prognosis as well as potential importance in defining biologically meaningful subgroups and clarifying fundamental mechanisms underlying this disorder."
Stevens, 2000[8]	96 elementary school children with autism, classified as high- or low-functioning	Retrospective study of preschool factors associated with high-functioning status in elementary school	• Nonverbal IQ in preschool was the single best predictor of outcome • The high-functioning school-age group showed social and behavioral abnormalities at preschool that were comparable to those of the low-functioning group, but these subsided by school age, leaving only mild residual social symptoms.

Table A.1 (cont'd.)

Author(s); Year	Subjects	Methods	Results
Seltzer et al, 2003[9]	405 subjects, age 10–53 years (mean age 21.7 years) all of whom had been diagnoses with ASD in childhood	Cross-sectional assessment of current symptom severity using ADI-R	"The findings of this study point to large improvements…across domains in the functioning of adolescents and adults who as children received a diagnosis on the autism spectrum. When current scores were used, only about half of the sample met ADI-R criteria for Autistic Disorder, and…11.9% showed a pattern of impairment on the ADI-R that no longer was indicative or any diagnosis on the autism spectrum."
Howlin, 2004[10]	68 adults, diagnosed with autism as children (average age at first visit, 7 years; range 3–15 years)	Average age at follow-up 29 years (range 21–48 years)	12% had "very good" outcome, 10% "good," and 19% "fair." Individuals with childhood performance IQ ≥ 70 had significantly better outcome than those with performance IQ < 70.
Coplan, 2005[11]	91 children with ASD, sorted into two groups based on nonverbal IQ and adaptive skills (IQ or DQ < 70, or ≥ 70)	Length of follow-up: 7 years	Children whose initial IQ or DQ was ≥ 70 showed significant resolution of atypical features; children whose IQ or DQ was < 70 showed no improvement in atypical features.

1. DeMyer MK, Barton S, DeMyer WE, Norton JA, Allen J, Steele R. Prognosis in autism: a follow-up study. J Autism Child Schizophr. 1973;3(3):199–246.
2. Bartak L, Rutter M. Differences between mentally retarded and normally intelligent autistic children. J Autism Child Schizophr. 1976;6(2):109–120.
3. Lotter V. Follow-up studies. In: Rutter M, Schopler E, eds. Autism: A reappraisal of concepts and treatment. New York: Plenum, 1978:475–495.
4. Gillberg C, Steffenburg S. Outcome and prognostic factors in infantile autism and similar conditions: a population-based study of 46 cases followed through puberty. J Autism Dev Disord. Jun 1987;17(2):273–287.
5. Szatmari P, Bartolucci G, Bremner R, Bond S, Rich S. A follow-up study of high-functioning autistic children. J Autism Dev Disord. 1989;19(2):213–225.
6. Venter A, Lord C, Schopler E. A follow-up study of high-functioning autistic children. J Child Psychol Psychiatry. Mar 1992;33(3):489–507.
7. Piven J, Harper J, Palmer P, Arndt S. Course of behavioral change in autism: a retrospective study of high-IQ adolescents and adults. J Am Acad Child Adolesc Psychiatry. Apr 1996;35(4):523–529.
8. Stevens MC, Fein DA, Dunn M et al. Subgroups of children with autism by cluster analysis: a longitudinal examination. J Am Acad Child Adolesc Psychiatry. 2000;39(3):346–352.
9. Seltzer MM, Krauss MW, Shattuck PT, Orsmond G, Swe A, Lord C. The symptoms of autism spectrum disorders in adolescence and adulthood. J Autism Dev Disord. Dec 2003;33(6):565–581.
10. Howlin P, Goode S, Hutton J, Rutter M. Adult outcome for children with autism. J Child Psychol Psychiatry. Feb 2004;45(2):212–229.
11. Coplan J, Jawad AF. Modeling clinical outcome of children with autistic spectrum disorders. Pediatrics. Jul 2005;116(1):117–122.

Appendix III: Psychological Assessment Tests

The list that follows is by no means exhaustive, but it includes the tests most commonly used for the psychological assessment of children. The examiner (psychologist, speech/language pathologist, etc.) determines which particular test instruments will best provide a detailed picture of your child's overall developmental level, plus his or her skills and weaknesses in specific areas (expressive and receptive language, nonverbal problem solving, executive function, atypicality, etc.). It is important that a child be tested with instruments that are appropriate for his or her skill level as well as age. Often it may be necessary for the examiner to select an instrument that begins at a lower age, even if this means administration or scoring needs to be done in a nonstandard fashion. Beware of less-thorough evaluations, based on just a few subtests—for example, the Kaufman Brief Intelligence Test (K-BIT), or the short form of the Wechsler Preschool and Primary Scale of Intelligence (WPPSI) or Wechsler Intelligence Scale for Children (WISC). These are fine to use when testing children at low risk for a developmental problem, but they are not up to the task of capturing the range of strengths and weaknesses in a child with ASD.

For additional information, try these links:

www.assessmentpsychology.com/testlist.htm

www.childpsychologist.com/mod/resource/view.php?id=22

http://ags.pearsonassessments.com/group.asp?nGroupInfoID=a30000

Intelligence

The purposes of these instruments include:

- To quantify your child's overall level of mental development
- To look for a split between verbal and nonverbal abilities
- To look for a split between crystallized and fluid intelligence
- To look for problems with executive function

Here are some of the more common instruments used for these purposes, arranged roughly in age order:

- Bayley Scales of Infant Development, 3rd Edition (BSID-III). The gold standard measure for assessing development in infants and young children, up to 3½ years of age.
- Stanford-Binet 5th Edition. Age range: 2 years–adult. A good instrument to use with children who are functioning at a preschool level, regardless of calendar age.
- Differential Ability Scales. Age range: 2 years 6 months through 17 years 11 months.
- McCarthy Scales of Children's Abilities. Age range: 2½–8½ years.
- Kaufman Assessment Battery for Children. Ages 2½–12½ years.
- Wechsler Preschool and Primary Scale of Intelligence, 3rd Edition (WPPSI-III). Age range: 2½–7 years 3 months.
- Wechsler Intelligence Scale for Children, 4th Edition (WISC-IV). Ages 6–16 years 11 months.

The WPPSI and the WISC are most informative if all optional subtests are given.

- Comprehensive Test of Nonverbal Intelligence (C-TONI). Designed to measure intelligence in children with severely impaired language skills. Age range: 6–18 years 11 months.

Adaptive Skills

The purpose of these tests is to quantify your child's day-to-day abilities in areas such as communication, self-care skills, and play. Often, children with ASD are untestable in a standard way, since they do not understand that they are being expected to perform. A detailed inventory of adaptive skills as provided by a caregiver familiar with the child can provide useful insight into a child's developmental level outside the confines of standardized testing. Adaptive skills are often somewhat higher than cognitive skills, since they reflect practiced, crystallized abilities.

- Vineland Adaptive Behavior Scales. Age range: birth–18 years.
- Scales of Independent Behavior, Revised (SIB-R). Age range: infant–adult.

Behavior

Instruments of this type are useful for looking at the qualitative aspects of your child's development: mood, cooperation, flexibility, and so on. Occasionally there are significant differences between parent and teacher impressions. This may be due to the fact that a child is under greater demands at school, leading to increased visibility of negative behaviors.

- Behavior Assessment Scale for Children, 2nd Edition (BASC-2). Ages 2–adult.
- Child Behavior Checklist. Ages 4–18 years.
- Conners' Rating Scales—Revised. Ages 3–17 years. For ADHD.

Atypicality

Instruments in this category are specifically designed to look for symptoms of autistic spectrum disorder.

- Autism Diagnostic Observation Schedule (ADOS). The most widely accepted tool for research purposes. Based on clinical observation of social, language, and play skills. For more on the ADOS: www.agre.org/program/aboutadosg.cfm.
- Childhood Autism Rating Scale (CARS). A 15-item rating scale of atypical features, rated from 1 (no abnormality) to 4 (severely atypical). For more on the CARS: www.pearsonassessments.com/cars.aspx.
- Gilliam Autism Rating Scale (GARS). A structured 42-item inter-

view of atypical features, covering the age range 3–22 years. Includes three subscales: Stereotyped Behaviors, Communication, and Social Interaction. For additional information, go to www.pearson assessments.com/gars2.aspx.

- Asperger Syndrome Diagnostic Scale (ASDS). A 50-item questionnaire designed to detect Asperger syndrome in children 5–18 years. For additional information, go to www.pearsonassessments.com/asds.aspx.

Language

Instruments in this group are designed to look at expressive and receptive language. The first three instruments tap single-word vocabulary, which can be very strong in some children on the spectrum, even when complex language skills such as pragmatics are delayed.

- Peabody Picture Vocabulary Test (PPVT): single-word receptive vocabulary
- Receptive One-Word Picture Vocabulary Test (ROWPVT): single-word receptive vocabulary
- Expressive One-Word Picture Vocabulary Test (EOWPVT): picture naming; the mirror image of the PPVT or ROWPVT
- Preschool Language Scale (PLS-4): measures receptive and expressive language abilities, birth through 6 years 11 months
- Test of Language Development, 2nd Edition: measures receptive and expressive abilities, ages 4–12 years
- Test of Pragmatic Language (TOPL): specifically looks at pragmatics (the use of language as a means of social interaction)

Academic Abilities

Instruments in this group look at your child's ability to perform the traditional academic tasks—reading, writing, and arithmetic.

- Wechsler Individual Achievement Test, 3rd Edition (WIAT-III): ages 4–19.11
- Woodcock Johnson III—Tests of Achievement: ages 2–90+
- Kaufman Test of Educational Achievement: grades 1–12

Appendix IV: Psychopharmacology in ASD

Here is a brief introduction to the drugs most commonly used in children with ASD. (I have omitted some of the less frequently used drugs, such as tricyclic antidepressants, benzodiazepines, pemoline, and beta-blockers.) This is highly technical material. But now that you have a child with ASD, you need to know a bit about the medications that might be able to help your child achieve his or her full potential. For additional information, see the references provided in the Resource List.

Terminology

All drugs have a noncommercial (generic) name and are also marketed under one or more brand names. Dexedrine is a brand name for dextroamphetamine, just as Shell is a brand of gasoline. There is seldom any difference between the brand-name product and the generic equivalent, but manufacturers naturally want you (and your doctor) to remember a drug by its brand name. However, we will refer to drugs by their generic names here, since drugs that are available today only as brand-name products will almost certainly become available as generic products when the patents expire. Furthermore, in cases where generics are already available, we do not want to imply that the brand-name version is better than the generic product. I prescribe drugs generically whenever possible. The biggest exception to this rule is for timed-release drugs, where I don't want to switch between different timed-release formulations of the same drug. (The active ingredient may be the same, but the time/action curve can differ.)

Drugs that enhance neurotransmitter activity are called *agonists* (as in drama, where the person who moves the action forward is the pro-tagonist), *mimetics* (since they mimic the target neurotransmitter), or may be identified by the suffix *-ergic* (*erg* means energy, as in "ener-gize"): Serotoninergic drugs enhance the action of serotonin; dopamin-ergic drugs enhance the action of dopamine, and so on. Drugs that block the action of a neurotransmitter are called *antagonists,* or *lytics* ("-lysis" means to destroy): For example, sympatholytics block the ac-tion of the sympathetic nervous system.

Mechanisms of Action

Each neuron is separated from the next by a tiny space, called the synapse. When a nerve impulse reaches the end of one neuron, it trig-gers the release of molecules called neurotransmitters into the synapse (Figure A.1). These neurotransmitter molecules spread across the synapse to the second neuron, causing it to fire, thus propagating the nerve impulse along the path to its ultimate destination. As long as neu-rotransmitter molecules are sitting in the synapse, they keep triggering the second neuron, causing it to fire. To prevent the second neuron from firing indefinitely, neurotransmitter molecules are collected by a reuptake system and returned to storage sites in the first neuron, ready for reuse. In addition, receptor sites on the first neuron, called autore-ceptors (since they regulate the activity of the neuron on which they are located), detect the presence of neurotransmitter molecules in the synapse and shut off further release of neurotransmitter.

Agonists increase the action of naturally occurring neurotransmit-ters by one or more mechanisms (Figure A.1):

- Enhance the release of neurotransmitter by the first neuron, in re-sponse to an incoming nerve impulse

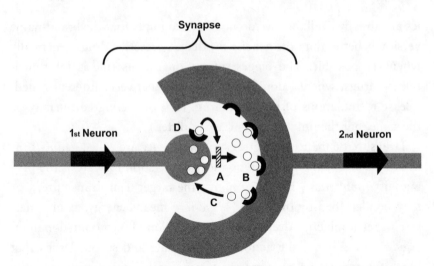

Figure A.1 Neurotransmission *In response to an incoming nerve impulse (heavy arrow), the first neuron releases neurotransmitter molecules (white circles) into the synapse (A). Neurotransmitter molecules diffuse across the gap and activate receptor sites (black semicircles) on the surface of the second neuron (B). In order to terminate firing of the second neuron, neurotransmitter molecules are taken up (C) and returned to the first neuron. Autoreceptors on the first neuron (D) detect the presence of neurotransmitter in the synapse, and shut off further release of neurotransmitter. Agonists and antagonists alter various aspects of this mechanism.*

- Mimic the action of the naturally occurring neurotransmitter at the second neuron
- Block the reuptake of neurotransmitter from the synapse. Drugs that work this way are called *reuptake inhibitors*. Selective serotonin reuptake inhibitors (SSRIs) such as fluoxetine block the reuptake of serotonin; norepinephrine reuptake inhibitors (NRIs) such as atomoxetine block the reuptake of norepinephrine.

Antagonists work as mirror images of agonists, decreasing the action of naturally occurring neurotransmitter, by one or more of the following mechanisms:

- Inhibit the release of neurotransmitter from the first neuron. One way to do this is by activating autoreceptors on the first neuron, since the natural function of the autoreceptors is to shut off release of neurotransmitter (the alpha-2 adrenergic agents, clonidine and guanfacine, work this way).

• Block the action of neurotransmitter at the second neuron. Naltrexone blocks the action of opioids by occupying the receptor sites on the second neuron. Risperidone blocks dopamine, in part, by occupying dopamine receptor sites.

Drug / Neurotransmitter Classes

We will discuss drugs by *drug class,* rather than individually, since the therapeutic effects and the side effects are broadly similar for all drugs in a particular class. There are notable exceptions, which I'll point out. Except for risperidone, none of the drugs discussed below have been specifically approved by the FDA for treatment of symptoms of ASD as of this time. There are few head-to-head studies of one drug versus another, and virtually no randomized controlled trials of multidrug combinations, even though many children with ASD are on two or more psychotropic medications.*

Dopamine / Noradrenaline / Adrenaline

Agonists
Dopamine (DA), noradrenaline (norepinephrine, NE), and adrenaline (epinephrine) are synthesized both inside and outside of the brain. Dopamine modulates four distinct systems within the brain: movement, cognition, emotion, and the endocrine system. Noradrenaline (norepinephrine) modulates arousal, working memory, the sleep/ wake cycle, and the brain's reward centers. This is what gives noradrenergic drugs such a high potential for abuse and explains why the stimulants (amphetamine, methylphenidate) are tightly regulated by

---

* Most research is paid for by drug companies, and there is always a risk in paying for research to compare your drug to someone else's. What if theirs turns out to be better? So most studies simply compare the new, brand-name drug to placebo. This is a tremendous impediment to figuring out what works best.

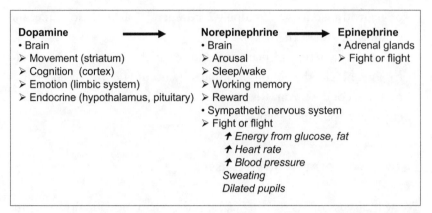

Figure A.2 Metabolic Pathway and Physiologic Roles for Dopamine and Its Derivatives *Excess dopaminergic and noradrenergic activity gives rise to hypervigilant, agitated, and "aggressive" behavior (exaggerated fight-or-flight response), and disordered sleep/wake cycles. Underactivation of the RAS (reticular activating system) due to inadequate noradrenergic input can lead to inattention, with resultant hyperactive, impulsive behavior. Treating a child who exhibits both agitation and hyperactivity is a challenge, since the drugs for agitation (dopamine blockers) and the drugs for ADHD (noradrenergic agonists) work at cross-purposes, pharmacologically.*

the FDA.* Outside of the brain, noradrenaline is the neurotransmitter for the sympathetic nervous system, your body's "emergency broadcasting network," that sets in motion the fight-or-flight response in response to a perceived threat. There are at least five major kinds of dopamine receptors (designated D1 through D5), and five major norepinephrine receptors (alpha 1 and 2, and beta 1, 2, and 3). The end result of stimulation by DA or NE will vary, depending on the type of receptor that has been stimulated (see Figure A.2).

Finally, the entire dopamine system is regulated by a tiny cluster of serotonin-producing cells located in the upper brain stem. Therefore, the actions of dopamine can be altered directly, by targeting DA receptors, or indirectly, by targeting serotonin receptors within the DA-releasing system, to increase or decrease DA release. The atypical

---

* The FDA classifies drugs based on abuse potential: Schedule I includes—among others—heroin; Schedule II includes cocaine and morphine; Schedule III includes short-acting barbiturates; Schedule IV includes diazepam (Valium); Schedule V includes codeine-based cough syrup. Amphetamines and methylphenidate are Schedule II drugs.

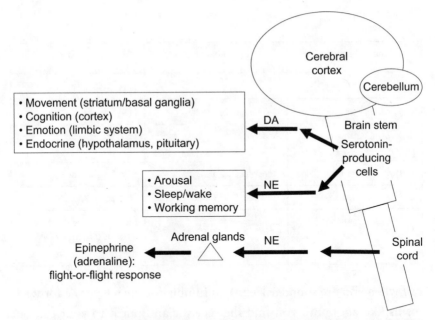

Figure A.3 The Dopamine System, and Regulatory Role of Serotonin *A tiny cluster of serotonin-producing cells in the brain stem control the release of dopamine (DA) and norepinephrine (NE) by the brain. This system regulates a vast array of cognitive, behavioral, and endocrine functions within the body. This explains why most of the drugs we use have side effects in areas we did not wish to affect with treatment.*

neuroleptics (risperidone, aripiprazole, etc.) work this way, as combined DA and serotonin blockers.

Sympathometics (Stimulants)

Stimulants increase the release of dopamine and norepinephrine or mimic their action at the second neuron; atomoxetine blocks NE reuptake. FDA-approved indications for stimulants include narcolepsy (sudden attacks of falling asleep) and attention deficit hyperactivity disorder (ADHD). Many children with ASD also manifest inattention, distractibility, and hyperactivity. Whether these constitute "true" ADHD or are simply a part of their basic ASD is an interesting theoretical question, but the practical aspects of management are the same in either case.

It may seem strange to use a stimulant to treat someone who is already "hyper." To understand why this is so, imagine getting a phone

Table A.1 Stimulants

Generic Name(s)	Brand Name(s)	Comment
Amphetamine	—	FDA Schedule II
Dextroamphetamine	Dexedrine, Dextrostat	FDA Schedule II
Dextroamphetamine + amphetamine	Adderall	FDA Schedule II
Methylphenidate	Concerta, Ritalin, Metadate	FDA Schedule II
Dexmethylphenidate	Focalin	FDA Schedule II
Atomoxetine, attentin	Strattera	Norepinephrine reuptake inhibitor (NRI), not FDA Schedule II

call when you are sound asleep. You fumble for the telephone for what seems like ages until you find the receiver and put it to your ear, but you are still half asleep, and you have to struggle to follow what the caller is saying. Eventually you become fully awake. In physiologic

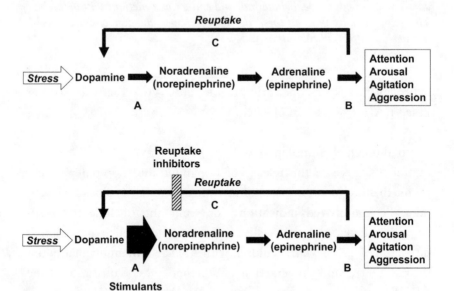

Figure A.4 Action of DA (Upper Panel) and Dopaminergic Drugs (Lower Panel) *Stimulants (dextroamphetamine, methylphenidate) enhance the release of DA or mimic its action directly at DA receptor sites; reuptake inhibitors (atomoxetine, for example) block the reuptake of norepinephrine.*

terms, the part of your brain that is responsible for *alertness,* known as the reticular activating system (RAS), has finally gotten revved up. Now that you are finally awake, you ask the caller to repeat the first part of the conversation. Imagine going through life with an underactive RAS: You stumble from task to task, have trouble following complex instructions, and have difficulty organizing your thoughts. Persons with ADHD have a chronically underactive RAS. Even though they are not physically sleepy, their brains are not fully alert. Stimulants work by "tweaking" the RAS, raising it to the desired level of alertness. (Too high a dose of stimulants produces perseveration, in which case the parent may complain that their child has been "turned into a zombie." The solution is to cut back on the dose slightly.)

Side effects of stimulants include suppressed appetite, headache or stomachache, and (if given late in the day) insomnia. Stimulants can also intensify anxiety, agitation, aggression, and obsessive-compulsive behaviors.

The biggest long-term side effect is slower growth. This can often be minimized by giving the child a "drug holiday" over the summer, to permit catch-up growth. If your child is on stimulants, he or she should take them seven days per week. Treating the child only on weekdays prolongs and aggravates side effects such as appetite suppression and insomnia.

BLACK BOXES

Stimulants have been used to treat hyperactivity for nearly one hundred years, with no known serious problems. Nonetheless, in 2006 the FDA issued a warning listing sudden cardiac death as a risk for children taking stimulants. There are no controlled data to show that the rate of sudden cardiac death in children on stimulants is any higher than the rate of sudden cardiac death for children in general. The conclusion by medical experts outside of the FDA is that the FDA may have gone too far:

- "There does not seem to be compelling findings of a medication-specific risk necessitating changes in our stimulant treatment of children and adolescents with attention-deficit/hyperactivity disorder."*

- "Despite public controversy and labeling changes to warn of extremely rare cardiovascular and psychiatric side effects, the evidence does not support the hypothesis that medication for ADHD increases risk for sudden death, mania or psychosis."[†]

---

* Wilens TE et al. Stimulants and sudden death: what is a physician to do? *Pediatrics.* 2006; 118(3):1215–1219.
† Pliszka SR. Pharmacologic treatment of attention-deficit/hyperactivity disorder: efficacy, safety and mechanisms of action. *Neuropsychol Rev.* 2007.

Antagonists

Some children with ASD have difficulty regulating their state of arousal, shooting right up to a state of extreme arousal with little or no external provocation. Parents may feel like they are walking on eggshells, and the child is always having meltdowns. This is not a good situation for anyone. This situation calls for drugs that can antagonize (counteract) the effects of dopamine and noradrenaline, both within the brain (centrally) and outside of the brain (peripherally).

Alpha-2 Agonists

Alpha-2 agonists activate autoreceptors on noradrenergic neurons, inhibiting release of noradrenaline into the synapse. Think of alpha-2 autoreceptors like the control rods in a nuclear reactor. Without them, our temper and blood pressure would go through the roof every time we were subjected to stress. The primary use for alpha-2 agonists is to treat hypertension (high blood pressure). Alpha-2 agonists also dampen the heightened state of arousal associated with the fight-or-flight response, making them useful in the treatment of impulsivity plus aggression. They are also useful in the treatment of impulsivity, and for

Table A.2 Alpha-2 Agonists

Generic Name	Brand Name(s)	Comment
Clonidine	Catapres	More sedating than guanfacine
Guanfacine	Tenex, Intuniv	

inducing sleep (in which case clonidine is preferable, since it has a stronger sedative effect than guanfacine). These agents also bind to alpha-2 receptors in the frontal cortex, where—it is theorized—they act to enhance attention and behavior. When treating a child with ASD plus impulsivity, I often try guanfacine before going to stimulants, because guanfacine does not aggravate anxiety the way stimulants often do. If someone has been on one of these drugs for a while, it must be tapered slowly, to avoid rebound hypertension.

Atypical Neuroleptics

Atypical neuroleptics function directly as dopamine *antagonists* by blocking D_2 receptor sites, and indirectly as dopamine *agonists* by blocking 5-HT_{2A} neurons, thereby triggering increased release of DA (Figure A.3). The actions of an atypical neuroleptic are determined by the relative balance of these two effects. Side effects of the atypical neuroleptics reflect dopamine's role in the regulation of the endocrine system and movement, and can include weight gain, insulin resistance, diabetes, changes in cholesterol levels, elevated prolactin (a hormone made by the brain), enlarged pituitary gland, involuntary movements, and neuroleptic malignant syndrome, a rare but potentially fatal condi-

Table A.3 Atypical Neuroleptics

Generic Name	Brand Name	Comment
Aripiprazole	Abilify	Relatively less risk of weight gain.
Clozapine	Clozaril	Causes bone marrow suppression.
Olanzapine	Zyprexa	Greater risk of weight gain.
Quetiapine	Seroquel	Greater sedation.
Risperidone	Risperdal	Greater risk of weight gain. Approved by the FDA in 2007 for the treatment of agitated behavior in children with ASD. Generic available.
Ziprasidone	Geodon	Relatively less risk of weight gain.

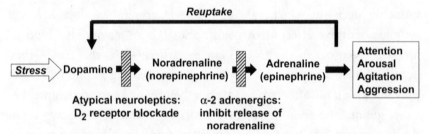

Figure A.5 Dopamine Antagonists (Includes Atypical Neuroleptics and Alpha-2 Adrenergics)

tion characterized by muscle rigidity and elevated body temperature. Children on atypical neuroleptics need to have routine monitoring of weight, blood sugar, insulin level, lipids, and prolactin, as well as monitoring for the presence of involuntary movements. Despite the potentially significant side effects, these drugs are often essential to treat severe agitation in children with ASD. (Ideally, we would like a more selective drug, one that only targets dopamine's role in cognition and arousal, without altering its role in endocrine function or movement.)

GABA and Glutamate

Gamma-amino-butyric acid (GABA) is an amino acid that inhibits neuronal transmission within the brain. Conversely, glutamate is an amino acid that increases neuronal excitability. Drugs that alter the balance between GABA and glutamate thus alter the overall level of excitabil-

Table A.4

Generic Name(s)	Brand Name	Comment
Carbamazepine	Tegretol	GABA agonist
Gabapentin	Neurontin	GABA agonist
Lamotrigine	Lamictal	Inhibits glutamate (excitatory amino acid)
Topiramate	Topamax	Inhibits glutamate (excitatory amino acid)
Valproate, valproic acid	Depakote	GABA agonist

ity of the brain. Seizures are the prime example of an overexcitable brain, with spontaneous firing of brain cells—a storm cloud of electricity. GABA agonists were first used (and continue to be used) as antiepileptic drugs (AEDs). In addition to controlling seizures, GABA agonists can also stabilize disordered mood; for example, GABA agonists are used to treat mania (the "up" swing in people with bipolar disorder). In children with ASD, GABA agonists or glutamate antagonists are sometimes used in the management of agitation and aggression. Children on these drugs need to be monitored for changes in function of the liver or bone marrow.

Opioids / Endorphins / Opioid Antagonists

Narcotic drugs (heroin, morphine, opium, etc.) activate opioid receptors within the body, relieving pain and causing a feeling of well-being. The body also makes its own, naturally occurring opioids (endorphins). Endorphins are released at times of great stress, enabling the person to withstand physical trauma without noticing. The so-called runner's high is due to a release of endorphins following physical exercise. High-intensity self-injurious behavior (SIB) may also result in endorphin release. The opioid antagonists (naltrexone, naloxone) block the action of morphine, heroin, and naturally occurring opioids. One use is to treat narcotic drug overdose. They are also sometimes used as part of the treatment of severe self-injurious behavior when SIB is self-reinforcing because of endogenous opioid release.

Serotonin (5-HT) and Serotoninergic Agents

Serotonin is synthesized within the brain from tryptophan, a dietary amino acid (this explains serotonin's other name: 5-hydroxytryptamine, or 5-HT). After release, serotonin is taken up by a serotonin transporter (SERT) and returned to the presynaptic neurons for storage, converted to melatonin (Figure A.6), or broken down to 5-hydroxyindoleacetic acid (5-HIAA; not shown).

Only a tiny number of neurons, all clustered together in the brain stem, make serotonin (Figure A.3). Yet these few neurons connect to all other parts of the brain, regulating a host of activities. There are seven

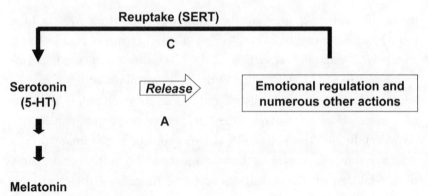

Figure A.6 Pathways for Serotonin

major classes of serotonin receptors ($5\text{-}HT_1$ through $5\text{-}HT_7$), and at least fourteen receptor subtypes. The location and nature of receptor subtype determines the effect of serotonin at that location: Buspirone, a $5\text{-}HT_{1A}$ agonist, is useful in the treatment of anxiety; sumatriptan, a $5\text{-}HT_{1D}$ agonist, relieves migraine headaches; ondansetron, a $5\text{-}HT_3$ antagonist, blocks nausea and vomiting from chemotherapy, and so on. As we mentioned in our discussion of the DA system, serotonin $5\text{-}HT_{2A}$ neurons inhibit the release of DA from dopaminergic neurons. In addition to its direct actions at various $5\text{-}HT$ receptor sites, the role of serotonin as a regulator of DA gives serotonin a wide range of effects.

Serotoninergic Agents

Selective serotonin reuptake inhibitors (SSRIs) bind to SERT, preventing the reuptake of serotonin. The therapeutic effects of SSRIs often take up to ten weeks to appear. This suggests that the SSRIs are doing something else besides just preventing the reuptake of serotonin from the synapse—perhaps altering gene expression within neurons. SSRIs are useful in the treatment of anxiety, depression, and obsessive-compulsive disorder. They are commonly used to treat anxiety, and cognitive rigidity in ASD, although not approved by the FDA for these purposes. The most common short-term side effect is "activation": a state of mild agitation and/or hyperactive behavior. In 2004, the FDA issued a warning on the risk of suicidal thoughts when SSRIs are used to treat depressed children and adolescents. (There are no studies showing an increased risk of completed suicide.) The risk of triggering suicidal thoughts in children

Table A.5 Serotoninergic Agents (SSRIs and Serotonin Releasing Agents)

Generic Name	Brand Name	Comment
Citalopram	Celexa	SSRI
Escitalopram	Lexapro	SSRI
Fluoxetine	Prozac	SSRI
Fluvoxamine	Luvox	SSRI
Paroxetine	Paxil	SSRI
Sertraline	Zoloft	SSRI
Trazodone	Desyrel	SSRI, also antagonizes 5-HT$_2$ receptors ($\uparrow$ DA release)
Buspirone	Buspar	5-HT$_{1A}$ agonist
Mirtazapine	Remeron	Blocks alpha-2 receptors $\rightarrow$ $\uparrow$ serotonin release

with ASD, where SSRIs are used to treat obsessive behaviors, stereotypies, and anxiety, is probably far lower, but has never been specifically studied.

- *Buspirone (Buspar).* Buspirone is a 5-HT$_{1A}$ agonist. FDA-approved indications for buspirone include short- and long-term treatment of anxiety. Buspirone is theoretically attractive for the treatment of anxiety or obsessive behavior in children with ASD, because it replaces

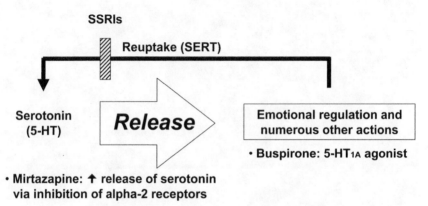

Figure A.7 Mechanism of Action of Agents Enhance Effects of Serotonin

serotonin, which is deficient in the brains of children with ASD. However, published data on its use in children with ASD are limited at this time.

• *Mirtazapine (Remeron)*. This drug is believed to work by antagonizing alpha-2 receptors, removing the brake on presynaptic release of serotonin (at low doses) and noradrenaline (at higher doses). Mirtazapine is also a postsynaptic $5\text{-}HT_2$ and $5\text{-}HT_3$ antagonist, and an antihistamine. Side effects include drowsiness and weight gain.

Index

About the Author

Dr. Coplan completed his undergraduate training at Dartmouth College in 1969, earned his medical degree at New York Medical College in 1973, and completed two years of pediatric residency at Hartford Hospital. After serving two years in the U.S. Public Health Service, Dr. Coplan completed a fellowship in child development at Johns Hopkins University in 1979. Dr. Coplan spent the next eighteen years on the faculty of the State University of New York—Upstate Medical Center, as director of training in child development, followed by seven years as director of training at Children's Seashore House of The Children's Hospital of Philadelphia. In 2004 Dr. Coplan opened a private practice specializing in the care of children with autistic spectrum disorders (Neurodevelopmental Pediatrics of the Main Line, PC; www.ndpeds .com). Dr. Coplan continues to teach physicians from the Department of Psychiatry and nurses from the Graduate School of Nursing of the University of Pennsylvania, and lectures frequently on the topic of autistic spectrum disorders.

Dr. Coplan has been married for thirty-six years; he and his wife have three grown children and one grandchild. When he is not busy with other matters, Dr. Coplan can be found in his backyard, working on his garden railroad.